MW00622530

The Amateur Hour

The Amateur Hour

A History of College Teaching in America

JONATHAN ZIMMERMAN

Johns Hopkins University Press

Baltimore

© 2020 Johns Hopkins University Press
All rights reserved. Published 2020
Printed in the United States of America on acid-free paper
9 8 7 6 5 4 3 2

Johns Hopkins University Press
2715 North Charles Street
Baltimore, Maryland 21218-4363
www.press.jhu.edu

Library of Congress Cataloging-in-Publication Data

Names: Zimmerman, Jonathan, 1961– author.
Title: The amateur hour : a history of college teaching in America /
    Jonathan Zimmerman.
Description: Baltimore : Johns Hopkins University Press, 2020. |
    Includes bibliographical references and index.
Identifiers: LCCN 2019057287 | ISBN 9781421439099 (hardcover) |
    ISBN 9781421439105 (ebook)
Subjects: LCSH: College teaching—United States—History. |
    Education, Higher—United States—History. | Learning and scholarship—
    United States—History.
Classification: LCC LB2331 .Z56 2020 | DDC 378.1/250973—dc23
LC record available at https://lccn.loc.gov/2019057287

A catalog record for this book is available from the British Library.

*Special discounts are available for bulk purchases of this book. For more
information, please contact Special Sales at specialsales@jh.edu.*

Johns Hopkins University Press uses environmentally friendly book
materials, including recycled text paper that is composed of at least
30 percent post-consumer waste, whenever possible.

For M. Paul Zimmerman
1934–2017
with love

CONTENTS

In 2008, when I was a faculty member at New York University, I received its Distinguished Teaching Award. There was a lovely dinner, where the four other winners and I received medals from the university's president. My daughters, wife, and parents were all on hand for the ceremony. It was—and remains—my proudest moment as a professor. I'll never forget it.

But until I started working on this project, I hadn't thought much about what happened that evening. Each of us was called up to the front of the room and introduced by our respective deans. When it was my turn, I took my place next to the lectern while my dean—who was also a friend—prepared to give a short speech in my honor. I looked down at her notes, illuminated by the small lamp at the lectern, and here's what I saw: a list of the books I had authored. And I suddenly realized, *she's going to tell them what I wrote!* At a dinner about teaching!

And so she did. I don't begrudge her for that, at all. What else could she go on, really? She had never been to one of my classes. And even if she had, how would a single visit—or two—help her say anything meaningful or important about my instruction? What other evidence could she invoke? What did she know about me as a teacher, really? What do any of us know about that?

Not much, which is why I wrote this book. Paradoxically, college teaching is a highly public act that has remained mostly private. Millions of Americans have taught in our gigantic higher education system, but we don't have shared standards or even vocabularies to describe what they do. And talking about our teaching isn't usually a part of our job, so we also don't hear much about it from each other. Our scholarship is a professional enterprise, resting on peer review and other long-standing collective practices. But when it comes to teaching, we're solo operators. We're flying by the seat of our pants.

We're amateurs.

That doesn't mean we teach badly, because amateurs can sometimes be really good. What it means is that we don't have codified understandings of "good" and "bad" in the first place. It also means that we don't have much in the way of a shared history of teaching, which has mostly remained behind the closed doors of our classrooms. And that makes it nearly impossible to evaluate the loud, often apocalyptic claims that permeate our present-day debates about higher education. I realized that a few years ago, while attending a seminar about online college instruction. One set of speakers argued that online technologies would make teaching better, and the other speakers worried that teaching would be worse. But to sustain either claim, you have to know something about what preceded us. You can't say that things will be better—or worse—unless you know what came before. And we don't.

So that's what this book tries to remedy. After a quick look at the nineteenth century, it explores how generations since then have imagined and experienced college teaching, and—especially—how they tried make it more "personal." Over and over again, Americans have condemned college teaching as routine, mechanical, and dismissive of their individual differences. Of course, there were substantive changes in teaching over the years: educational television grew rapidly in the 1950s, for example, and classroom encounter groups enjoyed a brief but passionate vogue in the 1960s and early 1970s. But the perception that college teaching was failing students—and, especially, that it was ignoring their individualities—has been a constant across time. I hope this book helps us think about what we want teaching to be. And the only way to do that is to figure out what it was, and why so many people thought it wasn't good enough.

The most important constant for me has been the support and care of the people who were at my teaching-award dinner, back in 2008. All of them are still with us except my father, who wore a dapper suit that evening and grinned from ear to ear. I'll never forget the lessons he taught me, about life and love. This book is for him.

ACKNOWLEDGMENTS

The standard practice upon completing a book is to thank the people who helped you to research and write it. But this is a book about college teaching, so I'd like to start by acknowledging my best college teacher. Four decades ago, Eviatar Zerubavel modeled for me the rigor and passion that are the hallmarks of all great professors. I remain grateful for his inspiration and example.

Most of the stories in this book have never been told, because they're buried in unpublished manuscript records. So I'm deeply thankful to the Spencer Foundation, whose generous grant allowed me to visit the 59 archives listed in the appendix. Thanks also to the Bentley Historical Library—for its own generous travel grant—and to my graduate assistant, Angus McLeod, who did yeoman's labor digging up college newspapers and other online sources.

Richard Arum, Elizabeth Knoll, Chris Loss, and Harold Wechsler all read early iterations of this project, and they all helped make it better. Sadly, Harold didn't live to see the book in print. He was a mensch, in every way. I miss him.

Greg Britton brought this book to Johns Hopkins University Press, where he shepherded it with characteristic grace and skill. Thanks also to Greg's terrific staff, especially Kyle Gipson, and to Hilary Jacqmin, Kathryn Marguy, Juliana McCarthy, Kimberly Johnson, and freelance copyeditor Jeremy Horsefield, who did wonders in cleaning up my notes (and much else). The book began when I was at New York University and took shape while I taught at the University of Pennsylvania. Thanks to Jim Fraser at NYU and to Pam Grossman at Penn, who have been constant supporters and true friends. I'm also grateful to Kathy Hall—the world's best colleague—and to Bruce Lenthall, whose tireless efforts at Penn's Center for Teaching and Learning inspired many of the themes in these pages. I rehearsed the argument in a freshman seminar at Penn, "Why College? Historical and Contemporary Perspectives," where my students contributed more to the book than they might have imagined.

My biggest debt is to Susan Coffin and to our two daughters, Sarah and Rebecca. And it only gets bigger as time goes on.

The Amateur Hour

Personality over Bureaucracy

The Paradox of College Teaching in America

In a 1911 speech comparing American and German universities, Max Weber proclaimed that the differences came down to one thing: bureaucracy. That was hardly surprising, given the German sociologist's lifelong focus on bureaucratic formation as the key organizational feature of modernity. What was surprising, however, was Weber's observation that American universities were actually *more* bureaucratic than their German counterparts. Whereas young lecturers in Germany were paid only via the fees of students they attracted to their courses, assistant professors in the United States received an official appointment and a regular salary. German lecturers could remain in academic limbo indefinitely as they awaited a permanent position, whereas young American faculty members were subject to dismissal—"the reverse side of bureaucratization," as Weber called it—after several years at their respective institutions. He expanded on this theme in a 1917 address published two years later as "Science as a Vocation," perhaps his most famous treatise on academic life. German lecturers had a much lower teaching load than American junior professors, Weber wrote, but they also had to lure students to their classes; otherwise, they had little chance of obtaining a full-time professorship, which Weber believed should reflect intellectual promise rather than classroom popularity. "Attendance at lectures is quantitatively tangible evidence whereas high quality in research is imponderable," he complained. "If it is said that a *Privatdozent* [lecturer] is a poor teacher, it amounts almost to an academic death sentence, even though he be one of the foremost scholars in his field."[1]

All of this was anathema to Weber, who deplored the unfounded assumption that failure in the lecture hall ensured the same in the laboratory or the library. "One can be very outstanding in research and atrocious as a teacher," he argued, citing the famed scholars (and famously bad teachers) Helmholtz and Ranke as examples. Most of all, Weber questioned whether the number of students attending a lecture reflected the teacher's scholarly quality or potential. "The fact that students flock to a teacher is . . . determined in unbelievably large measure by purely superficial factors such as temperament and even tone of voice," he wrote. "Democracy should be practiced where it is appropriate. Scientific training, however . . . implies the existence of a certain type of intellectual aristocracy." To be sure, research success also required a mysterious and unpredictable form of "inspiration," as Weber admitted. But at least scholarly claims could be assessed—and, inevitably, surpassed—by successive generations of scholars; that was not the case for teaching, which always rested on "highly personal" factors. In the United States, Weber added, young professors had so many teaching duties that they had often little time for research; in Germany, by contrast, they had more time to write because there was less opportunity to teach. Yet both of them would ultimately be assessed based on whether they could "pack the house" with students, Weber worried, which was an invidious way to judge anyone.[2]

Weber was right about the larger bureaucratic apparatus at American institutions of higher education, which were growing at a rate that would soon eclipse all of the other universities in the world combined. But he was wrong about the way Americans selected and evaluated their professors. Large private and public universities had already begun to hire and promote faculty members based on their scholarly publications, which inverted Weber's formula: *research* was deemed "quantitatively tangible evidence" of success, to quote his phrase, while the quality of their teaching was often seen as "imponderable." To be sure, smaller colleges and less prestigious universities—increasingly known as "teaching" institutions, to distinguish them from "research" ones—continued to hire and promote faculty based on pedagogical skill, at least in theory. But even at these institutions, there was almost no sustained organizational effort to judge or regulate how teaching was delivered. Financially strapped administrators took note of the enrollment in professors' classes, of course, but—contrary to German practice, and to Weber's assumption about America—they rarely assessed the faculty by that metric. For the most part, teaching was considered too ineffable and idiosyncratic—indeed, too personal—to be systematized at all. "Teaching is largely a matter of personal influence," education scholar Samuel P. Capen wrote in 1911, summarizing the received wisdom of the day. "If an educational institution or system adopts too many mechanical methods it may submerge personality and thereby interfere with the somewhat mysterious influence of teacher upon pupil."[3]

A future university president, Capen recognized the need to rein in—or even to remove—some of the "bunglers" and "pathetic failures" who taught in college classrooms. But he was also pessimistic about the prospects of real supervision of teaching, for several reasons. Even as university bureaucracies ballooned, he wrote, American faculty members had retained an extraordinary amount of freedom in their own classrooms. "Tradition sanctions the 'laissey faire' policy with regard to college teachers," Capen noted. "To break down the policy would probably cause deep resentment in many quarters." The resentment would be even greater if regulation came from specialists in education, like Capen himself, who were already regarded as the least scholarly members of the academic guild. Most of all, American professors simply did not regard teaching as something that lent itself to bureaucratic guidelines or parameters. The year after Capen's article appeared, a Carnegie Foundation official proposed that colleges establish "tests of the efficiency of teaching" by sending professors into classrooms, cataloguing "what appears to them to be the best teaching," and formulating standards around the results. The proposal went nowhere, because American professors persisted in viewing teaching as "personal" rather than "systematic," as the official wrote. So did their students, who likewise saw personality as the key to quality in college instruction. "The professor must be the personality that envelops an idea and makes it seem alive," a Vanderbilt student wrote in 1929. "His spirit, soul, understanding, call-it-what-you-will, will be keenly awake to the student." A university president confirmed that teaching rested on "that elusive and indefinable something we call personality," which was "impossible to define." All he knew was that it was everything, and nothing could stand in its place.[4]

This book hinges on a paradox that Max Weber did not foresee: as more and more of American higher education came under the bureaucratic umbrella, teaching mostly remained outside of it. It was a charismatic activity, which Weber saw as the opposite of the rational authority associated with bureaucracy. Charisma inhered in the "exceptional sanctity, heroism, or exemplary character of an individual person," Weber wrote, not in the impersonal rules and regulations that marked modern organizations. As historian William Clark has observed, the "academic charisma" of the research scholar somehow survived the rationalized world of academia. How else to explain the irrational competition for "star" faculty, whose publications established them as geniuses standing above the fray of the day-to-day? Yet scholarly charisma is also sanctified by its own elaborate set of bureaucratic rituals, including citation counts and reviews by fellow experts in the field. The charisma of the scholar surely exceeds these rationalized procedures, as Clark has noted, but it cannot exist without them. No so for teaching, which Americans saw as resting almost entirely on the personality of the instructor. In the nineteenth century, where this book begins, they defined the ideal teaching situation as

"Mark Hopkins on one end of a log and the student on the other"; if the professor had the right personality, like the beloved Williams College president did, everything else would take care of itself. Professors and students since that time have continued to describe college teachers in highly charismatic terms, praising or condemning them for their spirit, soul, call-it-what-you-will. "If a teacher wishes success with pupils, he must inflame their imagination," wrote a prizewinning teacher at Penn State in 1993, quoting the legendary early twentieth-century Yale professor William Lyon Phelps. "The teacher should put the classroom under the spell of an illusion, like a great drum."[5]

But that also made popular teachers suspect, precisely because their charisma lacked any real sanction in the scholarly world. Indeed, it could—and often did—count against them. William Lyon Phelps was a case in point: adored by generations of literature students for his dramatic lectures and kindly temperament, his colleagues charged that he had "stooped to conquer" by offering students entertainment in the place of education. They also questioned his scholarship, especially when he started writing for popular newspapers and magazines instead of for the academic journals that had become the sine qua non of professorial status and advancement. "Phelps, you're just the kind of man we don't want here," a Yale professor told him, when he was still an instructor. It took Phelps several tries—and the intercession of Yale's president—to obtain a regular professorship, over the objections of the faculty. In Germany, where professors were paid by lecture fees, poor student enrollment could become what Max Weber called the kiss of death, but in the United States, a strong student draw could play exactly the same role. When a lecturer became "popular" with students, Harvard professor Bliss Perry wrote, colleagues immediately pegged him for a *popularizer*. "They are sure if he talks well to a Woman's Club about the latest novel or the latest play there is something wrong with him; he will be giving 'radio hours' next, or writing for the Hearst newspapers," Phelps noted. It surely did not help William Lyons Phelps's reputation on the Yale faculty that he ended his career on a radio show, edifying the masses about literature. "The entire intellectual wealth of mankind is within reach of every humble person," Phelps told a 1934 radio audience. "Not every person can become a personage, but every person can become a personality."[6]

Echoing the burgeoning fields of psychology and advertising, the last comment imagined personality as a plastic form of selfhood that could be adapted—or manipulated—by social forces. It also mimicked the "personnel" perspective borrowed from industrial management in the 1920s and 1930s, when university administrators developed freshman orientation, mental health clinics, and other interventions designed to adjust diverse students to their new environment. When it came to teaching, however, students and faculty members more commonly used "personality" to connote the essential interior qualities of professors rather than their exterior—and evanescent—traits. Its meaning was closer to "character," a term inherited from the nineteenth century and often transmuted into "personality" in the twentieth. Like charisma, personality was a magical and mysterious substance that resided in the individual. A powerful personality could change students, when they came into his or her orbit. But the teacher's personality did not and could not change; nor could teaching, of course, if it hinged on personality. "One cannot disassociate character, personality, and teaching competence," a faculty dean at Princeton wrote in 1954. "In large degree, these qualities are God-given." Nearly two decades later, a Yale department chair echoed the same sentiments in a self-effacing spirit. "In general, I do not believe that teaching can be taught," he wrote. "I have found in my own case that . . . there is an unexpandable limit to my personal charisma which my students and I have to live with. Teaching effectiveness is very much dependent on temperament, as well as on the kinds of choices a professor makes—and I believe is entitled to make—among the impossibly conflicting demands that academic life places on his attention." The more Americans saw teaching as a personal act or decision, the less it could be organized or standardized—or improved.[7]

But Americans kept trying, as the ensuing pages will attest. From the dawn of the modern university into the present, reformers have struggled to make college teaching *more* personal. They especially lambasted the large-group lecture, which allowed for "the expression of the personality of the teacher"—as Columbia president Nicholas Murray Butler acknowledged—but was not itself a "personal method": placing hundreds of students in the same room, it deprived them of anything other than superficial contact with their professor. Indeed, as a Rollins College dean wrote in 1927, teachers and students could only become "acquainted intimately" in a smaller classroom setting. "Could any better plan be devised for the submerging of personality than the big college lecture grouping?" he asked. Rollins was in the vanguard of teaching reform in the interwar era, when dozens of institutions developed tutorials (sometimes called "preceptorials"), honors programs, and other innovations designed to elicit and engage the distinct personalities of students, as well as those of their teachers. The pattern would be repeated across the century, as growing colleges and universities sought to leaven the anomie of "mass" instruction with small-group experiences. But even these reforms depended on locating and cultivating the right faculty personalities, who needed the proper interpersonal skills to conduct seminars and discussions. Indeed, they needed *different* personalities than did theatrical lecturers, as students told a researcher in the 1930s. "In the seminar or preceptorial everything depends on the man himself, his sense of humor, his capacity to relax, as well as his enthusiasm," they explained. Occasionally, a single personality could light up both a large lecture hall and a small seminar room. More commonly, though, a teacher who succeeded in one environment failed in the other—and there was no predicting which was which. "Too commonly we think of the teacher as if he or she were something standardized, built according to specifications like an automatic shoe-making machine," another interwar observer wrote. But teaching always reflected "the inscrutable interaction of personalities," he added, "each the product of its own unique history."[8]

Other reformers aimed to replace classroom teachers via technology, even as they sought "better" personalities for the profession. In the 1950s and 1960s, foundation donors sponsored large-scale efforts to recruit stronger teaching candidates and also to develop televised classes that could supplant the weaker ones. "Let us not deceive ourselves into thinking that this would be another step toward impersonalization by replacing man in the flesh by a tape and machine," one educational TV enthusiast wrote, somewhat defensively. "What may actually happen is the replacement of what is often a novice by an expert or a dullard by a vibrant personality." Even without a dynamic figure on the screen, TV advocates added, instruction would be "personalized" insofar as students could watch it whenever they wished. Other forms of self-paced instruction also witnessed sharp rises in the postwar era, aided by "teaching machines" and—eventually—by computers. These reforms proposed a new definition of "personal" instruction, emphasizing the initiative and convenience of the individual student. But from another perspective they were also highly impersonal, separating students from their teachers and from each other. "Without student contact, I don't want to teach," one professor told researchers in 1967, denouncing televised classes. "Professors want to know their students; students need personal contact, because, after all, learning is a spiritual process of student-teacher relationship. It's better to have a poor instructor in the classroom than to have a good one on TV."[9]

Into the present, both forms of personalization have marked—and, critics claim, marred—American college teaching. Some professors turned themselves into "apostles of personalism" who emphasized close and empathetic relationships with their students, as sociologist David Riesman wryly observed in 1980. But they also sacrificed academic rigor, lest it interfere with the relaxed atmosphere they strove to establish in the classroom. "The going style is almost an aggressive 'hang loose' or 'laid back' approach," Riesman wrote. "The class is a rap session, and everything is related to the personal experience of students." Meanwhile, computer-assisted instruction and then online classes offered a different kind of personalism, tailored to the individual schedules and—theoretically—to the individual aptitudes of each user. The first brand of personal instruction was costlier, of course, requiring institutions to reduce class size and hire more teachers. So it was also more common at elite colleges and universities, whereas "personalized learning" via computers was increasingly dominant at community colleges, for-profit universities, and other institutions catering to the less affluent. By 2013, even a prominent champion of online education warned of a dystopia where "rich kids get taught by professors and poor kids get taught by computer." No matter how they envisioned teaching, though, most reformers assumed that students—not their professors—would be the driving force in determining its future. "Education is a business and educators often lose sight of this," a Florida community college professor flatly declared in 1998, defending online classes. "Students are our customers and the customer must be satisfied."[10]

The new consumerism in college teaching conjured the German fee system that Max Weber criticized, which had roots going all the way back to the medieval university: whoever attracts the highest student enrollment wins. It spawned declining student workloads in courses and runaway grade inflation, because keeping the customer satisfied generally meant giving her or him less work and higher marks. And it was reinforced by the massive rise of adjunct and contingent faculty, who could be let go whenever a student complained. Even for professors with the protections of tenure, meanwhile, assumptions about the personal, idiosyncratic nature of teaching continued to sandbag efforts at improving it. "Teaching is a highly personal matter, and criticism of one's effort is experienced and resisted as a direct attack on one's self," two scholars observed in 1975. When he became president of the University of Massachusetts in the early 1970s, Robert Wood began to wonder why professors "have been so casual and almost amateurish" in their approach to teaching. The answer was simple: it was personal. "It is a risky business," Wood wrote. "It does assault one's personality, one's identity, one's knowledge, one's confidence in oneself." So professors typically met critiques of their instruction by invoking academic freedom, which they translated as "my right to do what I want in my class," as one study of junior college faculty members noted. That freedom was never absolute: during the white-hot years of the Cold War, especially, professors narrowed or changed what they taught for fear of being labeled a Communist or fellow traveler. So long as they did not make too many political waves, however, professors were left alone in the classroom. They viewed it as their castle, one dean wrote, and for the most part they were correct.[11]

How do you change something that is essentially personal, especially when the persons involved can so easily insulate themselves from change? By the mid-twentieth century, calls for the reform of college teaching had already assumed a predictable pattern: committees would convene, statements would be issued, and most professors would continue teaching as they always had. Writing privately in 1957, one dean said that the entire process reminded him of a snow globe he had owned as a child: he shook it up and the flakes circulated, but then they settled down just as before. Many institutions developed administrative mechanisms to address teaching, including faculty committees and university-wide teaching centers. But most of these offices lacked any coercive organizational power, which Weber identified as the hallmark of modern bureaucracy; they were missionary efforts, appealing to the goodwill of professors whose careers would be determined by their publications rather than their pedagogy. Even as they proclaimed their dedication to quality undergraduate teaching, indeed, administrators privately advised junior faculty to "back off on the teaching a bit" and get some work into print, as a UCLA professor noted in 1976. "If I take time away from my students and my teaching, then I am cheating my students. If I take time away from my own research and publications, I am cheating myself," she confessed. "It has really been a crisis of conscience." Every professor had to resolve that crisis in her or his own way. But the fact that it was a matter of conscience—and not of compulsion— spoke to the peculiar status of undergraduate instruction in the larger realm of academia. Like teaching itself, the decision to change it (or not) remained a personal act. It all depended on the individual.[12]

The pages that follow document the extraordinary effort that many American professors devoted to teaching, simply because they believed in it. By the 1980s, across every kind of four-year institution, the amount of time faculty spent on teaching was inversely related to their salaries. The more they devoted themselves to instruction, the less they earned; the more effort they expended on research, meanwhile, the higher their pay and rank. But faculty members at every level threw themselves into teaching, despite—or even because of—its lack of material reward. "Many of us may be comfortable with the low value placed on teaching—precisely because that gives teaching autonomy from the relentless demands of universities," Northwestern University professor Michael Sherry admitted in 1994. "In that regard, what devalues teaching in professional terms may also be just what makes it valuable to us as individuals—it is *ours*, not the profession's." That also meant that there was little formal training or peer review for college teaching, as Sherry happily affirmed, echoing a consistent theme across the twentieth century. Even renowned teachers like William Lyon Phelps proudly admitted that they had never "rationalized their procedure," as Yale president James R. Angell told a colleague in 1932, echoing Max Weber's rhetoric of bureaucracy. Phelps himself bragged that he had not engaged in any systematic preparation for teaching; instead, he learned everything he needed on the job. "I may as well confess at the start that I know nothing whatever of the science of pedagogy," Phelps wrote, introducing his 1912 book about teaching. "I have never studied the 'psychology of the child,'" he added, punctuating his skepticism with air quotes, "and have never attempted to find the way to a boy's heart by scientific formula." Teaching was something that you learned from life rather than from study or from supervisors, a Stanford professor confirmed. "Each man must work out his own method for himself," he told a 1932 survey about college teaching.[13]

In other words, it was an amateur enterprise. When it came to scholarly activity, American academics developed strong and shared norms of professionalism: the PhD certified that professors had developed the skills of the guild, and peer review ensured that they maintained its standards. But on the matter of teaching, SUNY Binghamton president G. Bruce Dearing observed in 1965, the "mystique of amateurism" remained. "As a group, college teachers have been loftily contemptuous of courses in education and absurdly vain about their innocence of any formal instruction in curriculum design, testing techniques, and formal classroom procedures," Dearing wrote. Ironically, a former professor added, any suggestion that faculty members receive training for the classroom was dismissed as *unprofessional* because it conjured the lowly status of elementary and secondary school teachers. "College teaching is the only profession which does not require its members to prepare for their life's work," Alan Schoonmaker wrote in 1971, shortly after leaving the classroom. "We are amateurs and want to remain amateurs, despite the consequences our incompetence has for our students." In the early twentieth century, Max Weber worried that German universities might interpret success in teaching—especially as measured by student enrollment—as an indication of talent as a researcher. Americans made the opposite mistake, assuming that research skill would make for a good teacher. But as Weber correctly noted, "the coexistence of these two talents in the same person is . . . wholly a matter of chance." That is mostly how Americans have left it, up until today. Scholarship is a highly professional enterprise, marked by elaborate codes of credentialing and practice. But teaching remains a game of chance, conducted mainly by people who are not systematically inducted into it. Each man—and each woman—must work it out for themselves.[14]

Over the past 150 years, Americans developed the most elaborate and diverse system of higher education in human history. An enterprise that formerly served only white men—at a tiny number of colleges—evolved into a behemoth of over 4,000 degree-granting institutions, enrolling millions of students from an astonishing array of backgrounds. It has also generated a remarkable range of scholarly ideas, spurred by precisely the dynamic that Weber predicted: each scholar tries to surpass the last one. But teaching has stayed relatively static across time, even as the winds of change have swirled around it. If you think otherwise, try a little thought experiment: imagine that Henry Adams was raised from the dead and returned to the contemporary United States. In 1907, looking back at his own education at Harvard, Adams wrote what remains the most famous account of American college teaching. If Adams were suddenly transported into the twenty-first century, he would be astounded—or baffled, or appalled—by changes in patterns of communication, labor, family, and much else. But once he entered a university classroom, he would feel right at home. Surely he would notice new features, especially the gender and racial composition of the students and faculty and the strange new contraption beaming slides onto a screen; he might also note that the lecture-heavy methods of his own day had been leavened by periodic discussions and other classroom activities. But the cadence and rhythm of the class would be familiar to him, even if PowerPoint was not. Indeed, college teaching has probably seen *less* change than almost any other American institutional practice since the days of Henry Adams. "It continues to depress me, even as I teach my own classes, to think of the thousands across the country doing much the same thing in the same kinds of places at the same hour," University of Utah English professor Kenneth Eble wrote in 1972. Eble had just completed three years of visiting higher-education institutions of every type, ranging from community colleges and small liberal arts schools to large public and private research universities. But the amazing diversity of these institutions—and of their clienteles—was simply not reflected in their style of instruction. It was much the same thing, in the same kinds of places, at the same hour. The amateur hour.[15]

And precisely because it was amateur, it has also remained mostly out of sight. Professions write things down: they document and record and authenticate, all in an effort to maintain consistent standards and practices. By contrast, amateurism rests on inherited wisdom and tradition; it is more akin to folklore, passed down informally across generations. The amateur status of teaching has meant that it is rarely documented—or recorded, or authenticated—in the ways that a truly professional practice would be. That creates a special challenge for the historian of college teaching, as Henry Adams recognized many years ago. Writing in 1872, just 14 years after graduating from Harvard, Adams argued that "the history of instruction . . . should come directly from first sources." But such sources were in short supply, he added, except for official records produced by colleges themselves. Those documents revealed "a formal tale of boys' experiences"—that is, what students were supposed to do—without illuminating how or even whether they did it. "One wishes to know what the student thought of himself, of his studies, and of his instructors; what his studies and his habits were; how much he knew and how thoroughly; with what spirit he met his work, and what amount of active aid and sympathy he received from his instructors," Adams wrote. He ignored the growing body of memoirs by students, which could have cast light on their varied experience; three decades later, indeed, Adams would publish the most famous contribution to that genre. Yet the full story of college teaching would never be told, he insisted, because institutional records reflected the party line and student voices were rarely recorded at all. "The student must remain content to have no history of education written from his standpoint," Adams glumly concluded.[16]

This book tries to listen to a variety of voices—students, faculty, and administrators—by drawing on sources that Henry Adams could not have accessed. It relies most heavily on private letters and memoranda in 59 different college and university archives, which illuminate not only the "formal tale" of teaching (as Adams called it) but also the ways it actually operated. I also use student evaluations, which trickled into higher education in the early twentieth century but became commonplace by the end of it. All of these sources contain an obvious negative bias, because most commentators took note of undergraduate instruction only when it was blatantly inadequate. According to an old journalistic adage, "if it bleeds, it leads"; likewise, in the realm of college teaching, the worst examples often draw the most ink. So let me make my own biases as clear as I possibly can. Thanks to a growing body of research, I do believe that we can differentiate between good and bad instruction: the best teachers engage students in their own learning, and the worst ones simply ignore them. Across time, most college teachers were neither excellent nor horrible, but somewhere in between. Professors generally gave more attention to undergraduate learning at smaller colleges—where the research imperative was less insistent—than they did at larger universities. But these differences narrowed after World War II, when institutions of every kind recognized and rewarded publication over pedagogy. Even at the ostensibly "teaching"-oriented Assumption College, a small Catholic school in Massachusetts, administrators gave lip service to teaching but promoted faculty mainly on the basis of research. So male professors generally received higher salaries than women faculty, who "spend a lot of time with students"—as one female emeritus professor observed in 2012—and rose more slowly in the ranks as a result.[17]

I do not believe that this is fair or just, either for our professors or for their students. And surely it helps account for the poor overall quality of undergraduate teaching in the United States, which has been documented—and decried—by a small cottage industry of books and articles in recent years.[18] The problem is not a lack of knowledge about how students learn; to the contrary, the learning sciences have also witnessed a remarkable scholarly boom over the past few decades.[19] Instead, it is the absence of real incentives to translate what we know about learning into our day-to-day teaching. I am hardly the first historian to note how American higher education came to reward research over teaching. But these accounts rarely examine the actual teaching practices that professors employed, or the ways that they diverged from the *best* practices that research has illuminated.[20] American academics like to tout their evidence-based bona fides: unlike the great unwashed masses, who allegedly base their opinions on myth and error, we kneel before the altar of facts and science. But when it comes to teaching, we too often turn a blind eye to them. That is another thing marking us as amateurs, of course. The word is rooted in the Latin verb "to love," and many of us surely love teaching.[21] But we balk at making it into a professional project, which would require us to master new knowledge and apply it in our own classrooms. We are the real mythmakers, caught up in old stories that we pass down from generation to generation.

Many of those stories remain unpublished, which is exactly what you would expect for an amateur endeavor. In recent years, we have witnessed admirable efforts to professionalize college teaching via societies and journals devoted to exploring and improving it. But that project is a very minor satellite in the larger academic universe, as even its most zealous advocates will admit.[22] College teaching has taken place in public settings while remaining a private affair: it is "something you did when others weren't looking," several Penn State professors recently observed, which is yet another hallmark of amateurism. So my book is likewise based mainly on private sources, hidden away in thousands of boxes and awaiting the next scholar who will—in good Weberian fashion—prove me wrong. "There is no good history of teaching and no history of good teaching," Harvard president Charles Eliot complained in 1889, three decades after Henry Adams studied there.[23] This book tries to answer their challenge, by making the private—and the personal—as public as they can be.

CHAPTER ONE

Between the Two Ends of the Log

Teaching and Learning in the Nineteenth Century

In 1871, a future president of the United States delivered America's most famous tribute to a college teacher. Addressing a Williams alumni dinner at
the swank Delmonico's Steakhouse in New York, Ohio congressman James
Garfield (class of 1856) questioned the value of the new laboratories and libraries that the college was seeking to fund. "A log cabin, with a pine bench in it
with Mark Hopkins at one end and me at the other, is a good enough college
for me," Garfield declared, in a testament to the longtime Williams professor
and president. Years later, after Garfield was assassinated, his college friend
and US senator John James Ingalls (class of 1855) quoted Garfield as saying, "A
pine log with the student at one end and Doctor Hopkins at the other, would
be a liberal education." This is probably where we get the aphorism "Mark
Hopkins on one end of a log and a student on the other," which became the
standard maxim about the importance of teacher-student interaction in undergraduate learning.[1]

Hopkins inspired a quasi-religious devotion among generations of students
for the care he devoted to each one. In a typical testament, sent to Hopkins
shortly before he died, one Williams graduate praised the "moulding and guiding influences which your teaching and example have had upon my whole
life." (Soon, the former student confidently predicted, Hopkins would don "the
crown of glory"—in Heaven.) But Hopkins also went against the grain of
nineteenth-century pedagogy, which surely accounts for a large part of his
fame. Unlike most other professors, Hopkins did not require his students to
recite assigned texts in class; he instead peppered them with unscripted questions, designed to elicit their individual thoughts and beliefs. "The Doctor's
favorite question—What do *you* think about it?—was the key to his success as
a teacher," another student recalled; still another extolled Hopkins's "Socratic
method" and "genius of interrogation." Most college classes followed a predictable pattern of call and response, culled directly from a text that students had
committed to memory. But Mark Hopkins "makes a man *think*, and think
quickly too," as future Hampton University founder Samuel C. Armstrong un-

derlined in a letter to his family. Writing in his student diary in 1855, a young James Garfield likewise praised Hopkins's method of incessant inquiry. "We have been walking in the strong clear light of Dr. Hopkins' teaching which led us deeper down into the heart of things than anything we have had before," Garfield noted. "He is a real sky-clearer, a cloud-compelling Jupiter."[2]

Nor did Hopkins lecture, except on special occasions, which marked a second departure from the American college norm. In the early nineteenth century, when some students could not obtain books, lectures were often the only way they could obtain information; after the Civil War, when bigger classes sometimes made recitations difficult or impossible, lectures allowed professors to teach a large number of students at the same time. Most of all, as a new generation of Americans began to obtain advanced degrees in Germany, the lecture marked a professor as a scholar who had mastered a specialized body of knowledge. But not Mark Hopkins. His only degrees were from Williams and a nearby medical college, which was enough to qualify him as a professor of moral philosophy and rhetoric. Like several other college presidents, Hopkins taught a capstone class for seniors that explored "the great intellectual and spiritual problems of humanity," a student recalled; by the end of the course, the student added, Hopkins had demonstrated "the grounds of obligation and of belief in the being of God." So Hopkins was revered for being "undogmatic" while "teaching a course that was dedicated to the propagation of Christian dogma," as his biographer wryly observed. And he did so largely without reading or assigning books, preferring to rely on his students' commonsense intuition. "One danger of too much reading is that of encumbering the mind with thoughts of others, and thus destroying individuality," one student wrote in his notebook, recording a rare lecture by Mark Hopkins. Like reading assignments from textbooks, professorial lecturing threatened to diminish or negate students' personal passions and differences. Better to keep their minds open while prodding them with questions, which would—Hopkins faithfully believed—resolve into good Christian answers.[3]

Few college teachers inspired the same level of veneration that Mark Hopkins did. And few people knew that better than James Garfield, who—like Hopkins—served as a professor and president at a small college. Just a year after graduating from Williams, Garfield took the helm of Western Reserve Eclectic Institute—later renamed Hiram College—and taught English grammar, Latin, Greek, history, math, philosophy, rhetoric, and geology. He also conducted training sessions for his faculty, railing against the "slow torture" of rote methods in the classroom. Garfield was a popular teacher: even his geology class, which met at the ungodly hour of 5:00 a.m., attracted a loyal following. But he soon tired of the job, leaving it for the more lucrative—and less taxing—realms of law and politics. "You and I know that teaching is not the work in which a man can live and grow," he told a friend. Between the two sides of Garfield's log, a forest of material constraints—including meager pay and growing class sizes—made it hard or impossible to teach the way Mark Hopkins did. Nor did many professors evince either the will or the ability to do so. It was certainly easier to quiz the students in lockstep fashion or to lecture at them in a steady drone, which generations of young Americans grew to detest. The nineteenth century witnessed enormous changes in the professoriate, as gentlemen-generalists like Hopkins were replaced by specialists with advanced degrees in their disciplines. The one constant was the disdain of their students, who derided most of their professors as nasty sadists or pompous bores. Asked by his sister what he liked about his teachers at Kenyon College, Rutherford B. Hayes—another future president from Ohio—could only think of one thing: he liked being away from them. Indeed, the log of James Garfield's imagination probably separated professors and students more often than it brought them together.[4]

The Teachers: Recitation and Beyond

Like Mark Hopkins, most college teachers before the Civil War were ordained ministers drawn from the colleges they had attended. Between 1828 and 1863, 19 of 25 full professors at Dartmouth were graduates of the institution; 17 of them had also studied theology, all but three at nearby Andover Seminary. "The clerical office seems to be naturally associated with the office of instruction," one Dartmouth professor observed, because both enterprises aimed at "moral and religious instruction." At Amherst, meanwhile, president Julius Seelye highlighted the same goal to justify hiring alumni as faculty: Amherst aimed to create good men, so who better to teach students than Amherst men? As late as 1871, 21 of 27 professors at Williams were alumni of it; at Wesleyan, which was younger and smaller, alumni held five of seven professorships. Like James Garfield, they taught an astonishing array of different subjects. Between 1862 and 1912, Northwestern professor Oliver March instructed botany, geology, Greek, logic, mineralogy, physics, and zoology; from 1878 through 1912, Haverford's Allen Thomas taught US history, biblical literature, constitutional law, English history, English literature, political economy, and religion. Professors who specialized in one subject sometimes changed to another: at Williams, for example, a Latin professor switched to teaching mathematics when the grammar manuscript he was writing burned in a fire. Another professor who taught botany and mineralogy boasted that "he could go into any classroom at Williams and conduct the recitation," no matter the subject.[5]

The choice of words was revealing, because most teaching in the early nineteenth century *was* recitation. In the colonial era, students typically had to recite in Latin or Greek. English became the medium of instruction in the nineteenth century, when young men memorized and repeated long passages from books in literature, philosophy, mathematics, and science; the lone exceptions were the so-called classics, which continued to be recited in ancient languages. Students at Harvard rose for 6:00 a.m. chapel in the summer, which was moved up to 6:30 in winter; then came a recitation, followed by breakfast; and then two or three more recitations were held during the day, concluding at 6:00 p.m. with another round of prayer. At Dartmouth, the first morning recitation was omitted on Mondays, because preparing for it the previous day would have violated the Sabbath. Students typically recited three to five times a day, five or six days a week. Often they were called upon in alphabetical order, which excused students of any further duty or accountability; once they had recited, a Yale graduate recalled, they could daydream, sleep, or "read a novel." Starting in the 1820s, however, some professors began to select students via lots drawn from a box. Students sat anxiously until their name was drawn, stood up to recite, and then sat down again in pleasurable relief. Some professors returned the names to the box, to the chagrin of their students; that meant they could be called upon again the same day. For the most part, however, everyone knew when they were going to be called and behaved accordingly. They were alert when it was their turn to recite, a Dartmouth observer wrote, but rarely paid attention at any other time.[6]

Most of all, students rarely found interest or significance in what they were saying. The recitation system privileged memory over meaning, regurgitation over real understanding. In mathematics, a Williams alumnus recalled, students with "no conception whatever of geometry" could "recite every proposition by heart" and thereby satisfy their professor. Likewise, students tackled conic sections—possibly the most-hated topic in nineteenth-century education—by memorizing theorems, which were dutifully repeated in class. "Felt sick and unusually nervous . . . but was called up on general principles, and came off perfect," a relieved Amherst student wrote in his diary in 1848. "Thus ended conics, the bugbear of college mathematics, the long-dreaded and fearfully encountered; and after all, I *like them* real well." Other students took pride in reciting long passages in Latin but often remained only marginally aware of what they were saying. Future Cornell president Andrew Dickson White recited an entire book by Tacitus before his professor at Yale said anything about why it might be of value; after hearing a student recite from the same book, another Yale professor joked that the student had been repeating "one of the noblest productions of the human mind without knowing it." In philosophy and history, meanwhile, students more readily comprehended the words but affixed little import to them. "The text-book was simply repeated by rote," wrote White, recalling his course in "natural philosophy" at Yale. "Not one student in fifty took the least interest in it; and the man who would give the words of the text most glibly secured the best marks."[7]

Professors often declared the student's grade out loud and then recorded it in a notebook, which also served to enforce attendance: anyone who was absent had their recitation graded as a zero or failure, unless it had been excused beforehand. At the University of Minnesota, historian Harry Pratt Judson—later the president of the University of Chicago—would listen to recitations from the textbook and languidly declare "That's worth about a 3" or "That's worth about a 7"; the rare perfect score was deemed a 10. Although some professors accepted summaries or paraphrasing of the assigned book, others demanded a word-for-word repetition—especially if they had authored the text, as was sometimes the case. "It took me 14 years . . . to write this book," declared Harvard professor Levi Hedge, referring to his *Elements of Logick* text, "and I am sure you cannot do better than to employ the precise words of the learned author." Meanwhile, students developed their own vocabularies for rating—and ribbing—each other. Reciting well was called a "rowl"; students who stumbled and stuttered were said to "fizzle," while those who failed to prepare at all suffered a "smash." At some recitations, a Williams student wrote, up to half of the students replied "not prepared" when they were called. But that did not seem to bother their professors, who sometimes dismissed the class—normally an hour long—after just 10 or 15 minutes. In one memorable instance, the grateful student added, a mathematics recitation "lasted but seven."[8]

But students also recalled professors who used the recitation hour for discussion, quizzing students not on the precise words of the assigned text but on its implications for their civic and moral lives. At Union College, legendary president Eliphalet Nott—who served in that capacity for 62 years—was also renowned for conducting highly interactive classes, which students remembered fondly many years afterward. Following a "brief recitation of the text," to ensure that students had read it, Nott "occupied the remaining time in animated discussion on subjects connected with the lesson," wrote Union alumnus Francis Wayland, who later became president of Brown University. Likewise, Wesleyan president Stephen Olin famously pressed his students to analyze texts and encouraged other faculty to teach in the same manner. "It is obvious [that] the pupils here are taught to *think* and *reason*," underlined a visiting committee to Wesleyan in 1848. "Their recitations are not a mere parrot's part of uttering words without comprehension of their meaning. They are trained to analyze, to classify, to compare, to judge." At New York University, C. S. Henry—who held a professorship of "Mental, Moral, and Political Philosophy"—demanded that students articulate a position and defend it against critics. "His object was not to give us information but to equip us with power," a former student wrote. Similarly, the ex-student recalled, Henry's successor Benjamin N. Martin taught students "how to think" instead of cramming their minds with disparate facts.[9]

Other professors conducted formal debates, drawing on a forensic tradition that dated to the colonial era. As political tensions mounted in New England during the War of 1812, Yale president Timothy Dwight supervised student debates about capital punishment, religious tests for office, and whether America should have "a monarchical or a republican form of government." Professors also required students to produce compositions on controversial literary and political matters and then defend their claims in class. At Amherst, students wrote competing essays about a Byron poem: one argued that "the general tendency of the piece was immoral and infidel," while the other claimed that it "only followed nature and the Bible." Students prepared for these encounters by reading drafts of their compositions out loud and then critiquing each other. "We had quite a debate on the question of whether reformers were in advance of their age," an Amherst student wrote in his diary, "and concluded mostly that they were." The same student recorded that his professor had led the class in a debate on whether "writers or speakers" exercise "the most influence" on the world.[10]

The same question arose around the most important and controversial development in nineteenth-century pedagogy: the professorial lecture. In the early part of the century, upperclassmen (that is, juniors and seniors) attended lectures by senior professors, especially college presidents, who added context and analysis to the texts that students recited; for poorer students who could not afford to purchase them, meanwhile, lectures could substitute for the book itself. Students transcribed—often verbatim—what professors said in class; afterward, they compared notes and sometimes prepared a master copy of the lecture; and then they would make their own individual notes from that copy. The process could be painstaking for the professor as well. Future president John Quincy Adams, who taught rhetoric and oratory at Harvard while serving in the US Senate between 1803 and 1808, described his lectures as "precisely the labor of Sisyphus." But his work seemed to pay off: Adams's classes were often filled beyond capacity, and his final lecture—before he left to become ambassador to Russia—was moved to the college chapel, the largest space on campus, to accommodate the throngs of listeners. The most popular college lecturer in the first half of the nineteenth century was probably Yale chemist Benjamin Silliman, who honed his craft as a paid speaker on the so-called lyceum circuit. At Yale, where he lectured every day except Sunday, he became legendary for his accompanying experiments and demonstrations. Elsewhere, too, science classes offered excellent opportunities for crowd-pleasing stunts and tricks. During a lecture on anatomy at Hampden-Sydney College in Virginia, one chemistry professor brought in a live cat, placed poison on its tongue, and then caused the dead animal to jerk and even sneeze by applying electricity to its nerves. A professor at Williams put phosphorus on his students' faces and turned out the lights, making the delighted students glow in the dark.[11]

Lecturing became more common, as well as more specialized, after the Civil War, when a new generation of faculty who undertook graduate study in Germany started to replace the "God-fearing gentlemen" and "fine old characters" of the old-time college, as one student remembered. By 1880, one-half of the Harvard faculty already had a PhD; 12 years later, two-thirds did. The change occurred more slowly in the smaller colleges, but its direction was clear. Writing in 1878, a Greek professor at Smith—and an alumnus of Amherst—worried that new German-minted faculty in the colleges would abandon wide-ranging education (including "oversight of the morals of the students") in favor of more narrow academic goals. Trained as experts in new fields of scholarship, the younger generation of professors typically taught elective courses in their specialties rather than the broad array of required subjects that professors had formerly instructed. Most accounts of the rise of the elective system attribute it to Harvard president Charles Eliot, whose 1869 inaugural address argued that electives would allow students to cultivate their individual interests under faculty members who were developing knowledge in the same area. Well before that time, however, other institutions had experimented with electives: Thomas Jefferson encouraged the practice when he founded the University of Virginia, and Swarthmore already let juniors and seniors choose two-thirds of their courses when Eliot instituted his reforms. Other colleges allowed a small number of electives but held out against the more open-ended system associated with Harvard, which Bucknell's president denounced for "entrusting the choice of studies to the crude, the indolent, and the inexperienced." But here, too, the direction of change was unmistakable: no matter the institution, America's students increasingly took courses they had selected, taught by faculty who specialized in those subjects.[12]

They were also more likely to experience lectures rather than recitations, especially if their professors had studied in Germany. Some young teachers clearly sought to emulate the public style and charisma of their German *professoren*, who were often evaluated by the number and spirit of the students they attracted: as a young W. E. B. Du Bois observed, writing in his diary from Berlin, students signified disapproval of a lecture by shuffling their feet and applause by stamping them. The exigencies of new scholarship favored lecturing as well: in fields undergoing sharp transformation, faculty could not find up-to-date textbooks—especially in English translation—to assign to their students. In some instances, finally, growing class sizes made the lecture into "the only practicable form of instruction," as Harvard historian Albert B. Hart wrote in 1884. ("The classes are too large for recitations, even if proper textbooks exist," Hart added.) Many colleges and universities boosted their overall student numbers without adding commensurate facilities, which led to overcrowded classrooms. But the biggest factor was the elective system itself, which not only allowed faculty to lecture in their specialties but also let students vote (not just shuffle or stamp) with their feet. Popular professors like Harvard geologist Nathaniel Shaler attracted so many students that he simply had to lecture, which was just fine by his hordes of devotees: when Shaler described the movement of the polar ice caps, one student recalled, "you would have thought he had been there, observing from a mountain-peak." Other students chose classes based on how much work they assigned, creating big crowds for so-called "snap" or easy courses.[13]

But some critics charged that the entire trend toward lectures let students avoid serious work, especially when compared to the traditional recitation. As early as 1823, Amherst president Heman Humphrey worried that lectures allowed students to loaf. The same concern appeared in the Yale Report of 1828: best known for its staunch defense of Greek and Latin classics, the report also warned against lectures in any subject. A student in lecture "may repose upon his seat and yield a passive hearing . . . without ever calling into exercise the powers of his own mind," wrote Yale president Jeremiah Day. "Daily recitation, on the other hand, requires steady and earnest efforts." Such anxieties stepped up after the Civil War, as lectures became more frequent. At Cornell, one professor worried that the skill of two incoming lecturers would remove any incentive to study in their courses. "They will both be most brilliant I have no doubt," he wrote, "and the more brilliant they are, the less inclined our boys will be after hearing them to go back to the hard work by which alone any solid results can be attained." Other skeptics feared that American lecturers would echo the soporific styles of their German forebears, who were hardly the spellbinding orators of popular lore. Upon return from study in Germany, American philologist James Morgan Hart worried that "dry, didactic monologue" would become the norm on his own shores as well. Harvard historian Ephraim Emerton likewise recalled German lectures as a "dreary recitation of facts," often from a book that the lecturer himself had authored.[14]

Some American professors did borrow these practices, much to their students' exasperation. At Columbia, John W. Burgess was notorious for reciting one of his own history books from memory; students would sit in class with a copy of the book open in front of them, marking "omit" next to any passage that Burgess happened to skip. But other professors composed original lectures, exerting enormous energy—and anxiety—in the process. "Getting up a lecture of this sort is no child's play," Johns Hopkins historian J. Franklin Jameson wrote in his diary in 1882, after spending 11 hours preparing for just part of a single class. Jameson then shifted to conducting traditional recitations, which he found less exhausting but also less effective. So he changed course yet again, to "questioning upon assigned lessons" and "informal lectures." Here Jameson echoed Harvard's Charles Eliot, who encouraged faculty to combine the best aspects of recitation and lecture and to avoid the worst dimensions of each. "Recitations alone readily degenerate into dusty repetitions, and lectures alone are too often a useless expenditure of force," Eliot warned in his inaugural speech in 1869. He returned to the same theme a decade later, noting that recitation "gives an opportunity for personal acquaintance and sometime intimate intercourse" between teachers and students but could also spawn mechanical memorization. Meanwhile, lecture allowed the professor to share his expert knowledge but could also render students "listless" and "completely passive." The key was to leaven both methods with spirit and spontaneity, promoting maximal exploration and engagement. "If, in the recitation . . . there is something of the lecture, on the other hand in the lecture there is, ordinarily, a large admixture of the Socratic method," Eliot explained. "The lecturer does not read or speak continuously to himself, but frequently interrupts his exposition to address a question to an individual or to the class, or to invite the class to ask questions and suggest difficulties."[15]

Other spokesmen stressed hands-on observation and experiment, often drawing from famous child educators like Friedrich Froebel and Francis Parker. Going back to the 1830s, Amherst geologist and future president Edward Hitchcock led students on field trips to the top of nearby Mount Holyoke; during a flood, he also brought them to watch the Connecticut River flow over its banks. Similarly, Albert Hopkins—Mark's brother, and a fellow Williams professor—took students on a natural-history trip to Nova Scotia; upon their return, they classified and displayed the objects they collected. Albert Hopkins also built a new astronomical observatory for the college, absorbing three-quarters of the expense himself and raising the rest via "begging tours" (as he called them) among alumni. After the Civil War, professors in the new social sciences instituted their own field trips to different municipal institutions. Touting the virtues of "look and see," as the observational method was known, Johns Hopkins political economist Richard Ely took students to visit nearby factories; meanwhile, his psychologist colleague G. Stanley Hall led excursions to local schools and mental institutions. The most renowned purveyor of observational pedagogy in the nineteenth century was Harvard biologist Louis Aggasiz, who sometimes locked a student in a room full of specimens and refused to let him out until he had identified them. "I must teach and yet give you no information," Aggasiz wrote, explaining his technique. "I must, in short, to all intents and purposes, be ignorant like you." Henry Adams, who authored the best-known critique of nineteenth-century higher education, said that Aggasiz's course on the glacial period and paleontology had "more influence on his curiosity than the rest of college instruction put together." That spoke well of Agassiz, of course, but not of the rest of college teaching.[16]

The Students: Resistance and Rebellion

Only a tiny fraction of Americans went to college in the nineteenth century, and almost all of them were white men. In the early part of the century, they tended to be younger—between 14 and 16 upon entry—and often came from small towns and farming communities, reflecting the overall agrarian character of the country. As America urbanized and its social classes hardened, the colleges increasingly drew from the scions of wealth in large cities; near the end of the century, growing numbers came from the country's burgeoning middle class. A handful of students also attended women's colleges and institutions for African Americans, which multiplied after Emancipation. As age differentiation became more pronounced in American grade schools, meanwhile, college students tended to be older than before.[17]

They also bore one more trait in common: they typically disliked college, at least the part involving teaching and learning. Looking back at his years at Yale, psychology professor Harlow Gale recalled science classes that drilled facts without revealing "the real stuffs, forces, and laws of nature"; math was an "unadulterated discipline in self-denial," he added, while philosophy was "as indigestible to us as an ostrich diet." Likewise, Henry Adams (Harvard, 1858) described his education as tedious, vacuous, and superficial. His four years at Harvard were "wasted"; indeed, all four years "could have been easily put into the work of any four months." His fellow students accepted poor instruction, because they attended for status reasons rather than scholarly ones. "No one took Harvard College seriously," Adams remembered. "All went because their friends went there, and the College was their ideal of social self-respect." An earlier graduate of the college, future senator Charles Sumner, pronounced an even harsher requiem for it. "*Not one single thing* is well taught to the Undergraduates of Harvard College," Sumner underscored.[18]

To be sure, men like Adams and Sumner could hardly have achieved their literary distinction if their college experience was entirely devoid of educational value. But most students insisted that they had learned in spite of the instruction they received, not because of it. They reserved special disdain for recitations, which generated a toxic blend of angst and ennui. One Dartmouth student described how his professor sat in a chair and called the students up one by one, each carrying a little card; students who recited correctly received one kind of dot on their card and those reciting incorrectly received a different kind. "That was the end of it," the student recalled. "It was taken for granted that the student had learned his lesson, and that he was present at the recitation not to be taught anything." Indeed, as other students confirmed, recitations typically functioned to test rather than to teach. The result was horribly humdrum, as students recited the same passages while others daydreamed, slept, or carved graffiti on their wooden desks to pass the time. "Little was said or done outside the text book," another Dartmouth student wrote, making class "as even as [the] Sahara desert and almost as dry." Remembering his recitations at Yale, prominent book editor Henry Holt declared that "the most diabolical ingenuity could hardly have done more to make . . . scholarship repulsive." Indeed, Harvard's twentieth-century in-house historian reported that his many years of research failed to uncover any other kind of reaction to the college recitation. "Almost every graduate of the period 1825–1860 has left on record his detestation of the system of instruction," Samuel Morison wrote in 1936. "The Faculty were not there to teach, but to see that boys got their lessons."[19]

To make matters even worse, from students' perspective, faculty often delegated that task to the most hated figure in nineteenth-century education: the tutor. Mostly young men just out of college, tutors lived with the students— ostensibly to preserve discipline and morality—and often conducted recitations. Although some tutors did become professors, the position was not seen as an apprenticeship for academia. It was instead a form of servile labor, exploited by professors and despised by students. Four Harvard tutors led 2,364 recitations in 1825, while the college's 11 professors taught a total of only 824. Students abused them too, transferring their dissatisfaction with college instruction onto their hapless tutors. Williams students scraped their slates and groaned at tutors during recitation; if a tutor was known to fancy "a young lady in the village," they wrote her name on the blackboard to shame him; and they woke tutors up in the middle of the night, by rolling stoves down the stairs or howling into the darkness. At Dartmouth, students loaded a cannon with powder and fired it under their tutor's window. Three hundred panes of glass shattered and houses shook in the adjacent village, where citizens thought an earthquake was upon them. Assigned to carry benches into the tutors' room to recite, students at Harvard took the benches outside and burned them instead. Students also made fun of tutors' ignorance, correcting their errors in recitation to demonstrate the students' allegedly superior intellect and breeding. Tutors are "low-born despicable rustics, lately emerged from the dunghill," a Harvard student jibed, "who, conscious of their own want of genius, were determined to discountenance all who possessed it." Amherst student William Gardiner Hammond rejoiced that his recitations under a tutor were coming to a close, to be capped by lectures from faculty members. "Hereafter we bid adieu to tutorial sway, and come beneath the profs.," he wrote jauntily in his diary in 1847.[20]

But lectures proved unsatisfactory as well, echoing another common refrain of nineteenth-century students. "I must confess I have been disappointed in them," Hammond wrote, referring to a set of zoological lectures by Edward Hitchcock. "I have no clearer idea of the general principles of the science than I might have got in an hour or two from the encyclopedia." Henry Adams likewise disparaged the lectures he heard at Harvard, where professors held forth before growing audiences of bored young men. "Any large body of students stifles the student," Adams wrote. "The lecture system to classes of hundreds, which was very much that of the twelfth century, suited Adams not at all," he added, referring to himself in the third person. Another prominent Harvard product, Henry David Thoreau, sat through lectures by the brilliant mathematician and navigator Benjamin Peirce—so brilliant, one of Thoreau's classmates joked, that none of the students understood him. Told upon his graduation that he had "studied navigation," Thoreau expressed surprise. "Why, if I had taken one turn down the harbor I should have known more about it," he wrote. Thoreau did enjoy lectures by chemist John Webster, whose penchant for blowing things up in class earned him the nickname "Skyrocket Jack." Webster once exploded a copper vessel and sent a piece flying to the back row of his lecture hall, where it would have killed anyone sitting there; a few years later, ironically, Webster would be convicted and hanged for murdering a fellow professor. For the most part, however, Thoreau was bored by his teachers. He studied physics and astronomy with a tutor who required students to recite outdated French-language textbooks but never conducted a single laboratory demonstration or even encouraged students to look at the stars. Nor did Thoreau's studies in "navigation" expose him to any actual apparatus used in that enterprise, although Harvard almost surely possessed it.[21]

Indeed, most of the scientific equipment that colleges acquired—and proudly advertised in catalogs and promotional materials—seemed designed to enhance the prestige of the institution, not the education of its students. The same went for libraries, which students could only visit for a few hours a week if at all. When professors brought chemicals and gadgets into class, students observed experiments instead of conducting them. A few institutions did allow students to engage with scientific apparatus, but the results were underwhelming. Samuel Chapman Armstrong went to the Williams observatory on clear nights and looked at the stars; that was enough to earn class credit, a bemused Armstrong reported, even if he got little else from the experience. ("I am accountable to no one for my work," he admitted.) Chemistry students at Dartmouth conducted a handful of exercises in an "ice-bound" laboratory, one professor wrote, where freezing temperatures cooled any possibility of "mental action." Likewise, students often reported that their institutions' much-ballyhooed field trips—which later generations would call "experiential learning"—generated more discomfort than enlightenment. At Roanoke College, where the president led his geology class to a faraway mountaintop during a rainstorm, students said they could have learned all the material without leaving campus. "We all voted it a bone to have to hire a horse and ride 40 miles to see a few rocks, when there are plenty of the same kind in the cabinet," one student grumbled, in a letter to his mother.[22]

Finally, the end of each term brought the bane of every nineteenth-century college student's academic existence: examinations. In every era, of course, students have denounced the tests that faculty foisted upon them. But the complaint was especially prominent in the early 1800s, when students were examined in public and then ranked next to their classmates. Faculty conducted the exercises much like recitations, awarding the highest marks to the students who could memorize the most. Some colleges delegated the task to special examination boards, which students regarded with a mix of bemusement and terror. Composed of local clergy, with a few lawyers and grade school teachers thrown in, the visiting board sometimes knew less about the subject at hand than anyone in the room: at Dartmouth, for example, an examiner in German held his book upside down for the entire duration of the examination. Mount Holyoke students were examined by both professors and students at nearby Amherst, which occasioned no small amount of anxiety at the women's college. "Just to think of reciting History topics . . . to say nothing of being pumped on Geology before the man that *wrote the book*," one worried Holyoke student underlined, most likely referring to Amherst president Edward Hitchcock. After the Civil War, as lectures gradually outpaced recitations, written examinations came to replace oral ones: according to Harvard's Board of Overseers, so named because it conducted exams, written tests would encourage students to "master the subject" instead of simply to memorize. Students often found otherwise: if anything, they reported, it was easier to "cram"—that is, prepare at the last minute—for a written exam than for an oral one. The key difference was that written tests were private, as were the grades assigned to them. Many colleges did not even inform students of their marks, so long as they had passed, causing some students to pine for the strict grading practices of their grade school years. "The vague idea of some indefinite future culture is hardly enough to make me sit down and study Greek verbs," one Wellesley student wrote, "when I have a chance to go boating instead."[23]

No matter the institution, many students found better things to do than to engage in their studies. An Amherst student noted that recitations sometimes did not count in class standing, which obviously reduced the incentive to prepare for them. Nor did it normally take a long time to do so. Upon graduating from Harvard in 1853, future president Charles Eliot estimated that a bright student could ready for all of his daily recitations in a single hour; Williams student William Whitney, later a leading Sanskrit scholar, reported studying 90 minutes a day. Addressing Bowdoin's commencement in 1825, budding poet Henry Wadsworth Longfellow expressed surprise to discover that he was ranked fourth in his class "in as much as I have never been a remarkably hard student." His Bowdoin friend Nathaniel Hawthorne, another future literary standout, likewise remembered college as a time of leisure rather than study; pupils were "idle lads" who gathered blueberries, shot pigeons and squirrels, and caught fish in a nearby stream. To be sure, some students—especially those from less wealthy backgrounds—put in long hours of work: at the University of North Carolina, for example, one student made himself ill by reading until 2:00 each night and then rising at 4:30 a.m. for morning prayers. But such students were also routinely mocked by their peers, who sought to enforce a strict code of lackadaisical effort. Students who arrived early at recitation or stayed late to ask a question were derided as "bootlickers," while anyone who put in too much preparation was deemed "blue," "blue-light," or "blue-skin." Lest anyone miss the point, Harvard students put it to song: "We deem it narrow-minded to excel," their popular college tune explained. "We call the man fanatic who applies. . . . We long to sit with newspapers unfurled, indifferent spectators to the world." When Theodore Roosevelt entered Harvard in 1876, the campus paper warned newcomers against participating in class. But Roosevelt ignored the advice, earning the enmity of almost everyone around him. Most students tried to avoid anything that looked like academic engagement, as another Harvard freshman observed. When called upon, he noted, the best answer was always the same: I don't know. "This, then, must be the 'Harvard indifference' about which I have heard so much," he wrote, only half-facetiously. "I am trying for it now, and I hope to be an expert when I go home at Christmas."[24]

Another way to avoid work was to disrupt class, an endemic practice across nineteenth-century higher education. Colleges were plagued by student riots and rebellions, often over poor food and other amenities; Harvard alone had nine major protests, including the Bread and Butter Rebellion of 1805 and the Rotten Cabbage Rebellion of 1807. But students also protested academic instruction, especially if they found it too onerous. In the Conic Section Rebellion of 1830, Yale students revolted when professors required them to explain theorems at the blackboard instead of reciting from a textbook. Eventually 42 of 96 students in the class were expelled by Yale, which refused to recommend them for admission to other colleges. Students also protested classes that allegedly assigned too much homework, sometimes via "the bolt"—nineteenth-century parlance for a boycott—or, less commonly, through a petition: in 1856, for example, students at Williams appointed a committee to demand that history assignments never exceed eight pages per evening. Informally, meanwhile, students devised various measures to interrupt, disturb, and divert their professors. Pranksters at Dartmouth rang the college bell early, so professors would dismiss their classes prematurely as well; they blew horns outside of classrooms and then scattered before the professor could identify them; they even drove cows into a classroom and left them there overnight "with unfortunate results," as one observer sardonically noted. Students at the University of Virginia stamped their feet for 15 minutes whenever a new teacher arrived—not to signal approval, as in Germany, but to squander time. Princeton students drowned out a chemistry lecturer with renditions of "Swing Low Sweet Chariot" and other songs; they also sidetracked an incompetent professor and military veteran by asking him questions about his past, a time-honored method of student obstruction and delay.[25]

Finally, students relied on another venerable tactic to avoid hard study: cheating. Upon discovering that their written examinations were published in Philadelphia, students at the University of Mississippi hired agents there to help them see the tests before they were administered. Around the country, meanwhile, students developed elaborate ruses and schemes to cheat during recitation. They folded crib sheets a dozen times and concealed them in their shoes or belts; they hid so-called "pony" translations of Latin and Greek classics in their laps, while pretending to translate the originals at their desks; and if a professor didn't know all the names in the class, students sometimes bribed classmates to recite for them. Writing in 1871, recent Yale graduate Lyman Bagg compiled perhaps the most comprehensive account of "skinning," the common slang for cheating. Instructed to close their books, students put them on the floor and turned the pages with their feet. They also helped classmates recite—known as "skinning a man through"—by holding open books for them, or by pressing a finger or pencil on their backs to provide an answer in mathematics. When it came time for examinations, students sometimes copied an entire textbook on a "skinning machine" of two-inch-wide paper mounted on twin rollers "like an ancient scroll," Bagg wrote. College authorities fought back with new rules, requiring students to place all books on the professor's table when they entered the room; they also barred students from wearing cloaks when they were called to the blackboard, where it was easy to conceal a small book while working out a problem. As usual, however, student deception exceeded the colleges' ability to detect it. One enterprising Yale

student even set up a small printing press in his room, producing translations on small bits of paper that could be secreted into Greek and Latin
texts.[26]

The Two Ends of the Log

All of these schemes and ruses spoke to the distance between students and
their teachers, belying the romantic image of the avuncular nineteenth-century
professor bonding with his loyal protégés. Like Mark Hopkins, some professors surely evinced enormous personal care and concern for their students.
But they were the exceptions, as a dejected Ralph Waldo Emerson observed
in 1846. "The teacher should be the complement of the pupil; now for the most
part they are earth's diameters wide of each other," Emerson wrote. Another
Harvard alumnus echoed the same complaint in 1860, looking back regretfully
on his studies three decades earlier. "I do not think the professors and tutors
generally show enough personal interest and regard for their pupils to win
from them the true favor," Samuel Osgood wrote. "The two parties are too often found set against each other in mutual suspicion." Likewise, Williams
graduate G. Stanley Hall recalled his own professors as distant and forebod-
ing figures, not as devoted or friendly ones. "The professors seemed to us to
live in splendid isolation," Hall observed. "There was only a 'ten-foot-pole' relation between them and us." The gap probably increased in the late nineteenth century, when increasing numbers of faculty trained in Germany and
imbibed their professors' austere style and passion for research. In an address
to alumni in 1887, Amherst president Julius Seelye worried that the growing
emphasis on libraries, laboratories, and investigation might erode the intimacy
at the heart of learning. "Education is a wholly personal work," Seelye intoned.
"It is not gained by books, or by instruction alone, nor by anything in place
of the living inspiration of the living teacher."[27]

Seelye's comment recalled James Garfield's aphorism about Mark Hopkins
on one end of the log and the student on the other. And at one level, the relatively small size of the nineteenth-century college must have made it feel more
intimate and communal than later—and larger—institutions did. As Williams
graduate Washington Gladden remembered, every student at the college was
"personally known" by every faculty member, not just by Hopkins. Professors
were sometimes responsible for overseeing meals, study halls, and chapel services; others doubled as registrars or librarians. They also tended to work at
a single institution for a long span of time: in 1870, the average tenure of professors at Princeton, Bucknell, Swarthmore, and Franklin & Marshall ranged

between 23 and 30 years. So we can safely assume that most students knew their teachers, even if the teachers remained somewhat aloof and enigmatic. It is also likely that the overall quality of instruction became more creative and cooperative over the century, as some professors dispensed with lockstep recitations and one-directional lectures. That probably allowed more students to interact substantively with their professors, at least in class. "Formerly, the only business of a teacher was to hear recitations and make marks for merit," declared theologian and Harvard alumnus James Freeman Clarke, at the university's 1886 commencement. "Now, he has the opportunity of teaching. This is one of the greatest educational discoveries of modern times—that the business of a teacher is to teach."[28]

But the dominant modes of instruction in the nineteenth century had changed much less than Clarke allowed. Most forms of recitation remained mechanical and formulaic, with teachers and students playing their appointed roles, and most lecture classes were monologues by the faculty, who loomed as distant and austere figures atop their podiums. Overall, teacher-student intimacy seemed threatened in the late nineteenth century by the "drift of the age toward organization," as one of Mark Hopkins's former students worried in an 1888 tribute to him. "We belong to an era of appliances and adjustments," Leverett Wilson Spring observed. "Our educational affairs move on with the precision of clock-work." But, Spring continued, "there is one factor in education that has remained essentially unchanged from age to age. This fact is the personal—the native, indefinable something in the teacher that wins and inspires the pupil." Mark Hopkins had that "something," Spring wrote, as did Louis Aggasiz and several other nineteenth-century teachers whom he hailed. But as Spring also admitted, "the personal element" that defined good teaching was "so difficult to characterize and so impossible to measure." In the ensuing years, as the drift toward organization grew ever more relentless, it would become more difficult—and sometimes impossible—to retain the personal element. Teaching was surely a personal activity, but its intimacy was imperiled by a society that seemed to be dissolving the individual in the acids of bureaucracy.[29]

CHAPTER TWO

Scholarship and Its Discontents

Teaching and Learning in the Progressive Era

In 1900, the *Nation* ushered in a new century with an old jeremiad: college teaching had gotten worse. In earlier eras, the magazine said, figures like Mark Hopkins and Eliphalet Nott had made their mark "as instructors, rather than scholars." Yet the contemporary academy prized scholarship, to the detriment of instruction. The modern professor was "exceedingly learned" but "rarely succeeds in awakening the personal affection which marks the work of the great teacher," the *Nation* complained. Some institutions actually penalized their best teachers, who had to overcome "a pervading distrust" of their intellect and authority. "Broadly speaking, pronounced ability as a teacher . . . is not a passport to distinction," the magazine noted. "It very rarely leads to promotion." Overall, the *Nation* concluded, "the number of great teachers is decidedly less now than it once was." Lest anyone miss the point, the editorial's headline placed it in block letters: "THE DECLINE OF TEACHING."[1]

The editorial reflected nostalgia for the alleged virtues of college instruction in the nineteenth century, which had already become a recurring theme in American public life. The old guard were teachers, the story went, who were personally invested in their students; the new guard are scholars, committed to advancing specialized knowledge. That narrative inevitably distorted the past, which was never the pedagogical utopia that critics imagined. But it also spoke to real trends in the present. A minor key in the late 1800s, the PhD became a hallmark of faculty status and identity during the first decades of the new century; so did the lecture, which evolved into the central mode of college instruction. The twin developments were related, of course: hired on the basis of their expertise, professors were also more likely to proclaim it from a platform or stage. And they were less likely to conduct recitation, which lost its traditional dominance in college classrooms. "The time formerly spent by a professor hearing boys is now spent by boys in hearing a professor," surmised George H. Palmer, a Harvard philosopher whose career spanned the late nineteenth and early twentieth centuries.[2]

The emphasis on expertise was part of a much broader revolution in American life during the Progressive Era, which valorized scientific and technical knowledge in the service of the public good. Universities lay at the heart of this vision, producing the new skills and understanding that would—in theory—be harnessed by governments at every level to cleanse the country of disease, corruption, and inefficiency.[3] But the universities expended almost no energy in preparing professors for the classroom, nor was there any real effort to supervise or evaluate what faculty did once they got there. The outcome was a curious blend of system and anarchy, of expertise and amateurism. The same institutions placing renewed accent on technical skills largely ignored the techniques of teaching, leaving professors to instruct their students however they wished. "You will be absolutely free to conduct your courses as you see fit," a department chair at Stanford assured a newly hired professor in 1903. "Results are what we want, and I believe the best results can be obtained by allowing each man to work in accordance with his own ideas."[4]

But students and alumni told another story, as they always do. Left to their own devices, many faculty devoted as little attention as possible to the growing numbers of undergraduates in their charge; as the *Nation* declared in 1913, in another attack on college teaching, professors were "impatient of detail, careless in presentation, full of their own mental processes, and unaware of those of their students." The problem spawned many other exposés, along with several efforts at reform: most notably, under Woodrow Wilson, Princeton University instituted a preceptorial system designed to bring professors and students into more sustained and fruitful contact. But these efforts mostly foundered on the shoals of the university system, which inevitably drew students and professors farther apart. On the one hand, teaching was seen as a professorial prerogative that was too personal and idiosyncratic to be governed by university officials; on the other, the new scholarly imperatives—and the lack of real accountability—tended to diminish teaching or to bury it in impersonal routines, which took little regard of individuals. "Here is the weak point of all the great colleges, and even of the smaller ones—the lack of personal contact between teacher and student," wrote journalist Edwin Slosson in 1910, following a tour of 14 leading universities. "It is partly due to defective organization and partly to the development of a new school of teachers, who detest teaching, who look upon students as a nuisance, and class work as a waste of time." Like Humpty Dumpty, Slosson suspected, teacher-student relations had been fractured so deeply that all the king's horses—and all of the university's men—could not put them together again. "Teacher and pupil were not even on opposite ends of the same log," Slosson added. "They were at opposite ends of a telephone working only one way." In the Progressive years, the image of Mark Hopkins and the log continued to inspire a vision of college teaching that was ever more distant from the ways that most Americans experienced it.[5]

The Rise of the Scholar

In 1903, William James published the most famous critique of credentialism in American higher education. Although James had taught psychology and philosophy at Harvard for many years, he did not possess a PhD in either field. But colleges were increasingly demanding that degree of new faculty members, with deleterious consequences for teaching. "Will anyone pretend for a moment that the doctor's degree is a guarantee that its possessor will be a successful teacher?" James asked. "Notoriously his moral, social and personal characteristics may utterly disqualify him for success in the classroom." Many PhD candidates lacked the intellectual spark and enthusiasm to inspire others, James wrote, but were drawn by the status of the degree and its promise of a steady job. "We dangle our three magic letters before the eyes of these predestined victims," James warned, "and they swarm to us like moths to an electric light." But the real victims were their students, who suffered under the many weak bulbs in the professoriate. Authored for the *Harvard Monthly*, James's own university journal, his essay's catchy title—"The Ph.D. Octopus"—became a symbol of degree seeking run amok. It was reprinted in many places, including the *Educational Review*—a leading journal in its field—in 1918. "The conditions which it describes have been but slightly altered, if at all, in the intervening years," declared a plaintive editor's note at the start of the article.[6]

Actually, the trend accelerated as time elapsed. Ten years after James's essay appeared, West Virginia University professor John Harrington Cox observed that the PhD octopus had spread its tentacles even wider than before. "In the minds of college administrators-at-large, the magic Doctor's degree has become an all-potent talisman," Cox quipped, using a different metaphor to make the same point. To be sure, the move toward PhD faculty hiring was slower at small colleges and less elite universities like West Virginia. At Bowdoin, for example, President William De Witt Hyde declared that a PhD was "not essential" for joining his faculty; the most important qualification was "a great personality," which would draw students toward the professor, as well as to his subject of instruction. Elsewhere, too, colleges and universities sometimes selected "a good man in the bachelor's degree instead of a second-rate in doctor's silk," as Carnegie Foundation executive Frederick Keppel observed in 1917. But the drift toward the PhD was unmistakable, at nearly every type of institution. It brought status to professors as well as to their employers, marking both of them as part of the quest for the era's holy grail: science, investigation, and research. "There is something in the research virus which causes it to spread, and seek to dominate," wrote one observer in 1917, summarizing a set of self-surveys by colleges and universities. "Unless its relative value is definitely ascertained, with conditions for guiding and controlling it, research interest will supplant teaching interest."[7]

Like the selection of new faculty, promotion up the academic ladder increasingly turned on scholarly degrees, achievements, and reputation. "The young instructor has been urged to place as many printed pages as possible to his credit," Stanford president David S. Jordan admitted in 1910, "and in so doing has been encouraged to look with scorn on the 'mere teacher' who cares for the intellectual welfare of the students." Indeed, dedicated teaching could even count against a candidate for hire or promotion. "Many college professors are suspicious of a colleague who appears to be a particularly good teacher," a dean at Ohio State wrote privately, the same year. "There is a rather wide spread notion in American Universities that a man who is an attractive teacher must in some way or other be superficial or unscientific." To be sure, college presidents and other higher-education leaders gave lip service to the importance of teaching. But their off-the-record correspondence and conversation often revealed the opposite. Abraham Flexner, perhaps America's closest student of early twentieth-century education, quoted an anonymous dean who identified the best teacher on his faculty. When Flexner asked if the professor would be promoted, the dean replied quickly and firmly: no. "He hasn't done anything," the dean said, noting the professor's scant publication record.[8]

Some college officials and faculty members insisted that research and teaching went hand in hand: the best researchers were the best teachers, and vice versa. "As a general rule, the investigator will prove a more capable teacher than the non-investigator for the simple reason that he will be more apt to keep abreast with the progress of his studies," one University of Michigan professor insisted, rehearsing a defense that would dominate higher-education rhetoric for the ensuing century. But some professors openly proclaimed the inherent superiority of research over teaching, a less common—and more controversial—claim. "It is to the *discoverers*, in far greater measure than to the *transmitters* that the world is under obligation," underlined University of

Chicago classicist William Gardner Hale, in a much-quoted statement. The most famous advocate for this line of argument—and, as it happened, a famously poor teacher—was economist Thorstein Veblen, who openly disdained most undergraduate students. Research was "primary and indispensable," Veblen wrote in his renowned 1918 treatise, *The Higher Learning in America*; by contrast, teaching was secondary and usually superfluous. "It is this work of intellectual enterprise that gives its character to the university and marks it off from the lower schools," Veblen wrote, praising research. "The work of teaching belongs to the university only because and in so far as it incites and facilitates the university man's work of inquiry." The lone worthwhile form of instruction in higher education "trains the incoming generation of scholars and scientists for the further pursuit of knowledge," Veblen added. Everything else was grade school pedagogy, beneath the dignity of the true scholar.[9]

As the research gospel spread, indeed, many schools began to palm off their teaching duties onto a new breed of instructor: the assistant. Burgeoning PhD programs brought with them the kind of people Thorstein Veblen wanted to teach—that is, graduate students—who could in turn be enlisted to instruct undergraduates. Sometimes they were employed to grade essays, especially in courses on English composition. Mandatory for most undergraduate degrees, "English Comp" could generate between 20 and 30 hours per week of reading for the instructor. So it was tempting to hire an assistant, an "unseen public of one," who "comes into no personal contact with the pupil" and "touches the soul of the writer of a theme only through hieroglyphics on its margin," as one jaundiced Cornell professor joked in 1914. Other assistants taught their own composition classes while struggling—often, in vain—to complete their doctoral dissertations, which a second professor denounced as "academic serfdom." Still others taught "sections" of large lecture courses, another innovation of the Progressive Era. At Harvard, for example, "Economics A"—the introductory course in the subject—brought together 525 students for a lecture once a week; on two other days of the week, they met under a "teaching fellow," as assistants were called, in 21 sections of about 25 students each. The results were uneven at best. Teaching fellows "struggle manfully with their little sections," an alumnus wrote, "but they do not get under the skin of the undergraduate." Indeed, another graduate complained, his own teaching fellow seemed indifferent to teaching. "He was totally out of sympathy with his students," the alumnus recalled. "This is the main fault with the assistants—they don't care, take no pride with their duties, and work merely because it is a mild way of paying for their tuition." Like their professors, one English scholar surmised, teaching assistants (TAs) prized their own "research work" over the "menial work" of undergraduate instruction.[10]

In private, meanwhile, some university officials began to doubt whether they could bring both functions under one roof. "Personally, I believe that a good deal of our trouble comes from trying to maintain two ideals in the same institution, namely: Research and Teaching," the dean of the college at the University of Chicago told a correspondent in 1910. "These two things are always coming into collision. Either the graduate schools complain that their Research men are drafted for undergraduate teaching, or the College Deans protest against Research men as unfitted for Freshmen and Sophomore classes." Wherever they worked, professors still devoted the vast bulk of their time to teaching rather than research; status and promotion lay in books and articles, but day-to-day routines were dominated by the classroom. At the Universities of Wisconsin and Indiana, two institutions that had sharply enhanced their research profiles, surveys revealed that faculty gave about two-thirds of their time to teaching; the rest of their energies were split evenly between research and service activities, like serving on committees. Moreover, as a Wisconsin dean predicted in 1916, faculty teaching responsibilities were likely to multiply still further in the coming years. "There is an increased and increasing tendency to ask of teachers a large amount of personal attention to the intellectual life and development of their students," E. A. Birge wrote. "The teacher is expected to work with his students rather than to hear them recite." More and more courses would introduce "laboratory methods," he added, where students conducted their own research and experiments under faculty direction; and class size would decrease, to meet "the demand for personal guidance of the student in all studies."[11]

The Lecture System

Birge was right about the decline of recitation, but in almost every other way he was wrong. Universities became dominated during these years by the lecture system, which one contemporary observer called "the core of college teaching." And that surely made instruction less personal, rather than more so. Part of the reason lay in class sizes, which never declined (as Birge hoped) but instead rose steadily. To be sure, smaller colleges tended to have smaller classes. At Beloit, for example, nearly half of classes in 1910 enrolled between one and nine students; at Boston University, by contrast, just one in six courses were that size. But when John Erskine came to Amherst, upon earning his PhD in English at Columbia, he was surprised to find bigger classes at his new institution than he had encountered at his old one. "It was said that in a small college the student would receive his instruction in small groups and would therefore come into closer contact with the professors," Erskine wrote. At Amherst, however, he was immediately put in charge of two classes of 60 students each. A big university "could afford a faculty large enough to hold down the size of classes," Erskine explained, but smaller institutions—with lesser endowments—often could not. Down at Columbia, meanwhile, president Nicholas Murray Butler confirmed that classes were getting larger everywhere, and with ill consequences for teaching. In smaller settings, Butler wrote, "personal and intimate methods" were possible. But "as soon . . . as the group becomes moderately large," he warned, "there is a tendency to have recourse to the lecture alone."[12]

Worst of all, Butler charged, the lecture method recapitulated the same evil as the recitations it was replacing: rote memorization. Happily, he noted, "the parrot-like repetition of passages memorized from a text" had "largely disappeared from college teaching." But "the substitute . . . for the old repetition from a text-book is the lecture system," Butler added, which simply transferred memory work from written words to spoken ones. Students shuffled into dimly lit classrooms, heavy with stale air, and took their seats. The professor took the stage or platform, started to talk, and the students began the hated, all-consuming task of writing down what he said. "The slaves of the note-book toil like the slaves of the galley," wrote Frederick H. Pratt, a recent graduate of the college and medical school at Harvard. Note-taking was "largely a physical exercise" as evidenced by "the aching hand and arm," complained Pratt, who went on to teach physiology at several institutions. "It is *not* an intellectual exercise; for the student has become a note-taking machine." Enterprising students compiled and sold old sets of notes, which allowed their peers to skimp on note-taking or skip class altogether; since professors rarely changed their lectures from year to year, some students could pass end-of-term examinations without ever entering the lecture hall. Success on tests was the sole aim of the lecture system, Pratt wrote, and of college education writ large: no matter how the professor's words were recorded, students would "cram" them before tests and forget them shortly thereafter. "Students taught chiefly by lecture become effectively trained in but one subject—the passing of examinations," he wrote. "They work to pass, not to know," Pratt added, quoting Thomas Huxley's famous aphorism. "They do pass, and they don't know."[13]

Most of all, American students were bored by the incessant lecturing of the early twentieth-century university. Some professors delivered original lectures they had written, which often went over the heads of undergraduates; others read straight from the assigned textbook, which they had sometimes authored as well. Still others extemporized, casually and carelessly, which was certainly easier than planning out their remarks beforehand. Glancing at his watch, Columbia educational psychologist E. L. Thorndike realized he was scheduled to give a lecture in five minutes. "It would be fifty percent better if I spent this time in preparation," Thorndike admitted. "But let's compute another coefficient of correlation." The result was miserably humdrum, as countless students complained. "The majority of the faculty were pedants," Bowdoin alumnus Lloyd Osborn Coulter (class of 1918) flatly told a college official in 1955, recalling lecturers who dispensed disconnected facts and ephemera. "Most are dead, all are retired, so I shall speak frankly." His economics professor was "a gentleman, I know, and a Scholar, I'm sure, but a complete bore as a speaker," Coulter wrote. His Greek professor held forth on "rare irregular verbs" but "made no attempt whatsoever to arouse the plodding undergraduate to the glory that was Greece." Finally, the scholar who lectured on Shakespeare seemed "more concerned with the number of Roman conspirators who could stand on the dot of a colon" than in bringing the immortal Bard to life. Professors frequently mumbled, rendering them inaudible; others read out long columns of numbers, including tables of boiling points in chemistry class and dimensions of ancient buildings in art history, which cast a miserable tedium over the entire room. Indeed, professors often appeared every bit as bored as their students. "Our classroom is a race," one Yale student said, "to see who will get to sleep first, the class or the teacher."[14]

But there were also "wide-awake" lecturers, renowned for their exceptional stage presence and delivery. University of California historian John D. Hicks recalled inspiring lectures during his undergraduate years at Northwestern by Arthur Guy Perry, who "kept his students in a hypnotic spell throughout each hour" and "left them in a state of eager anticipation for the next." Perry spoke without notes, Hicks added, but his presentation was so organized and logical that Hicks's own note-taking was easy. Hicks also served as a TA at the University of Wisconsin for renowned lecturer Russell Fish, whose "bubbling wit" and "incorrigible ham-acting" caused some of his skeptical colleagues to "doubt his scholarship." But Fish knew his subject, Hicks recalled, and the students knew it as well: after each lecture, they saluted him with a "skyrocket," a long hiss followed by a boom and ending in a whistle and the chanting of his name. At Columbia, likewise, historian Carlton Hayes's lectures on European history provided "the most famous dramatic spectacle on the campus," as philosopher Irwin Edman—Hayes's former student—recalled. Audiences were thrilled by tales of Disraeli dropping his morning stick as the cannons boomed at Gibraltar, or even of Karl Marx writing the *Communist Manifesto* in the British Museum. Similarly, Hayes's colleague Charles Beard was somehow able to breathe flamboyant life into the otherwise dull machinations of American municipal politics. Lectures by Hayes and Beard were "first-rate theatrical performances," Edman remembered, "words shot out of emphasis, silences sustained for a moment, gestures and movements deployed like that of a good actor." Princeton professor Woodrow Wilson "gestured as if operating the handle of a spray pump" to douse students "with a shower of knowledge," a former student wrote, describing the future university and US president. At Atlanta University, finally, W. E. B. Du Bois mesmerized students with a lecture style that was less overtly dramatic but entrancing nevertheless. "He was a showman clearly aiming for effect," one listener remembered. Another student recalled "the way he walked, settled his shoulders, and his voice. You had to pay attention to him."[15]

Some Progressive Era faculty also mounted defenses of the lecture system, claiming that it allowed them to communicate material—especially in new areas of knowledge—that was not yet available in convenient print forms. "In an unorganized subject, like sociology, if a wide field is to be covered in a relatively brief time, the lecture method is indispensable," declared Charles Ellwood, one of the first sociologists at the University of Missouri. Other professors praised lectures as vehicles of inspiration, not of information. A good lecturer "gives what no book can offer, namely, vitalized intelligence," a Penn State professor wrote. "He breathes life into dead facts. . . . Books portray conditions, but the teacher should develop personality." Indeed, some advocates claimed, the lecture system infused long-lost values of personality—the professor's, of course—into the increasingly impersonal routines of the modern university. And the best way to display that spirit was on a big stage. "In the large courses students . . . can be taught a point of view, not facts," a University of California lecturer argued. "A stimulation comes from being in a crowd; clergymen do not divide their congregations into sections." Students would never forget a rousing messenger, whether they remembered his message or not. Praising his undergraduate psychology professor, one New York University scholar admitted that he did not understand much of what the man had taught. But he did recall the professor's "masterful and intense personality," which made his class "the most stimulating I have ever known." No recitation could ever rival the power of a strong lecture, he added.[16]

Recitation: Continuity and Change

The rise of the lecture system actually preserved recitations, despite premature announcements of their demise. Lecture classes were often attached to recitations, increasingly known as sections, which were typically instructed by a TA. No matter how they were structured, however, most classes built in some kind of routine quiz or test. In a 1910 survey of professors at Williams, where there were no graduate instructors or specially designated recitation sections, most faculty worked "to retain the recitation method of instruction" alongside lectures, as an astronomer noted. He spent the first 10 or 15 minutes of each class quizzing students on the material he had lectured about in the previous class; if there was assigned reading for the class, he also asked them questions about it. Likewise, a biology professor began each class with an oral recitation about his prior lecture. He also gave short written tests every other week, correcting wrong answers in red pencil and then quizzing students in class about their errors. Other faculty gave written quizzes only, marking the most important shift from earlier recitation traditions. A French professor started each class with a short written test, which required students to prepare "much more thoroughly than under any system of oral questioning which I have ever been able to devise," he wrote. A physics professor kept his students guessing by giving pop quizzes on most days, but not on all of them. "To ascertain whether the required work is being done, I give short written tests daily; or, at any rate, the student <u>expects</u> them daily," the physicist reported. In the prior year, he added, his students had taken 35 tests during their 46 class meetings.[17]

Many professors at universities routinely quizzed their students too, although not as commonly as faculty at smaller colleges did. The same year as the Williams survey, a questionnaire of University of Chicago faculty revealed that 25 of 122 replying professors gave some kind of quiz each day; 31 gave them each week, and 10 others did so every other week. The following year, in 1911, a survey of 188 economics professors around the country showed that 171 of them employed "oral quizzes" in class; only 60 of them used written tests. But students strongly preferred the written quizzes, which became more common by the end of the decade. Surveying undergraduates alongside faculty, the 1910 University of Chicago survey found that four of five students favored written tests over oral ones. A written exercise "gives time to think and organize, and present more logically," one wrote; another said it "calls for more preparation," while a third noted that it gives "less chance for bluffing." At Harvard, historian Albert Bushnell Hart started class with a 15-minute writing exercise that asked students to reflect on an issue in their assigned reading, such as "Was Jacksonian democracy the same as Jeffersonian democracy?" or "Did Jackson believe the judgment of the people better than his own?" Instructing four sections each, the five TAs for the introductory Economics A class at Harvard met weekly with course professor Edmund Day to design written quiz questions. Sections began with the written exercise, followed by an oral quiz in which every student was usually called upon at least once.[18]

The rest of the time in Economics A recitation was devoted to open-ended discussion, another important innovation of the Progressive Era college classroom. Most nineteenth-century recitations tested recall, as instructors asked scripted questions and students provided answers lifted more or less exactly from the assigned text. Early twentieth-century professors extended this tradition to their lectures, requiring students to take notes in class and to regurgitate them in written or oral quizzes. But faculty members and their assistants also conducted what several economists called "Socratic" discussions, usually after the formal quizzing had concluded. Under this schema, the quizzes ensured that students were "held to account" for lectures and assigned reading— as a Williams professor explained—while discussion helped expand their understanding. After testing students on "the essential facts," a second Williams faculty member wrote, he asked them about "doubtful points" requiring analysis and interpretation. ("Guidance and assistance are freely given in directing the student," the professor continued, "but he must draw out his own conclusions.") Indeed, a certain mastery of factual material was necessary for conducting any real discussion about it. At Yale, for example, legendary political economist William Graham Sumner—whom one student called "the greatest teacher since Abelard"—led his class in spirited debates about taxation, trade policy, and much else. But he also quizzed students on the information in his lectures, to make sure they were listening. "If you are going to make lectures amount to anything, you have got to follow them up . . . by the old-fashioned recitation method, so that a man who doesn't pay attention and doesn't acquire the matter will suffer for it in the usual academic way," Sumner wrote in 1907, shortly before he died. "I don't know of any better methods than the classes and exercises on which we were brought up in the old times."[19]

Actually, Sumner's own method radically transcended the rote techniques of prior generations. As he had written two decades earlier, in a critique of the "mischievous limitations" of nineteenth-century colleges, traditional recitation led students to "accept authority too submissively" instead of engaging in "analysis and investigation." His classroom reputation relied on his constant and often merciless critiques of students' facile assumptions, which they received with a mix of admiration and trepidation. As Yale professor Henry Canby wrote, recalling his own education at the same institution, many instructors continued to ask "trivial questions" of students who had either memorized the answers or bluffed their way out. Sumner, by contrast, "was like a rebel leader of a band of guerrillas, hovering on the flank of our complacent army." Not everyone enjoyed the attack. "He was brusque, and sometimes brutal," another student remembered. "People's feelings appeared to be no concern of his." Likewise, W. E. B. Du Bois promoted "open discussion" in his classroom but had "little patience with people who were mediocre," his students recalled; an "uninformed or unintelligent" remark would receive a "polite but mordant dismissal" from Du Bois, leaving the poor speaker "badly shaken." In some cases, indeed, the celebrated Socratic method could devolve into raw sadism. Yale English scholar Albert S. Cook met every student comment with the reply, "That's two thirds of the truth," winning him the nickname "Two Thirds True Cook." But he also seemed to take glee in exposing students' naivety and ignorance, which earned the enmity of big swaths of the undergraduate body. It even generated a retributive limerick, recited by several generations of Yalies:

> There was a professor named Cook
> Who thought he knew more than the book
> He shot off his mouth
> From Durfee to South
> To show what a great man was Cook.[20]

Meanwhile, professors who did aim to conduct engaged, mutually respectful discussions often lacked the skill to do so. Questions hung in the air, while awkward silence descended on the room; it was often punctuated by a single loud student, who talked so much that peers pleaded with their professor to shut him up. The challenges were greatest for younger faculty members and TAs, especially when controversial present-day political questions arose. Visiting several sections of Economics A at Harvard, an evaluator noted that the subject tended to generate strong opinions. But the TAs did not possess enough knowledge or experience to connect contemporary debates to the theoretical principles of the course, which tended to get drowned in "a maze of disputed facts." Indeed, he suggested that the instructors stick much more closely to class lectures or to the assigned text and leave debate and discussion for another day, or perhaps for another year. Many professors chose to do precisely that, either because they were lazy—as students often suspected—or because they believed that their own expertise enjoined them to hold forth, instead of indulging the puerile reflections of undergraduates. "The strong temptation . . . is to throw off our responsibilities as elementary teachers, and take our stands as pillars of the scientific ideal," one philosopher admitted, "distributing our wisdom to all sundry, and leaving our hearers to pick up such crumbs as they may find it possible to digest." Other professors fell back on traditional call-and-response recitation, which at least provided a predictable pattern of classroom behavior. Although there were exceptions, too many professors used recitation simply as a "method of finding out whether the student has swallowed a certain piece of knowledge whole," Woodrow Wilson told a group of educators in 1903. Nor would it do just to lecture, the Princeton president added, although he had done his fair share of that himself. The answer lay in a new method of tutorials, Wilson said, which would engage students fully in their learning—and would bridge the gap that still separated them from professors.[21]

Tutorials and Precepts

Actually, tutorials were not new at all. Going back to the colonial era, colleges had hired tutors—typically young men just out of college themselves—to conduct recitations. The tutors were the most despised figures in education, derided alternatively for their ineptitude and cruelty. The new feature that Wilson proposed was the hiring of recently minted PhDs, who would meet with small groups of students to discuss difficult questions rather than simply to drill the answers. Also known as the "conference method," a system of informal meetings was already underway at several other institutions. At Vassar, for example, historian Lucy Salmon held personal meetings with her students to "teach them how to think historically," which required close individual mentoring; at Bowdoin, meanwhile, the college hired a special Greek and Latin tutor in 1899 who met weekly with students in teams of five or six to "vivify" the instruction they received in class. With Bowdoin taking on more students, one observer added, the tutorial would "keep in the individual factor in education" and avoid "the temptation to deal with classes as masses." By 1910, professors in several departments at Bowdoin were conducting their own weekly conferences with students, outside of their regular class duties. "Teacher meets learner, man meets man, in groups so small that formal barriers are broken down, individuality is recognized; and teacher and learner touch each other through their common contact with the subject taught," Bowdoin president

William De Witt Hyde wrote. The meetings represented nothing short of "a revolution in teaching," Hyde boasted.[22]

But an even bigger revolution was happening at Princeton, Hyde also noted, where classes were too large to expect professors to lead these groups on their own. In 1905, three years after he became president of the university, Wilson hired 47 assistant professors to meet with students in groups of three to five; the following year, he appointed nine more. Wilson called these new teachers "preceptors," a term borrowed from England to avoid the negative connotations that Americans attached to tutors. The preceptorial system—as it became known—owed a good deal to Cambridge and Oxford, which Wilson had visited a few years earlier; he also sent one of his deans to Oxford in 1902, to examine instruction there. As Wilson told an audience that same year, he admired the British system of tutorials but not the way it selected tutors: hired for life, they inevitably "go to seed" after long years of meeting with students. So his Princeton precepts would be appointed for strictly limited five-year terms. They would neither lecture nor conduct recitations, which Wilson regarded as the dual evils of undergraduate education: one was the "pouring of learning into empty pitchers," while the other promoted "the memorization of certain facts" without any real understanding of what bound them together. Precepts, by contrast, would engage students in dialogues about a course and supplement it with new readings and information. Most of all, Wilson said, precepts would tear down the unnatural barriers that traditional teaching methods had placed between professor and student. They would act as "guides and friends," Wilson declared, not as orators or inquisitors; they would replace the "schoolboy idea" of a quiz about a lecture or textbook with the "grown-up" idea of a conference about a topic in a discipline. "Even in a great University, the close and intimate contact of pupil and teacher may . . . be restored and maintained," Wilson told Princeton's Board of Trustees in 1905. Indeed, he predicted, the new tutorial system would give Princeton students "the same sort of close and intimate council with his instructor that the undergraduate of the small college enjoys."[23]

Starting that year, then, students met with preceptors in small groups in order to discuss—and expand—the knowledge transmitted by professors in class. The students seemed to welcome the new arrivals, even hailing them in a 1906 song: "Here's to these preceptor guys / Fifty stiffs to makes us wise / Easy job and lots of pay / Work the students night and day." But in fact, it was the preceptors—not the students—who were radically overworked. A single preceptor was assigned as many as 35 students, whose work he was supposed to guide in six or eight subjects; hence, he had to read 10,000–12,000 pages in a term, just to keep up with his students. The reading and teaching load "nearly broke my back," one preceptor wrote; nor was it fair to students, who quickly recognized that the preceptors were in over their heads. ("At least *I* got an education," another preceptor quipped.) Princeton eventually limited the number of courses in which a preceptor was expected to teach. But that also required the university to increase the size of each precept, which inhibited the small-group intimacy that Wilson had sought. Meanwhile, the preceptors themselves languished in a kind of academic no-man's land. Hired on five-year appointments, as per Wilson's original directive, they struggled—often in vain—to produce the kind of scholarship that could earn them a job afterward; as they departed, meanwhile, the cash-strapped university increasingly hired instructors in their stead, with a salary and status below that of assistant professors. By 1913, a faculty committee already detected "a falling away from the ideals of preceptorial teaching that were so earnestly accepted at the inauguration of the Method." As the number of professors engaged as preceptors declined—and as the number of students in each section rose—the precepts often became "little else than a preparation for the final examination," the committee found. Nor did preceptors communicate effectively with the professors in charge of their courses, who often saw precepting as "hack work" of a "distinctly inferior grade."[24]

In their own teaching, meanwhile, the preceptors tended to fall back on the same traditional lecture and recitation methods that they were supposed to transcend. "Many a preceptor, impressed with the value of his own views, will present them as a form of denatured fireworks," Princeton's student newspaper complained in a 1915 editorial. When the preceptor was not delivering an "unofficial lecture," the paper added, he was too often drilling students from a textbook. "The preceptorial system was designed to educate by informal discussion," the editorial emphasized. "The student should neither be compelled to listen to a lecture—he already has enough of them—nor be subjected to a quiz process designed to draw information from him as a plaster extracts pain from a lame back. Preceptors should lead the mind, not lull it to sleep." The following year, one of Princeton's most famous literary voices scrawled an angry epistle to his own English preceptor in the back of a textbook:

> Gee but this man Griffin is terrible, I sit here bored to death and hear him pick English poetry to pieces. Small man, Small mind. Snotty, disagreeable. Damn him. "Neat" is his favorite word. Imagine Shakespeare being neat. Yesterday I

counted and found that he used the expression "Isn't that so" fifty four times. Oh what a disagreeable silly ass he is. He's going to get married. God help his wife. Poor girl. She's in for a bad time. They say Griffin has made more men leave the English department than any other praeceptor in College. The slovenly old fool! I have the most terrible praeceptors.

The preceptor was Nathaniel Edward Griffin, who had received his PhD at Johns Hopkins University with a dissertation on medieval versions of the fall of ancient Troy. And the objecting student was F. Scott Fitzgerald, a student in a course on the Renaissance that Griffin was precepting. The course allotted two weeks to *Hamlet*, which Griffin reportedly spent analyzing a single line in the play. The following year, Fitzgerald published a short story in Princeton's literary magazine, "The Spire and the Gargoyle," featuring a preceptor who was most likely modeled on Griffin—and whose own repulsive features were highlighted in the title. "His glasses, his eyes, or his mouth gave a certain grotesque upward slant . . . that branded him as of gargoyle origin, or at least gargoyle kinship," Fitzgerald wrote.[25]

Much of Fitzgerald's story (including its title, as a chapter heading) appeared in *This Side of Paradise*, the debut 1920 book that would establish Fitzgerald as one of America's rising young novelists. In the original story, the student protagonist flunks out of college after failing a makeup examination that the gargoyle-preceptor administers. When the student encounters the preceptor several years later, in a chance meeting in New York, he is surprised to learn that his tormentor has left campus as well, to pursue a better-paying job elsewhere. But the preceptor is still hoping to return to his position at Princeton, even after the student writes it off: "The gargoyle, poor tired little hack, was bound up in the fabric of the whole system much more than he was." Here Fitzgerald echoed the dismissive language around precepts—"poor tired little hack"—that the faculty committee at Princeton had deplored in its 1913 report. Renamed to avoid the negative aura of tutors, precepts could not escape the poor status accorded to teaching in the modern university. Sadly, they also began to imitate the distant authoritarianism of the professors who disdained them. One of the original 47 preceptors added to the faculty by Woodrow Wilson back in 1905, Nathaniel Griffin "lectured in precept instead of playing Socrates, which was the proper way to teach a precept," as another English scholar observed. But Griffin was also bound up in the fabric of the system, to quote Fitzgerald. Like other faculty members, he was a specialist on a narrow subject—in Griffin's case, medieval representations of ancient

Troy—who was asked to teach about very broad ones. The more he taught, the less he was valued by the professors and the students surrounding him. And playing Socrates was a dangerous game, especially in a system that neither taught professors how to do that nor rewarded them when they did.[26]

Supervising Teaching in the Progressive Era

Reflecting its low status, teaching was haphazardly supervised and evaluated during the Progressive Era. Higher-education officials clearly realized that college instruction was under fire, from students as well as the general public. All they had to do was pick up a newspaper or magazine, where headlines routinely indicted college teaching as inadequate and college professors as remote, selfish, and lazy. Indeed, leading university presidents often jumped on the same bandwagon: consider Nicholas Murray Butler's jibes at the rising fetish of research, or Woodrow Wilson's attack on lecture and recitation. Nor did they turn a blind eye to poor instruction under their own roofs, making repeated efforts to improve it. Most of that activity took place outside of public sight: like teaching itself, the supervision of instruction was mainly a private and idiosyncratic affair. In a 1911 article, based on a survey of 60 deans and presidents, Clark University professor Samuel P. Capen scolded institutions for failing to monitor college instruction. But the archived replies sent to Capen suggest more effort in these areas than his essay documented. Caught between a public that criticized teaching and a professoriate that was increasingly distancing itself from it, university leaders devised their own informal mechanisms of supervision and evaluation. Their attempts were scattershot and often ineffective, but they did not simply throw up their hands.[27]

The weakest form of supervision was also the oldest one: visiting committees of trustees and other alumni. Several institutions continued to host delegations of mostly older men for annual "inspections" and "examinations," just as they had since the early 1800s. These visitors sometimes enhanced publicity and fundraising for the institution, as a dean at Boston University acknowledged, but nobody believed they could evaluate or improve teaching. "The Trustees send a Visiting committee once a year to visit the class rooms and report on the work," Bowdoin president William De Witt Hyde told Capen. "Without wishing to be quoted, I may say that this examination is not very thorough or the results of it very valuable." A Tufts dean was more direct in his denunciation: the college's board of visitors was "worthless," rendering "superficial and sometimes decidedly erroneous" recommendations. Likewise, the "Board of Fellows" who visited Trinity College each year were "not professionally competent . . . to criticize the work of a professor," president Flavel S. Luther wrote. In the best case, officials said, these bodies did nothing. At Colby, president Arthur J. Roberts confided, the trustees "appoint every year a visiting committee who almost never attend to the business assigned to them."[28]

So officials devised their own semiofficial methods for attending to it. A few presidents visited classes on their own, a practice that also dated to the nineteenth century. At Colorado College, president William F. Slocum reported that he was "constantly in and out of classrooms"; at Dickinson, likewise, president George Edward Reed said he had "quite frequently inspected the class room work of professors and instructors." But visiting a professor's class was "rather delicate work to do," Haverford president Isaac Sharpless admitted, and most leaders were reluctant to do it. So they sometimes dispatched deans or department heads to observe or even to teach colleagues' classes, "perhaps the best way of ascertaining what the students are doing," University of Georgia chancellor David C Barrow wrote. (As a bonus, he added, "it also gives each student the benefit of the instruction of the Head of the department.") Overall, however, class visits were rare. Deans and other officials often lacked sufficient knowledge of a professor's field of study, one respondent explained, especially as more and more faculty developed specialized knowledge; nor could visitors know whether the class they witnessed reflected the overall performance of a teacher, who might change his practice when observers sat in. More than that, though, professors saw any kind of visit or inspection as a slight upon their independence. "The University ideal of academic freedom seems to be violated when a supervisor enters a man's classroom," wrote a University of Chicago dean in 1910, five years before the American Association of University Professors made its first statement on the subject. In most official accounts, academic freedom was supposed to protect professors' right to express ideas rather than keep faculty free of any oversight whatsoever. But many faculty members already interpreted the concept to mean that nobody could or should visit their classes, under any circumstances: the college teacher was "a law unto himself," Samuel Capen observed, or so many professors believed. "I think it may be taken for granted that college teachers would resent a system of direct supervision of their teaching," wrote Brown dean and future Amherst president Alexander Meiklejohn, who would also become one of America's leading civil libertarians. "The benefits which might be obtained in this way are obtainable in sufficient degree in other ways."[29]

The best way, university leaders said, was the informal collection of information—from alumni, other faculty members, and students. That was easier in a smaller college, and hardly foolproof anywhere. But officials often insisted that they knew who the best teachers were, even without any official system of evaluating them. "Where the number of students is small, there is no difficulty in forming a pretty fair estimate of the effectiveness of a teacher," Flavel Luther wrote from Trinity. "The impression that a man makes in faculty meeting, the general atmosphere of his lecture room, in particular after a year or two, the number and character of the men who choose his courses, the frank statements of very young alumni who have been under his charge, in rare cases the statements or even complaints from undergraduates, make it pretty clear what a professor is doing and how he is doing it." In one instance, Luther wrote, a group of students had come to him to protest the poor teaching of a professor, and "their action resulted in a change." But most students were understandably "reticent about such matters" and "reluctant to make complaints," Luther added, so officials needed to devise other methods to solicit feedback. As part of a 1908 survey about undergraduate education, the University of Chicago sent questionnaires to students and recent alumni and then shared anonymized information about specific courses with their professors. The study raised hackles among faculty, who questioned whether the college should credit the puerile impressions of randomly selected undergraduates. So officials more commonly relied on "confidential conference with mature students of good judgment"—as Oberlin president Henry King wrote—or simply kept their ears to the ground. "We depend much upon the information which comes to us incidentally, without seeking for it, especially from students," wrote a dean at the University of Minnesota. "If a man is thoroughly acceptable to students, not on account of giving 'snap' courses, but on account of making his work valuable and interesting, it is strong evidence that he is the kind of man we wish to encourage by promotion and increased pay. Whereas if a man is not acceptable to students, it is pretty good evidence that he does not fit the place."[30]

Privately, however, officials also acknowledged the difficulties and ambiguities of this process. Every college and university had an "underground railway" of student opinion and advice about faculty members, a scholar noted, but it could be notoriously callous and imprecise. ("For Heaven's sake, No," one piece of student wisdom held, regarding a prominent professor. "He may know his subject, but he spits on the radiator.") As per the Minnesota dean's warning about easy "snap" courses, meanwhile, it was never clear whether a positive student evaluation reflected the high quality of the instructor or the low workload he required. Nor could they rely on the grades professors gave, which varied radically within the same institutions and were hardly an assured indication of teaching skill in any event. At Harvard, journalist Edwin Slosson reported in 1911, the chances of getting an A in an introductory course ranged from 1 percent in the English department to 35 percent in Greek; at the University of California, 17 percent of students in physics and math classes received failing grades, but no students who took education courses did. Only a few institutions had imposed a normal grade distribution: for example, the University of Missouri required that half the students in each class receive a C, a quarter receive an A or B, and the other quarter a D or E. Faculty at most other places were on their own. A few institutions sent professors a graph of their grades plotted next to the average, to promote stricter standards among easy graders and leniency by hard ones. More and more, though, the graphs were revealing "a pronounced skew" to more As and Bs. "We may suppose that he is a teacher of such exceptional ability that he is able to stimulate all his students to supernormal activity," Slosson wrote, of the high-grading professor, "or his reputation is such as to attract only students of remarkable ability. Other explanations, perhaps equally plausible, will readily occur to the readers." Inflated grades in a class could reflect high quality or low standards, but it was hard to know which was which without more information.[31]

Given the scattered nature of this knowledge, most university officials were reluctant to act on it. As the president of the Case School of Applied Science (soon to become Case Western) admitted, he relied more on "rumors" than on "any systematic method" to evaluate teaching. Even new professors were generally judged on reputation, as a dean at Tufts acknowledged. "One of the weakest parts of our college system is the failure to properly supervise the instruction given by inexperienced teachers," he wrote. "They are commonly left to their own devices and not infrequently to their destruction." In a few isolated cases, however, professors were dismissed for poor teaching. At Princeton, Woodrow Wilson fired an instructor for failing to discipline "the very skittish colts in our classes"; then, he dismissed three full professors, including the notoriously easy-grading archaeologist Arthur Frothingham Jr. "Here's to Frothy our latest find, / He's gentle and easy to drive and kind," a student poem jokingly declared. "He had to make his courses hard / Or he couldn't play in Woodrow's yard." Students and alumni were more concerned about the dismissal of French professor Arnold Guyot Cameron, whose own father was one of Wilson's most despised teachers during his undergraduate years at Princeton; indeed, Wilson dated his hatred of recitations to Henry Clay Cameron, who required students to memorize line after line of Greek.

His son, by contrast, was a popular orator whom Wilson accused of playing to the crowd; to Wilson, Arnold Cameron's "sensational classroom lectures" marked him as a "charlatan" and a "mimic man" rather than a sober-minded academic. "His classes were amusing; he told stories; he talked about all sorts of topics; but he seldom taught any French," Cameron's department chair confirmed. There were also reports that he made off-color remarks in class, including that women were "good for raising bread, babies, and hell." When alumni rallied to the professor's defense, however, Wilson was forced to give Cameron a year's grace period before he left. After that, Woodrow Wilson never attempted to remove another professor for poor teaching.[32]

Elsewhere, too, nearly every professor who passed muster as a scholar was retained or promoted. Without any real system of teaching evaluation, it was next to impossible to fire a faculty member for his classroom performance. "I have sometimes thought that if the Trustees had more information concerning the work of inexperienced men some of the men who have been promoted would fail to secure promotion," a Dartmouth dean confided. "It would seem to me a proper thing for the president of the college to know more about the teaching power of his Faculty than most presidents know." At lower-ranked institutions, where PhD faculty and research were less common, almost everyone got passed along. In an extraordinarily forthright letter to Samuel Capen, the dean of arts and sciences at the University of Florida confessed that the poor status and pay of college teachers made him reluctant to fire anyone for poor teaching. "I think it must be conceded that there are many men and women in the profession who ought never to have taught a day," James Anderson wrote. "But what are we to do about it? Teaching is a difficult calling and there are not enough good teachers to fill the places." Even more, Anderson underlined, "people think that anybody can teach <u>and they pay accordingly</u>." That "drives talent from the profession," he explained, and made it difficult to purge the "unfit" from the classroom. "If a man does only tolerably well, the tendency is to keep him," Anderson confessed. "Besides, pity enters into the case. The teacher is not able to save anything, is <u>dependent</u> on his monthly salary, and we hate to turn him out." Teaching was a hard and thankless job, and the best way to improve it was to find more good people who were nevertheless willing to do it.[33]

Personality and Pedagogy in the Progressive Era

Anderson's letter prefigured a concern that surrounded college teaching for the next half century: how could institutions recruit the "best men" into it? That language remained unchanged as women inched slowly into the professoriate.

Although females made up a fast-growing fraction of the student population—at the University of Michigan, for example, they topped 40 percent in
1900—there were almost no female university professors in the entire country; roughly a quarter of American faculty were women, but nearly all of them
taught at women's colleges. With the entry of the United States into World War
I, universities worried that young male professors would leave the academy
and "faculties will be gradually feminized," as a Missouri educator wrote. So
the key was to locate the right people—ideally, the right men—early. They
could be identified by their "personality," college officials said, which usually
meant a combination of insight, energy, and enthusiasm. The best teachers
demonstrated a "hearty manly sympathy" with his students, Cornell president
Andrew Dickson White declared, ignoring the fact that growing numbers of
students were women. The Cornell student newspaper concurred, praising the
professor who was "a wide awake man of the world" rather than "the 'College
Widow' type." Especially in hard-to-teach courses like English composition,
which were dominated by younger faculty members, successful instructors
needed to exude the same "homiletic habit" and "evangelistic spirit" as circuit-
riding ministers, a Minnesota professor urged. But too many of them lacked
that spark, which was the sine qua non of successful teaching. Indeed, as a
Dartmouth observer added, "success or failure, under any system . . . depends,
of course, mainly on the personal impact of the man." It was not the system
that mattered; it was the person—and the personality—of the professor.[34]

But that also meant that there was no way to systematize teaching. In an era
that worshipped science and statistics, as Progressive reformer William H. Allen observed, "personality" remained remarkably hard to measure or even to
define. "If personality can win appointment, promotion, dismissal; if it . . .
causes students to flock to or from an instructor's courses; if it draws students
like a magnet for conference; if it drives them away like a sign marked 'third
rail'; if it wins confidence; if it compels and expresses thoroughness; why, pray,
is it impossible to describe it?" Allen archly asked. Like height or eye color,
moreover, personality was usually considered immutable. So most college officials and faculty balked at any kind of special preparation for teaching, which
could not make people into better teachers any more than it could give them
better personalities. Indeed, critics worried, any such training might actually
inhibit the teacher's personality by imposing a system on it. "Teaching is largely
a matter of personal influence," Samuel Capen concluded, summarizing this
objection. Any required or standardized training regimen for teaching threatened to drown that influence in impersonal rules and regulations.[35]

Preparation for college teaching also conjured normal schools, the institutions that readied elementary and secondary instructors for the classroom. Near the bottom of the academic status ladder, normal schools seemed to embody the bloodless, bureaucratic routine that threatened academic personality and spontaneity. "The normal schools produce a mechanically efficient teacher in most cases for primary and secondary work," Trinity president Flavel Luther conceded. "Yet I question whether there is not a loss of individuality on the part of some teachers due to their normal training." To be sure, several university leaders supported the idea of teacher preparation for college professors: Boston University president William Edwards Huntington said that all faculty "should have a thorough elementary training in pedagogics," while other officials suggested coursework in the history and philosophy of education. Still others argued that teaching experience in elementary or secondary schools should be a prerequisite for a doctorate, so TAs and newly minted faculty were not complete strangers to the classroom. "Some teaching should precede Ph.D. training," a New York University professor urged. "A little pedagogy is not a bad thing." But no institution required teaching experience or preparation, which was widely disdained by the professoriate. Indeed, even widely praised college teachers took pains to distance themselves from it. At Yale, English professor William Lyon Phelps—perhaps the institution's most celebrated teacher—proudly boasted that he had never received any formal preparation for it. Phelps went on to compare pedagogical training to phrenology, the discredited science of skull shapes. Just as a businessman could discover more about a job candidate via an interview than by measuring his skull, so could a professor learn more about students by interacting with them than by reading the allegedly "scientific formula" of so-called experts on education.[36]

Ironically, Phelps was one of a small group of professors in the United States who were renowned precisely *for* their pedagogy, rather than for their publications. But they were famous less for what they did than for who they were— in short, for their personalities. To be sure, students praised Phelps's unapologetically dramatic lectures—"There is something distinctly histrionic about the teacher's art," Phelps wrote—as well as his skill in leading discussions. Most of all, though, students adored "Billy" Phelps for the concern he evinced for them. Yale alumnus and prominent novelist Sinclair Lewis declared that Phelps had "the greatest love of human beings" of anyone Lewis had ever encountered, with the possible exception of Socialist leader Eugene Debs. "He has been to each generation of college students the Best Neighbor, the kindliest older friend of the whole faculty," Lewis added. But the rest of the faculty was not so kind to Phelps. He published almost no scholarship yet remained deeply popular among undergraduates, which made peers suspect that he was more of a charmer than an educator. In many ways, he was the last of his breed at Yale. Although Phelps did not possess a distinguished academic pedigree, another observer wrote, he brought something to the classroom that other professors often lacked: "the ability to love."[37]

So did Harvard's Charles T. Copeland, who was often paired with Phelps in popular tributes. Like Phelps, "Copey" (as students called him) filled lecture halls with his theatrical presentations on great literary figures of the past. He also gave frequent public readings of his favorite authors, a formerly common practice that was going out of style with the advent of film and radio. But what really won the hearts of his students were the long hours of individual attention that he gave them. He required students to write 400–800 words every week and then to visit his room in Hollis Hall to read the essay aloud. (A lifelong bachelor, Copeland lived on campus while he taught there.) What ensued was a "wrestling match," journalist Walter Lippmann recalled, with Copey challenging each imprecise word or phrase and the student doing his best to parry the attacks. Copeland could be withering in his critiques, telling one embarrassed young man that he "wrote like a High School girl"; another disciple described these sessions as "mental torture," which "scared the bejazus" out of him. But Copey's close analysis made indelible impressions on his long roster of famous former students, who included John Reed, Van Wyck Brooks, T.S. Eliot, and John Dos Passos, as well as Lippmann. Writing in 1935, nearly three decades after he studied with Copeland, Lippmann praised him as a pioneer of a new pedagogy that had "revolutionized the method of instruction" at colleges around the country. "Thirty years ago he was already acting on the assumption that teaching is not the handing down of knowledge from a platform to an anonymous mass of note-takers, but that it is the personal encounter of two individuals," Lippmann wrote. Indeed, Copey's method was "a continuing demonstration against mass instruction and the regimentation of learning," Lippmann continued. "Copey was not a professor teaching a crowd in the classroom. He was a very distinct person in a unique relationship with each individual who interested him."[38]

Lippmann wrote amid widespread efforts to "individualize" college instruction in the interwar period, including a movement to revive Woodrow Wilson's dream of conferences between professors and students. But the "cult of Copey"—as many observers called it—actually illustrated the opposite of what

Lippmann claimed. Hardly a harbinger of things to come, Charles T. Copeland was a reminder of how far higher education had strayed from the personal ideal that his venerators proclaimed. Like William Lyon Phelps, Copeland lacked scholarly publications; he even lacked a doctorate, which Copey—conjuring William James's octopus—mocked as "the Ph.D. death-rattle." But that also made him a target of disdain among his Harvard colleagues, who derided him as a mere elocutionist (for his public readings) rather than a real scholar. Denied a full faculty position for many years, like Phelps, Copeland eventually received the same chair in Rhetoric and Oratory that John Quincy Adams had held. Yet he always remained an outlier, because he left his mark via people rather than publications. "A man is always better than a book," Copeland said, in a remark that his students often quoted. But books—and scholarship—were in the saddle, and Copey was not. He spent his last years in a Cambridge hotel, where former students would stop by to hear him read aloud once again. He might have "personalized" college education, as one alumnus wrote, yet his voice echoed across a world that had mostly left him behind.[39]

CHAPTER THREE

The Curse of Gigantism

Mass-Produced Education and Its Critics in Interwar America

In 1924, a group of seniors at Dartmouth College released a report denouncing the low quality of teaching there. The report came in the wake of an investigation of undergraduate education by a Dartmouth faculty committee, which had concluded that students were too distracted by fraternities and sports to take their academic work seriously. Nonsense, the seniors replied: if students were disengaged in learning, the fault lay with the "mass-production system of teaching" at Dartmouth. "The teacher becomes an impersonal ladler-out of assignments, facts, and quizzes—a hurler of boomerangs—which return shod in blue books," the student group wrote, referring to the already-ubiquitous notebooks used for examinations. The student, meanwhile, was saddled with regurgitating whatever the professor had required. "Memory is good and necessary, but *it is not enough*," the seniors underlined. "A parrot can be taught to repeat things, but no one claims that this is evidence of intelligence." Like other colleges and universities, Dartmouth had accepted more students in the new century and had increasingly warehoused them in large, impersonal lecture courses. The only solution was to break up large lectures into small classes, which would replace the "mass system of education" with "a vital, personal relationship between teacher and student." Otherwise, one senior committee member warned, the college student would become a machine and the faculty member its operator.[1]

In many ways, these complaints echoed long-standing jeremiads at American colleges and universities. Instruction was too rote driven, privileging memory over meaning; classes were too large and impersonal, drowning the individual in a sea of anonymity; colleges were urged to create smaller and more intimate environments, bridging the chasms that had too often separated teachers and students. But there were several elements that also marked new chapters in the history of undergraduate instruction. The first was a broader critique of size—or "Gigantism," as critics called it—across higher education. College enrollment rose more sharply after World War I than it had in any place—and at any time—in human history; by 1930, there were more students in college in the United States than in the rest of the world combined. That created enormous challenges for an institution that had formerly served a very small slice of the American population. The most apparent change was the rise of massive lecture classes, which topped 1,000 students at some schools; as a jaundiced Cornell professor observed, it was obviously much cheaper to pay one professor $5,000 a year to lecture to 1,500 students three times a week than to pay "even very modest salaries" to 100 professors "who would teach those students properly." Increasingly, critics borrowed the language of modern industrialism to denounce these new arrangements. Teaching was not simply impersonal—as prior generations had complained—but automated and mechanized; the university was a factory, which mass-produced students just like Henry Ford built cars. The year after the Dartmouth report, indeed, a student magazine issued an attack on "Fordized Education" in American colleges.[2]

Second, the interwar years witnessed an unprecedented burst of student protest around undergraduate instruction. College student revolts in America were as old as America itself, as the *Boston Globe* observed in a column about the Dartmouth report. But the focus of protest had shifted from food and housing to teaching and learning. "The old Redskin chief, who has served for so many years as the mythical mascot of 'the Big Green teams,' is clearly bewildered," the *Globe* wrote, in a teasing mood. "And why shouldn't he be? He has never before seen Dartmouth undergraduates raising a rumpus because they weren't being taught the way they liked to be." To be sure, many "good, traditional 'he-men'" continued to neglect or ignore their studies, in the time-honored fashion; indeed, as a Dartmouth professor told the *Globe*, undergraduates "still regulate their lives according to the motion picture shows" rather than their daily class schedules. But student activism surrounding academics was new, the paper observed, and it was hardly restricted to Dartmouth. The year after the seniors' report, delegates from twenty colleges met at Wesleyan to discuss the deficiencies of undergraduate teaching. "It is not that college boys have ceased to have a good time on the campus," explained the *Globe*, which sent a reporter to the conference. "It is rather that an increasing proportion of them are wondering what college is all about and why they are there." The students heard a rousing speech from historian James Harvey Robinson, who said that most college instructors were "insufferable bores." He urged students to "stand up and kick" against poor teaching, because "college belongs to them."[3]

Students continued to do precisely that, organizing new protests across the interwar era. They also devised a new mechanism of critique: written evaluations of professors and courses. Bubbling up slowly from student organizations and publications, course evaluations were occasionally adopted—and, as student critics claimed, co-opted—by college administrations. But student evaluations provoked loud objections among the faculty, who kicked back with as much force as students attacked them. Like the 1923 Dartmouth faculty committee, professors insisted that the real problem in college teaching lay with the people whom they taught. In the 1920s and 1930s, students came from a wider array of backgrounds—with a wider range of skills—than ever before. Drawing from the popular language of intelligence testing, some critics claimed that the new students simply lacked the innate ability to succeed in the classroom; others said students were too distracted by extracurricular activities, which also experienced an unprecedented boom. So both professors and students blamed each other, a venerable tradition that reached a kind of apogee in the interwar years. Its spirit was neatly captured by a 1932 editorial in the *Argus*, the student newspaper at Illinois Wesleyan University, which accused both parties of "shifting the blame for their own inadequacies onto some one else." Students who blasted their professor's boring or disorganized lecture often did not prepare for class themselves, which "allows one to attend to the movies or basketball games with a clear conscience," the *Argus* caustically observed. At the same time, the professor who indicted students as distracted or disengaged "does not pause to question his teaching method," the newspaper added. "'Passing the buck' is as much a panacea for the troubles of the teaching class as it is for the student class," the *Argus* concluded. As mass-produced education exploded across the country, creating new industrial-scale challenges for teaching and learning, students and professors found it easier to malign each other than to look in the mirror.[4]

The New Students

In 1924, a veteran professor at Penn State praised the "democratization" of higher education in the United States. Whereas the European university "still caters pre-eminently to the upper classes," economist Oswald Boucke wrote, American universities had "opened their doors to the lower as well as to the upper strata of society." Like many such generalizations, the claim contained elements of both truth and hyperbole. Student enrollment skyrocketed five-fold between the two world wars, from 250,000 to 1.3 million; 15 percent of 18- to 20-year-olds went to college by the advent of World War II, up from 5 percent at the time of World War I. They included growing numbers of women—who made up 47 percent of college students in 1920—and many more middle-class students than before. But they were hardly "drawn from families and homes of every conceivable type and kind," as Columbia president Nicholas Murray Butler boasted. Most obviously, African Americans were radically underrepresented: in 1937, when roughly 12 million blacks lived in the United States, only 35,000 attended college. The advent of the Great Depression in 1929 also diminished college opportunities for working-class students, who frequently had to drop out of school to support their families. Still, the shift in student population—both in size and in diversity—was unmistakable. As a University of Chicago professor summarized in 1939, "An institution once devoted to the preparation of a chosen few for the learned professions has become a training school for life for a large section of the youth of America."[5]

Unlike Oswald Boucke, however, many faculty saw this trend less as a flowering of democracy than as a dagger at the heart of the university. By opening its doors to a wider swath of students, the argument went, colleges had also brought in more people who were "unfit" for college-level learning. "A great many students are not intellectually capable of assimilating even the minimum of so-called education required to get a college degree," a Kansas professor groused. Here faculty often invoked the burgeoning pseudoscience of eugenics, which suggested that nature had placed a cognitive limit on what students could accomplish. "I now have some beginning students who are doing satisfactory work, but they have C-grade brains, inherited from C-grade parents," a Beloit professor explained. "Modern hereditary studies show that you cannot raise the natural inherited brain grade." Many college students were inclined to agree, although of course they never placed themselves in the "unfit" category. Speaking at the Wesleyan student conference in 1925, Dartmouth student leader (and future Hamilton College president) William H. Cowley stated flatly that "40 to 60 percent of college students are morons; that is, they are mentally unable to do the work." Other students attributed the poor quality of their peers less to heredity than to environment, including inadequate secondary school preparation. But the upshot was the same: colleges were taking too many weak students, who could not learn what the colleges were trying to teach. "Entrance requirements are far too low," a fraternity at the University of Virginia complained, in a confidential letter to its dean. "The University . . . has gradually degenerated intellectually to such a plane that it is hardly more than an advanced county high school."[6]

Ironically, many observers targeted fraternities—and other extracurricular activities—as the central culprit in this degeneration: whatever their ability levels, critics said, students came to college mostly for a good time rather than for a good education. That made them much harder to reach—and to teach—than prior generations, or so many professors believed. "Intellectual life has to meet far hotter competition than 75 years ago," wrote Stanford medievalist John S. P. Tatlock in 1922, citing contemporary diversions like sports, movies, and cars. Of course, professors had denounced distracted and intellectually disengaged students for many years; most recently, and most famously, Wood-row Wilson had complained that the sideshows of extracurricular fun and games at Princeton had swallowed up the main tent of academics. The change, again, was one of scale. With more and more students coming to campus—and more and more opportunities for entertainment and amusement—colleges seemed overwhelmed by social activity as never before. "Large numbers of students, when rounded into classrooms, can not concentrate their thoughts on anything but fraternity politics, dance dates, football rallies, and the next week-end party," wrote Caltech's William B. Munro, who chaired an American Association of University Professors (AAUP) committee on teaching in the 1930s. "Serious study, in far too many American colleges, has been tacitly permitted by administrative authorities to become submerged by profitless 'activities.'"[7]

Many students admitted as much, forsaking academics for leisure with a nod and a wink. At Beloit, students openly told faculty that they could have a *really* good time in college were it not for their classes. Looking back at his own undergraduate years, a 1938 Bowdoin graduate joked that he "learned bridge, poker, and how to hold my liquor." ("Any college that does not afford these opportunities is a failure," he added.) Students who took their academic work seriously were mocked or ostracized by their peers, another recurring theme in college history that peaked in the interwar era. Even at the University of Chicago, an institution proud of its intellectual climate, students who asked questions in class—or who tried to talk to the professor afterward—were taunted for trying to "get in on the ground floor," a student survey reported, using a common euphemism for toadying to the teacher. Other hardworking undergraduates were excluded from fraternities and other high-status social entities, which preferred the easygoing and the athletic to the serious and studious. "The very finest students are not in the clique organizations," a Rollins College student complained; a diligent scholar "certainly cannot feel a part of the school," he added, "and one cannot blame him." Indeed, to many observers, it seemed that America's colleges had come under the spell of their least committed students. "Just now the college is the haunt of a lot of leather-necked, brass-lunged, money-spending snobs who rush around the campus snubbing the few choice spirits who come to college to seek out reason and the will of God," eminent journalist William Allen White observed in 1924. The headline of his article—"Why Students Are Stupid"—told the whole story, so far as he was concerned.[8]

But other students blasted their peers for turning a blind eye to academics, which complicated this dismal narrative. On the one hand, their rhetoric echoed faculty complaints about lazy students who had substituted leisure for schoolwork; on the other, their voice and presence suggested much more academic engagement than the faculty critique allowed. "We believe that Dartmouth College is not an institution of higher learning, but a social institution where good fellows may get together for four years or more and waste time and money in having a good vacation before launching forth upon the sea of life," an anonymous student broadside declared in 1923. "There is scarcely any spirit of learning at Dartmouth," the leaflet continued. "Men at Dartmouth do not want to learn. They have not come to Dartmouth to learn. They want to enjoy themselves in other ways—picture shows, basketball games, drinks. . . . They do not think. They do not want to think! They shun thinking in others. They seem to despise and ostracize men who think." Three years later, a student committee at the University of Oregon fired a similar volley. "We believe, quite frankly, that the university 'atmosphere' is not intellectually vitalizing; that scholarship, the essence of education, is not the coveted goal of the mass of students," the Oregon committee wrote. "Far too much time and energy is spent in the distractions of student activities and in the whirl of collegiate social life." At Harvard, a student journalist confirmed, the highest status went to members of the football team; next came other sports, followed by the glee club, the dramatic society, and the comic weekly. "Scholastic excellence" sat at the very bottom.[9]

The New Faculty

For faculty members, by contrast, scholarship was at the top. Since the late 1800s, universities had increasingly emphasized research and publication as criteria of employment and promotion. The trend accelerated in the interwar period, when PhD production in the United States increased sharply. But it could not keep up with the boom in the student population, which meant that large numbers of students would be taught by faculty members without doctorates. Indeed, as one observer noted in 1925, several institutions that had formerly required PhDs for their faculty no longer did so. The following year, a survey of nearly 9,000 faculty at 163 institutions in 19 states found that

33.9 percent had a PhD; 58.1 percent had no more than an MA degree, and 24.8 percent had earned only a bachelor's degree. In 1931, another study showed that 243 of 553 social science professors in the 11 former Confederate states had a PhD, 260 had only an MA, and 50 had only a bachelor's degree. Meanwhile, many observers worried that the new generation of professors—especially those lacking doctorates—also lacked the skill and sophistication to teach effectively in America's teeming college classrooms. An Indiana University student journal underlined "the economic law of academic Gigantism": "*When enrollment increases rapidly, it is necessary to hire a number of cheap men, instead of fewer high-priced men.*" Often that meant employing instructors on a year-to-year basis instead of full-time faculty; at the University of Chicago, 70 percent of large undergraduate courses in 1925 were taught by professors on one-year contracts. It also meant hiring people with lesser qualifications and thereby eroding the profession's "monopoly value," as the AAUP's committee on teaching worried. At Amherst, for example, a student left for two years to obtain an MA degree in economics and then returned as an instructor of the same. "I'm one step ahead of you but that isn't really enough," he told his class on the first day, "so you're all going to have to work pretty hard in order to get anything out of the course."[10]

By the late 1930s, as a University of Virginia professor recalled, a PhD degree had become the "union card" for permanent faculty at elite institutions; only "the dregs of the profession"—as he indelicately put it—taught without one. But it was hardly clear that possession of a doctorate made one a better teacher. "We wonder whether it is too many Ph.D.'s, or the lack of them, which is the cause of so much poor teaching," two professors quipped in 1935. Students, especially, complained that "the Ph.D. disease"—as one editorialist called it—had produced dull specialists who lacked both the general knowledge and the sympathetic character to succeed in the classroom. "Intensive and mechanical grubbing in a narrow field does not necessarily produce a broadly informed teacher, nor does it guarantee a competent scholar," the journalist added. One college senior recalled asking a specialist in seventeenth-century literature a question about a literary figure "who had the bad grace to die seven years before the century began"; the professor gazed back at her in "amazed disapproval," noting that his own knowledge started in 1600. "I have finally discovered that professors are not what they seem," she wrote. "My days of hero-worship and aspiration are over." Other students likewise described how they arrived at school full of energy and curiosity, only to see it stamped out by dry-as-dust PhD-bearing professors. The more specialized the teacher, it seemed, the worse he taught. The *Harvard Lampoon* published a satirical poem in the voice of a young scholar who "grubbed and delved in dusty research" to obtain his doctorate but then failed as a classroom instructor. "I received my degree / And lost all joy and desire of teaching," the poem concluded.[11]

Privately, meanwhile, many college officials concluded the same. "I have grown wary of the Ph.D.," an unidentified college president told an interviewer in 1924. "I look over the Ph.D.'s with special care to see whether their focusing on a detailed, narrow, and sometimes meaningless research subject has made them useless as teachers." Writing to a fellow college president, Wesleyan's James L. McConaughy insisted that people without doctorates could and did provide "excellent teaching." He was perfectly happy to hire and promote professors who did not have a doctorate, McConaughy confided; the real obstacle was his PhD-bearing faculty, "who may resent the promotion of a man who has not gone through all the apprenticeship of the guild and received its various degrees." In the 1930s, especially, some university leaders—and even some doctorate-wielding faculty—began to go public with their concerns. "I have seen very respectable college teaching done by instructors without so much as a single learned note with which to bless themselves," an English professor at the University of Colorado wrote in 1934. They were often superior to the "distinguished scholar" who was "too damned busy with his book even to go through the motions of a decent lecture!" he added, quoting a typical student complaint. By 1939, no less a figure than Columbia's Nicholas Murray Butler included a jibe at PhD faculty in his annual presidential report. A doctorate was "non-essential" for quality instruction, Butler wrote; indeed, its "high degree of specialization . . . is precisely that which is to be avoided in college teaching."[12]

Yet the same institutions that maligned PhDs continued to hire them, as University of Chicago classicist Berthold Ullman wrote privately in 1930. "Why is it that the colleges insist on this degree if they are not satisfied with the product that we send them?" Ullman asked. His letter found its way to university president Robert M. Hutchins, who told his faculty that they should offer two different degrees: one for students who planned to become college teachers, and another for those who wished to be scholars. That was a hard sell: five years later, in fact, Hutchins admitted that he had yet to find a member of the faculty who agreed with him. Status lay with research, and with the PhD that signified it. So every school aimed to bring in more faculty with doctorates, whether they could teach well or not. Writing in 1933, after visiting 45 colleges and universities for the AAUP's teaching committee, physicist Homer L. Dodge observed that universities were "striving to be research institutes," colleges were "trying to become universities," and even normal schools had refashioned themselves as teachers colleges. So teaching was increasingly "relegated to a subordinate position in favor of research," Dodge added, no matter the type of institution. It also meant that young professors often arrived at their jobs believing that teaching was "somehow unimportant," Knox College president Albert Britt complained, "and not a real life work." But none of that stopped him from pursuing people with PhDs for his faculty, as Britt privately—and sheepishly—admitted. "We have worshipped at the feet of the Ph.D. and still do," he told a colleague.[13]

Teaching in Interwar America
Lecture

As before, though, the bulk of professors' work *was* teaching. Despite the growing emphasis on research, most professors still spent more time in the classroom than they did in the library or laboratory. And most of that time was spent lecturing, which reached a new apex during the enrollment surge of the 1920s. "Gigantism, which is the prevailing disease in American universities, makes the lecture method inevitable," a University of Oregon student wrote in 1928. Faculty, too, admitted the cold practical reality that lay beneath this trend. "The reasons for the almost universal application of the lecture method are very simple," wrote Dartmouth chemist Leon Richardson, who surveyed undergraduate instruction at several different colleges. "It is attractive to the administration of a college because it is relatively inexpensive; and it is attractive to the teacher because it is easy." As in earlier eras, students reported that professors lectured from the same notes year after year or read directly from the assigned text. Others rambled from topic to topic, without any apparent plan or theme. An irreverent Indiana student journal called the *Vagabond* sent a "vagabond stenographer" into a large class and published the resulting lecture, which skipped from the lumber industry in Sweden to the professor's travels in the Philippines to his encounters with labor radicals. He paused at one point to ask whether the students had read an assigned chapter; when they did not respond, he continued on his merry way. "Violation of 'academic privacy' is justified only in the most extreme cases," the student paper wrote, prefacing its transcript of the lecture. "But we feel that the time has come for a showdown." Equally dismal lecturing "goes on every day of the academic year," it added. "The same rubbish could be duplicated in the classes of at least 20 other faculty members."[14]

The use of a stenographer in the Indiana exposé was ironic because many students around the country complained that the lecture system had indirectly forced them into the same occupation. Note-taking was the bane of the college student's existence, generating endless jokes and jeremiads. Newspapers featured cartoons of hundreds of students sitting in rows, hunched over desk chairs and writing furiously. "Forty, eighty, two hundred heads slanted over so many student note books; pencils mechanically recording facts—points one, two, and three—with important items underscored against the future day of reckoning. That is the lecture system," a student journal editorialized. Most of all, students complained that they neither understood nor cared about what they were writing—and that they forgot everything after their test or quiz, anyhow. Critics routinely described college as the place where the professor's lecture notes passed to the student's notebook, without passing through the brains of either. Although the quip was widely attributed to Mark Twain, there is no record of him saying or writing it. The first print version appeared in a 1927 book entitled *Creative Learning and Teaching* by educator Harry Lloyd Miller; it was recycled in many other places after that, most prominently by eminent philosopher Mortimer J. Adler. "Most of us are guilty of the vice of passive reading, of course," Adler wrote in the same passage where he cited Twain's supposed quip, "but most people are even more likely to be passive in listening to a lecture." Notetakers might be active physically, but the most avid student stenographer often failed to learn anything substantial about what he was writing down.[15]

Other students dozed off in class or gazed into space, content to borrow notes from a friend or to purchase the ones available for sale. Arriving for a year of study at Princeton in 1922, a British student was offered "a quite embarrassing selection" of notes, as he recalled; one service charged $4 per course, another offered six courses for $20, and a third "prided itself on a very specialized summary . . . a sort of *edition de luxe*." The colleges tried gamely to interdict the note-taking services, which a Dartmouth official—with a nod to alcohol prohibition—condemned as "intellectual bootleggers." But as the campus newspaper editorialized, the real fault lay in rote-driven classes that lent themselves to these kinds of shortcuts. "Outlines sell by the tens of thousands in Hanover," the paper declared, "and they seem likely to continue to do so just so long as factual courses predominate and memorizing makes or breaks a student scholastically." Other students stopped going to lectures, because they knew they could obtain the information elsewhere. "I have attended this class four times this term and have a straight B grade on the midterms!" a University of California student exclaimed privately in 1940. "I have done none of the reading! I obtained the lectures . . . for the spring term and they follow the teacher's verbatim." In classes where professors read directly from books, likewise, there was no good reason to show up. "Why attend lectures when you can read them in much more intelligible form?" a University of California senior wrote to his student newspaper in 1938. He signed the letter with a revealing pseudonym: "Bored '38."[16]

Indeed, among all the student critiques and complaints about lectures, boredom was first and foremost. In student publications, authors seemed to compete to see who could come up with the most interesting adjectives to describe uninteresting lectures: dreary, tiresome, tedious, wearisome, bleak, grim, and so on. "We are lectured to death," a College of Wooster student wrote. "The student . . . calls the classroom a bore. It is. He throws himself into other activities, which are his own." If students paid more attention to the sideshow of sports and fraternities than to the main tent of academics, as Woodrow Wilson had charged, it was the ringmaster's fault rather than their own. Other students took to verse to denounce the dullness of their teachers. "Here he sits droning / On some forgotten truth; / Heedless of Springtime, / Intolerant of youth," a 1926 poem began. At Stanford, a second poet indicted professors who induced sleep: "But when it comes to lecturing / Then chloroform's the proper thing." A critic observing 72 university instructors was stunned—and, of course, bored—by their soporific lectures. Here large class size became an advantage, he noted, because it allowed students to doze without detection. "Three times a week / You hold us helpless while you speak," another student poem declared. "Well, here we are, your hundred sheep, / Tune up—play on—pour forth—we sleep."[17]

To be sure, every campus had lecturers who were famous for engaging students rather than for boring them. Stanford historian Thomas Bailey had started out as a youth preacher, which taught him to be "clear, succinct, as concrete as possible—and audible," he wrote in a memoir. Likewise, UC Berkeley historian F. J. Teggart was both bemused and pleased when the campus newspaper praised the "evangelical zeal" of his lectures; although he had long since forsaken his faith, he continued to model his delivery after the preachers who held forth—with "fire in their belly"—during his childhood in Northern Ireland. Teggart had also been active in amateur theater, which helped him hone his voice, timing, and body language. Students often saluted Teggart with applause, which—as in the acting world—provided both a "reward and stimulus" for a good lecture, one of his former students recalled. Gardner Murphy, a psychologist at Columbia, spoke seamlessly using a few dozen words that he had scribbled on an envelope; seeking to evince Murphy's spontaneity, yet lacking his confidence, one of his former students typed out his lectures beforehand but tried to make it sound like he was talking off the cuff. Other professors spiced up their lectures with classroom demonstrations, a perpetual crowd-pleaser. A psychologist at Minot State Teachers College in North Dakota arranged for two students to break into class and "rob" him, to illustrate how observers could provide different accounts of the same event. Unaware of the ruse, several class members "pounced upon the intruders and pummeled them," as one witness recalled. A good time was had by all, even by the fake robbers.[18]

But some students and faculty also criticized popular lecturers for "playing to the crowd"—that is, for reducing education to entertainment. The interwar era witnessed a new cult of the spoken word, fed in part by Dale Carnegie's book *Public Speaking and Influencing Men in Business* and also by the rapid development of radio. From urban "town halls of the air" to Franklin D. Roosevelt's "fireside chats," more and more Americans took in information via their ears than their eyes. But that brought with it a renewed skepticism about public speaking as well, which was derided as frivolous and shallow. The critique found its way into university classrooms, where one observer complained that professors were echoing the "smooth corporation vice-president type." Faculty especially condemned the handful of colleagues who drew a following outside of the college gates, which seemed to confirm their essential superficiality. Students, too, often became skeptical of the "popular" lecturer: although they praised professors who held their interest, they also disdained those who forsook rigor for theater. The distinction lay at the heart of a Northwestern student poem, "Song of the Popular Professor":

I'm the popular professor of the Universitee
And I'm known among the students for my personalitee
When my lectures are concluded loud applause is always heard
I infer such popularity must surely be deserved.
Of the classes on the campus, none's a fifth as large as mine
Which proves that all the virtues of five teachers I combine
If a popular professor you have any wish to be

(The method is quite simple), take these formulae from me:

Dismiss five minutes early and arrive five minutes late;

Have your hair made sleek and curly, and wear clothes right up-to-date

Tell the class about your tennis games and pastimes energetic;

Or any other applesauce to make you seem athletic

Be ready to emit a joke at slightest provocation,

But never to the subject let it have the least relation

All these precepts closely follow, and I'll guarantee you'll be

The most popular professor of the universitee.[19]

Recitation and Discussion

The surge in lectures meant a corresponding decline in recitation, which had been on the wane since the 1890s. But some professors held firm to the method, even in very large classes where they could only call on each student once or twice a term. In smaller classes, meanwhile, daily or weekly quizzes—both oral and written—remained common. Sociologist Albert Keller, who began teaching at Yale in 1900, continued to start each class with a 10-minute quiz until he retired in 1942. So did a Beloit chemistry professor, who gave short daily quizzes to test his students' understanding and also to expose the "IWWs" (interwar collegiate shorthand for "I Won't Work") in the class. But most recitation duties at large universities devolved to teaching assistants, whose numbers skyrocketed as well. In 1928, 230 of 310 graduate students at Iowa State were employed as assistants by the university; and whereas all of them were engaged in some kind of instruction, they often lacked "real skill and understanding of the teaching profession," as the school's president wrote privately. Students confirmed as much, denouncing underqualified TAs and the cash-strapped universities that hired them. Sometimes the assistants taught classes on their own; more commonly, they served as "section men" (as TAs of both genders were called) for larger courses. "Many students are being subjected to high school pedagogical methods at the hands of earnest and well-meaning, but green, student assistants," a Johns Hopkins student journal complained. The assistants were often radically overworked as well: as the economy tanked in the 1930s, they took any job they could get. One Columbia graduate student rode the subway from his home in Brooklyn to take morning classes, rode back to Brooklyn in the afternoon to conduct a lab section at Brooklyn College, went back to Columbia to study in the evening, and then returned home to Brooklyn around midnight. Undergraduates recognized the assistants' plight but remained mostly unmoved. "It's all right to give deserving young scholars a boost, but it's not right to make a whole class suffer just so the University can pay living wages to a youngster," an Illinois student opined in 1932, at the height of the Great Depression.[20]

Other students took aim at the recitation system itself, which sparked a lively debate in the interwar years. As in earlier eras, critics denounced question-and-answer sessions as exercises in sadism and repetition. "The recitation was a series of mechanical shocks and jolts on the memories of the students to start a train of thought," wrote one classroom observer, after watching a geography professor lead his class through a series of tedious questions and trite responses. ("What factors made contact with the Orient quite easy?" the professor asked. "All the water routes," came the predictable reply.) Coupled with lectures, an Oregon student wrote, the recitation resembled the Lancasterian system devised to teach poor children in the United Kingdom and the United States in the early nineteenth century: the head teacher taught student "monitors," who in turn were charged with teaching other children what they had learned. In modern colleges, likewise, the professor dispensed wisdom and his "quiz master" assistants checked to see whether students had memorized it. But other students praised recitations for keeping them on task: as one Dartmouth journalist argued, most members of his class "would do no studying to speak of if not held to a rigid system of daily requirements." Meanwhile, psychologists cited a body of research suggesting that these exercises actually helped people learn. "It is sometimes said in criticism of recitations that they are useless repetitions of facts which the learners already know," University of Chicago education professor Charles H. Judd wrote. In fact, they were "useful means of fixing materials in the minds of learners." When students recited rather than simply read materials over and over, Judd noted, "they learn faster and remember longer and more completely than they do when they do not recite."[21]

Yet quiz-style recitation continued its steady decline in favor of discussion, which was widely hailed as the hallmark of "true teaching"—to quote Dartmouth's Leon Richardson—after World War I. The difference between the two methods was summarized by the eminent poet Robert Frost, who was also a beloved professor at Amherst and several other institutions. "Long ago I gave up the idea of asking my students to tell me what I knew just that I might discover if they knew as much as I did," Frost told an interviewer in 1925. "Now in classes I ask questions in the correct sense of the word, for I want them to tell us something new, something I do not know." At Wellesley, likewise, famed literature professor Vida Dutton Scudder proudly reported that she had never asked a question with a yes or no answer; truly educational questions had many possible replies, requiring students to come up with their own. Students often reserved their highest plaudits for skillful discussion leaders, who made them use their heads as well as their tongues. "You are an instructor, not a dictator," one student wrote to Kimon Friar, a Greek scholar and translator who taught English at the University of Iowa. "You bring up questions for deep thought and all opinions are welcomed regardless of conflicting ideas." The student went on to praise Friar's easy manner in discussion, so different from the stress of recitation: "One can relax, act human, and express his real ideas in your class since it seems just a meeting of friends." A second student called Friar's pedagogy "revolutionary," because it required "original thinking" rather than repetition. Tongue firmly in cheek, a third student teased Friar about his method of inquiry. "The worst of all are the discussions. Those are terrible," the student jibed. "I may get some new ideas, and it may start me thinking sometimes, and you do conduct them very well and present quite a few new angles, Mr. Friar, but after all—oh, I guess they aren't so bad."[22]

But other students leveled more serious critiques of Friar's technique, highlighting problems and challenges facing even a skilled discussion leader. Too many students failed to read the assigned material before class, leading some of their peers to plead with Friar for a bit of traditional quiz-master recitation. "Usually the class discussions are weak, due to the fact that only a very few persons take part," a student told Friar. "This problem could be remedied, I believe, by having more short quizzes, for strange as it seems . . . better association with the material at hand would bring better discussions." Another student suggested that Friar keep a written record of responses in class, which would incentivize both preparation and participation. As a third student added, "there would be some embarrassment for some until they learned that they would have to read their lesson," but it would be worth it, "making possible a more interesting discussion because they would then know what was going on." Still others criticized Friar for letting students veer into irrelevant tangents, which wasted valuable time that could have been spent learning about the assigned topic. "Arguments and view points are brought forth, but one thing leads to another and the original issue is left hanging in the air with no definite conclusion," a student wrote. "The discussions have left one feeling that the head of the nail has been hit a little on the eccentric. A good lecture about once every two or three weeks would help everyone immensely."[23]

Elsewhere, too, students complained that instructors let discussions devolve into "bull sessions" instead of exerting their professorial authority. "Sometimes

I wanted the *teacher's* viewpoint rather than a fellow student's, not to tell me *what* to think but to measure my own resulting thoughts against," a New York University student underlined in a class evaluation. Other students in the same class complained that "a few motor-minded individuals do all the talking," which allowed "the shirker" to "lie down on the job." Likewise, University of Chicago students said that their abler classmates monopolized discussions, the better to hear the sound of their own voices. "Too much opportunity is given to the student to express himself; he is eager to attach too much importance to his own opinions," one angry student wrote, blasting the loudmouths in his class. Other observers criticized professors for taking up too much airtime themselves, instead of allowing students to talk. Sometimes the teachers returned to the old question-and-answer format, especially when they could not spark more spontaneous dialogue: as one Bowdoin alumnus quipped, recitation was another name for "discussion held with uncooperative students." Others simply lectured, which was the easiest way to fill the vacuum. The problem was especially acute in sections led by TAs, who often imitated the didactic style of their own professors. But even faculty who aimed to provoke discussion often failed to generate the "peculiar blend of dominance and self-effacement" that the method required, as one professor at Hampden-Sydney College admitted. "The teacher must be like an orchestra leader bringing out now the winds and now the brasses," he added. Too often, though, discordant noise ensued. Discussion demanded "very great skill on the part of the teacher," he concluded, and most teachers simply did not have it.[24]

Still other instructors were probably afraid to allow real discussion in their classrooms, lest it stray into dangerous political realms. Dozens of professors had been dismissed or pushed out during World War I, typically for seeming "soft" on the German enemy. In the 1920s, battles over evolution made religious subjects especially perilous to address in the classroom; then came the Great Depression, which raised the specter of socialist and Communist alternatives to capitalism. Most professors probably danced around these topics or avoided them altogether, to the consternation of their more politically minded students. "Why this cowering fear of 'controversial topics,' anyhow?" an Indiana student publication asked in 1925, on the eve of the Scopes Trial over evolution. The answer was obvious: they could get you fired. In 1935, University of Pittsburgh historian F. E. Butel reported that he was forced to resign after publically denouncing "inhumane conditions" in the Pennsylvania coal mines; however, the school chancellor claimed that he was fired for espousing the theory of evolution in class. Overall, statements made while teaching received less protection than those made in publications, and most faculty members seemed to accept that distinction. The majority of respondents in a 1923 survey said they should have unrestricted freedom in their research, but fewer than half believed they should have similar protection for teaching; meanwhile, over two-thirds said that professors should restrict in-class comments in accord with the dominant political and religious beliefs of their institutions and communities. College officials and right-wing citizen groups sometimes sent stenographers into classes, to make sure professors hewed to the conventional wisdom. But most of them were doing that already, as Columbia philosopher Irwin Edman joked in a 1942 satirical poem:

> A teacher should impart what's true
> At least when they allow him to;
> A college teacher should not vex
> His pupils with his thoughts on sex;
> He should keep mum if he has odd
> Views on the character of God.
> He should dismiss as red inventions
> All but the three well-known dimensions.

Lest anyone miss the point, Erdman concluded with a reminder that faculty who followed these rules could assure their continued employment. "And keep for you, though, far from clever / Your job—and what a job!—forever!"[25]

Student Protest and Teacher Evaluations

To many students, by contrast, "forever" was far too long: like the poor of scripture, it seemed, bad teachers would always be with them. Since the birth of American colleges, indeed, students had criticized poor college teaching. But in the interwar years, they began to denounce it in an organized, intercollegiate fashion. The first salvo was fired by the National Student Forum, which brought together 50 student leaders and college newspaper editors in Hartsdale, New York, in late 1922. They were unanimous—and unforgiving—in their attacks on college instruction. "To put it baldly a great deal of college is just so many hours of deadly boredom," the students declared; entering college to "gain some insight into human problems," young people were "presented with a pile of textbooks and some more or less untidy diagrams on a blackboard." Then came Dartmouth's senior Committee on Undergraduate Education, whose furious 1924 report triggered similar student investigations—and indictments—around the country. "This is no isolated phenomenon," the *New Republic* proclaimed, in the wake of the Dartmouth report. "Everywhere are rumblings against 'the system,' minor revolts, polite petitions, and persistent, dogged sabotage." Some students had "pledged to flunk out" rather than "bend the knee to what they regard as childish routine"; others had taken up pen and typewriter, determined to expose the scandal of college instruction and to change it for the better. As a Pittsburgh scholar observed, students across the country were issuing an "insistent call for freedom" from dull, tyrannical, and inefficient instruction.[26]

Indeed, as *Time* magazine confirmed, "every conscious college in the land" had witnessed some kind of collective protest on the subject. Students at the University of Oregon released a blistering 1926 report denouncing "spoon feeding" and "rubber stamp procedure" in the classroom. The same year, a student committee at Harvard condemned faculty for teaching in "the mechanical way" of high schools, including "dry monotonous lectures." And in 1929, students at Indiana University issued a humorous but revealing call for revolution in college instruction. "When in the course of human events it becomes necessary for one student and another to sit through classes hour after hour with faces as long as a Rolls Royce automobile and as sad looking as that pebble in Egypt they call the Sphinx . . . I deem it advisable to promote legislative action," one wrote. By 1931, students at 14 different institutions had produced protest letters and reports about college teaching. They ranged from large public schools like the University of Nebraska to small private colleges like Swarthmore, where a student committee denounced professors for reading straight from the textbook—even in tiny classes—and for rehashing old lectures year after year. What held these various campaigns together was an unrelenting focus on the classroom, as the Dartmouth report's lead author confirmed. "Nothing can straighten out the college question except good teaching," William H. Cowley declared. "Everything else is besides the point."[27]

Meanwhile, many of these same students took the lead in demanding—and, often, in designing—student evaluations of teachers. If teaching was the key function of college, and students were its intended beneficiary, who better to stand in judgment of it? Championing teacher evaluations, one student journal published a pointed 1922 letter by the English playwright George Bernard Shaw. "As far as I can gather, if the students in the American Universities do not organize their own education, they will not get any," Shaw wrote. Faculties were unlikely to evaluate themselves, Shaw wrote, nor would trustees or other college officials dare to do so. "The remedy is co-operative organization by the consumers: that is, by the students," Shaw wrote. If the American baker gave customers "what he liked instead of what they liked," Shaw added, American bread would be as indigestible as American university education. So students had to make their wishes heard, in a sustained manner, which was the only thing that would improve the product. At Dartmouth, angry students suggested the formation of a committee of seniors to visit classrooms and "fumigate the faculty" of its worst members. But in the same breadth, they acknowledged that college officials and professors were unlikely to agree to such a plan. "We realize the faults of the above system," the students wrote, "but we feel sure that some system is necessary whereby the mental garbage which contaminates the intellectual atmosphere of Hanover can be removed." The simplest solution, another student added, were written evaluations. Students could organize them on their own, without any approval or oversight from college authorities. And rather than providing a snapshot of a professor's performance, the surveys would collate a wide swath of opinion and "determine whom the students consider most efficient and effective in their work."[28]

Student newspapers took the lead, distributing questionnaires and publishing results in their pages or in special book-length guides. The first and most prominent was Harvard's *Confidential Guide to Freshman Courses*, which the *Harvard Crimson* started issuing in 1924. Initially restricted to freshman courses, the "Confy"—as generations of students called it—billed itself as a way to inform course selection for new arrivals. It affected a jocular, inside-scoop tone that provided "personal impressions" rather than "exhaustive, final judgments," as a 1925 press account noted. "This course in elementary logic probably does as much good for the brain as swinging Indian clubs in the Hemenway Gymnasium does for the body," the Confy quipped, reviewing a philosophy course. "And both forms of exercise are equally exciting." (The course "consists of parroting a number of logical rules of thumb," the evaluation continued, "by which the valid may be distinguished from the fallacious with as little thought as possible.") By the following year, student newspapers at Cornell and at the Universities of Wisconsin and Illinois had all established their own course guides; Yale and Stanford would follow shortly after that. "Student criticism of college courses has emerged from the bull sessions and established itself in the college paper, where it can be more effective both in warning the uninitiated student and in assisting the professor whose teaching is not 'getting across,'" one student journal declared. It gave special plaudits to the Cornell guide, where "adverse criticism was served unsparingly." A review of an animal biology course, for example, warned that it will "deaden the interest of all save the most pedantic students"; it also required lengthy dissection of a frog, which "produces utter ennui and final disgust." Student guides might not be scientific, the Harvard Confy admitted, but at least they gave voice to the victims. "The merit of these statements is that they are not 'official' and that they are written by men who have taken, not given, the various courses," it declared in 1934. "They give 'the dope.'"[29]

Meanwhile, a handful of institutions were establishing precisely the kind of "official" student evaluation systems that the Confy abjured. As student guides sprouted around the country, Oklahoma Agricultural and Mechanical College initiated a formal survey that would be "much more satisfactory than allowing rumors coming from a few students to give the rating of a teacher's ability," as the dean who devised the questionnaire wrote. Students were promised that only the dean and the relevant instructor would see their evaluations, and only after the students had received their course grades. Several other institutions developed "rating sheets" that were in turn adopted by other schools, marking the first cross-collegiate movement to evaluate teachers. The most famous was the Purdue Rating Scale, which asked students to judge professors' "presentation of subject matter," "sympathetic attitude towards students," "fairness in grading," and several other traits; four decades later, in the late 1960s, some colleges were still administering the instrument and sending the results to Purdue University, which developed a side business in scoring them. Another popular scale was designed by Oberlin, which rated professors in clarity, accessibility, "richness of course content," and "general influence on student morale." Other institutions continued to create their own surveys, which they gave to alumni as well as students. The University of Idaho sent questionnaires to everyone it graduated between 1924 and 1928, asking them to identify their best and worst professors, as well as the qualities that made them so. The results were shared individually with the faculty, which "gave more attention to the subject of teaching than they had formerly done," the university president proudly asserted.[30]

But student evaluations also spawned organized faculty resistance, which stalemated or even reversed the nascent movement to "grade the professors," as press accounts inevitably called it. The sharpest revolt took place at the University of Washington, which instituted a student questionnaire of all classes in 1931 but abruptly shifted course when professors rallied against it. Even at Oberlin, which developed one of the common rating scales, efforts to implement student evaluation backfired. A faculty committee rejected it in 1930, insisting that "the value of student judgment of a teacher's work is a moot point." Undergraduates' "immaturity and inexperience" rendered their opin-

ion "unreliable," the committee added, "and any effort to obtain it systematically is dangerous." College president Ernest Wilkins then decided to survey
the previous five years of alumni, tabulating the results by himself and keeping the entire project a secret. But when the faculty found out, they howled.
Wilkins had taken "unfair advantage" of professors by distributing the questionnaire, they said, which would give disgruntled ex-students a chance to "get
square"—that is, to exact revenge—on faculty "who in their judgment had
been unfair to them." Student evaluations also earned the ire of the AAUP's
committee on teaching, which worried that the trend would encourage professors to dilute their standards and expectations. "Occasionally a teacher
achieves a high place in the estimation of his students by doing most of their
work for them," the committee noted; other undergraduates were "unduly influenced" by a professor's personal appearance, mannerisms, and "other
things which have little or no relation to the real effectiveness of his classroom
work." Even faculty members who administered their own informal surveys—
an increasingly common practice—almost always opposed institutional ratings, as UC Berkeley German professor Franz Schneider observed.[31]

Schneider himself represented a notable exception to that rule, uniting with
students behind standardized teacher evaluation and triggering the interwar
era's loudest controversy over the practice. By his own estimation, Schneider
was not "a great scholar in the ordinary sense" but aimed to live up to UC
Berkeley's motto, "Let there be light." That meant eliciting and distributing information about his colleagues' teaching effectiveness, much to their anger
and annoyance. Schneider made five different proposals to the faculty senate
to institute a formal system of student ratings; rejected all five times, he worked
with students to distribute surveys on their own. The first one went out in 1938,
when 12 students blanketed the campus with a questionnaire that Schneider
designed; they eventually collected 1,620 evaluations of 250 professors, which
he anonymized and reproduced in a self-published book the following year.
The year after that, Schneider distributed 15,000 reaction sheets—mainly via
student clubs and fraternities—and received about 4,000 in return, which he
duly published as well. The evaluations reflected the same jocular and often
snarky tone of other student reports—one professor "has yet to say something
during class time which is either original or stimulating," an angry student
wrote—and sparked predictable enmity in the faculty senate, which voted to
censure Schneider in 1940. But he continued unbowed on his quest, confident
that he was "helping all good people throughout the State" and that history
would vindicate him. "Some of my colleagues won't like me any better for

holding up the mirror to their nature, but I cannot help it that they are not as good looking as they ought to be," Schneider told a colleague. "I want them to do a better job of teaching toward the children of our people whose money they take under the assumption that they will teach them."[32]

Students rallied behind Schneider, meanwhile, praising his courageous stance against his colleagues and echoing his consumerist arguments for evaluation: as payers of tuition, they also had a right to rate their teachers. "A certain professor who drives a big gray Buick convertible sedan seems to think it beneath his dignity to venture out in the rain in time to attend his 9 o'clock class," a student wrote to the *Daily Californian* in 1938. "Every time it rains we come to class only to find that our professor has not shown up. What did we pay our $26 for?" Two years later, amid the battle over Schneider's rating sheets, the *Daily Californian* again called on the university to elicit and respect "the consumer's angle"—that is, student opinion. "The Academic Senate is naturally concerned with the privileges of the faculty, but we are just as naturally concerned with the rights of the students," the paper editorialized. "Who is to protect them against poor teaching?" But it was hardly clear that student evaluations would do that, as even some supporters admitted. Especially when students collected them, the ratings were often slapdash and incomplete; many of them remained anonymized, which reduced the pressure on professors to change; and many faculty members proudly declared that they would ignore the ratings anyway, dismissing student evaluation as "campus gossip." For their own part, students seemed to use published guides as a way to locate easy courses, not necessarily good ones. Harvard's *Confidential Guide* actually warned against that practice in 1934, endorsing president James B. Conant's campaign against so-called "snap" courses. But it proceeded to identify them anyway, especially those where professors and assistants allowed windy and imprecise answers on quizzes and tests. The 1940 Confy called a class on the English Bible "a snap course which tends to stress bull-slinging"; the following year, it said that exams in Introduction to Psychology were "comprehensive but easy to bull on," while those in Modern Government were "easily passed by the use of quantities of hot air." The same students who condemned professors as lazy and indifferent often displayed the same traits themselves, reinforcing the cycle of blame that had hounded college teaching from the start.[33]

Impersonality, Everywhere

But on one matter—and one matter alone—students and faculty seemed united: college instruction was becoming radically impersonal. In the era of mass education, critics said, individual differences and desires were being submerged by mass production. "It reminded me of Henry Ford—just production with no human interest," a University of Michigan student wrote, citing the state's most famous industrialist. Another Michigan student called the university a "huge, heartless place," while a third decried the "lack of personal contact with instructors." An Oklahoma student made the same point with a more agricultural metaphor, complaining that "the individual during this period is shuttled through a machine like a bundle of straw." Part of the problem lay in professors' commitment to research and its "spirit of disinterestedness and detachment," a University of Pennsylvania student newspaper suggested, which ran counter to a deeply personal endeavor like teaching. But the bigger issue was institutions' growth in size, which simply did not allow for the kind of individual exchange and intimacy that successful instruction demanded. "Instead of being a person . . . I am now merely a suit of clothes pinned together by four or five seat numbers," a Yale student lamented, referring to the number of classes he took. Faculty concurred, frequently bemoaning their lack of real contact with their students. At the University of Chicago, one professor worried that students would not comprehend or care about "impersonal knowledge" unless teachers found a way to connect it to their personal concerns. "More opportunities should be made for the student to know his instructor, and vice versa," the professor wrote. Yet that too would be unlikely or impossible if the universities kept growing, a Tulane professor despaired. "Most of our administrators, captivated as they are by American ideals of bigness, are leading us toward depersonalization, disintegration, elephantitis," he glumly predicted.[34]

Even at the smaller colleges, critics said, bloat and bureaucracy were blotting out individuality and idiosyncrasy. "The business methods of efficiency and standardization, relentless as a steamroller, crush the rebel spirits," a College of Wooster senior wrote in a typical jeremiad. At Swarthmore, for example, students decried the lack of a "personal element between professor and student" and demanded "less lecture work and more individualism"; at Bowdoin, likewise, an alumnus recalled that nobody on the faculty seemed "sufficiently interested" to get to know him. Some critics attributed the change to the research gospel, which was infecting every kind of institution—and diminishing the teaching function—in the interwar years. "The first-line universities, like major planets, exercise a tremendous attraction," three observers worried, "and their emphasis on research tends to deflect some liberal colleges from their supposedly fixed orbits." But the biggest culprit was the curse of bigness itself, even at little schools. Colby College was forced to raise class sizes in English composition above 30 for the first time in 1923, the department chair wrote; that was "too large for effective composition work," he noted, "for a student's needs in learning to write are individual needs and cannot be met by mob instruction." Three years later, the college added 165 students but only one new English instructor; so "paper marking suffers," the chair complained, "and the students' poor English remains unimproved." Noting rising class sizes in the psychology department as well, its chair worried that the weaker students would be neglected and that "indifferent" ones would not be sufficiently prodded or challenged. "Wholesale education lowers the standard and defeats its aim," he warned.[35]

The most personal instruction in the interwar years probably took place at junior colleges, which grew steeply from 50,000 students in 1928 to 200,000–13 percent of total higher-education enrollment—in 1940. Offering two-year degrees in a mix of academic and vocational subjects, junior colleges often held classes in high schools; their instructors were frequently high school teachers as well, whom students sometimes mocked for their professorial pretentions. But these teachers were on the average better instructors than college professors, several observers wrote, precisely because they engaged with their students—like secondary teachers did—instead of simply talking at them. "The merely ordinary, if admitted at all to do college work, have their rights," one junior college dean wrote. "One right that should be 'inalienable' is the right to be shown," he added, contrasting his "high school method" of illustration and explanation to one-way lectures in most four-year colleges. Asked to identify the advantages of junior colleges, a 1931 survey of their students named low costs, smaller classes, and "personalized instruction." A professor at an all-female junior college in Virginia instituted a "thesis-response" method, requiring students to react to several claims in the assigned reading and explain themselves in class. "It gives a chance to express your own opinion and to defend it even though it disagrees with the thought of the professor or the textbook," one student said; another reported that the method "challenges the mind of the student by making [her] think rather than 'ramble' or 'parrot.'" At Stephens College in Missouri, another junior college for women, students kept diaries to record their personal reactions to readings and shared them with professors and peers. "In every course . . . instructors are trying to make the teaching material as close to the experiences of the girls as possible," one observer wrote.[36]

At women's four-year colleges, too, instruction was generally more personal than the interwar norm. Like junior college teachers, large numbers of professors at women's colleges had previously taught in elementary or secondary schools. Hence, they lectured less often, preferring to engage their students in activity and discussion. "I don't mind the essential teaching, tho' I abominate 'lecturing,'" confessed Wellesley English professor Katherine Lee Bates, who became famous for writing "America the Beautiful." Bates's seminar on Elizabethan literature was renowned for extending to four or even five hours instead of the scheduled three, as Bates questioned and debated her transfixed students. During these years, women's colleges had more female professors at the lower levels and roughly equal numbers of men and women in senior-faculty roles. In a 1924 survey, female faculty and deans reported that women were "usually more conscientious" than men in their teaching; a student in the same study reported that "women try to find out what you know; men to show what they know." As a rule, that meant that female professors got to know their students more intimately than male ones did. But it also meant that even female students often favored male teachers, because men were less demanding; women also said they could "work" male professors, charming their way to *less* work and higher grades.[37]

At black colleges, finally, the small communal environment of the institutions—and their status as distinct segregated communities—sometimes spawned closer personal connections between students and faculty. But rising class sizes eroded that intimacy, just like it did at other colleges and universities during these years. At Howard, most notably, alumni and students blasted President Stanley Durkee for embracing "the idea that bigness necessarily implied greatness," as one critic wrote. "A big college, unless a wealthy one, is very likely to be a big sham." Opponents especially slammed Durkee for hiring graduate students and even advanced undergraduates to teach overcrowded introductory classes. "Though education has wandered somewhat from the beaten path, instruction is still one of its aims," another critic wrote. "This means teachable classes and real teachers." The tradition of close professor-student rapport lived on in smaller black institutions like Wiley College in Texas, where legendary English professor Melvin Tolson modeled his instruction after Socrates. That sometimes meant mocking weak student responses and especially any sign of lackadaisical effort, which Tolson said would prevent students from succeeding in a society that was already stacked against them. "You know where white folks put information they want to hide from you?" he asked a stunned class. "Books and magazines and newspapers—that's where!" Tolson really knew his students, frequently hosting them at his house, so they knew they could not dodge him. At other black institutions, however, professors with less skill and empathy than Tolson humiliated their students out of sadism and rage. Sociologist Horace Clayton recalled colleagues at Tuskegee Institute demeaning their students as "ignorant sharecroppers," which created a "strict caste line between students and faculty."[38]

No matter the size or type of institution, it seemed, students and professors were drawing apart. But some teachers always found ways to bridge the divide. Surveys of college officials throughout the interwar period identified their best teachers as the ones whose personalities allowed them to relate to students, and vice versa. "I have come to the conclusion that the distinguishing characteristic of the great teacher is . . . that elusive and indefinable something we call personality," Birmingham-Southern College president Guy E. Snavely wrote in 1929. The more he thought about personality, Snavely admitted, the harder it became to capture or describe. Yet down in Florida his friend Hamilton Holt was "building up a Faculty of Golden Personalities" as part of a radical experiment in "individualizing instruction" at Rollins College. Holt's system replaced classes with small conferences, where faculty and students would work together on common problems. Personality was elusive, in short, but it was not unattainable. The question was whether American colleges and universities could reform themselves to bring personality into practice, instead of burying it in the grave that mass education had prepared for it.[39]

CHAPTER FOUR

"Teaching Made Personal"

Reform and Its Limits in Interwar College Teaching

In 1932, the head of a national study of undergraduate teaching described two different and somewhat contradictory campaigns to improve it. On behalf of the American Association of University Professors' Committee on College and University Teaching, Homer L. Dodge had visited 45 different institutions over the previous year. Many of them were aiming to "individualize" instruction via small-group tutorials and conferences, independent study, and special honors programs. But many of these same schools were also clustering students in large classes, where research had demonstrated that students could sometimes learn more than in smaller settings. "The most important trends are, curiously enough, towards the two extremes," wrote Dodge, a physicist and dean at the University of Oklahoma. But they were also related, he noted, because institutions needed to offset their "individualization experiments" with "mass instruction" in order to balance the books. "Economies must be effected everywhere," Dodge explained. "If the colleges are to ask society to support a more individualized type of instruction, college professors must be willing to learn the technique of handling large groups of students." Several institutions were taking new steps to prepare faculty for big classrooms and also to incentivize better instruction, via teaching awards and other evaluative efforts. More such experiments were surely on the way, Dodge predicted, as the colleges worked to tailor teaching to each individual and also to improve it on a mass scale.[1]

Indeed, as another college dean observed, the interwar years witnessed "a real renascence of college teaching" such as America had never seen. Under pressure from dissatisfied students, colleges established smaller classes and a host of other innovations aimed at more intimate educational experiences. Meanwhile, as enrollments continued to climb, schools sought to hire and promote stronger teachers with an eye to improving "regular"—that is, large-scale—classrooms. But both efforts were stillborn, generating more debate and discussion than real change. Tutorials and conferences required instructional skills that professors and teaching assistants often lacked; likewise, many students did not possess the initiative or maturity to succeed in these novel environments, especially without steady mentorship from the faculty. Nor did most institutions succeed in changing the larger culture of teaching on campus, which continued to take a back seat to research. A third dean noted that "reforms are abroad in the land" but would not bear fruit until good teaching was rewarded; but that, in turn, was unlikely so long as the colleges failed to document or even define it. "Well, sir, what is good teaching?" an Alfred College math professor asked in 1931. He wasn't sure, and neither was anyone else. "We know little about causes and effects in education," a Tulane scholar admitted in *Scientific Monthly*, three years before that. "We are in a pre-scientific age respecting education and we are attempting to function as if we were in a scientific age."[2]

Colleges had also entered a bureaucratic age, of course. But they were attempting to function as if they were in a pre-bureaucratic one, using impersonal levers to make teaching more personal. The tension was neatly captured by journalist John Palmer Gavit, in a 1925 book on the changing American college. "It was Socrates who asked: 'How can a man learn from one who is not his friend?'" Gavit wrote, praising efforts to bring teachers and students into closer dialogue. But he added a note of skepticism about how—and whether—institutions could promote such teaching, which depended on individual qualities rather than organizational ones. "The genius of it is that it is *not* a system," Gavit underlined, describing teaching. "In its best expression it is Socrates incarnate." Likewise, Harvard political scientist William Bennett Munro—whose scholarship examined the development of government institutions—wondered if teaching lent itself to official policy or analysis at all. "Pedagogy is like politics in that anyone can tell you how to do things better than they are being done," Munro wrote in 1928. "But teaching is an art, and true art can never be enslaved to formal rules. Teaching is an intensely personal thing; it cannot be standardized any more than leadership can." Here Munro cast a dubious eye on tutorials, conferences, and the rest of the "catalogue of panaceas" touted by interwar reformers. "Education does not succeed or fail on the issue of methodology but on the capacity and personality of the teacher himself," Munro concluded. The following year he took a new position as president of the California Institute of Technology; three years after that, he became chair of the AAUP's Committee on College and University Teaching. Here, as a functionary in a large organization, Munro would attempt what his own words suggested was impossible: to systematically change something that was not—or should not be—systematic. Indeed, many critics came to believe that the interwar campaigns to make teaching more personal threatened to destroy the individuality that lay at its heart.[3]

The Age of Experiment

In 1931, Charles F. Thwing, the former president of Western Reserve (later Case Western Reserve) University in Cleveland, took to the *New York Times* to proclaim a revolution in American college teaching. "Higher education is giving itself to experimentation," Thwing happily declared. Harvard had instituted a tutorial system, bringing its undergraduates under the guidance of a set of young scholars; the University of Chicago evaluated students not by course credits but by a comprehensive examination; a new branch of the University of Wisconsin—dubbed, naturally, the Experimental College—replaced lectures with seminars; and at Rollins College in Florida, courses were dispensed with altogether in favor of a "conference" system, in which faculty and students worked on shared topics and questions. What bound these experiments together, Thwing wrote, was a new emphasis on "individuality in the educational process." Formerly structured around shared goals, college instruction was being reoriented toward each student's interests and needs. Headlined "College Problems under Wide Attack," the article's subtitle referenced the shared solution: "Teaching Made Personal."[4]

Of course, the tutorial was as old as college itself. Princeton had revived it under Woodrow Wilson, renaming the tutors as "precepts" to avoid the negative connotations that had hounded them since the colonial era. Other schools instituted their own version of the tutorial after World War I, led most prominently by Harvard. Students met with a tutor individually—or, at most, with one other peer—each week to assess their progress, answer questions on old assignments, and develop new lines of inquiry; unconnected to specific classes, the tutors helped students prepare for the end-of-college comprehensive examinations that Harvard also instituted during these years. The tutors were mainly junior faculty and graduate students, who often held class in their rooms or in other informal settings. Assisted by a grant from the Carnegie Corporation of New York, Colgate assigned every freshman a preceptor, each sophomore an adviser, and all juniors and seniors a tutor; whatever their titles, these mostly young faculty members would provide friendly advice and counsel, not just technical or intellectual instruction. Lacking the same resources, other institutions more often linked tutors to particular courses—as in Princeton's system—and grouped them with six or eight students, instead of just one or two. But to Harvard philosopher Ralph Barton Perry, tutorials were the wave of the future everywhere. "The tutorial method . . . now seems to be as inevitable in America as was the elective system a generation ago," Perry wrote in 1924. "It may be conservatively described as the next great experiment in American higher education." It signified "increased liberty for the individual student," Perry added, as well as a new kind of relationship to teachers. No longer would the student sit at the teacher's feet, soaking in knowledge; instead, they would seek it together. "The tutorial code calls for fraternity rather than paternalism," Perry concluded. "American colleges should and will adopt [it] *provided they can afford to do so*."[5]

But as Perry's highlighted warning suggested, tutorials were also very costly. As the country descended into depression, they often became untenable for even well-endowed institutions. In a 1934 interview, Stanford president and former US secretary of the interior Ray Wilbur questioned whether tutorials—an import from the United Kingdom—could survive in the United States, which was "going into a period when we are likely to have less rather than more funds available for such extra expenses." Nor was it clear that tutorials were worth the money, he added, even if it could be found. The system required "such care in the selection of the tutors, that only especially favored universities could hope to make it a success," Wilbur cautioned. The key was to find faculty members who had broad enough knowledge to advise students on a multiplicity of topics and deep enough interest in the students themselves to care about the outcome. But young scholars studied increasingly narrow and arcane subjects, which did not necessarily equip them for the wide-ranging discussions that the tutorial system imagined. They also lacked experience in conducting such exercises, often reverting to the more familiar lecture method. "The student attends to clear up points which, in his reading, he has been unable to understand," a Harvard student committee explained. "To spend his hour listening to the tutor's opinions . . . is besides the purpose of the system. Tutors should not devote the conference hour to lecture practice." Even worse, another Harvard student panel noted, the regular Harvard faculty mostly eschewed tutoring; focusing on their research, they shunted tutorials to part-time instructors seeking permanent positions or to graduate students trying to complete their doctorates. So tutors were also radically overextended, which reduced both their effectiveness in the classroom and their prospects of steady employment in the future. "I am a happy supporter of the tutorial plan and I am deeply interested in the problem of giving the best possible education to our undergraduates," a Harvard dean wrote privately in

1934. "On the other hand, I believe that we cannot give them the best possible education except with the best possible men and I am sure that we cannot hope to have the best possible men if they are overworked or if they must work without proper chance of promotion."[6]

By the early 1940s Harvard's tutorial system was "nothing but a shadow on paper," as one embittered alumnus complained. The university instituted a "plan B tutorial," as critics called it, restricted to sophomores and to juniors and seniors of "exceptional ability": the plan allowed everyone to experience the tutorial as underclassmen, but only people who truly merited such attention would receive it after that. President James B. Conant also removed the handful of faculty who had served mainly as tutors "because they have not their Ph.D.'s or did no research work in Tasmanian Archaeology or some such thing," as another disgruntled alumnus wrote. So tutoring devolved almost exclusively to graduate students, who often saw tutorials as an annoying distraction from their doctoral research. Other colleges limited or eliminated their tutorials as well. The University of Washington restricted tutorials to seniors and imported their tutors mainly from Oxford, ironically, declaring that English scholars were more likely to possess the broad education and culture that the university wanted. Princeton's preceptorial groups billowed to as many as 12 or even 15 students, which seemed to defeat the whole purpose of the enterprise; although professors still taught the groups, unlike at most other institutions, "each man has too many students to do really effective work," one faculty member complained. Even at "progressive colleges" where faculty had initially welcomed the tutorial system, Columbia historian Jacques Barzun observed, they turned away from it when they realized the amount of work it involved. Meeting with students individually in half-hour tutorials for a full day was enough to turn any instructor into a "gibbering idiot," Barzun noted. Quoting a common student joke, Barzun noted that teachers at more forward-looking institutions tended to "die young" from overwork; at more traditional ones, by contrast, the students died from boredom. "That seems to be the basic difference between old-fashioned and Progressive Education," Barzun concluded.[7]

The Educational Vanguard

Here Barzun hailed a group of small private colleges in the vanguard of educational change, including Antioch, Reed, Swarthmore, Bennington, and Rollins. Yet rather than simply adding tutorials, as Barzun implied, they sought to refashion the entire structure of undergraduate teaching and learning. They often drew on the doctrines of John Dewey and other Progressive theorists, who were more commonly associated with primary and secondary schooling. Dewey himself served as chair at a conference on college teaching at Rollins in 1931, joking that his own work in graduate-level instruction (Dewey rarely taught undergraduates) gave him the requisite "degree of ignorance" for the task. But the assembled delegates—and the different reforms that they reported—spoke to an advancing body of knowledge and experience. At Antioch, the "Autonomous Plan" allowed students complete freedom in choosing how they learned. Receiving a syllabus for each course, they could attend weekly lectures and seminars or simply read on their own; they could also set up conferences with professors or informal discussion groups with their peers. Reed dispensed with course grades and substituted comprehensive examinations, which were modeled on graduate schools; its founder imagined Reed as a "Johns Hopkins for undergraduates," replacing lecture classes with small research seminars (where attendance was always optional) and individual meetings with professors. Behind these experiments lay the Progressive idea that education should be centered upon students—not teachers—and organically connected to their experience, as a participant at the 1931 conference emphasized. "The ideas of John Dewey . . . are evidently beginning to pervade the realm of higher education," the speaker observed. "Here we have seen lifted out of their hitherto elementary school settings the notions that education is life and vitally connected with life in its broader meanings."[8]

The most radical experiment probably took place at the institution hosting the conference, Rollins College. It was the oldest postsecondary institution in Florida, founded in 1885 by New England Congregationalists who hoped it would "be to the South what Harvard and Yale have been to the East." It drew little national attention until 1925, when journalist Hamilton Holt agreed to become its president. Holt soon instituted his "Conference Plan," which eliminated formal classes in favor of meetings that were modeled on Holt's own experience at editorial meetings of the *Independent*, the liberal weekly magazine he ran for over 20 years. Although Holt had degrees from Yale and Columbia, he said he learned almost nothing from the dull lecturers and quizmasters he encountered. So he refashioned the classroom as a kind of intellectual salon, where students and professors would work together on common problems. In a psychology conference, one visitor reported, students sat around a table and debated the "relative part played by environment and heredity" with their professor. One student had been asked to read a few chapters of a book on the subject and report to the class; others had been given a set of readings they could use to prepare for the discussion. And so it went, from an economics conference that deliberated the nature of vocations, to a human relations conference examining why many Christians despised Jews, to a Bible conference about why the serpent approached Eve rather than Adam. "You should have heard the discussion on the relative power of men and women to resist temptation," the impressed visitor wrote.[9]

Students, too, recorded enthusiastic accounts of the Rollins experiment. "I like the contact we have with the professors—really personal and not just 'gazing from afar,'" one student wrote, in a 1929 survey. Others raved about the selection of faculty, who were chosen for their "Golden Personalities" (as Holt liked to say) rather than for their research acumen. Indeed, Holt canvassed every job candidate's former students and turned away anyone who received a "thumbs down" from them, he wrote. "Holt looks not for professors highly commended by other professors, but for men and women highly commended by students who know them," a visiting journalist wrote. "After all the student is the test of the professor and of the college." Many of the professors seem to have passed with flying colors, taking a deep personal interest in the people under their charge. "Here faculty and students are truly pals who still admire and respect each other," wrote a junior transfer student. "I have acquired faculty friendships which I am positive will endure thru life. And how fine it is to be able to work for one's friend—not one's boss." Others appreciated the freedom and independence that Rollins afforded them, especially compared to other colleges. Students did almost all of their work during the conferences, which met for two hours three times a day. That left the rest of their days—and, especially, their evenings—free. "There is time to enjoy life and not grind every night for the next day's preparation," a student wrote. Unburdened by late-night cramming for recitations and examinations, students "approach their work each morning with rested minds," another observer added.[10]

But some of them also also took the opportunity to "slack," as several students privately admitted. Only the most committed students did "outside" reading, which was recommended rather than required; the rest completed in-class assignments quickly and perfunctorily, saving their energy for their real priority: social life. "They have something they want to do every night, so this system works very well for them," one student quipped. Others found that the faculty slacked off as well, failing to engage students in the substance of their fields. "I guess I had the idea that the professor was to really teach and give us the best of his ideas, thoughts, and experiences," a disgruntled transfer student wrote. Professors chosen by Holt for their reported instructional skill had taught in traditional classrooms, so they were often at a loss for how to gainfully use their two-hour conferences. While he consulted with one student, a professor wrote, the others engaged in "monkey business" that distracted their peers. Other students simply refused to do any reading in class "unless it be the sports page or the 'funnies,'" another professor groused. Often he felt like a kindergarten teacher, using "games" to keep the students engaged and interested. But such gimmicks tended to lose their power after meeting with the same students for two hours every day of the week, he admitted. So professors began to dismiss class early, especially when the Florida weather turned unbearably hot; others reverted to the old lecture-and-recitation method, which the Conference Plan was designed to replace. "I'm too old to learn these new tricks even if I really believed in them," one professor privately admitted. "Besides, I've got my good results the old way and what we want is results." Facing a faculty revolt, Holt returned Rollins to a traditional one-hour class format—with lectures and recitations—in 1942. But he remained committed to his reform model, even if it had not worked at his own institution. "The Rollins Conference Plan has never been tried one hundred percent at Rollins any more than Christianity has been tried in churches," a dejected Holt surmised.[11]

In fairness, as Holt's biographer wrote, few other colleges had challenged "accepted academic procedures" as radically as the Conference Plan did. The closest rival was probably the University of Wisconsin's Experimental Program, which started with similar fanfare but met an even more abrupt end. It was the brainchild of philosopher Alexander Meiklejohn, who was pushed out of the presidency at Amherst in part for terminating professors who were poor teachers and for demanding a more integrated undergraduate curriculum. He moved on to Wisconsin, where he was given free rein to create a new college that would "find our way out of the confused wilderness of unrelated specialisms," as he said in 1926. Limited to freshmen and sophomores, the Experimental College focused on ancient Athens in the first year and modern America in the second; "advisers" (as the professors in the program were dubbed) met individually each week with students and gave periodic lectures in their specialties. Attendance at these events was optional, and the only graded requirement was the comprehensive examination at the end of the second year. So the program was "an adaptation to higher education of the project method that has been worked out in primary and secondary education," Meiklejohn declared: it was self-paced, student centered, and focused on a shared set of activities and problems. But it was also poorly regulated, marred by vandalizing in the dormitories (where all of the college's students lived together) and, especially, by academic ennui and laziness. "Quiet hours are flagrantly violated, lectures are poorly attended, conferences cut, vacations extended, and little attention paid to work," a student committee found in 1930. "This college, instead of sponsoring individual responsibility, is engendering selfishness, lack of social unity, and utter lack of ambition." Two years later, the university's faculty senate eliminated it. Its demise was sealed by the same "privatization of learning" that had ended the Rollins experiment, as a historian at the Florida college later observed. Freeing individuals from the moribund hand of tradition was supposed to enliven education, but it could also allow students—and faculty—to evade it.[12]

Other Reforms: Comprehensive Exams and Honors Programs

The "Great Plans period in college history"—as one journalist called it—surely left its mark on interwar teaching, even if few of the plans came to full fruition. The most obvious influence occurred in the realm of comprehensive examinations, a centerpiece of most so-called progressive institutions. Without course grades—or, even, without courses at all—the only way the schools could evaluate students or recommend them for graduation was with some kind of capstone test. At Reed College, where upperclassmen spent just eight or nine hours a week in class, juniors had to pass a written comprehensive exam in their major field of study. That cleared them to write senior theses, which they had to defend—in a two-hour oral examination—as a precondition for graduation. Antioch required a six-hour departmental test in the major, as well as a "General Examination," which took 12 to 15 hours. Its aim was to determine whether students "can analyze complex situations" by drawing on knowledge from different fields, as president Arthur Morgan wrote; for example, one question asked students how they would address "the smoke problem in large cities." At the University of Chicago, finally, President Robert Hutchins's "New Plan" required students to take a comprehensive examination at the end of each year of college. Class attendance was purely voluntary, and students could also take their exam whenever they felt prepared for it. "Whereas some universities are trying tidbits and spurs . . . Chicago has begun to treat the undergraduate as though he really desired an education and needed only the sign-posts to help him get it," one journalist wrote, in praise of the New Plan.[13]

Yet dozens of colleges with more traditional formats also developed comprehensive examinations during these years. Unlike the vanguard schools, which required the exams across the board, other institutions often allowed departments to decide the matter on their own. Harvard's division of History, Government, and Economics initiated the university's first comprehensive examinations in 1915–16; other departments followed after World War I, so that by 1923 two-thirds of the graduating class was subject to a comprehensive exam. Nationwide, the number of institutions using a "comp" (as students everywhere called it) in at least one department rose from 3 in 1900 to 73 in 1932 and to 94 in 1935. Syracuse University's School of Citizenship and Public Affairs replaced a required senior thesis with a comprehensive examination; the thesis "aggravates undergraduate over-specialization," a faculty committee wrote, whereas comprehensive tests "obviate the very danger which the senior thesis perpetuated." Even more, it added, end-of-college exams were "recognized by leading educators everywhere as the next step in a progressive educational system." To be sure, some institutions adopted comps because they wanted to liberate students from arcane educational routines. But others developed the tests because they wanted to raise academic standards, especially at schools that were known for weak ones. "Colgate is no longer a country club for seniors," wrote one observer, praising its eight-hour end-of-college exams. "Fraternity men explained that they could find no substitute for study." Other professors said that comps would require students to display more synthetic understanding than the standard "objective" tests they took in their different courses. Still others hoped that the new tests would keep away weaker students, who would gravitate to other departments that did not demand such a taxing exercise.[14]

In practice, however, comprehensive examinations often reinforced many of the problems they were designed to solve. Professors rarely coordinated their courses with departmental colleagues, so students struggled to connect these classes: at one comp, a student raised his hand and asked his professor if he could use information he had acquired in another instructor's course. Nor did the tests themselves typically require that type of intellectual integration, students and faculty confirmed. Instead, like final course exams, comps required students to regurgitate material they had memorized. "We are merely driving them back to their notes and textbooks," one professor wrote; to another, the comps had become "just one more hurdle in a reckless Marathon." Faculty at Colby complained that comps encouraged students to take more courses in their majors and to eschew electives, which inhibited exposure to "the broad field of knowledge and inquiry," as a survey underlined. At the University of Chicago, meanwhile, professors found that the comps led students to neglect their coursework altogether. When they attended class, it was only to "pick up some extra bits that will help them on the exams," one professor observed; freed from the daily grind of courses, they became slaves to the "single devastating experience" of the comp. "Theoretically they like learning for its own sake, but actually they tend to ignore any course, any reading, any field of knowledge which will not help them pass the comprehensives," another instructor confirmed. Even at an institution proud of its unique intellectual bona fides, the tests became exercises in recall rather than in real thinking. "Do you honestly know of any type of examination that is more dogmatic than the so-called 'true-false' type?" an angry student asked a dean. "Yet, the University of Chicago preached academic freedom and strives (?) to stay away from dogmatism. I wonder?????," he added, punctuating his skepticism with extra question marks.[15]

Other colleges limited comprehensive examinations to honors programs, another hallmark of teaching reform in the interwar era. The programs were typically open to juniors and seniors who had demonstrated the requisite skill and independence in their earlier coursework. "A system which is necessary to spur on the average student may clip the wings of the born student," a Stanford senior wrote, in praise of honors programs. "Detailed assignments, fortnightly quizzes and the like are necessary to keep the ordinary student occupied and working, but marks and quantitative standards only dampen the ardor and dwarf the imagination of the few intellectuals." Like Stanford's "Independent Study" plan, most honors programs allowed members to draw up a course of study and fulfill it however they wished, including optional classwork and tutorials; the only hard-and-fast requirement was passage of a comp at the end. A smaller number of schools established separate honors-level courses, tailored to their clientele. The best-known example was Swarthmore College, where honors students met in two weekly seminars—often at their professor's home—and usually prepared a paper about a shared reading assignment. Other professors required them to perform their own research and to present it to the group, which would teach students more than they would learn "from fifteen arbitrary assignments (however good) made in advance by [the] teacher," as one enthusiast argued. Swarthmore did not restrict comprehensive examinations to its honors students, but it did devise a separate comp for them; demanding more sophisticated mastery of the subject, the honors comprehensive was also graded by specially hired examiners from other institutions. "The teacher is a guide and a companion, an honest critic of the student's ability. But he is not to be the final judge," one observer wrote. "The student and teacher are both to be judged by an outside court."[16]

By 1924, 44 different institutions already offered some kind of special honors program or instruction; seven years later, in 1931, 81 schools did so. But the programs sparked dissent and controversy everywhere they took hold, belying the triumphal tone that marked many press accounts. At Swarthmore, honors students complained that their assignments and other activities were not distinct enough from regular class work; meanwhile, faculty argued that too many students were being admitted to the program, which diluted both its exclusivity and its effectiveness. As one professor noted in 1934, the original goal of the program was to "have a considerable gulf fixed between honors and pass students." Yet "the tendency of the faculty . . . has been to lift pass work toward the honors level," he grumbled. Another Swarthmore professor said he had cultivated a core of seven superb students in his honors seminar—including future novelist James Michener—but only by neglecting the less able half of the group. "I have never been so excited and never have felt that my teaching was so worth while," he told Swarthmore president Frank Aydelotte, forefather of its honors program. "In order to do that I refused to have anything to do with the other eight students." But still other faculty members denounced the program for establishing a kind of caste system on campus, reserving the best academic meals for the honors students and serving a weak tea to the rest. If instruction in seminars and original sources were better than lectures and textbooks, one professor asked, why not give them to everyone? The honors system was antithetical to "democratic community," he added, where "each person has the right to demand the best which the community has to offer."[17]

The remark echoed John Dewey's famous formulation that what "the best and wisest parent" wants for their child we should want for all children; anything less was "unlovely," Dewey wrote, and "destroys our democracy." It found its way into other attacks on honors programs, especially as the economic downturn of the 1930s brought more attention to inequalities of every kind. Canvassing the country in 1932 to investigate college teaching on behalf of the AAUP, Homer Dodge met students who denounced honors programs on the grounds that all students—no matter their ability—deserved the kind of instruction that the programs promised; meanwhile, some faculty critics told him that "the necessary expense of so favoring the brilliant few is not justified in our democratic system." Eight years later, an Iowa State student in a "regular" class pleaded for "more of the methods used in conducting so-called honors classes," which stressed "creative inspiration" instead of "a rehash of what someone else knows." But others questioned the quality of the honors programs themselves, which came under renewed scrutiny in hard economic times. At Harvard, graduate student and future best-selling historian Bernard DeVoto charged that the honors system—designed to "free the superior student from technical requirements"—had simply added a new set of tests, quizzes, and examinations to their lives. Indeed, as one scholar found, only a quarter of eligible students around the country chose to take honors work at all; the rest decided that it was too much work and that their time would be better spent engaging in extracurricular activities. "If one is going into business, as most of us are, it is more important to be a student-leader than an outstanding scholar," one student explained. Nor was it clear that they were wrong, as the AAUP's 1933 report frankly admitted. "Whether these honors systems have contributed much, if anything, to the general improvement of teaching is a matter on which opinions vary," the report noted. The only way to know, it added, would be to collect more data on them.[18]

Reforming Mass Instruction
Research and Evaluation

The last remark spoke to a perennial dream in interwar higher education: that research on teaching could improve it en masse, which was how most Americans received it as well. Relatively few students had access to tutorials, honors programs, or any of the other "individualized" reforms that dotted the higher-education landscape. Of the 81 honors programs in 1931, for example, only six enrolled 60 or more students. As college enrollments surged around the country, especially at large public institutions, the vast majority of instruction continued to take place in traditional fashion: large lecture classes, punctuated by smaller recitation sections. So college teaching would succeed—or fail—depending on what happened in those settings, as the AAUP's Homer Dodge emphasized. Funded by a $20,000 grant from the Carnegie Corporation, Dodge and his team visited dozens of institutions around the country; they also collected information from AAUP chapters, which held special meetings to discuss his project and the larger problems of college teaching. According to a Carnegie press release, Dodge's study would provide "a systematic examination of actual conditions of instruction with a view to setting up principles of discrimination between good and bad teaching." Despite the research boom in higher education since the 1890s, Dodge noted, there had been little interest in research *about* higher education. The AAUP study aimed to change that, he wrote, generating renewed cooperation between "academic professors" and "technical experts trained in the methods of educational research." One day, he predicted, the AAUP's effort would be "looked back upon as a turning point in the history of American education."[19]

There was good reason for optimism, at least at first glance. In 1920, an educator surveying research about college teaching declared that "the field is almost virgin." But by 1931, on the eve of the AAUP study, another scholar counted 600 articles and books on the subject. Nearly 50 institutions reported that they operated offices of institutional research, up from just two in 1924. The lodestar was the University of Minnesota, which sponsored 59 studies between 1924 and 1927 on the central question in teaching-related research: class size. Using standardized tests, which also enjoyed a vogue in the 1920s, 46 of the studies—that is, over three-quarters—found that the students in larger classes learned more than similar peers in smaller ones. The implications were obvious and directly countered the small-group mantra that marked so many other interwar reforms. "Small classes are expensive; large classes relatively cheap," a dean at the university privately told its president in 1927. "If large classes achieve equally desirable results with small units, there can be no justification for the retention of the latter." A physics professor at Minnesota conducted his own experiment on the same question the following year, choosing two groups of 12 students "of equivalent ability" and teaching one as a separate class while incorporating the other into a 150-student lecture course that he also taught. The students in the big class scored better on his tests, much to his surprise and chagrin. "I began to question my ability as a teacher because I had fully expected that the results would be the reverse of what they were," he admitted. But the cost per student in the small class was $36.29, compared to $4.34 in the large one. As a citizen as well as a scientist, he concluded, he could not rationalize the added expense of small classes any longer.[20]

But most faculty members continued to insist that small classes were superior, invoking the same rhetoric that had powered tutorials and other interwar teaching innovations. "I still firmly believe that the personal contact that comes from each professor knowing his individual students is one of the most important parts in his getting good results in teaching," a City College of New York professor told an AAUP conference in 1932, dismissing studies that suggested otherwise. Others pointed to questionable methods and assumptions in the college teaching research, which investigators freely acknowledged. As scholars at Minnesota admitted, creating equal control groups in this type of research was almost impossible. If you compared different classes taught by the same instructor, how would you know if the professor taught the same way in each one? And might students meeting earlier in the day achieve less, because they were less alert? The other big problem lay in the measurement of achievement via true-false and other "objective" tests. Some critics said that these exercises revealed more about the test-taking ability of students than about what they learned in the course; others said that the tests documented "informational gain"—that is, factual recall—instead of real understanding, as one skeptic wrote. Most of all, observers noted, there was no real consensus on what constituted good—or bad—college teaching. After visiting the classroom of a famously dull mathematics professor who mumbled through a lecture, a researcher was shocked to learn that the professor's students received the best marks in the department on its shared final examination. "No one knows what good teaching means," the visitor admitted, noting that the professor had already been asked to resign because of his allegedly poor instruction. There was "no general agreement on determinants of the quality of teaching," he added, and "no universally adopted score cards on these determinants."[21]

The same problem afflicted institutional efforts to evaluate college teachers, which sparked a great deal of discussion—but much less action—during these years. A small number of colleges used student evaluations, which remained hugely unpopular with faculty and administrators alike; institutions employed such ratings not because "they believed it to be the best way," the AAUP's 1933 report noted, but rather because "there did not seem to be any other way." The AAUP went on to recommend peer evaluation, which sprouted slowly around the country in the interwar era. At the Hall-Moody Institute, a Bible college in Tennessee, a "faculty critic" visited all professors in their classrooms and presented a report about his observations at a public meeting; that "enabled every teacher to profit from the teaching methods and ideals of every other member," the college president wrote, and "raised the standard of teaching of every teacher." A faculty committee at Oberlin recommended "frequent visitation of classes" by colleagues, listing the characteristics and qualities that the visitors should evaluate: mastery of subject matter, "ability to call for the active cooperation of the students," and so on. Class visitation was most common at teachers colleges, where one study found that 40 percent of institutions had some sort of "inspection" of instruction; it was especially high at historically black teachers colleges, where presidents often visited classrooms on their own. At San Jose State, a former teachers college, the president hired a "consultant in college teaching" to visit classrooms and confer with faculty. By 1939, a survey of 61 colleges and universities found that 10 of them employed a specialist to supervise teaching. However, only 18 others reported any kind of supervision or evaluation of faculty instruction, which remained the exception rather than the rule. "Is it any wonder that good college teaching is so rare?" one advocate for supervision asked.[22]

The greatest obstacle to classroom evaluation was the faculty, of course, which saw any such effort as an attack on their discretion and independence. "I think one important idea to strive to abolish—I have largely failed here— is the idea that a man's class room is his castle, which no one else can invade," Wesleyan president James L. McConaughy wrote privately. McConaughy did "a little visiting" on his own, he added, but found it difficult to evaluate a teacher "by spending an hour in his classroom." The solution lay in peer review, he said, which was a nonstarter for his faculty: senior professors refused to visit junior ones, who in turn were reluctant to visit each other. Some faculty said that any kind of evaluation would inhibit their academic freedom, which they took to mean the right to teach in whatever way they wished. Others worried that classroom visitors would prevent faculty from experimenting with new methods and approaches. "A young teacher should be allowed to develop his technique without nagging or the exercise of a spy system," an AAUP chapter at Williams College resolved. Still others denounced visitation schemes as yet another banal and costly organizational exercise, especially when performed by a new functionary. "To set up a special official for supervision would be just an extension of the current tyranny and lunacy of bureaucracy over education," a Beloit professor wrote. "'Efficiency experts' had their little day of strut and bluster and quickly evaporated, being exposed as neither expert nor efficient." Nor was there any real consensus on what constituted good teaching, as Wesleyan president McConaughy admitted in public several years earlier. Without a shared target, critics asked, how could officials evaluate faculty for hitting—or missing—it?[23]

Yet McConaughy also established teaching awards at Wesleyan, which marked the final—and, mostly, fruitless—administrative effort to improve college instruction during these years. The first award was established in 1930 by the University of Chicago, which used a gift from an anonymous donor to fund between 5 and 10 annual teaching prizes of $500 each. The prize promised not just to recognize skilled teachers but also to boost the overall status of instruction, as college dean C. B. Boucher told the donor. "During a period of several years, not so long ago, the instruction of our undergraduates, and particularly of Freshmen and Sophomores, was grossly neglected or positively scorned," Boucher admitted. "Our students were the innocent victims." But awards for teaching tended to elevate research, at least indirectly. Announcing an award to two foreign-language instructors in 1932, the university emphasized that they had set forth their "remarkably successful methods and techniques" in a series of books and articles; in 1940, a nomination letter noted that one candidate for the prize had been "handicapped in getting advancement and promotion" because his teaching activities reduced his "research productivity." So the teaching award—which went up to $1,000—would actually be a consolation prize for someone who came in second in the research sweepstakes. Few professors, it seemed, could win in both realms. "He is an extraordinary ingenious and lucid educator, and what is rare among superior pedagogues—keeps out a good personal research program," declared another nomination letter for the prize, which was selected by the dean based on faculty recommendations.[24]

Similarly, the Wesleyan teaching prize was funded by a gift from a donor. However, it provided a three-year salary increase—not just a one-time boost—and, most importantly, it was selected via a poll of the faculty and of alumni who had graduated in the past 10 years. In 1930–31, the first year of the prize, 25 faculty members (two-thirds of the total) and 605 alumni replied to the poll; based on their choices, six professors received a salary increase of $2,500 and another eight received $1,250. But the award was controversial from the start, generating sharp dissent from alumni and faculty alike. Some alumni feared that the prize would favor members of "popular" departments, like English and history; others worried that it would divide faculty from each other, especially at a moment of massive economic insecurity. "The salaries of all are too low; if and when money becomes available it should be made available to all," one alumnus told McConaughy, shortly after he announced the prize. Faculty who did not receive the award would feel slighted, another graduate noted, which would reduce overall morale. "Philosophers and Scientists are still very human as are also their wives," he wrote; better to employ the "Army plan of uniform compensation in each grade." ("There are many points of similarity in army and college communities," he added.) Likewise, a faculty committee argued that the prize would injure "that democratic *spirit de corps . . .* which has traditionally been enjoyed at Wesleyan." Even worse, a professor argued, it would encourage faculty members to "campaign" with slick appeals to sentiment. So it would favor "the bond salesman type," he argued, not "the real teacher."[25]

In response, McConaughy argued in a meritocratic vein: faculty who did better work should get better pay. "Professors are not equally useful and valuable," he wrote. "To pay them a labor union, fixed, equal salary is one of the worst things I know of in academic circles." But the tide was turning against him. The Wesleyan controversy made national news and sparked hackles inside the AAUP, where members worried that "Little Jack Horner" awards—as detractors called teaching prizes—might be used by administrators to reward politically conventional faculty and to punish professors with more unorthodox beliefs. Similar faculty concerns were raised when Williams announced it would replace its uniform salary scale with a "merit" system for teaching. At the University of California, Berkeley, meanwhile, professors denounced a proposed teaching prize on the grounds that it would go to the "best dramatist," not the best teacher. Back at Wesleyan, meanwhile, James McConaughy's teaching prize sank slowly toward its demise. His successor, Victor Butterfield, was an opponent of the award even though he received it himself shortly before ascending to the presidency. The prize echoed the "bonus system used by industry," Butterfield wrote, but "business principles" did not apply to higher education. "Too much emphasis on the materialistic aspects of the job can be disastrous," he argued. "When a teacher begins to let his eyes shift too much from his student to his pocketbook, the student had better look for another teacher." A 1944 survey found the Wesleyan faculty evenly divided on the prize, with 14 in favor and 13 opposed; even the eight recipients of the prize that year were split down the middle, with four supporting the award and four opposing it. Shortly thereafter, Butterfield eliminated it. The prize had "a devastating effect on the morale of the faculty," he recalled. "You get better teaching on the whole—even from your average teachers—by not thus trying to separate the sheep from the goats."[26]

Faculty Selection and Training

But all colleges and universities separated sheep from goats when they hired new faculty, which also received new attention during this era. Indeed, widespread professorial resistance to evaluation centered even more concern on the question of who became a professor in the first place, as well as on how institutions could identify the "right" candidates. "It is natural for people not to want to know the truth about themselves, especially if they are the objects of unfavorable criticism," one scholar wrote to Franz Schneider, who spearheaded the campaign for student evaluations at Berkeley. "The people who are now in the saddle cannot so easily be reformed." So the university should focus instead on "cadet teachers," he added, making sure it got the best people for the job. The problem began in graduate schools, which evaluated students based on their research potential rather than their capacity for teaching. "If at least our better graduate schools could have some standard of admission which stressed personality as well as college grades, we might debar from the profession the men who are usually the most lamentably failures—exceedingly erudite scholars, often the 'pets' of their graduate teachers, absolutely incompetent to teach college undergraduates," wrote Columbia's graduate dean. Elsewhere, too, college officials sang the virtues of "personality" over other kinds of qualifications. "It may be Utopian, but I hope some day graduate schools will be more exacting in their standards," Wesleyan's James McConaughy told his counterpart at Oberlin, Ernest Wilkins. "Men deficient in personality and human interest may be trained to be scholars but somebody is wasting society's energy in training such men to be teachers." Too many graduate students were "hopelessly uninspired" and "hopelessly immune to any real inspiration," a Dartmouth professor noted. No institution could possibly make a teacher from someone "whose personality is unattractive," he added.[27]

So the question became how to identify such individuals, both for graduate programs and for college faculties. The University of Iowa developed a rating scale to rank PhD applicants in personality; it also administered a physical examination, which included tests for "psychopathic tendencies." Faculty hiring committees likewise began to pay more attention to personality, drawing on the burgeoning science of personnel management. "Many colleges are finding it possible to factor student personality," one observer wrote, noting the rise of "personnel offices" that sorted and advised students based on a battery of tests. Surely, then, colleges could do the same with faculty candidates. "Why is instructor personality undecipherable?" he asked. He went on to recommend a study called *Personality Culture by College Faculties* issued by the Institute for Public Service, which aimed to recruit "the ablest and noblest personalities into the teaching profession." Author David E. Berg observed 72 university instructors and compiled a compendium of 10 different teacher personalities, ranging from "sympathetic and open-minded" to "senile and decrepit." As Berg noted, industrial corporations and public school districts routinely employed personality tests that had been developed by universities, which also administered such tests to their students. But university professors had been "slow to admit that what's sauce for the goose is sauce for the gander," he added. Faculties should "try their own medicine" and "diagnose their own personality needs," which was arguably the only way to ensure better teachers—and better teaching—in the future. "Teacher personality can be selected as easily as seed corn and can be consciously improved as easily as can student personality," Berg insisted.[28]

It is hard to know how many institutions used such scales to select either graduate students or new professors. However, they clearly placed more emphasis on identifying and recruiting faculty who had proper personality for the job, as numerous officials wrote. "It is the personality and character that count in the professor and not the knowledge on tap," Rollins president Hamilton Holt wrote, in a typical statement. At Rutgers, likewise, the university president emphasized the need to find the right people—not just the right scholars—for his faculty. "Education, which means the development of the student's whole personality rather than his intellect alone, is achieved, not solely out of books nor in lectures, but in personal association with gifted men and women who are themselves the kind of people we want these young persons to become," he noted. Other college officials cited surveys from students, who were more likely to invoke personality than academic qualifications when asked to identify the qualities of a good professor. Especially at elite universities, however, research productivity and potential remained the prime criterion for professorial selection; "personality" came in a distant second, in part because—like good teaching—it was so difficult to measure. Despite hundreds of studies listing the characteristics of effective classroom teachers—and despite the growing use of scales and tests of personality—the concept served "as a blanket designation to cover those factors deemed desirable, though not readily definable," as sociologist Logan Wilson wrote in 1941. Even more, he added, people tended to regard it as a static quality that inhered in an individual. Although personnel specialists like David Berg said that personality could be improved, most college officials continued to regard it as inborn.[29]

That assumption hampered efforts to provide preparation for college teaching, another widely discussed—but rarely implemented—reform effort in the interwar years. If college teachers were born rather than made, it made no sense to train them for the task; either they possessed the right personality, or they did not. Although the born-not-made doctrine was also common in elementary and secondary teaching, City College of New York president Sidney Mezes observed in 1920 that instructors at those levels still received "training for their life work." Only college teachers could enter the classroom without any such preparation, on the specious grounds that they already knew what they were doing or would learn how to do it on the job. "No plan of training for college teaching is in operation, and no discussion of such a plan can be found," Mezes complained. But that was about to change. In 1922, the Land-Grant College Association resolved that all candidates for college faculty posts should be required to have at least six semester hours of "professional training," including courses in educational psychology and methods of teaching; seven years later, in 1929, the Association of American Colleges declared that every graduate student intending to teach at the college level should receive "an adequate training in methods of teaching as applied to the particular department of knowledge in which the student is working." University leaders took up the cause too, vowing to ensure that graduate students learn how to teach. In their inaugural addresses, Robert Hutchins and Robert Sproul—presidents of the University of Chicago and the University of California, respectively—both called on PhD programs to prepare scholars for the classroom, not just for the library or laboratory. "To say that a college teacher needs no particular training . . . is just as ridiculous as to say that the painter, the sculptor, the musician, or the actor needs no instruction or training in the technique of his profession," Brown dean Otis Randall declared.[30]

Although teacher training never became de rigueur for future faculty, as these officials imagined, it did become slightly more common in the interwar years. By 1928, two states—Tennessee and Rhode Island—required coursework in education for anyone teaching in public colleges and universities; in Florida, new faculty members needed to have experience teaching in elementary or secondary schools. As the economy soured in the 1930s and academic jobs dried up, PhD candidates often took education classes in order to qualify for more plentiful high school teaching positions. Meanwhile, scattered universities began to design courses tailored specifically for college teachers. At Iowa State, the Bacteriology Department required all of its graduate students to participate in a seminar entitled "The College Teaching of Bacteriology"; other institutions offered more generic courses—typically through schools of education—on undergraduate instruction. Purdue established a class entitled "Psychology of Learning and Teaching Applied to College Work"; New York University offered "Improvement of Instruction in Colleges and Universities"; and at Penn State, students could take "Problems of Collegiate Education." For the most part, however, these classes were voluntary rather than mandatory. "Is it too much to ask that in this program of graduate training the student should be required to give some attention to the problems of education—problems which will constitute the student's chief concern once he is launched on his professional career?" asked W. W. Charters, who taught a course on methods of college teaching at the Carnegie Institute in Pittsburgh. Students in his class observed "superior" professors and discussed lesson planning, "methods of handling discussions," testing and grading, and more.[31]

But as Charters's frustrated tone suggested, faculty members generally resisted efforts to institute teacher training for future professors. One history professor noted that PhD students were already "trained by the apprentice system," serving as teaching assistants and observing faculty in action. For four-fifths of new professors, he maintained, "that is all the training necessary"; the other one-fifth "can never be made good teachers," no matter what they did. "We would not insult the intelligent four-fifths by making them attend a formal course on 'How to Teach History,'" he added. Likewise, a University of Chicago chemist insisted that courses about teaching condescended to their targets. "It is supposed that any man with the intelligence demanded for graduate work in the department, who is planning to go into teaching, will be able to 'direct' himself to observe the techniques of the members of the staff," he wrote; the department's graduate students should be "treated as rational and self-reliant individuals," he added, "and not led by the hand as children would be." An economist recalled asking his mentors in graduate school if he could take some coursework on the "problems of teaching" and being roundly rebuffed. "The feeling seems to be that the School of Education has nothing worthwhile to offer in this line, that teaching is something you have to learn by absorption or by experience anyway, and that a 'science' of education is rather to be smiled at, at least in connection with university teaching," he wrote, summarizing his professors' skepticism.[32]

As the final remark illustrated, professors in the arts and sciences associated any kind of teacher training with the lowest institution on the higher-education status ladder: the education school. Part of the issue was that ed schools typically taught broad-gauge "methods" courses that rarely applied to specific disciplines. "Method is tied up with the subject taught," a Stanford professor told the AAUP's Homer Dodge. "General method . . . is of doubtful value." But the biggest problem was the allegedly dismal intellectual quality of education schools, which offered nothing of real value to future professors of anything other than education itself. The Tulane chapter of the AAUP passed a unanimous resolution condemning "the movement to require courses in 'education' of prospective college and university teachers," punctuating its distrust with air quotes. "Education courses are often poorly organized, with meager subject matter, and low academic standards," it added. All one needed to do was to look at elementary and secondary schooling, which lay in "complete control" of the education schools—and continued to send weak and un-prepared students into the colleges. If the "professional educationist" had failed to improve grade school instruction, a University of Colorado professor asked, why should anyone believe that "he can help the college professor?" A Beloit economics professor and former high school teacher concurred, noting that she had taken 16 hours of education classes and learned almost nothing from them; instead of improving teaching, she said, those courses existed mostly to create jobs for education professors. Elsewhere, too, faculty denounced efforts to impose "high school methods" in the graduate schools. "I personally shall <u>resist</u> the professional instruction of college teachers in any such manner as secondary school teachers have been trained," one professor flatly told Homer Dodge.[33]

Meanwhile, atop the AAUP's Committee on College and University Teaching, chairman William B. Munro struggled to find a "middle ground" between "the educationist and the academician," as he told the AAUP's convention in 1932. Like Dodge, Munro had concluded that "no formal courses in education ought to be required or even encouraged" for future college teachers. Instead, he said, the academic departments themselves should take care of preparing graduate students for teaching. That would require them to establish "some way in which good teaching can be discovered and can be rewarded" in their disciplines, he added. But that was precisely what so many departments resisted, he admitted, precisely because it conjured the trite banalities of education schools. Most of all, Homer Dodge's interviewees told him, any such effort would inevitably erode the individuality that lay at the heart of all instruction. A Stanford professor told Dodge that he "does not believe there can be found a method of discovering the good teacher," because teaching was too idiosyncratic, variable, and ineffable for that. "No standardization is possible or desirable," the professor added. Even William Munro, at the conclusion of three years of study, concluded that "good teaching is a matter of men rather than of method." The more that teaching was imagined as a personal act—indeed, as a function of personality—the less it could be organized, standardized, or changed.[34]

CHAPTER FIVE

Expansion and Repression

Cold War Challenges for College Teaching

In 1949, the dean of the graduate school at the University of Minnesota imagined falling asleep and waking up in 1984. The first thing he saw was a newspaper, which did not reference any of the "Orwellian horrors" that George Orwell's novel about that year had predicted. Instead, the front page hailed massive improvements in undergraduate instruction at American institutions of higher education. "AMERICAN COLLEGE TEACHING REACHES A NEW HIGH," a banner headline declared. The article below it was divided by subheadings, also in all caps, each one capturing an important reform:

- IMPORTANCE OF COLLEGE TEACHING NOW RECOGNIZED BY ALL
- SKILL OF NEWLY TRAINED COLLEGE TEACHERS IN CLASSROOM AMAZES COMMUNITY
- NEW COLLEGE TEACHERS DEEPLY INTERESTED IN STUDENTS AND IN LEARNING PROCESS
- TEACHING ASSISTANTS AND APPRENTICES REALLY LEARN SOME-THING ABOUT TEACHING
- ALL FACULTIES SPONSOR IN-SERVICE PROGRAMS FOR VITALIZING COLLEGE TEACHING
- SUPER PULITZER AWARD ANNOUNCED FOR DISTINGUISHED COL-LEGE TEACHING[1]

Despite the note of hope, all of these proposals highlighted the weak state of college teaching in the wake of the Second World War. Undergraduate enrollment witnessed another enormous surge, powered by federal assistance to veterans under the G.I. Bill and by the overall prosperity of the era. But that also put new strains on the colleges, which both students and faculty indicted for failing to provide adequate instruction to the burgeoning undergraduate population. Much of the teaching was delivered by graduate students, whose numbers also swelled amid the overall increase in research dollars and opportunities during these years. Increasingly, their professors neglected or eschewed undergraduate instruction in favor of research and publication. Hence, the college student became "the forgotten man of higher education," as Sarah Lawrence president Harold Taylor admitted. Rhetorically, American educators and politicians stressed higher education as part of the "national effort to strengthen democracy," as President Harry Truman wrote in releasing the first report of a 1947 commission on the subject. Denouncing discrimination on the basis of race and gender—as well as economic constraints on the poor and working class—the commission decreed that any capable citizen wishing to attend college should be able to do so. But it also warned that universities would be unable to fulfill this mission in a meaningful way unless they improved the selection and especially the training of college teachers. "No program can be better than the people who operate it," the commission declared in its report, pointedly entitled *Higher Education for American Democracy*. "A teacher must know how to make his subject matter alive and understandable to others."[2]

But to do that, a teacher also needed the freedom to explore controversial subject matter with students. Over the next decade, as Cold War fears spread across America, a pall of repression settled over its college classrooms. Government and private spies monitored classes, sometimes in plain view of the faculty. Handfuls of professors were fired for statements they made while teaching; more commonly, they simply kept their ideas to themselves. "Now I no longer say what I think, but what I'm told to say," one professor told a researcher in 1955. One could never be sure who was watching or listening, another professor added, so the smartest move was to avoid anything even remotely contentious. "It's pretty obvious that one could not discuss issues in a classroom that you could have very easily carried on in my own undergraduate days in the 1930s," he said. "Some perverted versions of what you said would go out and could create repercussions. Subtle forms of pressure that could be brought to bear on you could result in whether you'd be promoted or not." In both obvious and subtle ways, then, college teachers were inhibited from teaching in a full and frank manner. Their horrors were less Orwellian than quotidian, a day-to-day set of pressures and reminders to toe the straight and narrow. College classrooms became more "democratic" in this era, insofar as they catered to a wider clientele. But they also became less so in practice, as San Jose State College president John T. Wahlquist acknowledged in 1954. "In American democracy it is our boast that we exalt the individual, provide for freedom of thought, cultivate the open mind, inculcate respect for differences of opinion, provide for freedom of the opposition, recognize the rights of the non-conformist," Wahlquist wrote. "But, as a general rule all of these procedures and noble ideals are violated or ignored in the college class-room." The contradiction would become even more evident by the early 1960s, setting the stage for a new set of reforms in undergraduate instruction.[3]

Cold War Students

On the eve of World War II, 1.5 million Americans attended college; by 1947, two years after the war concluded, their numbers had swelled to 2.1 million. Half of all students were military veterans, who created the greatest short-term enroll-ment surge in US history. The number of college students rose steadily—if less sharply—after that, topping 3.5 million in 1958. By then, one in three Americans between the ages of 18 and 21 attended college; as recently as 1940, only 1 in 10 did. Educational researcher Martin Trow likened the growth of college at-tendance to the boom of secondary schools between 1910 and 1940, when the fraction of 14- to 17-year-olds attending high school skyrocketed from 15 to 75 percent. Millions of Americans who had never considered college for them-selves now expected it for their children, as Trow told a conference in 1959. "There is good reason to believe that it will approach nearly universal experi-ence," he predicted. "That is at once heartening and frightening, the source of our best hopes for the future of our civilization and at the same time the source of our most acute fears for the future of our colleges and universities."[4]

For many college professors, the biggest fear of all was that the new students would not have the skill or talent to succeed at college. That was an old worry, of course, going back to every increase in student population since the mid-nineteenth century. But there had never been a rise as steep as the one after World War II, which triggered even greater anxiety about the background and ability of the newcomers. "Half the pupils have no desire for learning, three-quarters are poorly prepared . . . and only a small minority have come from homes where the love of books was cultivated," a Trinity College physicist complained in 1945. Students often arrived unable to write in "correct and clear English" or to understand their textbooks, a historian at Clark University ob-served, adding that the school had been forced to offer courses in "remedial reading." Unlike prior generations of carping professors, Cold War faculty members typically blamed students' poor secondary school preparation rather than their supposedly inherent deficiencies. But the result was the same: there were too many students, and many of them should not be there. Writing pri-vately to University of California president Clark Kerr, historian Page Smith urged that the school drop "the bottom one-fourth of our undergraduates who are not truly qualified for university-level work." Perhaps, he allowed, they could attend a less rigorous state college. But at almost every school, professors questioned the qualifications of the people they taught. "Admitting incompetents to college . . . and watering down our teaching to the level of the lowest intelligence in the class is not democracy; it is idiocy," a Miami University professor warned. "To dilute and destroy *higher* education in the name of a moronic conception of 'democracy' eventually will destroy real democracy."[5]

Even when students had the requisite skills for college, other observers charged, they lacked real commitment to the academic enterprise; they came to have fun, not to learn. That was an erstwhile complaint as well, going back to Woodrow Wilson's worries about the extracurricular sideshows overcoming the scholarly tent. But it, too, reached an apogee in the Cold War years. An internal 1955 study at Bowdoin found that many students "of considerable or even great ability and promise" had "not been roused to their best efforts" in the classroom; instead, they were "more interested in the prestige offered by the extra-curricular or social activities of the College." The report took special aim at fraternities, which enlisted over 90 percent of Bowdoin students and diverted them from "college work." Serious-minded undergraduates echoed this complaint, repeating a pattern from the 1920s; in both eras, Columbia classicist Gilbert Highet wrote, academically oriented students blasted their peers for "dissipating their energies and wasting their gifts." But they were a minority voice, ridiculed or simply ignored by students who regarded college "as a prolonged opportunity for drinking, sexing, and roistering," as Harvard's *Confidential Guide to Freshman Courses* observed. At Purdue, "it is not considered smart to study and to make good grades," one observer wrote; indeed, a University of Michigan professor added, students who worked hard struggled to avoid "conspicuous display of academic achievement" lest they lose the approval of their classmates. Peer pressure against scholarly engagement was also sharp at all-women's colleges, where students feared that it would weaken their currency in the marriage market. "A girl who got serious about anything she studied . . . would be peculiar, unfeminine," a Smith student told alumnus Betty Friedan, who returned to the college in 1959 to conduct research for her now-classic 1963 book *The Feminine Mystique*. "I guess everyone wants to graduate with a diamond ring on her finger. That's the important thing."[6]

Other critics indicted students' "conformity," echoing a standard sociological critique of Cold War America. Even students who tried hard in their classes did so not to get an education, the argument went, but to get ahead. Most students saw colleges as "meal tickets" rather than as routes to personal enlightenment, as sociologist Christopher Jencks observed during a national tour of colleges in 1961. So they were also intellectually docile, keeping their heads down—and their pencils moving—on the road to a good-paying job and a life of consumption. Indeed, one journalist wrote, students had come to see college itself as a kind of commodity that they purchased in exchange for social mobility. "They're so accustomed to a passive role. . . . They submit to authority," one professor observed; another condemned students as "'yes' men to their teachers for grades." Yet professors also faced widespread student reproach of their instruction, which suggested more gumption—and less "conformity"—than the standard critique allowed. Military veterans were especially vocal in condemning weak college teaching, contrasting it to the superior instruction they had received in the armed forces. "If pedagogic desks were reversed and the veteran in college now were given the opportunity to grade his professor, he would give him a big red 'F' and rate him as insipid, antiquated, and ineffectual," one observer wrote. Although faculty derided the young people in their classrooms as "distracted, uninterested, shallow, and impudent," as a University of Pennsylvania sophomore noted, they rarely paused to ask how their own teaching might have shaped students' poor behavior and attitude. "The student response is directly proportional to the amount of effort expended by the instructor," the Penn student argued. If professors wanted better results, he added, they needed to step up their own game.[7]

Cold War Teachers

The boom in student enrollment forced colleges and universities to hire thousands of new instructors, which raised almost as much anxiety within these institutions as the growing undergraduate population did. "It is very difficult to determine whether our greater problem is the flood of new students or the flood of new teachers," Hope College president Irwin J. Lubbers told a conference in 1948. The previous year, 39 percent of higher-education institutions reported that they were "unable to obtain qualified faculty members"; many colleges also said they had to "lower their standards" to meet demand. That meant employing fewer PhD-credentialed professors, who were not numerous enough to service America's booming student population. In 1948, 55 percent of college instructors held an MA as their highest degree; more remarkably, perhaps, one-third had only a bachelor's degree. The PhD continued its decline on faculties in the 1950s, unable to keep up with soaring enrollments. Between 1954 and 1959, the number of PhDs teaching in colleges dropped by 25 percent. Most of the slack was taken up by candidates with MA degrees; as late as 1961, however, 17 percent of new college teachers still held less than a master's degree. Many of them were former high school teachers who worked at junior (increasingly known as "community") colleges; others were in technical or engineering fields, where the graduate-degree tradition was not as strong. In 1962, the new television show "Meet the Professor"—designed to advertise college teaching as a career choice—featured the head of the Department of Electrical Technology at the New York City Community College of Applied Arts and Sciences. His highest degree was a BS from the City College of New York, where he had also served as an instructor following graduation.[8]

Across different institutions, meanwhile, professors debated how much degrees actually mattered. Writing in 1947, a University of Illinois instructor blasted institutions for holding fast to the "Ph.D. fetish." Even amid "the greatest teacher shortage in history," he added, most colleges balked at hiring faculty "who lack the mystic blessing of three degrees." But there was also some softening on that score in the 1950s, as it became clear that the supply of doctorates could not keep up with demand. Bowdoin's 1955 self-study report explicitly rejected the idea that the number of PhDs on its faculty was "an index of effectiveness"; indeed, it noted, one-third of full professors at the college did not possess the doctorate. Likewise, Earlham College decreed that the PhD "should not be a union card" for faculty employment; the most important thing was to find committed teachers, whether they held doctorates or not. In a more jocular vein, the eminent novelist Vladimir Nabokov—who taught at Cornell and several other institutions, without a PhD—told his students that the acronym stood for "Department of Philistines"; more often than not, Nabokov claimed, it signified intellectual narrowness and a lack of "culture." To its defenders, by contrast, the PhD was the mark of a learned human being and hence the most desired degree in every case. "It introduced a certain amount of rigor which separates its products from the dilettantes, the hacks, the retired clergy finishing off their careers in a small college, and the grade B− Mr. Chipses," the graduate school dean at Northwestern declared. Hence, most institutions continued to seek the PhD-bearing professor, whether they could find one or not. Kalamazoo College decided that it would accept faculty with MAs, but "only if the man is going to earn Ph.D. subsequently," its president told an interviewer. By 1958, at least seven professors at the college were working toward their doctorates.[9]

Another option for addressing the teacher shortage was to hire women, whom most institutions (except all-female ones) had avoided or barred in prior eras. During World War II, when millions of men served in the armed forces, the proportion of PhDs earned by women rose from 13 to 20 percent. But it dropped abruptly when the war ended, falling to less than 10 percent by 1948. The fraction of MAs awarded to women showed a similar pattern, rising to an astonishing 57 percent during the war but falling to less than one-third after that. By 1955, nevertheless, 22 percent of American faculty were female, including 16 percent of professors at public universities. They were hugely over-represented in some fields—especially home economics, where they composed 96 percent of professors—but nearly absent in others: less than 5 percent of engineering and philosophy faculty were female, while the fields of religion and agriculture had no full-time women professors at all. Part of the problem was the enormous skew in awarded doctorates, especially in scientific and technical fields: between 1950 and 1961, for example, only 140 of 2,500 math PhDs went to women. But even qualified female candidates faced enormous hurdles. Anti-nepotism rules often prevented them from obtaining jobs at the same institutions as their husbands, while other colleges barred them from teaching while they were pregnant. "Schools complain about the shortage of qualified people and then refuse to hire those who are just waiting [for] a chance to teach," one frustrated female academic wrote. Arriving at Yale in 1949 to study for a PhD in English, Patricia Meyer Spacks was dismayed to discover that the university did not allow women to serve as teaching assistants. Consequently, she transferred to the University of California, Berkeley, which did.[10]

But Berkeley—like other colleges across the country—also exploited TAs, who were the easiest and cheapest solution to the teacher shortage: when universities could not find a real faculty member, they simply hired an assistant. The official rules of the California system decreed that assistants should not be the sole instructor of classes. But a 1947 survey of 15 departments at the University of California, Los Angeles, found that 11 of them required some or all of their TAs to teach full courses instead of discussion or laboratory sections—and for a fraction of the pay that a regular faculty member received. "We realize that this situation is a result of the University's desperate need for instructors," an officer in the Los Angeles Federation of Teachers' College Section wrote to the UCLA graduate dean in 1947. "But the fact remains that teaching assistants who now do the work of instructors are not being paid in proportion to the kind and amount of work done." Eleven years later another UCLA survey found that TAs had "virtually the sole responsibility for instruction" in 166 sections of 25 courses, despite the "questionable legality" of the practice. Even when TAs taught sections of a regular faculty member's lecture course, they were immensely overburdened. Although UCLA's policy stated that assistants were required to work 18–20 hours a week, a 1946 survey found that some TAs spent up to 190 hours per month—roughly twice the official requirement—preparing labs, grading quizzes and papers, meeting with students, and teaching their sections. That left little time for their own studies, the Teachers' Federation officer wrote, yielding "low morale and poor performance." So did their dismal pay, he added. Graduate students who served as "readers" of undergraduate tests and papers at UCLA received just 75 cents an hour, less than clerical workers or any other university employees; at Berkeley, meanwhile, they made less than local Safeway clerks.[11]

Under such conditions, critics noted, universities could not hope to attract "the best men"—to quote the gendered language of the day—as TAs. The most talented graduate students sought research assistantships, which were both more lucrative and more prestigious than TA posts. "The good researchers go into research," a Johns Hopkins biochemist observed, describing PhD students, "and the others go into teaching." Some institutions established grade point average (GPA) requirements for TAs but waived the rule upon request of desperate departments, which sometimes questioned whether there should be any GPA restrictions at all: as one UCLA chemist suggested, perhaps the best TAs had lower grades in graduate school because they were exceptionally devoted to their undergraduate students. "The sole real qualification for an Assistant should be his aptitude for his assigned duties," another chemist argued. "Superior grades in advanced work are less important than the qualities that make for good teaching." But most universities made little effort to improve or even to monitor TA instruction, leaving the assistants to fend for themselves. In a 1947 survey, over half of TAs at UCLA reported that their teaching was "not supervised"; meanwhile, only 10 percent said they received "detailed instruction by which to teach" from professors directing their courses. "When we hire young fellows and assistants, we ask ourselves only one question: Is the young man capable of going ahead and doing good research as a graduate student?" Rice University professor George Williams frankly admitted. "We don't give a damn about his teaching ability. We let the students sink or swim; it's their affair, not ours."[12]

But it was also the affair of undergraduates, of course, who frequently complained about the poor quality of their TAs. Harried TAs often exuded a "get away, I'm busy" attitude, as one Harvard student wrote; like the professors they served, they were eager to get back to their laboratories and libraries. "It is almost commonplace for the section man, when asked a question, to beg off by saying that he has not attended the lectures, has not done the reading, and is too busy with his own studies and research to keep himself properly informed," a military veteran and recent Harvard alumnus wrote. "No self-respecting high school would permit its students to be exposed to such slipshod pedagogy as that delivered by many Harvard section men." At the Illinois Institute of Technology, likewise, students complained that their TAs were more interested in their own research than in fulfilling their teaching responsibilities. Gamely, some university leaders tried to defend TAs; at Wisconsin, for example, president Conrad Elvehjem insisted that he had done his own best teaching when he was a graduate assistant. But other faculty and administrators admitted that TAs were "second class staff," assigned to handle the "dirty work in university instruction"—like laboratory sections and English composition—that nobody else wanted to do. "Exploitation of teaching assistants and fellows as 'slave labor' in blind unguided assignments is morally indefensible and practically wasteful of human potentialities," Kentucky political scientist Gladys Kammerer flatly admitted in 1959. But it would continue unabated, she predicted, until universities improved the overall quality of teaching in their classrooms.[13]

The Cold War Classroom

From the dawn of the republic, students denounced the poor instruction they received in college. The difference, in the Cold War, was that professors like Kammerer got in on the act as well. A veritable cottage industry of criticism arose around college teaching, spawning book-length exposés and critical articles in both the academic and popular press. Its authors included leading scholars like New York University philosopher Sidney Hook, a protégé of John Dewey, which gave the critique added intellectual heft. "Practices are countenanced in colleges which would not be suffered for one moment in any good elementary or secondary high school," Hook wrote in 1946, as thousands of new students flooded into universities. Part of the problem was simple overcrowding, which stuffed the students into poorly lit lecture halls while they strained to see or hear the professor at the front of the room. But the biggest obstacle was the professors, who lacked the preparation, incentive, and skill that good teaching required. As Rice University's George Williams quipped, a new professor was like someone who was briefed about the mechanics of an airplane's internal combustion engine and then told to fly the plane. "Tragedy for the pilot is almost inevitable; in the case of the young instructor, the tragedy befalls his students," Williams wrote. But most professors did not seem to mind, as Hook sadly observed. "Many college teachers, especially if they feel secure because of length of service or publication, profess not to care if they are good teachers or not," he grumbled.[14]

Hook and others proceeded to remind them how bad they were, issuing compendia of poor traits and behaviors they had observed or experienced in college classrooms. William Godfrey, an English professor at the University of Detroit, even published a list of the "Seven Deadly Sins of Teaching" in 1951: failure to prepare, sarcasm, dullness, garrulity, tardiness, digression, and belligerence. The first item promoted many of the others, Godfrey noted: professors were tardy, digressive, or belligerent precisely because they were trying to cover for their lack of preparation. George Williams published his own seven-part inventory, which he enumerated as negative personality types: the "plain stupid" professor, the smug professor, the arrogant professor, the professor "who just does not care about people," the professor "who tries to 'pal around' with his students," the pretentiously "cultured" professor, and the dull "businesslike" professor. Just as there was only one way to make love but a thousand ways to commit murder, Williams quipped (with a nod to Dorothy Sayers), there was just one way to be a good professor but "at least seven ways to be a bad one." University of Missouri communications professor Loren Reid reduced the list of bad professor types to four: the Ghost, the Wanderer, the Echo, and the Autocrat. The Ghost discouraged questions and left right after the bell, so students never got to know him; the Wanderer was disorganized, rambling in lecture and ambiguous about assignments; the Echo simply repeated what was in the textbook, which students could read instead of attending class; and the Autocrat graded arbitrarily and otherwise treated students "as if they were inmates in a penal institution."[15]

Many students felt as if they were captives as well, suffering under cruel and domineering professors. Similar complaints dated back to student riots against "tyrannical" colleges in the antebellum era, which typically focused on food, housing, and rules of decorum. The Cold War critique centered more squarely on teaching, which students denounced as capricious, dictatorial, and otherwise inconsistent with the democratic rhetoric of postwar higher education. A University of Missouri economist began his class by admitting that none of its students wanted to take his course, and he did not expect them to succeed; at Yale, English professors routinely asked students who failed to answer a question if they were stupid; and at Rice, one student recalled, professors treated her like "a total idiot" if she could not grasp a new concept. "There is such a thing as sadism in educational life," Sidney Hook confirmed. "Teachers have enormous powers to make students miserable." Students especially despised professors who evaluated them in an arbitrary or punitive fashion, making grades into a weapon of domination and dread. "My freshmen [*sic*] year in college was the most painful period in my whole life," one recently graduated University of Michigan alumnus wrote in a 1949 survey. "It's a wonder I didn't develop ulcers from a constant state of nerves." Professors often began her courses by warning that two of three freshmen would flunk out, which put her immediately on edge. "It was a living night mare [*sic*] of fear and pressure," she recalled. "Why do college people deem it necessary to frighten young people into learning?"[16]

Other students found that professors were more likely to bore than to scare them, especially via dull and disorganized lectures. Going back to the Progressive Era, of course, students had condemned teachers who lectured poorly. But massive student enrollment increases—and related teacher shortages—in the Cold War era made lectures ubiquitous as never before; indeed, as a Harvard student committee underscored, "lectures and the lecture system are assumed to be *the* educational device" for postwar college teaching. At Berkeley, half of lower-division instruction occurred in classes of over 100 students, and 20 percent took place in classes of 400 or more; other universities reported similarly huge classes, which could only be taught via lectures. The critique of them accelerated too, especially at larger schools. Some students offered a kind of passive resistance, reading the newspaper or playing cards during lectures; others simply cut class, reasoning—often correctly—that they could obtain the same information from the textbook. But still other students mounted a much more explicit and vocal attack on the poor delivery and content of the lectures they received. Students especially bridled when professors spoke in monotones or in whispers, rendering them inaudible. Other teachers distracted audiences with annoying mannerisms, like rattling coins in their pockets or repeating the same word or phrase over and over; in one hour-long class meeting, students counted a professor saying "heretofore" 96 times. Prefiguring a common intervention in the 1970s and beyond, when many college teachers watched videotapes of their instruction, an angry student at the University of Southern California proposed that all professors be forced to look at a film of themselves at the front of a classroom. Then and only then might their lectures improve.[17]

As the critique of college teaching spread into the professoriate, faculty members and administrators increasingly denounced the lecture system as well. Even small colleges had caught the lecture disease, they noted, spreading apathy and ennui across campus. "Are students going to be lectured to death?" Amherst president Charles W. Cole asked, in a particularly pointed attack. The problem was not just one of pedagogy, faculty critics said, but one of democracy: lecturing was an "authoritarian" method, more suited to America's global enemies than to its own classrooms. "For a lecturer to dictate material and pour out his own conclusions, day after day, upon twenty defenseless students (or one hundred or five hundred!) who do nothing but listen and absorb, may be excellent training for young Fascists and Communists," Bates English professor Robert Berkelman wrote, "but such procedure is certainly gravely questionable in a democracy that prides itself upon cultivating initiative and combating regimentation." At an American university in France, established to provide college courses to US soldiers after World War II, another professor mounted a similar critique of the lecture method. "It gives the learner no opportunity to express his own reactions, and is therefore less democratic than some other procedures in teaching," J. G. Umstattd wrote in 1947. "It promotes the authoritarian type of instruction and minimizes the importance of the learner and his views." (Besides, Umstattd added, the school's older and "tough-minded" students—tempered by the experience of war—simply would not stand for it.) A psychologist at Arizona State University went even farther, declaring that the professor who lectured was himself a tyrant who embodied values antithetical to the ones America was trying to spread around the world. "He is the dictator of the classroom; the Stalin of the chosen few," the professor charged.[18]

Other lecture critics associated the method less with global dictatorship than with cheap theatrics, fearing that some professors were substituting amusement for academic rigor. Every campus had professors who were renowned for their spellbinding podium performances. Harvard English professor Walter Jackson Bate—author of a Pulitzer Prize–winning biography of Samuel Johnson—was famous for crying each year at the lectern as he described Johnson's death; to one listener, it seemed as if Bate was describing the loss of a friend. Stanford poet Yvor Winters mesmerized audiences by reading verse out loud, which revealed "the intensity and passion of his commitment to the art," as a former student recalled. But faculty often cast an arch eye at colleagues who were "performers," especially if they lacked the literary pedigree of figures like Bate and Winters. At Columbia, Dean Harry Carman—a vocal critic of "dull, routine instructors"—also blasted professors who tried to amuse their students. "We do not want teachers who are showmen and entertainers," Carman wrote. "One can be a master teacher without being either a glamour boy or as conventional as a church deacon." Meanwhile, students praised professors who held their interest but condemned those who condescended to them with stale humor or overstated melodrama. "Mr. D. is a brilliant and fluent lecturer, although he tends towards the thumb-in-waistcoat school of oratory with considerable unnecessary histrionics," one Yale student wrote, evaluating political scientist Cecil Driver; in a Shakespeare class, meanwhile, others complained that the professor overemphasized sexual imagery in a "play upon Yale emotions." A Missouri student government leader wrote that as a rule students "enjoy jokes but not vulgarity, obscenity, or horse play." A little levity was good, but too much seemed to make a joke out of teaching and learning.[19]

In response, other professors and students mounted a qualified defense of "entertainment" in education. "There will always be among teachers some who disapprove of human happiness, who will insist that any instruction which gives pleasure to the instructed, probably does more harm than good," wrote Columbia English professor John Erskine, who was also a popular public lecturer outside of the university. But a good lecture could provide pleasure and instruction, he argued; unless it entertained, indeed, students were unlikely to learn anything from it. Likewise, Reed College ex-president Dexter Keezer blasted faculty who seemed threatened by anything that hinted of enjoyment or amusement. "Too few professors respect . . . their obligation to make their teaching as interesting as possible," Keezer wrote in 1949. "Indeed, some of them seem to me to take the position that it verges on the quackish for college teachers not to be dull." University of Pennsylvania political scientist D. Lincoln Harter noted that "the first principle of selling is arousing interest," citing advertising professors at Penn's Wharton School. After Josef Stalin seized Czechoslovakia, Harter appeared in class on May Day—the Communist holiday—with a sickle sticking out of his back, along with a blood-red caption: "Joe got me!" If students forgot everything else from his class, Harter predicted, they would always remember that. "It is no sin to make education alluring," he concluded. Students concurred, seeking out professors who could entertain and educate at the same time. According to one Yale student, Robert D. French's famed lecture course on Chaucer made audiences believe that French *was* Chaucer. "The teaching methods employed by French are not particularly new; here they don't have to be," the student wrote. "There is unfortunately little discussion, but the lectures are presented in such a delightfully, lively way, that much of the value of discussion conferences is retained."[20]

The last remark highlighted a key irony in Cold War college teaching: although lecture became the dominant method, discussion was the approved one. The same critics who lambasted the teacher at the lectern celebrated the teacher at the roundtable, who engaged students as equals in the quest for knowledge. At Stephens College, professors organized their classrooms "more like living rooms," one impressed visitor observed. Instead of chairs and desks being aligned "with military precision, row upon row," they were set around tables seating four to eight students; the professor rotated between them instead of remaining behind his own desk. "It becomes impossible for the instructor to develop professional airs and to assume a sense of infallible superiority in such an informal atmosphere," the visitor wrote. Other professors retained the traditional row arrangement but led discussions anyway, even in very large "lecture" classes. Yale philosopher Paul Weiss conducted all of his courses—regardless of size—as dialogues, starting each class with a "bald, usually controversial statement" that provoked a "storm of questions," a student journalist wrote. Likewise, Harvard philosopher Raphael Demos was famous for turning a large lecture into a "super-size section-meeting," one student wrote. Historian Arthur Schlesinger Jr. could lead a "lively discussion" with a group of 300 students as effectively as a tutor could with three of them, an impressed Radcliffe parent observed. At a meeting of the American Council on Education's (ACE) Committee on Teaching, several members noted that skilled instructors could generate "intimate involvement of students" even in a lecture-type setting. Better to have a few such superstars than many weak teachers, each "communicating with mediocrity in an intimate environment," they argued.[21]

Yet real exchange was surely more common in smaller classes, committee chair O. M. Wilson noted. So if good teaching was "defined as 'discussion,'" he warned, colleges would need to lower their student-faculty ratios in order to improve it. That was a difficult proposition amid the hothouse growth of postwar higher education, but several smaller (and wealthier) private schools managed to pull it off. Brown established small discussion-based seminars for underclassmen, with the help of a grant from the Carnegie Corporation. ("This sort of education is expensive," a journalist noted, "since there will be no mass lectures of I.B.M.-corrected examinations.") A Carnegie grant also allowed Earlham College to create weekly tutorial meetings between a professor and three to four students, which would "prevent the sacrifice of essential educational values as the new 'bulge' of students hits our campuses," as one college representative wrote. But most institutions lacked the endowment or foundation support to preserve small-group settings in an era of mass education. "A tutorial or semi-tutorial relationship between an instructor and a small number of students represents the most desired and effective pedagogical situation, and the least realized in our present curricular structure," a UCLA faculty committee on "improving the effectiveness of instruction" flatly declared. The only way to free up more faculty time for small seminars was to create ever-larger lecture courses, a Berkeley committee added, "to compensate for increased time spent on tutorial work."[22]

Meanwhile, critics began to question whether all of this work—and expense—actually delivered on its promises. In theory, a Harvard student group wrote, small-group discussions would promote the kind of spirit John Dewey envisioned in his classic book *Democracy and Education*; other advocates of discussion cited psychoanalysts like Carl Rogers, who urged teachers to let students explore their own problems—and come to their own conclusions—in the same manner as a therapist drew out a patient. In practice, however, many professors lacked the will and the skill to conduct meaningful discussions with undergraduate students. Some faculty dismissed the technique as "high-schoolish" and "not sufficiently dignified for college classes," where the professor was supposed to hold forth. Other teachers aimed to elicit discussion but failed, reverting to lectures when the silence became too much to bear. "Too many questions asked in class are either superficial, out-of-focus, or too general," a department chair at Rensselaer Polytechnic Institute wrote, in a memo to his faculty. Nor did most professors wait for a reply, he added; instead, "they prefer to rudely interrupt and give their own answer to their own rhetorical questions." Even in classes labeled "seminars," as sociologist Nathan Glazer observed, professors took up most of the airtime. At the University of Chicago, where officials boasted about the shift from lectures to discussion as the "dominant mode of instruction," a 1949 analysis of 25 recorded classes led by different professors found that each of them talked for at least half the time and some for considerably longer than that. The students who did participate represented only a small fraction of the class, moreover, which annoyed and irritated their less voluble peers.[23]

Most of all, as Chicago psychologist Benjamin Bloom found, many students were distracted and disengaged from the entire process. Bloom played back the recordings a week after class for student participants, who reconstructed what they were thinking at the time. Fewer than half of their recalled impressions reflected "active thinking relevant to the subject at hand," Bloom discovered. Many students had been watching the clock, "wondering how much longer the class would be"; others asked why the instructor was wasting time eliciting information from students, when he "should have given it himself." Indeed, as many observers noted, students often preferred lectures over the much-ballyhooed discussion method. "The habitual pattern is still that of the teacher being a pitcher that pours information down 'the minds of students' instead of a participation process," wrote one Brooklyn College economist, who tried—mostly in vain—to provoke discussion. "I must do more explanation of my method of teaching because I am convinced that it results in a more effective learning process!" Turning the tables on their undergraduates, frustrated professors said that *students* were too "authoritarian" to accept free-flowing discussion: they "wait for the pearls of wisdom to drop prettily from my mouth," one University of Chicago instructor complained, revealing "an almost psychopathic desire to hand back 'the right answers.'" Some students worried about achieving a good grade in the discussion system; for them "democratic methods seem unorganized and ambiguous," as noted by one professor. But others simply believed that they would learn more via lectures, and in certain circumstances they were probably right. "Is it better to have a group of students talk about something they knew very little about than to have a structured lecture by a professor who does?" a Swarthmore alumnus asked, deriding the "cult" of discussion. At Sarah Lawrence, another school proud of its "democratic" character, a graduate said that her best course had been a straight-lecture class given by English professor and mythology expert Joseph Campbell.[24]

The Great Fear: Political Repression in College Teaching

Another constraint on discussion came from the larger political climate of the United States, which discouraged professors from addressing contentious or divisive issues in their classrooms. Writing in 1954, a panel of scholars examining undergraduate instruction took faculty members to task for pulling their punches. "There was a widespread belief in university and college circles that a teacher should be 'objective' at all costs, and that he should therefore hide his convictions on important and controversial issues from his students," the panel reported. But that was morally dishonest as well as pedagogically ineffective, it argued: students needed to learn how to "wrestle with social, economic, moral, and political issues," and they would be unable to do so if professors hid their own opinions under a veil of false neutrality. Indeed, the report concluded, the professor who avoided controversial political questions was "a traitor to the cause of a liberal or liberating education." But during these years, especially between 1950 and 1955, professors who took up such questions in

class were themselves denounced as traitors. Just a year after the report was issued, one professor reported that he had been fired for telling his students
that the United States should recognize Soviet Russia; another was dismissed
for arguing in class that railroads should be publically owned. In America, academic mythology held that professors were free to say whatever they wanted
in their own classrooms. But reality told a very different story, severely restrict-
ing the scope and meaning of "discussion" in college teaching.[25]

Much of what we know about political repression in the classroom during
this era comes from the work of Columbia sociologist Paul Lazarsfeld—the
leading survey researcher of the period—and his graduate student, Wagner
Thielens Jr. Published in 1958 as *The Academic Mind*, their research was based
on a questionnaire administered to nearly 2,500 social science professors
around the country. Twelve percent of respondents said they had become
more careful about "assigning potentially controversial works in their classes,"
and 20 percent said they were less willing to express "unpopular political
views" in the classroom. Yet the mostly unpublished faculty comments that
Lazarsfeld and Thielens collected suggest much more fear and repression than
their quantitative data revealed. Dozens of professors said that their classes had
been monitored by student or political watchdog groups; others suspected that
agents of the Federal Bureau of Investigation were observing them; several
others said they had been interviewed by the FBI, in its quest to expose "subversive" colleagues and students; and still others were harassed by their own
students, who reported suspicious faculty to college officials. Whether or not
they admitted on surveys that they had self-censored their own political opinions, they clearly avoided potentially contentious subjects. "We know if we
are wise we will not discuss controversies," a professor at John Stetson University stated. Although faculty were reluctant to discuss controversial questions in class, a University of Washington political scientist added, they were
also loath to admit that fact. "They don't say they don't have the courage to do
this but the effect is very easily seen," he underlined.[26]

The most frequently avoided topic in class was Communism, of course.
"We don't discuss Red China; instead, we discuss whether the student should
wear shoes or not!" quipped a professor at Antioch College, which was famous
for its bohemian atmosphere. At the Louisiana Polytechnic Institute, meanwhile, a geographer reported that he had stopped teaching about the Soviet
Union "because it can't be discussed objectively." When Communism did
come up, professors either changed the subject or exaggerated their anti-
Communist attitudes in order to play it safe. "I say that I am giving both sides

on the question when I am really protecting myself," a University of Maryland professor confessed. "I approve the recognition of Red China but I find myself presenting the other side more strongly than I otherwise would." Likewise, an economist at San Francisco State College admitted that he was "even more critical of the Soviet Economy" than he had been in the past; at the Massachusetts Institute of Technology, a third professor said he inflated his distaste for Karl Marx. "I feel I must remind students that Marx was a clown," he wrote. At DePaul University, even chemistry and physics instructors were afraid to tell their classes that "the Soviets have made progress" in these fields, as one professor observed. The wariest professors were probably those who taught courses about Marxism or Communism, which were still offered at a handful of universities. Professors teaching "Critical Study of the Philosophy of Marxism" at Yale made tape recordings of every session, to defend themselves against potential charges that they were advocating Communism instead of analyzing it. "You'll notice the word 'critical' has to be in the title," one Yale professor archly noted.[27]

Others were afraid to discuss federal relief measures that had passed during the New Deal, which Senator Joseph McCarthy and other conservative critics had tainted as "Red" in spirit. "Quite often I'm a little afraid to say anything about Social Security, etc. that may be interpreted as leftist," a historian at Louisiana Polytechnic Institute admitted. Even at Swarthmore, an institution renowned for its liberal identity, professors balked at revealing outright support for the liberal state. "When I discuss TVA, the New Deal, I think I tend to tred [*sic*] softer, go more slowly," a historian there acknowledged. "Normal statements that are not really controversial have become controversial." Professors also tried to avoid topics connected to religion, where any critical or skeptical remarks might alienate devout students and raise the specter of "Godless" Communism. A professor of social psychology at Western Reserve University considered playing a tape recording of a famous faith healer, to illuminate "methods behind religion," but he quickly thought better of it. "I was afraid to chance it," he jotted on his survey. Thirty years after the Scopes Trial, meanwhile, the theory of evolution remained verboten in many college classrooms. "It is the vilest of heresies according to the administration here," one professor noted. Students had complained to college officials that he taught about evolution, which earned him a warning from the institution. "Now I teach what I'm told, not necessarily what I think," he gloomily admitted.[28]

As the last example illustrated, students often served as the informal guardians of political propriety in college teaching. To enforce the boundaries of acceptable topics and comments, administrators had to know what was happening in the classroom, and, for the most part, the only way for them to find out was for students to tell them. A historian at South Dakota State College of Agricultural and Mechanical Arts was called in for a talk with his department chair and dean after students reported him for telling them that accused spies Julius and Ethel Rosenberg would not have been convicted if public sentiment had not been against them. He did not say they were innocent, he emphasized, but rather that the evidence against them was "flimsy." To his critics, however, raising any questions about the Rosenbergs' guilt was tantamount to exonerating them. "I've been asked to 'pussy-foot' and tone down my remarks," the historian wrote. At Hunter College in New York City, a professor changed a reading assignment related to Marxism after one of her students complained to her adviser, who in turn told the president. Altering the assignment was the only real option, the professor explained, because refusing to do so would become part of her academic record and "would come up at time of promotion." A University of Tulsa professor was reported by students as a "New Dealer" to the trustees, who made him produce his course syllabus; a Grinnell College student made a similar report to his father, an Iowa Supreme Court Justice, who told the university president that his son was "getting too much Roosevelt in his classes"; and at the University of Colorado, a student gave a state legislator his class notes to illustrate his professor's skewed teaching. "The best Gestapo is the student," one dejected instructor concluded, denouncing undergraduates who reported on their professors.[29]

But other faculty worried about people from outside their classes, who occasionally showed up inside of them. At Yale, for example, the director of the Center of Alcohol Studies received unannounced classroom visits from representatives of the distillery industry and the Woman's Christian Temperance Union (WCTU). "The WCTU says we're agents of the distillers," the professor wrote. "Distillers are afraid on the other hand of taxes. The distillers and the WCTU hate each other, yet they join with each other to fight us." Other faculty reported visits from right-wing watchdog groups with names like Students for America and Youth for America, who relayed allegedly subversive comments to local police or to state lawmakers. Still other faculty were convinced they were being watched in class by spies from the FBI, or that the watchdog students were FBI agents themselves. Intelligence agencies investigated hundreds of allegedly radical or subversive university professors, who were fired or pushed out for their past Communist affiliations or for their refusal to discuss them. So faculty had good reason to suspect that they were being spied on in classrooms, whether they were or not. In 1946, "it was more or less common knowledge . . . that a student was reporting to the FBI on certain teachers," a Williams professor recalled. "I know who the boy was—I had him in class and I had the distinct impression on many occasions that he was trying to make a complete transcription of everything I said." Other professors began to think that any new face in their classroom—or even the man washing its windows—could be a spy. "That's the vicious part of it—it could come from anybody or anywhere," one instructor fretted.[30]

A smaller fraction of right-leaning faculty members welcomed the added classroom surveillance, whether it came from students or even from spies. "Professors are more worried. And I think that's a good thing," one instructor and self-described admirer of Joseph McCarthy wrote on a survey. "I personally am less worried. Depends on which side of the fence you are [on]." Reflecting the high level of support for McCarthy within their faith, Catholic professors often endorsed political scrutiny of the classroom as a needed constraint on left-wing colleagues. "It may have checked some of the radicals," a Catholic faculty member at Massachusetts State Teachers College wrote. "Some teachers may have gone over-board and they may have had influence on their students." Beyond that, Catholic professors said, the surveillance of faculty had enlightened the broader American citizenry about the perils posed by "subversive" college teachers. "I think it has shaken off much of the apathy—it has brought the general public face-to-face with some of the dangers in our own country [and] some of the fruits of the leftist teachings," a Gonzaga professor wrote. So there was also growing popular pressure to limit such teachings in college classrooms, as a professor at St. John College in Cleveland happily reported. "If the public is alert you are not going to have professors careless in what they say," he explained. "If people are alert professors are going to be fair and honest in their dealings with students more than if people outside are not interested."[31]

To be sure, professors across the political spectrum sometimes aimed to indoctrinate students into the teacher's own point of view. Conservative students, especially, complained that liberal professors spouted democratic rhetoric but acted like intellectual autocrats. At the University of Southern California, students denounced a faculty member who "talks about being democratic yet demands that his students 'cooperate' with him," one student wrote. "What he really means when he asks us to cooperate is to do what he says." In 1949, the new chairman of the *Yale Daily News* took to its pages to condemn an anthropologist who allegedly mocked religion in class. "In undermining religion through bawdy and slap-stick humor . . . he is guilty of an injustice to and imposition upon his students," wrote William F. Buckley Jr. Two years later, Buckley would produce a book-length indictment of the many ways that faculty members allegedly undermined religious faith (hence his title *God and Man at Yale*) and spread liberal orthodoxies like Keynesian economics. Yet in their course reviews, which were collected and edited under Buckley's direction at the *Yale Daily News*, other students condemned professors for their *conservative* prejudices. A statistics professor was "somewhat repetitious and biased towards Republican policies"; an economics professor was "very conservative," proclaiming ideas "from the last century" instead of exposing students to newer theories by Keynes and others. But the students also knew where their bread was buttered, often echoing professors' views in an effort to win higher grades. "It just doesn't pay to disagree with them," a junior at the University of Kansas told a researcher in 1959. "The thing to do is to find out what they want you to say and tell them that."[32]

Varieties of Cold War Teaching

That same year, eminent educator John W. Gustad warned against generalizing across the enormous differences in American higher education. Praising a film by the ACE to recruit new talent into college teaching, Gustad also questioned whether any single account could do justice to the profession. "There are such great differences in the kinds of jobs which one might get in higher education," Gustad told an ACE official. "If one is to be a research professor of nuclear physics at MIT, he has a very different situation that [*sic*] a man who teaches freshman English at West Overshoe Tech." Private institutions could maintain vastly lower student-to-faculty ratios than large public universities could: in 1949, for example, the ratio of students to each full-time professor at the University of Wisconsin was 35.3, as compared to 8.7 at Yale and 5.9 at the University of Pennsylvania. That obviously gave professors at private colleges more opportunity to work closely with individual students, as one journalist observed. Reviewing *The Art of Teaching*, a popular 1950 book by Columbia classicist Gilbert Highet, William D. Patterson noted that most college teaching positions looked nothing like Highet's enviable Ivy League lair. "He writes . . . from an academic tower, unfettered by some of the major problems that harass the average U.S. educator," Patterson wrote. "The spacious pursuit of intellectual improvement and student stimulation that he urges upon teachers from his own spacious university background must have a hollow sound for professors trapped in the grinding routine of a large state university." Indeed, as scholar Martin Trow warned, American higher education was moving in a dangerously bifurcated direction. As more and more students sought postsecondary degrees, he predicted, the United States might witness "a pattern of negative selection of less able, less bold and less imaginative men to the faculties of the junior colleges and the lower-status, mass 'people processing institutions' that are bearing the brunt of the greatly increased enrollments."[33]

Actually, there was some evidence that the men—and women—who taught at junior colleges were more effective in the classroom than their peers at other institutions. A 1954 study found that students ranked their experiences with professors highest at junior colleges and lowest at universities, with smaller liberal arts colleges in the middle. University officials reacted defensively, noting that they employed large numbers of TAs and that it was unfair to compare them to institutions "staffed by full-time experienced teachers." Yet junior colleges employed many part-time instructors, particularly high school teachers. What differentiated them was a stronger commitment to student learning and growth, as a middle-aged student at East Los Angeles Junior College wrote in her campus newspaper in 1951. Returning to college for the first time in 30 years, she found that teachers were less likely to "command student fear" or to center instruction on themselves; instead, they tried to ground it in students' own interests and experiences. "The position of teacher and student reversed," she wrote. "Old 'seen and not heard' is replaced by 'have you any ideas or suggestions?'" At smaller private schools, likewise, teachers typically devoted more time and attention to students than did faculty members at big research universities. "Intimate, quality teaching is the prime thing Bowdoin has to sell and she should never forget it," wrote a Bowdoin alumnus who served as assistant to the president at Bucknell. "In fact, that is the thing that all private colleges should try to sell in the future." Bowdoin's president, dean, and admissions officer all taught undergraduate courses. That was a testament to the college's commitment to "the primacy of the teacher," as its 1955 self-study report declared.[34]

But there was also evidence that colleges of every type were starting to neglect teaching on behalf of research, as Oberlin physicist Lloyd W. Taylor admitted. Even at an institution noted for its emphasis on undergraduate instruction, Taylor wrote, professors lacked "higher pride of profession" in teaching. "We are physicists who happen to be teaching; we are artists who happen to be teaching art," he confessed. "We accept altogether too passively that utterly vicious proverb, 'Those who can, do, and those who can't, teach.'" At Vassar, likewise, English professor James Early admitted that the "noble ideal" of research had spawned "the downgrading of teaching," particularly at women's colleges formerly dedicated to it. "The famous ultimatum 'Publish or Perish' hangs over the fledgling instructor in all the major universities and in many of the liberal arts colleges," Early wrote. "Teachers are hired, ostensibly, to teach but are judged by what they produce when not concerned with teaching." Stanford education scholar and former Hamilton College president William H. Cowley concurred, explaining that faculty at most institutions "give their primary allegiance to research and consider teaching a chore to bypass." Even more, professors exerted a perverse kind of peer pressure to enforce that new consensus: the rare individual who put instruction first "has to contend with the criticisms of his in-the-saddle, research-minded colleagues who scoff at him as 'a mere teacher,' 'a damned popularizer,' 'a hippodrome artist,'" Cowley added. Unsurprisingly, then, "great teachers seem to be almost as rare as southpaw shortstops," he concluded.[35]

Even at small colleges, limited funds often prevented schools from hiring a sufficient number of teachers or from attracting talented ones. That was particularly true at historically black colleges and universities (HBCUs), which struggled to locate and retain good teachers during these years. At Lincoln University in Pennsylvania, one professor simply gave his class the textbook and left it at that; another noted his low pay and "apparently reasoned that not enough money was being paid for a first class job," a student journalist wrote in 1947. To be sure, black colleges had outstanding professors like Adolph Reed, who mesmerized students at Southern University with his lectures about Frederick Douglass, Sojourner Truth, and other warriors for racial justice; at Spellman, meanwhile, Howard Zinn handed out loyalty oath cards to debate their constitutionality and held a moot Supreme Court to re-create the free speech trial of socialist Eugene V. Debs. Significantly, though, both professors were forced out of their jobs for supporting the civil rights struggle. As protests and demonstrations for racial justice swept HBCUs, students increasingly targeted weak professors in their own midst. "The students need an education now! Right this minute! We cannot afford not to have it," an anonymous Lincoln University student wrote in 1962. "How about the teachers who are supposed to help us get it? Some apologize, some sleep, and some do nothing at all. How can dedicated men shirk their responsibility?" Across American higher education, critics highlighted the same problem. Their solution was twofold: to bring more dedicated men (and sometimes women) into the profession, and to develop new machines and technologies that might replace them altogether.[36]

CHAPTER SIX

TV or Not TV?

Reforming Cold War College Teaching

In 1955, the Fund for the Advancement of Education (TFAE) brought together 14 prominent college administrators and professors to discuss the improvement of college teaching. They considered—and eventually rejected—the creation of a new teaching-focused PhD, fearing that it would "endanger a man's reputation . . . and thus defeat the very purpose for which it was created." But the group endorsed the TFAE's efforts to recruit "better men" into academia and to enhance their preparation for teaching once they got there. Several universities used grants from the TFAE to add courses on education—and a supervised teaching stint—to their standing PhD programs. Others created "Internships in College Teaching" for new faculty members, who attended a seminar on instructional strategies; they also observed classes taught by senior colleagues, who in turn observed the new teachers' classes. Established four years earlier by the Ford Foundation, the TFAE compensated colleges so they could lighten professors' teaching loads and free them up for the new pedagogical programming. "Your group has come nearer to crystalizing the shape of future preparation of college teachers than anything I have seen," one college dean told Clarence Faust, president of the TFAE.[1]

The same foundation was also working on ways to deliver college instruction more widely and efficiently, especially via technology. A few months after its conference on graduate school preparation, the TFAE announced a new Committee on Utilization of College Resources. Its biggest focus was educational television, which promised to relieve teacher shortages at the same time that it made "the greatest teachers of the age . . . available to students everywhere," as TFAE vice president Alvin Eurich told a reporter in 1956. The TFAE also supported the development and implementation of "teaching machines," which would supplant much of the activity currently performed by college instructors. Their most prominent advocate was Harvard psychologist B. F. Skinner, who received a TFAE grant to build 10 "college-level teaching machines" and install them in a "Self-Instruction Room" in a building on Harvard Yard; he also taught his popular introductory course on behaviorism using the machines. To Skinner, preparing "better" teachers—or even beaming the "best" ones over television—was a fool's errand. "The number of people in the world who want an education is increasing at an almost explosive rate," he told the TFAE, in his final report on the project. "It will not be possible to give these people what they want merely by building more schools and training more teachers." In most other fields, he added, growing demand had led to "the invention of labor-saving devices." Now education needed to follow suit, harnessing technology to enrich—or even to replace—what human teachers did.[2]

These episodes highlight the central and somewhat contradictory themes in the reform of college teaching during the Cold War era. Widespread dissatisfaction with "mass education"—and with inept instruction—spawned new initiatives to improve teacher selection, preparation, and evaluation. Meanwhile, another set of reforms aimed to alter the content and delivery of instruction via new technologies, especially television. By 1959, over 100 different colleges and universities provided nearly 500 televised courses to half a million students around the United States. Some of these classes were offered on campus, through closed-circuit TV; others were broadcast on the public airwaves, allowing students—and any other interested viewers—to tune in wherever they wished. Both sets of efforts received enormous aid from the foundation world, which marked an important shift in its own right: whereas prior efforts to improve college teaching came mostly from within the university, the Cold War brought important outside players into the reform arena. Like the Ford Foundation, which had seeded the TFAE, the Carnegie Corporation of New York (CCNY) invested millions in what one 1953 observer called the "renaissance" of college teaching. Its best-known beneficiary was the Woodrow Wilson Fellowship, which provided thousands of graduate scholarships to lure promising undergraduates into college teaching. As the CCNY's president told the *New York Times*, "The central ingredient in any education was the teacher." So the only way to improve instruction was to improve the instructors. Lest anyone miss the point, the *Times'* headline drove it home: "Teacher Put First by Carnegie Fund."[3]

Gamely, the champions of technological innovation tried to make the same case: television would showcase the personalities of leading teachers, while teaching machines would free instructors from dull classroom routine and allow their real pedagogical character to shine. As always, however, practice told another story. After the initial rush of celebrity passed, professors who appeared on television reported that they missed the "person-to-person contact from the teacher-student relationship," as one Penn State faculty member said. So did students, who "felt no need to pay attention out of courtesy to the instructor," as another Penn State professor wrote. So they slept, read newspapers, or stared into space rather than at the TV screen flickering in front of them. "Television as a mass media of education would seem to be an efficient method, but is this a *college education*?" a third Penn State instructor asked. Across the country, most faculty and students gave the same answer: no. "Having a TV class (pupils on TV) does not add to my learning," an Ohio University student wrote, after taking a closed-circuit course where he watched the professor interact with students in a TV studio. "I felt as if the teacher was talking to them and not me, giving a feeling that I was looking thru a window at the class." During these same years, students routinely denounced the anonymity and impersonality of large lecture classes. Television reinforced the problem instead of alleviating it, replacing a distant professor on the stage with a remote image on a screen. Even as reformers tried to put teachers first, bringing stronger personalities into the classroom, new technologies made teaching even less personal than it was before.[4]

Better People, Better Teachers

In 1947, the President's Commission on Higher Education predicted that America would need 250,000 new college teachers by 1960. Appointed the previous year by Harry Truman, the commission made headlines by insisting that any capable American who wished to attend university should be able to do so. But it also worried about recruiting enough "quality" people to instruct the teeming student population, especially given the low pay and high teaching loads at many colleges and universities. The average salary for a full-time professor was half of what a physician earned; even real estate salesmen made 60 percent more than faculty members did. Writing privately, a UC Berkeley department chair noted that undergraduates who were attracted to such a poorly compensated job were "likely to be deficient" themselves. Facing acute teacher shortages, however, the colleges often had little choice but to hire them. "We employ everybody nowadays who has two arms, two legs, and two eyes," an Ohio State dean confessed. The most urgent task was to locate and attract stronger teaching candidates, as the Truman Commission argued. "The expansion of facilities, the adjustment of curricula, and the elimination of attendance barriers, cannot guarantee an effective system of higher education in America," the commission warned. "The fundamental issue is that no program can be better than the people who operate it."[5]

That was also the rationale of the Woodrow Wilson National Fellowship, the brainchild of Princeton classicist Whitney J. Oates. A former officer in the Marines, Oates was struck by the "rare qualities of mind and heart" of the military veterans who flooded into his classrooms as World War II concluded. But he also worried that most of them would choose more lucrative careers in medicine, law, engineering, or business rather than in the field where they were most needed: college teaching. Working with Princeton's graduate dean, Oates raised money from friends and alumni to establish first-year fellowships for PhD students on the theory that "a year's exposure to academic life" might induce them to join it permanently. Next, he began to search for "young men whom he could 'save' for teaching," as a history of the Wilson fellowship recalled. Oates was able to fund four fellows the first year—including future Princeton president Robert Goheen—and 20 the next; by the third year, he had raised enough money to place fellows at other universities, not just at Princeton. The CCNY pledged $500,000 to the program in 1952, when it came under the sponsorship of the Association of American Universities; then came a vastly bigger infusion of $24.5 million from the TFAE, which funded 1,000 fellowships each year at dozens of institutions across the country. Soliciting recommendations from undergraduate advisers, officials selected fellows "as much for personality as for intellect," Whitney Oates emphasized. The goal was not just to find the men with the best grades but also to find the best grade of man.[6]

A similar purpose and spirit marked the Carnegie Teaching Fellowships at Yale, which received a CCNY grant in 1958 to hire promising undergraduate seniors to remain at the university as instructors for another year. Unlike the Wilson Fellowship, which provided scholarships for full-time graduate study, the Carnegie award was mainly for teaching: fellows instructed two sections of a college class and also took a single graduate-level course, to get a taste of PhD-level work. Critics inside and outside of Yale worried that recent college graduates would lack sufficient knowledge and maturity to teach students barely younger than themselves. Yale officials retorted that the Carnegie fellows were supervised by the professor in charge of the course they taught; after completion of their fellowship year, moreover, the vast majority of them chose to enter a PhD program. Facing the prospect of five or six years in graduate school, many top undergraduates eschewed college teaching. The Carnegie fellowship allowed them to "try it out before finally committing themselves" and—most importantly—attracted the kind of high-grade candidates that the field needed, officials said. Before World War II, as Yale president Whitney Griswold observed, colleges and universities had not made a "systematic effort . . . to recruit undergraduate talent" like businesses and other professions did. The Carnegie Teaching Fellowships would remedy that, recruiting what a Yale dean called "young men of brains, imagination, integrity and personality" into college teaching.[7]

Elsewhere, too, college and university officials sought to attract teaching candidates who possessed both intellectual potential and "that elusive thing called personality," as former University of Idaho president Frederick J. Kelly wrote in 1950. But too many people who were drawn to the professoriate were *only* intellects, he worried, so they lacked the genial affect and attitude that successful teaching demanded. "The dull dog who thinks only in terms of marks and attained them without much else to commend him is very likely beyond redemption," historian Dexter Perkins warned, in his 1956 presidential address to the American Historical Association. "We need to think more of the total personality and less of the score sheet and the aptitude test in selecting and encouraging our graduate students." According to a 1953 study of college teaching, faculty lounges were "filled with well-meaning but often dull and routine people." So the profession tended to attract students of similarly lackluster temperaments, instead of people who could seize the undergraduate imagination. "The college teacher . . . must be the right kind of person himself before he can deal with persons," a UCLA dean wrote. "It is a lot more important to get the personality with not too many brains than to get brains and no personality." But the more that officials emphasized personal qualities as the key to good college teaching, the less it seemed amenable to improvement and change. If teaching "involves problems of personality," several Harvard faculty members wrote, then "effective teaching cannot be taught to the apprentice college teacher."[8]

Preparing the New College Teacher

But other observers rejected the idea that "teachers are born, not made," as a University of Chicago faculty committee noted. Instead, it claimed that "teachers are made, but are now being made badly." Here the committee echoed Harry Truman's presidential commission, which combined its call for recruiting better teaching candidates with a pointed warning about their inadequate training for the job. "The most conspicuous weakness of the current graduate programs is the failure to provide potential faculty members with the basic skills and the art necessary to impart knowledge to others," the commission declared. "College teaching is the only major learned profession for which there does not exist a well-defined program of preparation directed towards developing the skills which it is essential for the practitioner to possess." Other critics went back much further in time, quoting Brown president Francis Wayland's 1830 plea for teacher preparation: "If there be any art as the art of teaching, we must ask how it comes to pass that a man shall be considered fully qualified to exercise it without a day's practice, when a similar attempt in any other art would expose him to ridicule." The problem seemed vastly more serious in the era of mass education, when millions of students were exposed to untrained teachers. To Reed College president Peter Odegard, the use of "poorly qualified instructors" in higher education was "so widespread as to constitute an academic scandal." University of Minnesota education professor Ruth Eckert went even further, deeming it a betrayal of democracy. Student enrollment was already 50 percent higher than it was before World War II, as Eckert highlighted in 1947, but colleges and universities had done little to prepare faculty to teach the new faces in their midst. "The utter urgency of education in this atomic age should force every graduate faculty to re-examine the training provided for prospective college teachers," Eckert implored.[9]

Some observers called for new graduate degrees in college teaching, which would theoretically supply future faculty with the instructional skills and practice that the PhD had failed to provide. It would also pave a new route into academia for people who wanted to be teachers, rather than researchers. As Johns Hopkins historian Sidney Painter argued, PhD programs wasted untold millions trying to make "productive scholars" out of "men who will never produce." Better to create a new degree for those interested primarily in instruction, who would spend their careers spreading knowledge instead of adding to it. By 1949, 9 of 97 graduate schools responding to a survey had established separate PhD tracks or degrees for future college teachers. At Harvard, a new PhD in social science required study in at least three separate departments, as well as a thesis "which may be interpretive rather than investigative," as one observer wrote; the implicit goal was to prepare graduates to teach in any of their selected fields, whether they did research in these areas or not. Michigan State University was more direct in its approach, establishing a "Doctor of Philosophy for College Teachers" that allowed students to choose a broad area of study—biological, physical, or social sciences—but limited their coursework in any single department to half of their total credits. That would guard against "narrow specialization" among students, who also participated in a seminar on higher education and taught an undergraduate class under supervision of a faculty member. The best-known college teaching degree was the doctor of social sciences at Syracuse University, which started the program with a grant from the CCNY in 1945. With the impending establishment of the State University of New York system, Syracuse president William Tolley realized that there would be a large market for college teachers. But institutions were not turning out enough PhDs to meet the demand, in part because too many doctoral candidates dropped out before completing their degrees. The new degree program at Syracuse would help close the gap, as Tolley argued. It mandated 30 hours of study in one social science—and 18 in two others—along with a course entitled "The Teaching of Social Science in Higher Education" and a supervised teaching stint. There was no required dissertation, however, so students starting the degree were more likely to finish it.[10]

But most other universities that considered such degrees rejected them, sensing—correctly—that employers would favor regular doctorates over any new teaching-focused credential. At Berkeley, for example, the chemistry department declined a proposed degree in the teaching of the subject "because the colleges do not want to accept anything less but a Ph.D.," as one official wrote. The president of Wheeling College, a Catholic institution in West Virginia, likewise dismissed new "crash-program doctorates," noting "in all reverence"—and with tongue in cheek—that the PhD remained "an outward sign of inward grace" across higher education. In an interview with University of Chicago social scientist Bernard Berelson, prominent historian Richard Hofstadter admitted that the doctorate was "not functional to what was done later" because most recipients did little research after graduate school. But "it is un-American to accept status differentiations that exist anyway," Hofstadter warned, so few universities were likely to create separate teaching and research degrees. Following a two-year study of graduate education commissioned by the CCNY, Berelson came to the same conclusion: the PhD was "still champion," and no other degree could unseat it. "Blame it on institutional vanity," Berelson wrote, "or on the fact that those who set the requirements are themselves products of the system—but there it is." The new teaching degrees would never provide a "true doorway into respectable academic society," Allegheny College president Louis Benezet confirmed. So the only viable way to improve college teaching was to "keep working on the Ph.D. itself," he urged.[11]

Many universities did exactly that, enhancing the teaching-related dimensions of doctoral training during these years. The University of Chicago took the lead, using several grants from the CCNY to "prepare holders of the doctors degree for teaching without impairing their training for research," as a dean somewhat defensively announced. Up to 50 PhD students attended a seminar on college instruction and taught under the supervision of professors "who have had marked success as undergraduate teachers," university officials noted. With assistance from Carnegie, likewise, the University of Oregon designated several PhD students as "Fellows in College Teaching," who supplemented their regular doctoral coursework with "special preparation" for classroom instruction. Vanderbilt established a "Program for the Preparation of College Teachers," using funds from the TFAE to give interested PhD students another year of graduate school to focus on teaching; by 1959, one-quarter of doctoral students at the university had elected to do so. Meanwhile, dozens of universities created courses and other activities aimed at enhancing undergraduate instruction. As early as 1949, a federal survey found, 52 graduate schools offered "courses in professional education for prospective college teachers" and 34 provided "workshops devoted to the problems of college teaching." The most popular class on the subject was held at Cornell, where it enrolled 160 graduate students; topics included theories of learning, ability differences, and grading. The University of Michigan offered a course on "current problems in higher education," taught jointly by the deans of the schools of education and of arts and sciences. Several departments at Michigan also provided methods classes, focused on teaching in their respective disciplines.[12]

Knowing where their bread was buttered, however, most PhD students eschewed these classes. Nor did many attend noncredit courses and workshops about teaching, which also proliferated in these years. At the University of Chicago, the handful of graduate students who came to noncredit seminars on teaching did not do the assigned reading beforehand. At Harvard and Radcliffe, which offered a joint noncredit course on teaching, faculty speakers reminded participants that their academic stars would rise or fall depending on publications rather than pedagogy. After providing several pointers for successful instruction, Harvard biologist Kenneth Thimann stressed that "the young teacher must always keep in mind the importance of doing individual research which is essential to his career," which was surely one lesson that PhD students had already learned. At another session, Thimann urged students to get as much teaching experience as they could while they were still in graduate school. He told the story of an American medical officer stationed in Japan, where he diagnosed a soldier in his unit with appendicitis. Having never performed the requisite operation, he captured a dog wandering near his base and removed its appendix; after that, "he was ready to operate on the man." Similarly, he said, PhD students should experiment on undergraduates to prepare themselves for teaching jobs down the road. These metaphors spoke volumes about the low status of teaching—and of teaching assistantships—at Harvard, where a 1960 survey found that the strongest doctoral students avoided TA opportunities in favor of research-related ones. Although graduate schools were surely attempting to "leaven the highly specialized loaf" of PhD training with instruction about teaching, as Colgate president Everett Case observed, most graduate students turned a blind eye to that effort. Anyone could see that research mattered and teaching did not.[13]

Here the students were surely influenced by their own professors, who roundly ridiculed new campaigns to address teaching as "high-schoolish" or—worst of all—as "educationist." The latter term conjured schools of education, which had occupied the lowest rung on the academic status ladder since the 1920s or earlier. But their reputation descended even further during the white-hot years of the Cold War, when journalistic exposés of K–12 education suggested that "Johnny Couldn't Read" and—even worse—that he was falling behind his Soviet counterpart. Many Americans blamed ed schools, which allegedly trained future teachers in "life adjustment" and other anti-intellectual bromides while forsaking the rigors of the disciplines they would actually instruct. Courses and workshops about college teaching—many of which were designed and taught in schools of education—would repeat and reinforce these transgressions, critics worried, afflicting graduate schools with the same "inflation of the obvious" that characterized education courses for K–12 teachers. Schools of education "bear the responsibility for passing on the poorly prepared students" who became primary and secondary teachers, one professor complained, neglecting any role that poor college instruction might have played in this process. Now they aimed to stick their noses into college teaching as well, which was the surest route to debasing it. "I get a little horrified at the thought that we might embark upon such an institutionalization of the teaching profession as we have already had in secondary schools," New School president Bryn Hovde warned. Many students concurred, especially if they had been exposed to education courses themselves. Addressing the American Council on Education's Committee on College Teaching in 1952, a student described her 20 hours of "professional education courses" as a "waste of time." She implored the group not to visit such classes upon future college teachers, eliciting applause from the mostly friendly audience.[14]

Only education faculty demurred, rising in defense of their beleaguered profession. "Are we to assume that useful insights into the nature of students, the ways of presenting material, and the like cannot be taught?" retorted Walter E. Hager, president of Wilson Teachers College in Washington, DC. Six years later, at an ACE conference on the preparation of college teachers, the handful of education school faculty and officials again found themselves under fire. But after listening to several hours of invective from disciplinary scholars, each casting aspersions on education schools and courses, Ohio State College of Education dean Donald P. Cottrell had enough. "The line of argument into which we are falling here is fatal," Cottrell intoned. "The business of the college teacher is not exclusively with his subject. I know I am taking a terrible chance here because somebody will say, 'You are just a methods man who doesn't know what he is talking about.' But there *is* such a subject as education." To teach well, Cottrell insisted, college teachers needed to know about that subject, as well as whatever discipline they instructed. Some university officials gamely tried to forge compromises between "subject-matterists and educationists," as one University of Chicago dean noted. But it was slow going because stereotypes on each side were so deeply entrenched, as Allegheny College president Louis Benezet explained. "We will view with alarm the encroachments of the educationists, who would reduce graduate school curriculums to a series of courses on How to Teach History of Physics to Sophomores in Colleges Over One Thousand Students West of the Alleghenies," Benezet quipped. "A few then among us will venture to suggest that perhaps subject matter people have a few skeletons of their own, in the dry-bones closets of doctoral research." It was always easier to caricature your enemy than to reflect on how you might have contributed to the conflict.[15]

Supervision and Evaluation: The Ongoing Struggle

Likewise, employers of new faculty members rarely owned up to their own responsibilities in readying young hires for the classroom. "To blame our slowness in preparing college teachers wholly on the resistance of the graduate school, has become a bit of academic buck-passing," Benezet cautioned. "Is our own house in order?" The answer was simple: no. Thanks to the TFAE, to be sure, several colleges developed formal mentoring programs that paired new professors with "older and more experienced members of our faculty," as an Amherst dean wrote; in Southern California, seven liberal arts institutions created a joint seminar to help newly hired professors become "more broadly-trained college teachers"; and at Rutgers, faculty members with less than five years' experience were invited to join PhD students in a semester-long course on undergraduate instruction. For the most part, however, the institutions that hired new teachers did little to assist them in learning how to teach. "The college faculty has failed even worse than the graduate faculty in its job of helping the teacher to improve," Carnegie president O. C. Carmichael complained. "It is little short of inexcusable that we have no really systematic way of helping the young teacher get oriented in his task." Concluding his study on graduate school training, which questioned whether PhD programs could improve the preparation of college teachers, Bernard Berelson urged the colleges to pick up the slack; in this scenario, Berelson imagined, graduate schools would "train in *what* to teach" and "the first employing institution" would help novices learn how to teach it. Likewise, a University of Michigan dean said that employers should "intern the product" rather than relying on graduate schools to "produce the finished teacher."[16]

But that was also unlikely, as many observers noted, so long as the colleges themselves lacked real systems of faculty supervision. The problem was not simply that new professors were not coached or evaluated; *no* professors were coached or evaluated, at least not in a rigorous or systematic fashion. "Supervision of teaching at the college level has always been a touchy subject," a 1956 study of teaching at Miami University surmised, "and one which normally is solved by college administrators through the 'avoidance technique.'" Hiring and promotion letters routinely stated that "the individual is a good or excellent teacher" without presenting any real evidence for the claim. ("There are no indications that any candidates are average or below average," he added. "How can they all be excellent?") Professors especially bridled at visits by colleagues or administrators to their classrooms, which they decried as a slight on their professional discretion and independence. Like the farmer who told an agricultural agent that "he already knew how to farm twice as well if he wanted to," one observer quipped, most faculty members knew that they could improve their instruction. But they interpreted "academic freedom" to mean that nobody could—or should—require them to do so. "The professor who will invite his colleagues to analyze critically his research . . . takes a different attitude about his instruction," two Penn State professors observed. "The privacy of the classroom is held to be sacred. The concept of 'academic freedom' [is] used as a blanket of defense spread over all matters."[17]

Punctuating their skepticism with quotation marks, the Penn State scholars went on to plead for "objective, analytic, systematic, and quantitative" efforts for evaluating teaching. But the handful of experiments in that direction foundered on the shoals of faculty resistance, which was even stronger than reformers imagined. At Berkeley, where Chancellor Clark Kerr had warned in a confidential 1954 memo about the poor quality of undergraduate teaching, officials proposed that department chairs rank their faculty members by teaching ability into upper, middle, and lower tiers. That would "force the gathering of evidence as to teaching competence," advocates said, and—most of all—it would "reward the good teachers and punish the poorer ones." The faculty had other ideas. To critics, the proposal was "contrary to the free spirt of universities" and carried "a 'Gestapo' connotation": it would subject professors to abuse by administrators, who were themselves unqualified to evaluate something as subjective as teaching. The only institutions that successfully implemented classroom supervision and evaluation were military academies like the Air University in Alabama, which provided an "Academic Instructor Course" to prepare Air Force officers for college and university teaching. Invited to attend the course, University of Tennessee professor Ohmer Milton was both humbled and gratified by the close critiques of his instruction that he received: he talked too quickly, said "ah" or "um" too often as he grasped for words, and so on. But he also failed to attract other faculty around the country to the Air University course, which did not "measure up so well to our standards of instructional and educational competence," as a Princeton dean brusquely wrote. For his own part, Milton took away a different—and more dejecting—lesson. "Faculty members as a group are not especially interested in improving their teaching behavior," he concluded. As the military academies demonstrated, Americans had the knowledge to improve college teaching. They simply lacked the will to do so.[18]

But even professors and administrators who shared Milton's wish to reform teaching often rejected his premise about it: despite all of the sound and fury over poor instruction, universities still lacked a real knowledge base to upgrade it. Awarded a yearlong sabbatical by the TFAE to study college teaching around the country, University of Virginia psychologist Frank Finger admitted that he could not confidently distinguish good instruction from the bad kind. "And finally a confession. I don't know what I'm talking about," Finger told an audience at Brown, ending a talk about reforming undergraduate teaching. "But I don't feel too bad about it, because nobody knows what I'm talking about." Likewise, Northwestern dean Moody E. Prior dampened the mood at a conference on college instruction by questioning whether universities knew enough to change it. "While the group has been talking about 'more effective teaching' . . . it has not clarified what is intended by this term," he warned. "What is good teaching?" If universities could assess "the outcomes of instruction," former University of Idaho president Frederick J. Kelly replied, they could answer the question; in the absence of such data, however, it remained an open one. "It is difficult to determine good teaching because it is difficult to measure the effects of good teaching," concluded Bowdoin College's 1955 "Self-Study" report, conducted with a grant from the TFAE. "Moreover, teaching methods are relative; what is good for one teacher is bad for another." The problem went back to the interwar era, when the University of Minnesota produced a "five-foot shelf of books on teaching methods," as a member of its faculty quipped. Two decades later, effective teaching—like goodness or beauty—remained mainly in the eye of the beholder. "We perhaps can recognize it when we see it," the Minnesota professor observed, "but we cannot draw up a bill of particulars beforehand."[19]

Other critics came to doubt whether universities really wanted that kind of information, which threatened to expose the poor practices in their classrooms. At the University of Chicago, physiologist Ralph Gerard designed a study to compare learning outcomes among three groups of matched students: one entering his university, another attending other colleges, and a third that did not go to college at all. The goal, Gerard wrote, was not simply to evaluate his own institution's instruction but to address broader questions about college teaching: whether it can be "judged objectively," which attributes "make a good teacher," and how much teachers contributed to student development. "Only as educational hypotheses and methods are tested by their results can they be subjected to rational experimentation and progressive modification," Gerard explained. "This is the scientific way." He embarked on a 14-college tour in 1947 to enlist participants in the study, including stops at Princeton, Columbia, Yale, and Harvard, along with Bryn Mawr, Haverford, Vassar, and Smith; he also mailed invitations to several other elite schools, but almost every institution turned him down. Brown officials said their students had already been "tested to death," especially via the Graduate Record Examination; a Harvard dean worried that his faculty—accustomed to essay-style examinations—would reject the objective questions in Gerard's test; Bennington cited a "manpower shortage" that would prevent the college from administering it, and so on. So the study never got off the ground, and knowledge regarding college teaching remained moribund. Writing privately two years later, Stanford higher-education professor William H. Cowley confessed that "nobody knows anything fundamental about higher educational teaching." Cowley did not teach a class on the subject because he did not know enough about it, he admitted. Neither did anyone else.[20]

Cold War Student Evaluations

Yet one group of people continued to insist that they *did* know how well—or how poorly—professors taught: their students. The Cold War witnessed another push for student evaluations of faculty and courses, which dated to the interwar period. The movement picked up considerable steam after World War II, spurred by rising student enrollments and especially by the large numbers of veterans in school. "Our returned service men . . . are in a restless mood," a Boston University sociologist wrote in 1947, noting their demand for student ratings of professors. "Some of them find many of us hopelessly dull." That same year, Harry Truman's presidential commission on higher education endorsed student evaluation of professors, as did the newly formed United States National Student Association, which also published a rating form that universities could adopt. As in the prewar period, some college students continued to operate their own rating systems. But the trend was moving toward officially sponsored evaluations and away from the "prankishness" that marred student-run ratings, as an Alfred University professor observed. By 1949, 59 of 408 colleges and universities replying to a survey employed student evaluations in all of their courses; two years later, in 1951, 196 of 634 institutions—over 30 percent—reported doing so. Universities borrowed liberally from each other, to save money and time. Three different institutions in Virginia used a rating sheet developed at the University of Pennsylvania, which asked students to evaluate faculty based on speech, "handling of class discussion," "ability to arouse interest in the subject," and the frequency and fairness of quizzes and tests. Bemoaning the lack of student evaluations on their own campus, student editorialists at Lincoln University—a historically black college—invoked the era's growing language of civil rights. Student ratings were "a democratic procedure," one wrote; students had the "right to criticize teachers," another added, "if they feel they are not getting as much out of a course as [they] have a right to."[21]

More commonly, though, students invoked their rights as consumers rather than as citizens: since they were shelling out money for college, the argument went, they had a right to judge its quality. "Students are not paying $500 tuition to provide a dole for research specialists," a Princeton student journal declared; regardless of a professor's "scholarly qualifications," it added, "he is not a worthy member of the Princeton faculty if he is a failure as a teacher." Likewise, parents proclaimed their status as taxpayers—and as consumers—in pleading for better instruction. "If the University is primarily interested in research and only secondarily interested in teaching, let this be known to the public so that parents can plan accordingly," a father of two students at Berkeley wrote to its chancellor, Clark Kerr, after denouncing the poor teaching they had received. Dissenters at Berkeley cited the irrepressible German professor Franz Schneider, who had championed student ratings since the 1930s. On the eve of his retirement, he collected various evaluations into an "Educational Consumers Guide" for students; he also started a campus reference bureau, which would serve as a "clearing house for educational consumers." Citing the leading business information service, Schneider imagined his bureau as "a kind of Dunn and Bradstreet" where students could "exchange information on classes and instructors." That was also the goal of the "Evaluation Service Center" at Syracuse University, which collected ratings of faculty and shared the results with them. "The guiding principle is simply the belief that the opinion of consumers is a good thing to know," one advocate explained. "The effectiveness of teaching may increase as teachers know how the consumers are reacting to their efforts."[22]

But many faculty members took issue with the metaphor, especially its implication that the buyer was always right. "There is everything to be gained and nothing to lose by finding out what effect you're having on the customers," a Brooklyn College professor acknowledged. "But as for the absolute validity of students' opinions, I am very doubtful." Most students "are really like potted plants waiting for the teacher to sprinkle them with knowledge," a colleague at the college wrote. "And then these inanimate individuals pass judgment on their teachers!" Using a gastronomic metaphor to counter the consumerist one, a University of Washington professor imagined a French chef accidentally arriving in a small midwestern American town. He cooks a wonderful meal, which "the yokel diners" douse in ketchup. Would student evaluation supporters "conclude that the chef was unworthy?" the professor asked. "Many of our students are yokels." Some professors worried that students would reward teachers who demanded little work and inflated grades; somewhat contradictorily, others warned that students would give high ratings to "drillmasters" who resembled the "grammar school pedagogues" of their youth. Still others denounced rating sheets as another form of McCarthyite "spying" in their classrooms, fearing that students would downgrade professors for unorthodox political opinions. "You live in a fish bowl here; the students publish a critique of your courses, and work you over," one professor privately complained. "If they think a prof. is teaching 1912 Republicanism, or say communism, they come out and say so." Like anonymous "visitors" to their classes, another professor complained, student evaluations violated "the dignity of the profession."[23]

Most of all, professors feared that the entire scheme would subordinate faculty to the students. "It is rational than an instructor's performance should be judged by his peers, or, better, by his superiors; it is not right that it should be judged by his disciples," an angry English professor wrote. "Education, whether we like it or not, is not in most senses of the word democratic, and nothing can make it so." Yet most faculty also resisted evaluation by their colleagues or by department heads, who were often regarded as "glorified office boys rather than executives," as one University of Washington instructor noted. Unless professors conceded to some kind of peer review, St. Michael's College president Rev. Gerald E. Dupont warned, student ratings were inevitable. "No one likes to police learning—least of all a college administrator who was certainly once a teacher himself—but in these days when the eyes of the public are focused on all classrooms, the teacher should be willing to adopt the open door policy and forget the old bugaboo of supervision as a teachers' college device," Dupont urged. "If we cannot depend on student opinion . . . then let us begin to base our evaluation of good teaching [on] visitation of classrooms." There was a third option, others noted, which might be even worse. If teachers did not step up to observe each other, they might come under surveillance via a new medium of instruction: the television set. "Can CCTV [closed-circuit television] be thought of as a one-eyed spy on the professor?" a Minnesota sociologist asked. "The problem is largely of who is to be the master, who is the slave." The biggest threat to faculty autonomy lay not in students' rising voice, he added, but in the flickering screen in some of their classrooms.[24]

College Teaching on Television: Origins and Development

Like the boom in postwar student enrollment, which was sparked primarily by returning veterans, the rise of educational television at the American university had roots in the American military. College officials took note of the pervasive use of film, charts, and other audiovisual aids in the armed forces, which were "a great educational organization in themselves," one Columbia professor wrote. As Gen. George C. Marshall quipped, World War II had accelerated the development of two important weapons: the airplane bomber and the motion picture. As early as 1943, Hollywood had already supplied the federal War Department with over 10,000 training feature films and a similar number of "shorts"; according to military instructors, the films had fast-forwarded learning among millions of trainees by 25 to 35 percent. That same year, University of Minnesota dean Malcolm Willey told a Navy official that universities would have to learn from the military as well. "If the teaching aids you are developing are as significant as they appear to me to be, then certainly our methods of college instruction are going to undergo profound changes," Willey wrote, "and the institutions that do not seize upon these new teaching devices will be left behind." To be sure, most large universities had already established audiovisual departments that helped acquire and screen films, slides, and other aids. But the armed forces experience promised to revolutionize instruction altogether, Willey noted, in ways that nobody could foresee. "I am quite sure that out of this mass teaching of enlisted men there will develop some important and efficient teaching methods and devices which sooner or later the universities will have to adopt," he predicted.[25]

The most important device arrived in the early 1950s, with the mass manufacture of television sets and the surge of commercial TV stations. A third of American households had a television by the end of 1952, up from less than 1 percent in 1948; by 1960, 90 percent owned one. The explosion of this new medium seemed to set the stage for precisely the kind of pedagogical revolution that Malcolm Willey had imagined. "In 1492 Columbus launched ships to open fresh geographical horizons to the Old World," Federal Communications Commission chairman Paul A. Walker told a 1952 conference in Columbus, Ohio. "Those of you gathered here in Columbus should launch television to open fresh educational horizons to the New World." True, he admitted, educational television would cost a great deal of money to develop. But so did the little red schoolhouse, the centralized high school, and the modern university. Television was "the latest way of trying to keep pace with the onrush of progress," Walker proclaimed, and nobody wanted to be left behind. Leading educators and politicians eagerly jumped on the TV bandwagon, predicting that it would improve instruction and spread it more widely. That was especially true for higher education, where poor teaching remained a common problem. According to Johns Hopkins president Milton Eisenhower, brother of the president of the United States, television would allow colleges and universities to replace "mediocre" professors with "the greatest teachers" of history, math, science, and medicine; it would also encourage them to prepare lectures and demonstrations more carefully, lest they lose face in front of enormous audiences. California governor and future Supreme Court chief justice Earl Warren imagined a future where anyone could "sit in the quiet and comfort of his living room" and receive a college education. "It is not entirely fantastic to consider the possibility that courses given on television could even lead to a degree," Warren told his audience at a 1952 conference.[26]

Seven years later, over 100 colleges and universities were teaching roughly half a million students via television. At a single institution, Penn State, 3,700 of the school's 14,000 students were registered for one or more of 13 courses taught via closed-circuit television at its University Park campus. Other universities beamed courses on broadcast TV, which could be taken for credit (and for a fee) or simply watched by anyone who was interested. The most prominent example was *Sunrise Semester*, a slate of courses offered by New York University (NYU) over the city's local CBS affiliate starting in 1957. The first course was a comparative literature class taught by professor Floyd Zulli, who "wandered through an attractive book-lined setting"—as one reporter noted—while holding forth on Stendhal or Balzac. (He also triggered a run on New York bookstores, which quickly sold out of the assigned novels by both authors.) *Time*, *Newsweek*, and several other major media outlets devoted glowing coverage to the course, which generated a notable *New Yorker* cartoon. "There's no question in my mind," a doctor tells a weary female adult patient, in the cartoon. "You either have to give the 'Late Late Show' up or give up 'Sunrise Semester.'" To get credit, students who registered for the course had to complete two take-home tests and appear in person at the university for a final exam; they also had to submit a term paper and pay a fee of $75. *Sunrise Semester* expanded to four courses the following year, each of which drew about 100,000 viewers; that was more than the *Today Show* and also more than *Continental Classroom*, NBC's competing lineup of televised courses. Students could also attend voluntary in-person discussion sections with their TV professor on NYU's campus; if they could not get there, they could contact the instructor by letter or phone. By 1964, a year after *Sunrise Semester* joined CBS's national network, 141 stations in 49 states broadcast the program, and 43 colleges outside of the New York area offered *Sunrise Semester* courses for credit.[27]

Across the country, meanwhile, dozens of other institutions experimented with closed-circuit courses, open-access ones, or both. Many of them received assistance from the Ford Foundation, which committed nearly $25 million to educational television by 1957. Four universities in Oregon used a $200,000 grant from the Ford-built TFAE to create a closed-circuit consortium, allowing classes offered at one of the institutions to be broadcast to the other three. Stephens College employed its own TFAE grant to develop a required liberal arts "teleclass," *Ideas and Living Today*, featuring well-known professors from around the country in televised lectures; after each lecture, students would meet for discussion with Stephens faculty in 50 small groups scattered around the campus. Starting in 1957, the University of Miami telecast daily lectures in accounting, psychology, and chemistry into 10 CCTV classrooms of 35 students each; four years later it opened an octagonal state-of-the-art "Audio-Visual Building," featuring eight 300-seat classrooms arranged like pie pieces around a central projection room. Los Angeles City College held conventional classes in its TV studio and beamed them into other classrooms on campus, where "monitor teachers" took questions from the students and broadcast them back to the studio lecturer. "The closer the contact between the TV lecturer and the student, the better," explained University of Detroit professor Eugene Grewe, who directed the school's closed-circuit classes in freshman English. "'Remotes' [on] national networks are simply too much removed from the students and from administrative control of the institution accepting the work for credit."[28]

Here Grewe took issue with the burgeoning trend toward broadcast television courses, which were already offered by 35 universities in 1955. The number spiked in the late 1950s with the expansion of *Continental Classroom*, which was broadcast by 155 NBC stations by 1960. Participating colleges charged their own fees, gave and graded their own examinations (although they could also elect to use the tests provided by *Continental Classroom*), and set their own requirements regarding homework assignments, face-to-face meetings with the instructor, and so on. Other institutions broadcast their own courses, which proved especially popular among nontraditional students. At Chicago City Junior College (CCJC), which broadcast 25 hours per week from the city's educational television station, 27,000 students registered for TV courses between 1957 and 1963; only 10 percent of them were between 18 and 22, the age of traditional college students, and 40 percent listed themselves as "housewives." In 1957, 22 television students at CCJC were inmates of the State Reformatory for Women; three years later, the college held a special graduation ceremony for five male TV students at the Stateville Penitentiary. Not surprisingly, the vast majority of people who tuned in to open-access TV classes did not take them for credit: according to some estimates, indeed, just 1 out of 1,000 viewers of a televised course actually registered for it. "The very fact that a presentation bears the credit label seems in itself to attract a certain audience not at all concerned with earning credit," a 1955 report found, "but interested because the program content bears this academic stamp of approval." Students who did take a TV course for credit were more likely to complete it if they had met in person with the instructor or participated in telephone office hours, a standard practice at many institutions. But many TV students were reluctant to phone their professors—especially if that involved a costly long-distance call—and most could not miss work to come to campus. Nor could their professor be reasonably expected to develop a real, face-to-face rapport with them, as two CCJC evaluators wrote. "He moves into a new kind of teacher-pupil relationship—the impersonal, yet intimate relationship of TV," they observed, describing the modern-day "televised professor."[29]

TV, Pro and Con

The last comment pointed to a central debate in Cold War higher education: did television make education more "personal," or less so? Just as new recruitment programs would bring better personalities into the classroom, TV advocates argued, television would transmit them onto a vastly bigger stage. Indeed, one UCLA official enthused that television was "the most efficient, the most economical, and the most personalized teaching method available." A single gifted teacher could instruct thousands of students at the same time— no matter where they lived—and every student would get a "front row seat." Indeed, an NYU report insisted that TV teaching was *more* personal than regular classroom instruction because the teacher became more "vivid" on the screen. "Clearly, a televised lecture can 'bring the instructor close' even when the students have no personal contact with the televised lecturer," the report stated. Some students in TV classes concurred. "You have a more personal feeling of relationship to the instructor than you would have from the rear row seats of an overcrowded room," a student participating in NYU's *Sunrise Semester* insisted. Another *Sunrise Semester* student waxed more poetically, praising literature professor Floyd Zulli as he would a longtime mentor. "I do get up every week-day morning at 6:15, perform the essential ablutions; genuflect before the electronic image of Prof. Zulli," he wrote. "Gone are the ivy-covered towers; the classrooms overcrowded. . . . Instead of these we will have individual teaching (Just as Professor is so kind as to teach me individually) done by the select best." Many college teachers "lack the spark of teaching talent," he added, so students had to suffer through "the hesitant, the fumbling, the mealy-mouthed." Thanks to television, however, "the unquestioned great in wisdom and teaching capacity will be available to everyone." He did not know Professor Zulli personally, of course, but that did not matter. He was exposed to Zulli's personality, and that was enough.[30]

Likewise, many professors who taught a televised course raved about the experience. Zulli clearly enjoyed performing on *Sunrise Semester*, where he used his "native histrionic talent"—as the show's producer observed—to bond with his audience. ("Whether you like it or not, we are in show business," the producer added. "If we put on a scientist, a professor or a showgirl, the rapport between viewer and speaker is extremely important.") After teaching a TV course that was broadcast in St. Louis, Washington University philosopher Huston Smith noticed that he was recognized by strangers on the street and even by the electrician working at his house. Teaching the TV course "was the most exhilarating experience of my life," Smith wrote, calculating that his weekly audience of 100,000 was 10 times greater than the number of students he could otherwise have taught across a 50-year career. Other TV professors said that they taught better on television, which required them to prepare more extensively; in that sense, as NYU television teacher Hollis Cooley observed, TV had the potential to improve conventional classes as well. "The necessity of tightening one's lectures, avoiding careless impromptu remarks, and seeking out desirable visual aids may lead to greater care and sounder performance in all teaching thereafter," Cooley wrote. Before taping a lecture in the statistics course that he co-taught for *Continental Classroom*, Harvard professor Frederick Mosteller practiced it at home—"boring his wife and children," he admitted—and then did three rehearsals at the NBC studio; although each class was just 30 minutes long, producing one took half a day. Mosteller learned to speak more slowly and to limit his writing on the blackboard, which helped improve his in-person classes as well. But his TV course reached 5,000 for-credit students at 325 different institutions, as well as untold other viewers, who sent him hundreds of letters with questions about his lectures, suggestions for improving them, and more. "In all this, I see no threat to the teacher," Mosteller concluded. "I see an opportunity to come closer to [Mark] Hopkins' idea of personal attention—one student, one teacher, one log."[31]

Other faculty members were highly dubious about television, dismissing Mosteller's allusion as a distortion of the past as well as of the present. "Mark Hopkins on one end of a log and a student on the other has given place to discussion of a latter day Mark Hopkins and the entire resources of a television studio on one end of a coaxial cable and thousands of students on the other," a skeptical professor jibed. In fact, critics claimed, television placed new barriers between teachers and students: already separated by the anonymity of large lecture classes, they became even more estranged when the professor appeared only on TV. "Although our staff frequently could project them-selves from the screen," a chemist at Penn State wrote, "I believe it would re-quire a George Gobel capacity and staging staff to achieve at each perfor-mance the audience contact which one normally has in the average university lecture hall." Like Gobel, a leading comedian of the era, a handful of profes-sors had the charisma and dramatic skill to hold students' attention on tele-vision. But most of them could not, even with careful stage instructions from campus TV studio directors. "Relax," a University of Missouri "Guide for Tele-vision Teachers" urged. "Try to be yourself. Remember that the TV camera projects your natural personality best, and the more relaxed and natural you are, the better you will reach your viewers." Male teachers should wear "con-servative" ties, advisers added, while women should avoid necklines or hem-lines that might "cause discomfort or embarrassment" if they leaned over a counter or sat in a low chair. As much as the directors told faculty to "be themselves," their instructions bespoke the opposite: professors were in a new play now, and they needed to act the part.[32]

That kind of advice raised the specter of "entertainment," a long-standing taboo among American professors. Going back to the Progressive Era, critics had warned about glib teachers who amused students without really educat-ing them. Television would magnify that danger, providing a new and much bigger stage for "the Billy Phelps type, who can attract half the student body to his humorous, anecdotal lectures on *the Novel*—meaning of course pop novels," Temple professor Earnest Earnest warned. Here he alluded to William Phelps, the legendary Yale literature professor who was beloved by his students—for his dramatic lectures and winsome personality—but derided by colleagues for the same reasons. Whereas TV enthusiasts imagined the new medium "multiplying a good man" by projecting the best teachers to the masses, as University of Louisville president Philip G. Davidson wrote, doom-sayers predicted the opposite: it would create more opportunities for "show-men," and less for everyone else. "It is not difficult to foresee in a faculty the development of a small group of TV 'personalities' and a proletariat of section hands and paper graders," Earnest worried. The "personality" of the television teacher was a chimera, another critic warned, manufactured by an industry designed to sell people products they neither wanted nor needed. If TV took over higher education, it might replace many regular teachers altogether. "What does the future hold for the professor who is not photogenic or a 'TV personality?'" a University of Chicago professor asked. Often promoted as an antidote to the college teacher shortage, TV would create a new scarcity by eliminating teachers.[33]

Other faculty feared that televised instruction would further erode their precarious freedom in the classroom. Already, lecture halls were monitored by student watchdog groups and anonymous "visitors"; television would introduce a new spy in the form of "Cyclops, the one-eyed mechanical man," as one skeptic warned. "Not only is the medium easily subject to censorship—most drastically by cutting off portions of a program—but programs are easily recorded and the 'evidence' against a professor inescapably marshalled," a Bryn Mawr literature professor feared. "I for one would be much more careful about what I said for recording than what I said in the unrecorded freedom of a classroom." At the University of Oklahoma, a government professor admitted that he self-censored when he taught on television. "Knowledge of the kind of society I live in told me I could not say on T.V. (open circuit) what I might in a college classroom," he wrote. After he criticized the role of Christian missionaries during a televised course on African culture, Michigan State professor Ram Desai faced blowback from "'public relation' minded but ignorant administrators," as he privately wrote. At Oregon State, finally, English professor H. C. Childs admitted that his literature course—beamed to four campuses, as part of the state's closed-circuit consortium—was "a source of deception," because of the ways he disguised "the whole truth" on TV. "Literature . . . deals with controversial questions in economics, politics, religion, and sexual conduct," Childs wrote. "Even the ordinary classroom instructor must try to avoid such open discussion in these areas as will unduly shock his students." On television, that imperative was still greater. "Because of the heterogeneous audience, the lecturer must avoid even mildly shocking his listeners," Childs explained. "He must not discuss certain topics and he may not even assign a large proportion of the literature written in the 20th century."[34]

Students, meanwhile, remained sharply divided about educational television. Nontraditional students tended to favor the medium for its convenience, which allowed them to earn college credit—along with higher degrees and salaries—without the hassle of going to class. They could also avoid the rah-rah aspects of the collegiate "social experience," as one *Sunrise Semester* viewer noted, which held out little interest for older students anyhow. Regular on-campus students were typically more critical of televised instruction, because they "missed the discussion possibilities of the group and the more personal contact with the instructor," as an NYU official observed. Many students complained that they could not concentrate while looking at a screen, which engendered passivity and laziness. "When I watch TV, I expect it to entertain me," an Ohio University student wrote. "Unless a real classroom situation is achieved, I will take off my shoes and relax, and not learn a thing." Others dismissed the entire effort as a scam designed to "cut costs and increase profits at the expense of adequate instruction," as a Miami of Ohio student raged. A second student said he would have chosen a different college if he had known that Miami used television to teach; a third called his television course a waste of his time and money. "The business of learning demanded that we embrace the electronic goddess and that we voice extravagant claims of her miraculous powers," a former NYU TA recalled. "Never mind that the students went to sleep. Never mind if this experiment destroyed rapport between teacher and student. Every emperor chooses the clothes with which to cover his nudity."[35]

Teaching Machines: Beyond Personality?

To still other reformers in the Cold War era, the goal was to free students *from* teachers. That was the mantra of Harvard psychologist B. F. Skinner, who argued that most of the teaching enterprise—at every level—was itself a kind of empire without clothes. His skepticism dated to a 1953 Father's Day visit to his daughter's elementary school, where he saw that her teacher was violating "two fundamental principles" of education: she did not reinforce correct answers immediately, and she did not allow students to proceed at their own pace. The more advanced students were bored, and the less skilled were struggling to keep up. "How could a teacher reinforce the behavior of each of 20 or 30 students at the right time and on the material for which he or she was just then ready?" Skinner asked. Later that afternoon, two graduate students arrived early for a lecture by Skinner and found him sitting in an empty auditorium, cutting up manila folders. "I'm making a model of a teaching machine," Skinner announced. The concept dated to the 1920s, when Ohio State psychologist Sidney Pressey invented a machine that would correct students' wrong answers and reward them for right ones. The experiment foundered during the Great Depression, when massive teacher unemployment dampened the demand for a labor-saving device: its manufacturer withdrew Pressey's machine from sale, and his personal life took several sharp turns as well. (His wife divorced him, and then he married her best friend.) To insulate his own teaching machine from the fickleness of the market, Skinner looked to a steadier source of support: the foundation world. Using a grant from the TFAE's new committee on "effective utilization of faculty resources," Skinner developed 10 box-like machines that exposed students to course material via disks containing small items called "frames." Students would respond to questions in each frame and then immediately learn whether they were right or not.[36]

Whether that promoted real learning and what that really meant were different questions altogether. At times, Skinner and his champions argued that his machine placed more responsibility on students; at others, that it would provide an "automated individual tutor" for each of them; and at still other times, that the device would free professors from routine drudgery and allow *them* to engage in more substantive, one-on-one teaching. Students in Skinner's introductory class in behavioral psychology became the first "experimental organism" (as he quipped) for his teaching machine, which supplemented his lectures and the assigned readings. As Skinner might have put it, the experiment was inconclusive. Describing the teaching machines for Harvard's student-run *Confidential Guide*, one student proclaimed that "THEY WORK"; another called them "fascinating at first, but somewhat of a drag after a while." Some students binge-watched Skinner's entire set of 48 disks in two days, while one completed 31 disks in a single marathon session. According to Skinner's own survey of his class, 32 percent of students said they "learned much more on the machine"—compared to studying the course textbook—and 46 percent said they "learned somewhat more." They continued to denounce Skinner's disjointed and confusing lectures, which belied his claim that teaching machines would improve "regular" instruction; they also condemned him for failing to return their midterm exams, which flouted his own emphasis on reinforcement as the key to learning. But students sensed that his partially automated course reflected the wave of the future, for good or ill. "B. F. Skinner, the brains behind teaching machines, is—to students and to colleagues—either a saint or a sinner," the *Confidential Guide* declared. "Anyway, he is a man who will probably have a revolutionary effect on education before long."[37]

Similar claims dotted triumphal press accounts of teaching machines and "programmed learning," rivaling the breathless reports that had greeted educational television a decade earlier. *Time* magazine declared that programmed learning "promises the first real innovation in teaching" since movable type; *Science Digest* went even further, predicting that teaching machines would trigger "the greatest educational revolution in history." One of the earliest adapters was Hamilton College, B. F. Skinner's alma mater, which received a TFAE grant to modify Skinner's machine for the teaching of philosophy. The machine aimed "not to take the teacher out of teaching, but to put the learning in the learner," Hamilton philosopher John Blyth explained: providing opportunities to "practice" concepts outside of class, it would give students more responsibility for their own education. Earlham College used a TFAE grant to develop programmed instruction in statistics, genetics, music, and Russian; eventually, as one official told a visitor, "the entire campus" would adopt it. Hollins College in Virginia received a generous gift from the CCNY to teach math and foreign languages via teaching machines at the college and at area high schools. In a phone conversation with Hollins officials, a delighted B. F. Skinner predicted that "automated teaching will sweep the country in the next few years" and that Carnegie's assistance to it "will make the Ford Foundation's support of television look SICK." Actually, as a community college teacher in Philadelphia claimed, the revolution had already arrived. "Everything these days is introduced as SKINNERIAN," she told B. F. Skinner, after corresponding with officials at Hamilton and Earlham about teaching machines. "You have really turned psychology inside out, upside down!"[38]

But actual teaching practices at most colleges remained little affected by the Skinnerian revolution, much to the chagrin of its eager vanguard. Part of the reason lay in the mixed research on programmed learning, which never demonstrated the gains that advocates had predicted. Thanks to grants from the federal government and various foundations, programmed learning and teaching machines received enormous attention from researchers: one educator in 1964 counted 190 different studies since 1954, with 165 of them published since 1959. As in the case of research on television, however, most studies showed little or no increase in learning when teaching machines were employed. To some supporters, even the null hypothesis argued in favor of the new technologies: since his institution's own data showed that students learned about the same amount in televised and conventional classes, one University of Alabama professor asked, why not use TV and save money on teachers? The answer lay in another set of studies, emerging from opinion research, which revealed a strong preference among students and faculty alike for face-to-face instruction over both TV classes and programmed learning. "We should resist the substitution of television and other gadgetry for the teacher-student relationship," an educator told a 1957 conference on college teaching for Purdue University faculty. "We must resist dehumanizing the teaching and learning process to the point that it could be branded as assembly-line or machine-made education." To B. F. Skinner, the teaching machine promised to free instructors from mindless tasks; but to many professors, it reduced teaching itself to "routine mechanical operations" and the teacher to "a routine mechanic," as another observer wrote. "It's hard to believe satisfactory substitutes will ever be found for a human teacher's warmth and encouragement, worldly experience, and ability to demonstrate subtle distinctions in taste," a third critic wrote. "Was the dehumanized Brave New World really with us, I wondered. Is it 1984 already?"[39]

The writer mixed literary metaphors, combining Aldous Huxley and George Orwell. But the point was clear: teaching was a personal endeavor, and technology threatened to drain it of personality. The same national magazines that ran adulatory articles about televised and programmed learning also published paeans to famous college teachers, who were marked by their indelible individual characters. *Life* magazine devoted a full-length feature to "Great Teachers" in 1950, after asking student governments at 52 leading colleges to nominate their best instructors. One professor led his geology classes on backpacking trips; another entered his classics classes singing folk songs; a third performed an annual Christmas reading of poetry and fables. Wellesley philosopher Thomas Hayes Proctor was so cherished that students often returned to campus to have him perform their marriage ceremonies; at Northwestern, meanwhile, students launched a write-in campaign for beloved political scientist William McGovern to become a candidate for Congress. (Politely, he declined.) "The professors who earned greatest respect were those who, whatever their field and however great their ability, give of their hearts as well as their minds," *Life* surmised.[40]

To be sure, such accolades generated the same skepticism that had always greeted popular teachers. Just six years later, in fact, McGovern's own dean at Northwestern questioned whether colleges should—or could—make supposedly "superior" teachers available to more students via big lecture classes or television. "There is a point at which a mutation takes place and the superior teacher becomes the great performer," Moody E. Prior warned. "I distrust the cult of the Great Teacher as I do the cult of the Hero or The Great Man." Likewise, University of Chicago president Robert Hutchins dismissed the quest for "great personalities" in the classroom as "a formula for educational futilitarianism." But Americans believed in the power of personality in teaching, above and beyond any system for improving it; indeed, their emphasis on personality often suggested that systematic improvements were impossible. Writing to B. F. Skinner, Yale psychology department chair Claude Buxton praised Skinner's efforts to develop teaching machines and—more broadly—to augment theoretical knowledge about how learning could be reinforced.

But in the same breath, he doubted how much it would really matter. "While I think a decent theory of teaching is absolutely essential, the longer I administer as well as profess, the more I think the problem is basically one of getting the right people to take on the task of teaching," Buxton asserted. "Such people, given any opportunity for learning at all, are the ones who will shape responses and re-enforce them effectively, whether they know that type of language or not." Theory was important, to be sure, but it would always take a back seat to personality. The question was still how colleges could find or develop the right personalities, how any system could promote that, and whether the "system" itself might harm or destroy the human element at the heart of teaching.[41]

CHAPTER SEVEN

The University under Attack

College Teaching in the 1960s and 1970s

In September 1970, a presidential commission on campus unrest blamed it— in part—on poor college teaching. Appointed by Richard Nixon in June, after National Guardsmen killed four antiwar protesters at Kent State University, the commission noted that 30 percent of college campuses had witnessed "some degree of strike activity" in the wake of the Kent State killings and the US invasion of Cambodia that spring. Over 8,000 bombings or attempted bombings had been reported by colleges and universities, more than 7,000 people had been arrested in protests, and over 30 states had enacted laws to address campus disturbances. But no law was likely to quell the unrest, as the commission—chaired by former Pennsylvania governor William Scranton— pointedly warned. It urged an end to the war in Vietnam, which had done more than anything else to trigger student protests. It also demanded better training for local law enforcement officers and stronger campus security forces. Most of all, the Scranton Commission (as it became known) called upon colleges and universities to upgrade undergraduate instruction. University faculties "have become so involved in outside research that their commitment to teaching seems compromised," the commission declared. Unrest was "most prominent in the larger universities," which had "failed [students] in a larger moral sense" by subjecting them to dull classes with disengaged professors. The commission concluded that universities should establish regular evaluation of teaching, which should count more in faculty tenure decisions; they should also rely less on teaching assistants, who needed stronger training and oversight. Anything less promised yet more student unrest, a Michigan professor warned William Scranton. "Had the universities and college administrations even ten years ago given attention to able teaching (in salary or prestige) most of this wave of discontent . . . could have been avoided," he added.[1]

But other professors blamed the universities for admitting too many students, which was a formula for disappointment and disorder. As a Spanish professor at Waynesburg College told Scranton, many of the people in her classes came to Waynesburg "not because these students are 'college material,' but because they will need a college degree in order to get a job." When the college required higher standards than many students were able to attain, they indicted poor teaching; that way, they could hide their own inadequacies. Still other faculty members blamed the *decline* of academic standards, which freed up bored students for campus protest. "Faculty are allowing the University to become a 'four-year vacation,'" University of Wisconsin engineering professor Edward Obert wrote to Scranton, noting that average grades had skyrocketed even as student workload decreased. His engineering students rarely attended protests, he added, because they had "tests and homework" to engage them. "In our day there was no place on the campus for ugly girls, or for below-average students in intelligence and/or appearance, or for minority-group students, or for children from broken homes," Obert wrote President Nixon, in an angry letter he forwarded to William Scranton. "Today, not so. The ugly girl (better: the plain Jane) adopts hippy garb and the ugly boy, long hair and beard. These students, plus the embittered minority groups, then smash a few windows and presto—<u>acceptance by the group</u>." Campus unrest was less the fault of the poor teaching than of the larger culture of the university, which privileged "student rights"—including the right to protest—over student learning.[2]

To be sure, the faculty-student blame game dated to the birth of universities themselves. But it gained unprecedented strength in the 1960s and early 1970s, when the question of college teaching became linked to larger protest movements and—even more broadly—to the fate of higher education itself. To evaluate or improve college teaching, as one professor told a researcher of the subject, you had to decide what colleges were supposed to do. "<u>Why in the world do we have colleges?</u>" he asked, underlining for good measure. "That is the fundamental, radical question." Inspired by the era's civil rights and feminist campaigns, some observers replied that the first order of business was to promote equality across race and gender. Student bodies diversified significantly during the 1960s and 1970s, when new forms of federal assistance—especially government-backed loans—sparked another huge boom in enrollment. But that also generated new resentments—as Edward Obert's jaundiced missive illustrates—as well as new challenges, forcing colleges to reckon anew with their oldest dilemma: how do you adjust teaching to new students? One answer was the creation of more community colleges, which multiplied dramatically during these years; another was the revision of course requirements and grades, which were loosened to accommodate new student populations. "Everybody has a right to a vote, to a minimal wage, and it must follow, to a university education," British author Anthony Burgess wrote in a 1972 column addressed to his students at City College of New York, which had established open admissions two years earlier. "If everybody has this right, it seems reasonable to fit the crown of scholarship to the head that seeks to wear it." He probably should not have passed a student essay describing Shakespeare's Cressida as a "cock-teaser" or Ophelia as "going crazy because of her dad's being wiped out," Burgess admitted. But he did, of course, and so did many of his colleagues around the country. To meet student "needs" in the era of protest, universities sometimes denied them their greatest need of all: a rigorous education.[3]

College Students in the 1960s and 1970s

The 1960s brought millions of new faces into the American college classroom. Total undergraduate enrollment soared from 3 million in 1960 to 5 million in 1964, a two-thirds increase in just four years; it would double over the next decade, reaching 10 million in 1973. Before World War II, no American university had over 15,000 students; by 1970, there were 50 institutions of that size, and eight of them enrolled more than 30,000 students. The percentage of African Americans aged 18–24 attending college doubled from 10 to 20 percent between 1964 and 1972, spurred by court cases and laws requiring formerly segregated institutions to open their doors to nonwhites. By 1970, roughly 378,000 black students were attending predominantly white institutions. The sharpest increases occurred among female students, whose numbers quadrupled between 1958 and 1970; by the mid-1970s, they had achieved parity with men in college enrollment. Most of all, the 1960s higher-education revolution brought more working-class and lower-middle-class students into college classrooms. Thanks to the Higher Education Act (1965), over two million students received government-backed loans and grants by 1970. Four of five freshmen enrolled in community colleges, formerly known as junior colleges; with the assistance of the federal Higher Education Facilities Act (1963), one community college opened every week by the late 1960s. "In American education, the twentieth century may be known to history as the 'Century of the Community-Junior College,'" two scholars predicted.[4]

But to critics, it had already assumed a different name: the century of mediocrity. According to frustrated faculty members, the new legions of students lacked the skills and background that college learning required. The biggest challenge was at minority-serving institutions like Bronx Community College, where 70 percent of entering students could not read or write at the college level; one English professor used sixth-grade reading materials borrowed from his mother, an elementary school teacher. At every type of college, however, faculty complained about poorly prepared students. At the University of California, Berkeley, which doubled in size between 1960 and 1965, a professor noted that one-quarter of entering freshman could not identify the secretary of state and half owned fewer than 15 books at home; a Yale English professor who moved to Virginia Commonwealth University recalled that some students were "literally not literate" and that their "mental capacity was a little slow"; and at the University of Arizona, a sociologist wrote that he was "tired of babysitting intellectually inadequate marriage majors." Meanwhile, dejected professors noted that even students with the ability to succeed in college often lacked the motivation to do so. "Too many students drive through college in cars they don't need, soaking up booze they can't handle, then complaining that they can't afford the tuition," a part-time professor and father of three college students wrote. "They should have to work harder for it." Students at the University of California, Santa Barbara, refused to do the assigned reading, forcing their instructor to provide them with a "watered-down version" in class. A Princeton professor wrote that his students expected to be entertained, instead of to engage seriously with ideas. And at Harvard, a student flatly admitted that he and his peers had given up on study. "Nobody believes in work, nobody does final drafts of papers," he wrote. "Everybody's bored. A professor can't keep people interested for sixty minutes if he does a song and dance act."[5]

Other students engaged in open disrespect instead of passive resistance, which was—from the faculty's perspective—even worse. At Ithaca College, one student would not sit anywhere except the floor; his professor then refused to teach and did not resume the class until the defiant student dropped it three days later. Students around the country read magazines and newspapers in class, a time-honored way to challenge faculty authority; others wore risqué or inappropriate outfits, which allegedly distracted their peers. "To the side of me a girl in this time's fashion, bare thighs to the world," a male professor wrote, observing a colleague's class. "Every time the teacher steps before the class he has to prove himself in the face of varied and unceasing competition." Shocked by "indecent" shorts on women, University of Iowa professor Robert Caldwell barred students of both genders from wearing shorts to class; he had nothing against men wearing them, he told the student paper, but "to avoid discrimination" he "appealed to the class as a whole." When the student body president challenged the rule, Caldwell discovered he had failed to take a course prerequisite and moved to drop him from the class. "Professor Caldwell has no right to interfere with the student's individual choice of clothing," the student president wrote. "It is a personal thing, not to be institutionalized or dictated." To famed Brandeis psychologist Abraham Maslow, all of these conflicts reflected the "severe authority crisis" pervading universities and American society writ large. When he introduced a course and listed assigned readings, one student replied, "I'll read them if I want, and I won't read them if I don't want." And when Maslow corrected an incorrect statement in class, another student asked, "Who are you to tell us what is correct and what is not?"[6]

At the same time, ironically, still other professors attacked the new generation of students for being too accommodating—not too antagonistic—to authority. Blasting students for "apple-polishing" in search of better grades, education professor Sidney Simon also indicted their "rampant silence" about the "bad instruction" they received. "Where does it get you?" one student told Simon, who would later be fired by Temple University for refusing to submit letter grades for his classes. "Why should I be the one to jeopardize my grade? I'm not a martyr." At Stanford, meanwhile, William Cowley fondly remembered his own student protests at Dartmouth in the 1920s against "academic deficiencies" but found Stanford students reluctant to play that "gadfly" role. "I hope to get something started around here, but so far the students don't seem to be thinking in that groove," Cowley told a reporter in 1965. When psychology professor Alan Schoonmaker assigned two competing interpretations and asked students to evaluate them, they demanded the "right" answer; some even accused him of forsaking his teaching duties, because he was "supposed to tell them *the truth*." The problem began in the earliest years of school, as UC San Diego provost Paul Saltman claimed, when teachers imposed "educational conformity" and avoided controversial questions. Upon arriving at college, then, students aimed to please—and to succeed—rather than to critique or challenge. "The fact of the matter is that the great majority of the students in every university are just delighted that they're coping with the System," Saltman observed. "And that's enough. Their grade point average is adequate. Don't make waves. Don't question. Don't stir up intellectual ferment."[7]

Yet even Saltman's own protest-inflected language ("the System") suggested that there was more ferment about college teaching than his account allowed. Going back to the Port Huron Statement of 1962, the first salvo in a decade of student protest, author Tom Hayden indicted universities for boring and irrelevant instruction that ignored civil rights, nuclear disarmament, and the other pressing questions of the day. Colleges should "import major public issues into the curriculum" and "make debate and controversy, not dull pedantic cant, the common style for educational life," Hayden's manifesto declared. Two years later, during the Free Speech Movement at Berkeley, student leader Mario Savio blasted not just the university's repressive policies around free expression but also the poor quality of teaching in its classrooms. Drawing on a language of dissent that dated to William Cowley's generation in the 1920s, Savio denounced Berkeley as a "knowledge factory" that treated students like "raw materials"; he also invoked a more recent technological metaphor, complaining that huge impersonal classes made the contemporary student "little more than an IBM card." But how could "the System" have generated such a rich vein of student opposition, if it was as mechanistic and authoritarian as its critics claimed? In the wake of the Free Speech Movement, Berkeley historian Lawrence Levine recalled that his students became more critically involved in their learning; hardly the childish rebels or conformist drones that Abraham Maslow and Paul Saltman imagined, they transformed his classroom by questioning his theories, his assignments, and everything else. But as the war in Vietnam picked up steam, students increasingly disengaged from the classroom. In a 1970 survey, one-third of students said that the war had caused them to place less value on college education. "Everybody is fatalistic," a Harvard student dolefully admitted. "Nobody really expects to be alive in ten years."[8]

College Teachers in the 1960s and 1970s

These were also years of ferment among college professors, but for a different reason: there were not enough of them. As a 1963 report by the National Education Association noted, student enrollment had almost doubled in the prior two decades but faculty hiring had not kept pace. Hence, "the only course open to the employing officials will be to lower the standards," the report's author worried, "and thus concede the necessity for accepting a lower quality of teaching performance." The fraction of new college teachers with a PhD actually went down, from 31 percent in 1954 to 25 percent in 1963. Meanwhile, some institutions struggled to find anyone whom they could reasonably place in front of their crowded classrooms. The teacher shortage was especially acute at community colleges, where 40 percent of instructors came from the ranks of high school teachers; most of them had an MA degree and lengthy teaching experience, causing some school officials to denounce a "brain drain" from secondary schools to community colleges. (When the newly formed Harper Junior College in Illinois lured away five of his best teachers with "the greener pastures of higher salaries," the local school superintendent issued a semisatirical broadside against "Harper's Raid.") Other community colleges hired high school teachers on a part-time basis, especially in high-need fields like mathematics; in Los Angeles, for example, some math teachers taught an 8:00 a.m. class at a community college and then returned to their high schools by 9:00. At four-year universities, meanwhile, officials searched in vain for qualified applicants. The PhD was still the desired degree, as in prior years, but many schools were willing to take almost any warm body. "I don't want to employ a second-rate chemistry teacher, but what can I do?" the president of a liberal arts college in the Midwest told a reporter. "The men I would like to get are already teaching elsewhere—or they simply don't exist."[9]

As the president's gendered language illustrated, most institutions still sought male teachers. But women made important inroads into the profession during these years, powered by the feminist movement and also by federal laws and court decisions barring discrimination on the basis of sex. By 1972, when the landmark Title IX measure passed, 350 institutions holding federal contracts had already received sex discrimination complaints. Women's representation on college faculties rose to 25 percent that year, up from 18 percent in 1963. Nevertheless, enormous obstacles and prejudices remained. Many institutions sought to save money by hiring part-time "fringe-benefit" women—as they were derisively called—who were married to deans, professors, or graduate students. They constituted an "elastic labor pool," sociologist Jessie Bernard observed, and could be hired or laid off as needed; they also assumed a big fraction of the "backbreaking introductory work" of college instruction, especially English composition classes. For pioneering women on the full-time faculty, meanwhile, ridicule and exclusion were routine. One of the first female professors at Dartmouth drew curious visitors to her class on Father's Day weekend in 1961, including one student's father who asked her whether students listened to her or looked at her legs. When she presented herself at the college's Faculty Club, moreover, she was asked to leave and not return. Sixteen years later, in 1977, female professors at Dartmouth were still so rare—and so stigmatized—that a student walked into historian Mary C. Kelley's classroom and asked, incredulously, whether she was the professor. When she said yes, he replied "Not to me" and turned on his heels. Even at Vassar and Smith, all-women colleges where female faculty were commonplace, male faculty were called "professors" and women were known as "teachers."[10]

Others claimed that women would actually make *better* teachers, because of their allegedly maternal instincts. At Harvard, a female graduate student told a committee on the status of women in 1971 that the number of female professors would never increase until the university placed more emphasis on undergraduate instruction. To the committee, however, any claim about women's innate superiority as teachers would reinforce both their low academic status and the poor esteem of teaching. "We thus reject the argument that women should be recruited for the faculty because of their female personality traits, or that faculty standards should be changed *in order* to hire more women," the committee resolved. Three years later, however, a survey of incoming freshmen at the University of California, Santa Cruz, found that male and female students alike expected women professors to be "more approachable" and "less demanding" than male faculty members; however, the women were also less likely to "command respect." Three years after that, in 1977, eminent sociologist David Riesman wrote privately that female professors were, indeed, better teachers. "Most women faculty even in the liberationist era, which would lead them to deny it, are more painstaking, more supportive, more conscientious," Riesman asserted. Later associated with "second-wave" feminism, these kinds of claims were mostly scorned by the first generation of women professors. As barriers against women fell, stereotypes and generalizations about them were "disappearing like the so-called 'Uncle Tom' of yesteryear," one female professor wrote in 1972. "The hand that rocks the cradle is rocking the boat, and the campus will never be the same again," she added, putting the maternal metaphor to a different use.[11]

African American faculty members also increased during these years but remained radically underrepresented—and, in terms of degrees, less qualified—than other professors. Most of them remained concentrated in historically black colleges and universities in the South, which struggled to find and retain credentialed staff. In 1968, fewer than 1 percent of PhDs in the United States were awarded to African Americans. The handful of blacks with the doctorate or an MA often went to better-paying majority-white schools in the North, which led to charges of racial betrayal back home. "It is time that we consider what effect this is having on the colored college, where the need for academically trained faculty is growing more acute," the *Baltimore Afro-American* editorialized in 1968. "Those few who survive the system sufficiently to obtain a degree must consider using their skills for the good of the entire colored community." Assisted by the Woodrow Wilson Fellowship and the Southern Teaching Program, a nonprofit that placed graduate students and professors in black colleges, HBCUs increasingly hired whites as part-time or full-time faculty members. But that dynamic created tensions of its own. Several white teachers were fired for encouraging students to engage in civil rights protest, against the wishes of the more conservative African Americans who ran these institutions. "They seem to have the idea that they came down here for social revolution," one black college president complained. "Some of them must be sick, frustrated young fellows." One white instructor was attacked by black colleagues for telling students that African American styles of speech represented a legitimate dialect rather than "bad English." To the black faculty, that was a formula to "keep the colored down" instead of raising them up.[12]

The Problem of Teaching Assistants

No matter how hard they searched, most institutions could not find—or afford—enough full-time faculty to teach the millions of students flooding into American classrooms. So they increasingly turned to TAs, the "forgotten faculty"—as one sympathetic official called them—who did the dirty work of the modern American university. Colleges and universities had already hired large numbers of TAs in the late 1940s and early 1950s, to meet the big enrollment increases triggered by the G.I. Bill and the end of World War II. But the late 1950s and early 1960s saw an even sharper rise in TAs, who became the de facto answer to the college teacher shortage. The increase was especially dramatic at public universities, where the total number of TAs tripled—from 11,000 to 31,000—between 1954 and 1964. Whereas prior TAs had typically taught sections of another professor's course, the new generation of "assistants" often instructed their own. At UC Berkeley, 31 percent of all undergraduate classes in 1965 were regularly taught by TAs; by 1972, nearly 40 percent of lower-division (that is, freshman and sophomore) classes at the University of California, Los Angeles, had a TA as the sole teacher. Other TAs continued their traditional service as so-called section hands, who multiplied as well. At the University of Wisconsin, 59 percent of TAs taught sections or labs in 1968 that were connected to a course taught by a full-time professor, while one-quarter taught classes where they were the only instructor; all told, underclassmen at Wisconsin received 76 percent of their classroom teaching hours from TAs, while juniors and seniors got 44 percent of their instruction that

way. "The 'warm body problem' of putting an instructor in front of every undergraduate class was readily solved by using the teaching assistant," two
scholars surmised in 1967. America did not really have a college teacher shortage, they added; it had a college *professor* shortage, which it remedied by
making graduate students into teachers.[13]

But many of them lacked the time, skill, or will to succeed in the role. That
was a long-standing problem, but it magnified radically as the number of TAs
grew. "The discussion groups are worthless," a 1963 Yale student course evaluation declared, in a typical complaint. "Nothing pertinent ever gets said, and
the result is an hour that alternates between periods of uneasiness on the one
hand and 'talk for talk's sake' on another." Even worse were the classes where
the TA lectured, often because the regular professor was absent. Arriving to
their economics class, Yale students often left when they realized that the lecture would be delivered by a TA; others stayed "for the laughs," a course evaluation noted, "enjoying the chance to admit to each other and the jovial replacement how little they know." Most of all, students deplored TAs who used
their discussion sections to lecture. "Everyone went to it as a drudgery and did
not discuss," a University of Colorado student wrote, describing a history section. "It was more or less an added lecture." Then there were the regular
classes taught entirely by TAs, which were often the worst of all. At the University of Kentucky, TAs were assigned to teach sections of remedial math—
known colloquially as "bonehead" math—with unfortunate results for everyone involved. "Having graduate students teach enormous sections of
bonehead algebra with an inflexible syllabus is about the worst possible approach," one colleague told a math professor at Kentucky. The TAs would
surely despise the course, especially because they were not engaged in planning the class or selecting its textbook. And the poor undergraduates compelled to take the course would hate it even more.[14]

Here TAs often concurred, readily admitting their inadequate performance
as America's substitute college teachers. Recalling his Carnegie Teaching Fellowship at Yale, which allowed him to remain an extra year upon his undergraduate graduation and serve as a TA for a freshman literature class, author
Paul Monette recalled the year as a rank failure. Teaching *Heart of Darkness*
and *King Lear* to "overgrown high-school jocks who thought literature was
sissy stuff," Monette struggled in vain to convince them otherwise. "To them
it was just depressing and weird, and what did they have to know for the final?" Monette remembered. "Only four years older than they and painfully out
of my depth, I felt skewered by their boredom as they rolled their eyes at one

another, all of us counting the minutes till the bell rang." It did not help that the fellows were inevitably assigned to classes that met at 8:00 a.m. on Tuesdays, Thursdays, and Saturdays, mainly because regular faculty did not want to teach at such an early hour. (Until the early 1970s, many universities held classes six days a week.) Nor did the seminars Yale held for the fellows provide much practical advice or insight about how to lead discussions, how to interact with students, or any other dimensions of teaching; instead, they were devoted to professional academic concerns like publishing and even campus parking. But the teaching fellows at Yale had it easy compared to most TAs around the country, who often had to balance full-time graduate study with two, three, or even four classes that they taught. Historian Franklin Knight recalled routinely staying up all night to prepare for a class and then teaching it at 8:00 a.m. the next morning. "Having studied slavery, I was experiencing it," quipped Knight, a historian of the Caribbean world. His mentors helped him become a good historian, Knight added, but "developing the skills of a good teacher was a solitary assignment."[15]

Elsewhere, too, TAs reported that they received little or no training or supervision for teaching. Some TAs received their class assignments just a few hours before the term started and often in a subject outside their field of study, which forced them to scramble simply to read and understand the course material. Most of them met rarely if at all with the course professor, who—like everyone else—seemed content to let them sink or swim. A 1968 survey of TAs at the University of Wisconsin found that only 15 percent of them felt "very clear" about their duties and responsibilities before they started teaching; fewer than a third of the TAs said they had been observed in class while teaching, although 75 percent said they would welcome such oversight. Most of them also reported that they spent much more time in their teaching duties than the allotted hours their fellowships required. Hugely overworked and underpaid, 1,000 of Wisconsin's 1,450 TAs went on strike in the spring of 1970. The strike settled after 24 days, when the university agreed to provide a modicum of job security for the TAs by guaranteeing four years of support. Shortly after that, however, the university also pledged to reduce its dependence on TAs by getting more professors back in the undergraduate lecture hall. That would inevitably mean larger classes, TAs warned, without the face-to-face instruction and guidance TAs provided. "TA's do a real job: a job that either wouldn't get done or else would have to be done by someone else," the union admonished.[16]

It was also done by part-time faculty, whose numbers similarly soared in the 1960s. Like TAs, they were often enlisted to teach introductory or early-morning classes that the regular faculty eschewed. Others were hired as "emergency substitutes" when professors won research grants or consultancies that took them out of the classroom. That left a growing fraction of teaching to the great army of part-timers and hangers-on who gathered in college towns across the United States, as one scholar vividly described them in 1963: "young teaching personnel awaiting advancement, older professors surviving from days when undergraduate teaching was more esteemed, women, foreigners, able but doctorless souls, mediocrities with doctorates, and others who belong to the legion of the academically disenfranchised." Two years later, a survey of 26 departments at UCLA revealed that 11 of them assigned a "significant proportion" of their instruction to "temporary, part-time, or other personnel (excepting TA's) <u>not qualified</u> for permanent or full-time appointment." The exception was important, because at least TAs were enrolled in PhD programs and had often earned an MA before that. No so for many of the part-timers, who sometimes had no credentials at all. At Bennett College, a historically black women's college in North Carolina, the business department hired the school's bookstore manager, stenographic pool supervisor, and a secretary as part-time teachers. Valley State College (now California State University, Northridge) failed to fill 86 of 156 regular positions, hiring temporary staff who "generally lack the academic credentials of full-time professors," as one official admitted in 1968. That would start to change in the mid-1970s, when shrinking student enrollments and declining government aid to higher education turned the teacher shortage into a glut. By 1976, the National Board on Graduate Education predicted that only 1 in 10 new PhDs would secure a full-time faculty job in the next decade. Panicked young scholars began to take part-time positions wherever they could, piecing together courses at different institutions. Unlike most prior part-timers, they had the right credentials. They just could not find the right job, because jobs were disappearing.[17]

Teaching the "Mass Class"

Meanwhile, no matter their job titles, most college teachers in the 1960s and 1970s had to reckon with ever-larger class sizes. The problem was especially acute at big public universities like the University of Minnesota, where 2,000 students swarmed into an introductory psychology course. In 1972, 25 percent of all undergraduate instruction at Northwestern took place in classes of 100 or more students, and 15 percent in classes of at least 200. Classes bulged at private universities too: in 1965, fewer than 15 percent of sophomore course enrollments at Cornell were in classes of 30 or less. Ostensibly offering a more intimate learning environment, even discussion sections swelled to the point that they were "too large for good teaching," a 1972 self-study committee at Yale warned. Likewise, junior colleges—which often advertised their smaller classes and more personalized instruction—often found themselves incapable of providing either. "The average instructor or teacher is unable to give the student the attention he so desperately needs," a Los Angeles community college student journalist complained in 1972. "The student has lost his 'elbow room.' He is suffocated in the influx of clamoring fellow students." At Johns Hopkins University, where freshmen spent 87 percent of their time in classes of 100 or more, one professor worried that growing class sizes were eroding the school's historic character as a research-intensive school. "Outstanding scholars come to Hopkins and stay because they can teach small classes," he wrote. "Other institutions can teach the masses, if they want to."[18]

But almost *every* institution had to teach the masses, whether it wanted to or not. The "mass class"—as it was known—became ubiquitous in this era, accompanied by its erstwhile twin: the lecture method. Lectures had risen with every prior boost in student enrollment, of course. But they peaked in the 1960s and 1970s, when gargantuan class sizes made them imperative. Students often lined up before class so they could claim a seat in overcrowded lecture halls, where bolted-down chairs with arms for taking notes spoke to the sole pedagogical activity: the teacher talked—and talked, and talked—and the student listened. That was the theory, anyhow. In practice, students daydreamed or simply slept, which became the fount of endless jokes in the mass-class era. A George Washington student described an English professor as "one of the best anesthetists around"; Princeton students called their architecture professor "unbelievably tedious" and "sleep-provoking"; students at Methodist College in North Carolina were "wont to seek shelter in the arms of Morpheus, god of sleep," as one professor quipped; and at UC Santa Cruz, students dismissed a biologist's lectures as a "supervised snoring exercise" that at least provided an extra hour of rest. "I heartily recommend his lectures for insomniacs who can't find any other way to sleep," a University of Colorado student wrote, denouncing a chemistry professor. "[He] has got to be the most boring, uninteresting, and unenthusiastic lecturer this school has ever seen."[19]

Many professors simply repeated what was in the assigned textbook. That was condescending as well as soporific, another Colorado student noted, because it assumed that "nobody could read the book." Many students chose not to, reasoning—correctly—that they would get the same information in class. "You have to admit one thing; the lectures are much more interesting if you haven't read the assignment," several Yale freshmen noted, only half-jokingly. Others flayed the poor delivery and organization of lectures, which confused and bored them at the same time. One Colorado professor showed slides that were out of order and also upside down; another talked in a constant monotone, so that "ten minutes of lecture seemed like fifty"; a third "seemed to be talking to the blackboard"; and so on. Deluged with seemingly disconnected facts, students struggled to copy them down so they could duly regurgitate them later on. A Rice student described her biology class as a "lesson in speed writing and word for word memorization," little of which stuck with her later on. "The amount of forced feeding one has to take at Rice upsets me," she added. "In some courses the professors [*sic*] ideas have to be given back verbatim. Are we computers or human beings supposedly becoming educated? Is education merely memorization?" In a 1967 survey of college freshmen, which was updated by follow-up interviews in 1971, 70 percent agreed that "much of what is taught at college is irrelevant." It was also forgettable, exiting their minds almost as soon as it entered them. At UC Santa Cruz, a geology professor flatly admitted that his course was "analogous to memorizing telephone books." When Arizona sociologist J. T. Borhek discovered that students who had already taken another one of his courses could not remember its name—or anything else about it—he invoked a more pungent metaphor. "It is at this point that we begin to suspect that we have been merely entertainers and what we thought was 'force feeding' was, judging by its products, more like an enema," he wrote.[20]

The term "entertainer" reflected the long-standing anxiety that teachers were simply amusing students, not actually educating them. But some lecturers were skilled enough to do both, students and alumni insisted. Every campus had a handful of professors who were famous for superb lectures, which mesmerized large audiences every bit as much as other teachers bored them. Yale architectural historian Vincent Scully thrilled classes of 400 or even 500, pacing up and down on the stage and gesticulating at the screen with a 12-foot pointer. On one memorable occasion, he broke the pointer in two by slamming it against the screen; on another he fell off the stage, although Scully would later insist that he had jumped. At UC Santa Cruz, legendary calculus professor Ed Landesman made 300 students think that he was speaking to each of them individually. "RAVE RAVE RAVE RAVE RAVE RAVE RAVE!!!" a student evaluation booklet exulted. "Landesman can be very convincing when he puts on his big grin, and, staring into everyone's eyes, says, 'But it's all so fun!'" a class member added. Northwestern sociologist Bernard Beck began his career in improvisational theater, which helped him hone his craft at the lectern. "The whole [teaching] event resembles most closely a Borscht Belt comedian's act," wrote Beck, a Jewish émigré to the Midwest from New York, "and it succeeds or fails in the same way an act does. It depends on my energy, my sense of being present in the room, my contact with the patrons." As an experiment, the University of Southern California even hired a professional comedy writer and a television director to help coach a professor in the lecture hall; not surprisingly, student ratings of his performances rose significantly after that. "Our objective is to enhance the dramatic style of instructors of large classes," a USC dean explained. "Style is an important human activity, and it can be learned."[21]

But most large-class lecturers lacked either the natural charisma of Vincent Scully or the dramatic training of Bernard Beck, nor could they learn how to develop it on the job. To be sure, as student reports confirmed, some professors became better lecturers as time went on. But many of them continued to feel grossly inadequate, as a plaintive poem by an anonymous UC Santa Cruz professor illustrated:

Seems like summer just began
Yet tomorrow classes start
A hundred students—me in front
Some with eager shining eyes
Many bored with sleep-filled scowls
Dozens missing what I say
Hearing it go by too fast
For most others I'm too slow
There's no challenge—just ho hum
Some walk out to show disdain
Yet I like them—sometimes love
And I wish they loved me too.

Other professors openly reviled the mass class, which frustrated them as much as it did their students. A UCLA professor told a conference that "the quality of instruction at the university level is infinitely more inept than most people realize"; at the University of California, Santa Barbara, meanwhile, another faculty member denounced taxpayers who balked at the cost of smaller classes. "So it turns out that the biggest obstacle to the most desirable conditions of learning . . . is the democratic principle that pushes us toward the education of the masses in the most efficient economic (which is to say the cheapest) way possible," he wrote. Perhaps the most sorrowful account came from Arizona's J. T. Borhek. When he started out as a college teacher, Borhek wrote, he never imagined he would become one of the "old men who drone to their students from crisp, yellow notes." Then he confronted huge classes of bored and passive students, many lacking the ability or the motivation to succeed. So he droned on, a lonely voice on a huge stage, certain that most of his words were falling on deaf ears. "In the end we all become poor teachers, or at least come to know how poor we have always been," Borhek concluded. "In the long run we get to sleep in our own lectures. Thirty years of this will kill the liveliest of men."[22]

Still other faculty members took out their frustrations on their TAs or—more commonly—on their undergraduate students. Told by his TA that students could not understand his lectures, a Berkeley professor exploded. "You can't expect me to lower myself to their level," he raged. "This isn't high school you know." For the next week he stood in front of 800 people, filling the blackboard with incomprehensible graphs and ignoring his audience. "When the students start complaining, I turn my hearing aid off," another professor declared. Others lashed out directly at the students, creating some of the most painful and angry moments in American college classrooms. At California State University, Los Angeles, a professor grabbed a book that a student was reading during class and hurled it against a wall; another screamed at students in rage when they fell asleep; and a third grabbed a female student by the arm and returned her to her seat when she tried to leave early. Others publicly demeaned students, especially when they struggled to understand the material. A UC San Diego physicist made students stand and face the class of 300 to ask a question, and then replied that he had "already covered that in lecture"; students justifiably felt "stupid" for "holding up the class," an observer wrote, and were reluctant to ask anything else. Still other faculty ran their classes like prisons, using the threat of grades to beat students into submission. "This man is a power-hungry, greedy little boy," a University of Colorado student wrote, condemning his geography professor. "He gains sadistic pleasure from bullying members of the classroom each morning." The professor failed 65 percent of the class so he could "sock it to 'em," he bragged in class. "I was once interested in attending class, but now I'm too scared to be interested," the student added.[23]

Not surprisingly, many college students around the country simply stopped going to class during these years. Part of the reason was that lectures repeated what was in the textbook, as a Yale student wrote, "so you can easily 'get by' without one of the two." Others argued that inept teachers would actually inhibit their learning, which was better done curled up with the textbook at home. "She is so confusing in class, I'm afraid to go," a George Washington student wrote, denouncing an algebra instructor. But some professors still required attendance, sparking another sharp rift with students in the 1960s. "How many absentees are intellectually creative while playing hooky?" a University of Toledo sociologist asked in 1970. "Shouldn't the protesting militant, whose vast knowledge and wise judgment prevent him from attending class, instead be present in order to enlighten his ignorant professor and unthinking classmates?" Here he took aim at students who condemned compulsory attendance on philosophical grounds, not just practical ones. Students paid for class, a Lincoln University journalist argued, so they should also have the right to decide whether to go. "If a student can cut every class and still pass the final, more power to him," an Arizona student union added. "If a student wishes to fail, no regulation is going to stop him." Indeed, it continued, attendance requirements were really a way for faculty to prevent students from voting with their feet. "When attendance is poor it is usually due to bad lectures, bad lectures, or bad lectures," the union jibed. "If a course is good, students will come. If a course is bad, they might come. If they are forced to go, they must wonder why." Even in a class on "Motivational Factors in Personality," a George Washington student wryly noted, the course's dull professor gave students little intellectual motivation to show up.[24]

Testing, Grading, and Cheating

But professors still held the ultimate power, of course, which they exerted through the oldest motivational system in education: tests and grades. A handful of teachers continued the old tradition of periodic or even daily quizzes, either in their own classes or via their TAs. A Yale engineering professor began each lecture with a quiz about the previous one; he also graded all of the quizzes the same evening, so he "can tell how well the class understands the current topics, and adjust his lectures accordingly," a student approvingly wrote. But most students were much less appreciative, denouncing quizzes as "high-schoolish" and "insulting to college students," as several George Washington students wrote. Frustrated that his students were not preparing for class, UC Santa Barbara philosopher Harry Girvetz announced that they would receive occasional quizzes on the assigned reading. But he only dared to do so because a brave colleague had already instituted the practice, overriding strong student objections. "I don't think I would have had the courage to do it initially myself because, you see, we're really terrorized by students," Girvetz admitted. "They have ways of punishing us if only by that glazed look, not to mention adverse judgments on evaluation sheets!" But most other faculty members dispensed with quizzes, which they derided as a relic of the lost days of rote instruction. By the mid-1970s quizzes had largely disappeared from professors' classes and from TA-led "recitations" and "quiz sections," which were pointedly rechristened as "discussion" sections. As one scholar argued, quizzes were a "form of coercion" designed only to compel students into doing the reading. They were "essentially regurgitational," not educational.[25]

But so was a huge amount of teaching and learning in the 1960s, thanks to the exigencies of the mass class. Faced with growing numbers of students, professors often had little choice but to design tests and other exercises that evaluated recall, not real understanding. "I have found that I cannot mark with any pretense of fairness several hundred essays in the time allotted to me, and I do not think it right to leave to inexperienced 'readers' decisions which may affect a student's whole University career," a Berkeley professor explained. "I have therefore taken to 'objective' examinations demanding factual answers, which I dislike extremely but consider less unfair than badly marked essays." Satirizing a state initiative to "increase productivity" in higher education, Western Washington University economist Erwin Mayer recounted how he had used machine-scored tests in his 200-student introductory class; they required no grading on his part and also saved students "the arduous labor of thinking and writing," he quipped. But his "conscience as a teacher eventually caught up with him," Mayer wrote, and he decided to "revert to my old low-productivity days of using essay tests." With two TAs, he sat down to grade the first of 2,000 essays (10 by each student) and quickly realized the error of his ways. "I'm obviously working dumber, not smarter," Mayer jokingly concluded. In a mass-class environment, moreover, even essay tests devolved into rote exercises that could be easily checked and graded. "By 'essay,' the teacher meant 'list' or parrot back what he said," a Colorado student wrote, critiquing his economics professor. "No particularly original thinking was called for." In almost every class, students complained, they were judged based on their ability to "memorize, memorize, memorize," a Princeton student wrote. At Southern Illinois University, even badminton and tennis courses required students to read textbooks about the sports and reiterate them on a test.[26]

Worst of all, Southern Illinois students grumbled, some of the tennis-related questions were "unclear or tricky." That was another recurring complaint among students in the mass-class era, when many ostensibly "objective" measures reflected not recall but test-taking skill, or even just luck. "The objective questions were multiple guess," wrote a Colorado psychology student.

"The questions were ambiguous and, I felt, meant to 'stump' the student. Studying or not studying produced the same grade. . . . An essay exam would be better." But essay tests also lent themselves to more subjective judgments, which often reflected the whims and biases of the TAs who read them. "I have very little confidence in the grades turned in as a result of examinations read by 20 different teaching assistants, many of them grading for the first time, in a class of a thousand," a UC Berkeley professor wrote. Students shared his skepticism, of course. "Grading leaves much to be desired," a University of Arizona student wrote, critiquing a history course. "TA's vary in how they grade, leaving students in doubt as to what is expected of them: in other words, the same problem all large courses with TA grading have." Even when faculty did their own grading, enormous variation remained. At Bennett College, as a 1968 self-study report noted, some professors gave a "disproportionate number" of high grades and others a high fraction of low ones. The college did not seem to have a shared standard, any more than other institutions did. "What *are* Western's standards, anyway?" a Western Washington professor asked. "Can we standardize human behavior so that my 'A' means the same as your 'A'?" Almost everywhere, the answer was the same: no. As a Pomona College professor cleverly surmised, grade point averages were a "precise ranking based upon imprecise data."[27]

They were also rising, at nearly every institution of higher learning in America. Grade inflation was sharpest at elite private schools like Princeton, where the number of As rose from 17 to 30 percent of all grades between 1969 and 1975; the most common grade (45 percent) was a B, marking the transition from the "Gentleman's C" to the "Lady's and Gentleman's B," as one observer wrote. Stanford simply eliminated Ds and Fs, while Brown let students withdraw from any course—at any time in the semester—to avoid a poor mark. But the same trend was apparent nationwide, where the average GPA rose nearly half a grade between 1960 and 1973; the percentage of As awarded spiked from 16 to 34 percent, while Cs declined from 37 to 21 percent. The sharpest annual increases occurred between 1968 and 1970, reflecting professors' effort to "quiet down a restive student body during the highly emotional climate of the anti-Vietnam war demonstrations," one scholar wrote; subconsciously, perhaps, professors were trying to buy off student protesters by raising their grades. Others suggested that professors were loath to fail students because that might make them eligible for the military draft, which still exempted students in good standing. "No normal academician wanted to condemn a youth to possible death in the jungles of Southeast Asia because the victim didn't have intelligence enough or self-discipline enough to pass a given course," a Stanford professor recalled.[28]

Other easy-grading professors were probably more worried about saving their own jobs, especially at less prestigious institutions that needed to keep students—and their tuition dollars—coming through the doors. "The dean's power is wrapped up in a large enrollment," noted a teacher at a junior college in Chicago, which received $7.60 from the state for every student semester hour. "He won't hear of holding students out for not keeping up with the class." At Federal City College in Washington, DC, where some students lacked even grade school academic skills, pressure from both students and officials caused teachers to inflate grades. "Let's face it, you can't flunk *everybody*," a professor underscored. "Students are politicized and know how to organize against a strict instructor, so you don't dare flunk too many. As a result, as much as you hate to, you have to lower standards." Higher-status state institutions also reduced their admission requirements during these years, in order to keep enrollments high and—in some instances—to bring in more members of under-privileged groups. "Have you not wondered how disadvantaged students with poor high-school records can (and do) 'succeed' in college?" Wisconsin engineering professor Edward Obert asked, condemning grade inflation. But grades went up for everyone—even as assigned workloads went down— because institutions were competing for students, and nobody wanted to lose them. "The University finds itself in a buyer's market. It is trying to keep the enrollment up," a faculty committee at UC Santa Barbara explained. "But in a buyer's market one must give the buyer what he wants, and our customers, the students, by and large want 'fun' courses and good grades." In a democracy, the committee glumly concluded, grade inflation was probably inevitable. "The dogma that 'all are created equal' demands that ultimately everyone have a human right to an A," it asserted. "In this manner we have achieved the ultimate triumph of democracy—equality of mediocrity."[29]

To be sure, some institutions and professors struggled valiantly—and, for the most part, in vain—to hold the line on grade inflation. Marymount, a Catholic all-female women's junior college in Virginia, welcomed "borderline, unspectacular students" but refused to lower grading standards to accommodate them. "The grade of C—unspectacular, but thoroughly respectable . . . has become king, and the grade of F fatal," one official explained; indeed, as he proudly added, 21 of 180 freshmen entering in 1960 had been "dropped for academic reasons." Chicago State University reintroduced D and F grades after a two-year hiatus, winning accolades from African American syndicated columnist William Raspberry. Too many historically black schools like Chicago State "try to achieve academic excellence by declaration," Raspberry wrote, "leaving their graduates to blame it on 'racism' when they find themselves unable to compete in the real world." At Oakland University, a new institution serving mostly commuter students in the Detroit area, one-third of the students in the entering class received a failing grade in at least one course. "They deserved it," a professor argued. "We will damn well do it again! That's how we will get better students." But after officials warned that failing too many students would deter high school counselors from sending their best candidates to the school, grades began to rise. At more competitive schools, pressure tended to come from the students themselves. A Hartwick College professor reported that many faculty members got "worn down from the constant whining and complaining of students," holding firm on grades for a while but giving up in the end; at Cornell, meanwhile, students who got straight As in high school complained of "severe psychological trauma" upon receiving a B+. "And who amongst us wishes to traumatize an undergraduate?" one professor asked.[30]

At a meeting of HBCUs in North Carolina, finally, participants blasted the "lowering of academic standards" and a connected phenomenon: the rise of academic dishonesty. To be sure, student cheating dated to the dawn of colleges themselves. But it rose steadily during these years, when half of surveyed college students admitted cheating and 90 percent said they would do so if there were no risk of getting caught. The less that students believed in universities' testing and grading procedures, one student journalist noted, the more likely the students were to flout them. To many undergraduates, indeed, true-false and multiple-choice exams were an "invitation to academic dishonesty," as one scholar noted: if the tests were illegitimate measures of knowledge or ability, why *not* attempt to cheat on them? If college itself was a kind of joke, indeed, why play by its rules at all? In four years of school, one former Berkeley student wrote, undergraduates attended 1,200–2,000 "impersonal lectures," suffered through 300 "over-sized 'discussion' meetings," and took over 100 tests. "You must cheat to keep up," he argued. "If you don't cheat you are forced to perform without time to think in depth, and consequently you must hand in papers and exams which are almost as shameful as the ones you've cheated on." Most students realized that tests were regurgitation, he added, signifying nothing about their knowledge or understanding. So they cheated in all of the time-honored ways, secreting crib sheets into exams and obtaining copies of old ones that fraternity houses kept on file. One student reportedly wrote his crib sheets on throat lozenges, downing the evidence right after he wrote down the answers on his exam.[31]

Teaching versus Research

But faculty members turned a blind eye to cheating, critics said, even when it took place right in front of their faces. All they cared about was their latest book or article, which reflected its own form of academic dishonesty: professors gave lip service to teaching but routinely neglected it in favor of research. The charge dated back to the Progressive Era but reached a new pinnacle in the 1960s, when new funding opportunities—and new competition between institutions—led many of them to reorganize as "research" enterprises. To be sure, smaller colleges still placed a larger premium on teaching than big universities did: indeed, as a Virginia newspaper noted in 1964, "the higher you go in the world of formal education, the poorer you find the quality of teaching to be." But everywhere on the academic ladder, research received more attention and teaching got less. At the State University of New York at Albany, formerly known as a teaching-centered school, one department chair punished faculty who did not publish by doubling them up in offices and saddling them with large introductory courses. Most professors needed no such incentive, knowing full well where their bread was being buttered. Even at small liberal arts colleges like Carleton, which prided themselves on teaching, "the professors have come from the prestige graduate schools and are as lecture and research oriented as their colleagues in the university," wrote University of Utah professor Kenneth Eble, after serving as a visiting professor at Carleton. In a blistering 1966 address to the American Council on Education, classicist William Arrowsmith upbraided colleges for betraying their teaching mission in favor of research. "Instead of cleaving to the Socratic pretentions and traditions, the colleges have tended instead to become petty universities," Arrowsmith thundered. "We are rapidly junking pluralism for monolithic uniformity."[32]

The change was most apparent in tenure and promotion decisions, which increasingly rested on research at nearly every type of institution. The big exception was the junior college, where teaching remained the "paramount goal" and there was no pressure to "publish or perish," as one faculty member noted. That famous piece of academic alliteration had already entered the professorial lexicon in the 1940s, when sociologist and future University of Texas president Logan Wilson—in a prescient book called *Academic Man*—noted that "situational imperatives dictate a 'publish or perish' credo within the ranks." But almost everyone had adopted the phrase by the 1960s and 1970s, in practice if not in creed. A 1965 cartoon in the *Christian Science Monitor* showed students gathered at a professor's door, which bore the sign "Out for Research." Lest anyone miss the point, the cartoon's headline drove it home: "Teach, Publish, or . . . ?" Every reader—and, more to the point, every college professor—knew how to complete the sentence. A longtime Cornell professor reflected that in prior generations a faculty member's local employer was his or her primary community. But *Homo Academicus* had reoriented around scholarly communities, which could cement reputations on a national or even global scale. Prestige lay in publications not just because they could be counted but because they carried the imprimatur of a wider, more sophisticated audience. "A professor's bread is buttered by his relationships with his field, and they are established by research," a UC Berkeley official frankly admitted in 1967. "You don't get an international reputation by giving a great course at Berkeley."[33]

Indeed, several academic observers warned that dedicated teaching could actually harm one's career: it took away time from research, and it also potentially marked a professor as a weak scholar. "I hope I never get labeled in any student or faculty evaluation as a good man with undergraduates," a junior faculty member told a senior colleague. "Until my research record is unchallengeable, I can get farther by dull teaching of undergraduates. This will at least leave open the *possibility* that my research promise may therefore be high." Even better than poor teaching was no teaching at all: if you got grant money to buy out courses, your stock rose accordingly. By corollary, a professor with a full teaching load was often seen as something of a failure, "a wall-flower who has not been asked to go dancing around on government junkets," as Columbia historian Jacques Barzun quipped. In a series of books and articles, Barzun bemoaned the "flight from teaching" in the American academy. Starting in the early 1960s, teaching was "left to those few who, having seen it, still believed, and to those others who could not 'get an offer' from elsewhere or a grant," Barzun wrote. "Since such derelicts were not directing teams of research associates in studies of current social questions, or travelling on mission to settle the problems of Appalachian poverty or Venezuelan finance, there was nothing for them to do but teach." Even at Barzun's beloved Columbia, which was proud of its undergraduate core curriculum, faculty who actually volunteered to teach in this labor-intensive sequence were dismissed as "potential failures or real suckers," as one professor admitted. Across academia, the pressure to publish—and the corresponding disincentive to teach—became the subject for macabre humor. A cartoon in the *Chronicle of Higher Education* showed Christ being led to the cross, while his disciples looked on in grief. "He was such a good teacher," the caption read. "Too bad he couldn't publish."[34]

To students, of course, it was no joke. Starting in the early 1960s, protesters blasted universities for prizing "irrelevant research"—to quote the Port Huron Statement of 1962—over undergraduate instruction. The following year, the student union at UC Berkeley resolved that "there is an overemphasis on faculty research, at the expense of good teaching, on our campus." The year after that, during the Free Speech Movement, Berkeley students targeted the "low priority accorded to teaching," as the *New York Times* reported. The critique found its way into the Scranton Commission's 1970 report on campus unrest, which noted that students attributed poor undergraduate instruction to "university reward systems biased in favor of research and publication." Student leaders in Michigan slammed their university's tenure system for neglecting teaching; at Johns Hopkins, likewise, they blasted the school's "shameful overemphasis" on research and "the relegation of teaching to a perfunctory and often ignored exercise." In course evaluations and other campus publications, meanwhile, individual students around the country decried a system that placed publication before pedagogy. "He's so wrapped up in institutes and papers that he cares nothing about his class," a Colorado student wrote, evaluating his economics professor. "Why not pay him to research, but, please, not to teach *and* research?" A student journalist at UC San Diego turned the question around: if teaching was not valued, why did she go there? "Every year, California's graduating seniors are fed the same type of UC propaganda—'the UC system offers you a quality education,'" she wrote. "We accept these untruths and come to UCSD to find out that teaching is not the top priority here but rather research is number one." The UC schools valued "publish or perish" but not "teach well or perish," a UCLA student evaluation booklet confirmed. "Again and again some of the very best teachers on this campus have perished because they did not publish," it added.[35]

Teaching, Tenure, and the Limits of Student Power

The denial of tenure to popular teachers provoked some of the most bitter protests on American campuses in the 1960s and 1970s. The first major skirmish occurred at Tufts University, which rejected philosopher Woodrow Wilson Sayre's tenure bid in 1963. The grandson of America's 28th president—and of Princeton's 13th one—Sayre was widely regarded as an excellent teacher.

He had also gained national attention for his failed attempt to climb the world's tallest mountain, which Sayre described in his 1964 book *Four against Everest*. But the Tufts provost concluded that his publication record was not sufficient for tenure, overriding the recommendation of his department chair. "We are satisfied that you have been effective in the classroom, but the promise of scholarly contribution has not materialized," a dean told Sayre. The professor appealed, arguing that his book on Everest addressed "the nature of loneliness and the nature of friendship" and should be counted as scholarship. But he also maintained that his teaching record qualified him for tenure, regardless of the merit of his research. "There is no necessarily logical connection between the ability to publish and the ability to teach," Sayre told a reporter. "Socrates, one of the world's greatest teachers, would not have been hired, let alone given tenure by a college." Two weeks later, Sayre made "the case for not publishing"—as he called it—in the Tufts student paper. "In what circumstances is scholarly publication good?" Sayre asked. "Do the students benefit? By and Large, No. The more involved the teacher is in research, the less time the teacher will have for the student." Students and their families were paying thousands of dollars to attend Tufts, Sayre added. "Haven't they the right to expect that the main focus of the faculty will be the growth and development of the student, rather than the advancement of the faculty member through publication?" he queried.[36]

Students rallied on behalf of Sayre, picketing two administration buildings with signs proclaiming "Let Teachers Teach," "Socrates Never Published," and "Publish or Perish?" Sayre later recalled that several of the protesters shaved off their beards so onlookers would not associate them with riffraff like the Free Speech Movement protesters at Berkeley. He need not have worried. Picked up by several wire services, Sayre's case became a national cause célèbre that transcended both ideological and geographic divides. The *Boston Globe* and several other New England newspapers weighed in on behalf of Sayre, casting him as a victim of a research ethos run amok. "Has the Ph.D. tradition grown so strong that Mr. Chips is no longer wanted?" the *North Adams Transcript* asked. Southern papers that criticized sit-ins and other civil rights protests congratulated students for picketing in the Sayre dispute, which the *Greensboro News* in North Carolina depicted as an "academic Dreyfus case." Echoing Sayre, the *News* linked him to an ancient Greek martyr, as well as a modern French one. "Socrates himself would have real difficulty getting tenure in many leading halls of higher learning in America today," it warned. Sayre also won a vote of confidence from the voice of the conservative establishment, the *Wall Street Journal*, which quoted his claim that research and teaching ability did not always go hand in hand. It added a jab at the federal government for wasting taxpayer dollars on useless research, which lined professors' pockets but diverted them from students.[37]

But Tufts held firm in denying Sayre tenure, buoyed by strong support from professors at his own institution and around the country. A Tufts faculty advisory committee argued that teaching alone should not merit tenure; even if it did, the committee noted, "it is not at all evident that Prof. S's teaching so outshines that of his colleagues that he deserves tenure on that basis." Around the country, meanwhile, professors argued that teaching was a "private activity" that could never be judged by colleagues in the same fashion as research; somewhat contradictorily, others questioned whether a professor who did not perform research could succeed as a teacher. Still others condemned Sayre for "agitating" student protesters, whose praise actually underscored why he should be rejected. "Show me a man who tries to make his way as 'a great teacher' without supporting scholarly activity, and in nine cases out of ten I'll show you a man whose lecture notes are yellow with age, who pampers his students and tells them mildly off-color stories instead of forcing them to challenge him, a man who is passing familiar with many things but knows nothing," a Union College professor wrote to the *Berkshire Eagle*, in response to its editorial decrying Sayre's ouster. "The saddest performers in the classroom are the campus characters who substitute personality for knowledge, who waste their substance in pursuit of shallow popularity among callow undergraduates."[38]

The *Eagle's* editorial asked how many other gifted teachers—who were "not so newsworthy as the Everest-scaling grandson of Woodrow Wilson"—had suffered the same fate as Sayre. The next year brought a new one, Yale professor Richard Bernstein. Like Sayre, Bernstein was a philosopher—and an enormously popular teacher—who was denied tenure. A wunderkind who taught his first course at Yale when he was 22, Bernstein was rejected by his department and eventually by president Kingman Brewster, who refused to overturn its judgment. Students staged a three-day vigil in front of Woodbridge Hall, which housed Brewster's office. One of their signs asked whether Socrates could get tenure, echoing the Sayre protest; another declared that "Homer was a Two-Book Man," responding to detractors who noted that Bernstein had only published two monographs. In a semihumorous act of public theater, students also dragged an actual dead horse in front of Woodbridge for passersby to kick. Forged under the banner of a new organization, Students to Oppose Publish Perish Pressure, the protest would continue for two weeks. It also sparked nationwide press coverage, which linked the scuffle at Yale to the earlier one at Tufts. "Last spring a mountain-climbing professor at Tufts University, Dr. Woodrow Wilson Sayre, lost his footing on the precipice of tenure because he had not published enough scholarly works," the *Pittsburgh Post-Gazette* wrote. "Now the ivy-clad halls of Yale University are stirred by a similar controversy involving a popular 32-year-old associate professor of philosophy, Dr. Richard J. Bernstein."[39]

Like Sayre's tenure denial, the news about Bernstein triggered a wide public outcry. Some of it came from Yale alumni, who sent dozens of anguished missives to Brewster. "STRONGLY URGE RECONSIDERING THE DECISION ON PROF RICHARD B TENURE HE WAS MY BEST PROFESSOR AT YALE," one telegram read. Recent graduate Robert Connery agreed, calling Bernstein's course his most exciting experience at Yale. "He lit my own lantern far better than anyone before or since," Connery claimed. Other notes came from newspaper readers around the country who bore no connection to Yale but were outraged by its decision. "Some day my children will attend college if abilities and finances permit and I'd hope that the finest creative teachers will be their instructors," a mother of three near Buffalo wrote. "Good teachers can literally change your entire life, giving access to worlds you might never have entered." A correspondent from California praised the civility and dignity of the Yale protesters, whom he contrasted to student radicals on other campuses. "It is a welcome relief from the Mario Savio nonsense at the U. of Calif. Berkeley campus," he wrote. "Your students are right and your Administration is wrong." Here he echoed the *Wall Street Journal*, which praised the Yale students in the same vein as it had lauded Sayre's supporters at Tufts. To be sure, the *Wall Street Journal* noted, some student protest was "Communist-inspired, or just Cain-raising for its own sake." But the Yale action targeted "real rather than imaginary problems," especially the diminishing attention to undergraduate instruction at the "vast, over-bureaucratized, over-populated, undertaught, impersonal, factory-like institution that is so often the contemporary university."[40]

Inadvertently, perhaps, the *Wall Street Journal*'s invective summoned Savio's attacks on the modern university as a "machine" turning "raw materials" into passive consumers. But it also pointed to an emerging consensus about the problem of college teaching, which transcended many of America's dividing lines in the 1960s. University of California president Clark Kerr, Savio's chief antagonist during the free speech battles of 1964, actually presaged student critiques of poor instruction in a book published the previous year. "Educational policy from the undergraduate point of view is largely neglected," Kerr wrote in *The Uses of the University*, decrying large classes taught by TAs and professors who cared more about research than their students. "How to escape the cruel paradox that a superior faculty results in an inferior concern for undergraduate teaching is one of our more pressing problems." The pressure would mount as the decade continued, coming not just from students but also from politicians on both sides of the aisle. In 1965, Wisconsin Democratic congressman Henry Reuss convened hearings to expose how federal grants were "diverting scholars from teaching." Reuss received some pushback from university officials like Harvard dean Donald K. Price, who wryly testified that "a great many eminent scholars disliked teaching long before there were any research grants." Nevertheless, the committee concluded with a recommendation that faculty receiving federal dollars be required to spend at least part of their time teaching. In several state capitols, meanwhile, legislators introduced measures requiring professors at public universities to teach a minimum number of hours per week. Supporters included California governor Ronald Reagan, a frequent critic of student activists who nevertheless endorsed their campaign for more attention to undergraduate instruction. "Young men and women go to college to find themselves as individuals," Reagan declared. "All too often they are herded into gigantic classes taught by TAs hardly older than themselves. The feeling comes that they're nameless, faceless numbers on an assembly line." Only half-jokingly, a *New York Times* columnist called Reagan's comments a "paraphrase of the Free Speech Movement." Indeed, Yale psychologist Kenneth Keniston told the Scranton Commission that concern about poor college teaching was one of the only things that Reagan and his radical student opponents had in common.[41]

But as several observers noted, protests at UC Berkeley and other universities in the 1960s actually led to a *decline* in faculty instructional duties. To recruit big-name professors to schools that had witnessed student strikes and violent clashes with police, officials had to offer lower teaching loads and more money to conduct research. Students continued to protest on behalf of dedicated teachers who were denied tenure or promotion, occupying buildings at the University of Chicago, UC Santa Barbara, and several other institutions. But these efforts mostly came to naught, as faculty rallied to protect their own prerogatives. As the next chapter will detail, attacks on poor college teaching in the 1960s and 1970s generated an astonishing array of instructional reforms: new teaching degrees and awards, pass/fail grading, self-paced instruction, and more. But nothing could reverse the steady decline of teaching in status and power, relative to research, because tenured faculty had little incentive to alter a system that had *granted* them status and power. Interviewed by a reporter in 1983, upon release of the second edition of *The Uses of the University*, Clark Kerr noted that faculty were often liberals about political matters but deeply conservative when it came to their own affairs. "The academic changes of the 1960s originated in student bull sessions and in the minds and hearts of administrators who listened to students; they died in the faculty clubs," Kerr surmised. The comment was more than a little self-serving, exaggerating the openness of officials like Kerr to reform; it also ignored the very real changes that entered college classrooms, thanks in large part to student demands. But on the teaching-versus-research question, Kerr was correct. "With respect to the much broader matter of tenure itself, I find myself continually asking: WHY NOT PUBLISH OR PERISH?" a philosopher colleague of Richard Bernstein wrote to Kingman Brewster, using all caps to defend Bernstein's dismissal. "That's the 'name of the game' in university life." It was also a game he had won, of course, and he was not about to change its rules.[42]

CHAPTER EIGHT

Experimentation and Improvement

Reforming Teaching in the 1960s and 1970s

In 1971, the foremost scholar on American college teaching took note of two "experimental" reforms that had recently seized higher education: "T-group discussions" and the "Personalized System of Instruction" (PSI). A professor at the University of Michigan, Wilbert McKeachie was the author of *Teaching Tips*—the best-selling book on college instruction in US history—and also the founding director of the University of Michigan's Center for Research on Learning and Teaching, the first university-level teaching center in the country. For more than a decade, he had been promoting "best practices"—as he called them—in course planning, project-based learning, assessment, and the other standard features of college instruction. But T-groups and PSI represented new and more "innovative" changes, McKeachie noted. Also known as "encounter groups" or "sensitivity training," T-groups (the T stood for "training") came out of the humanistic psychology movement associated with Carl Rogers, who emphasized the development of emotional intimacy and trust in the classroom as a precondition for learning and growth. By contrast, PSI was a highly structured system in which individual students proceeded at their own pace through a series of written modules; when they passed a test in one, they went on to the next. Developed by experimental psychologist Fred S. Keller, a friend and champion of B. F. Skinner, PSI promised to unshackle students from oppressive classroom rituals. They would learn on their own clock, and in their own way.[1]

In some respects, McKeachie observed, these trends were "going in opposite directions": one called for deeper engagement in group dynamics, while the other sought to free individuals from them. But the reforms also bore several important elements in common. First, they imagined the teacher less as a source of information or enlightenment than as a "Planner, Consultant, Coordinator, and Facilitator," as McKeachie wrote: the best teachers set the conditions for education but did not dominate it, putting students at the center instead. Second, both reforms made the student—not the teacher—responsible for her or his own learning. The same features marked hundreds of different teaching innovations that dotted the higher-education landscape in the 1960s and 1970s, leading celebrants and critics alike to call it "The Age of Experimentation." From small liberal arts colleges to huge public universities, reformers developed courses and programs that promised to replace desiccated, lockstep traditions with a new emphasis on the individual learner. Dozens of entirely new colleges and universities sprang up as well, proudly proclaiming themselves "experimental" and emphasizing the growth and liberation of each student. "College teachers are living their last year in Valhalla," one graduate student at the University of Massachusetts declared. "Their unchallenged reign as classroom monarchs is about to end." He was himself a college instructor, teaching an undergraduate class entitled "The Future of Education." But unlike his own professors, he would put students—their interests, their learning, and their freedom—at the heart of his course, where nothing would be required but everything would be possible. "There will be a revolution next year," he predicted in 1970, "because students are tired of asking for the bread of living education and being given a stone."[2]

Predictably, the promised revolution—like all of the earlier ones—failed to materialize. "We have tried technology; we have tried student ratings; we have tried videotape feedback; we have tried behavioral objectives," McKeachie wrote in 1977, looking back at the experimental era. "None has resulted in revolutionary improvements. There is a danger that our excessive expectations will now result in excessive disillusionment." But there were also grounds for optimism, he added. Since the early 1960s, thousands of faculty members had participated in professional development programs to improve their teaching skills; dozens of institutions had established special teaching centers—following Michigan's lead—and also new teaching prizes for faculty; several universities had created new degrees designed specifically for college teachers; teaching assistants were more likely than before to receive training and supervision; and foundations had provided funds and sabbaticals to help faculty upgrade their instruction. Most of all, there was more overall discussion and concern about teaching in the profession writ large. Published by the center he founded at Michigan, the university's *Memo to Faculty*—containing news and suggestions about teaching—reached 20,000 readers around the country and the world by 1972. Several institutions even provided new faculty with complimentary copies of McKeachie's *Teaching Tips*, which went through seven editions by 1978; 10 years later, it had sold 100,000 copies and had been translated into Spanish, Japanese, Chinese, Polish, and Arabic. None of that heralded a revolution, McKeachie admitted. It was more like a slow march forward, which rendered teaching more personal and impersonal at the same time. Some reforms brought faculty and students into sustained and intimate contact, while others allowed individuals to learn and grow on their own. There were many false starts, and even a few steps backward. But despite the myriad attacks on teaching in the 1960s and 1970s—or, perhaps, because of them—there was more "active learning" than ever before, Mc-Keachie observed. America was "not going to make every teacher a Socrates or Jesus or Abelard or Mark Hopkins," he added, "but we can improve the general level of college teaching and we have made progress." He was probably right.[3]

Experiments in College Teaching

In 1966, Princeton historian Martin Duberman received permission to offer his undergraduate seminar on American radicalism as an "experimental course." Four years earlier, on the recommendation of a student, Duberman had read A. S. Neill's classic testament to educational freedom, *Summerhill,* and was struck by how children flourished when they could exercise it. So he decided to structure his college course along the same lines, which meant almost no structure at all. Students would choose what they wanted to read from a list of books Duberman suggested, but nothing—including reading, class participation, and attendance—was required. There were no papers or examinations, and—most radically—there were no grades. "Grading is but one way in which we turn potentially creative individuals into data-processing machines," Duberman wrote. But "more than grades must go," he quickly added. "The entire superstructure of authoritarian control in our schools must give way." Drawing on his own experience in group therapy, Duberman sought to create a "permissive, non-judgmental atmosphere" in class that broke down the "false distinctions" separating teachers from students. His students would call him by his first name, just like he did with theirs. To promote maximal dialogue, he divided the 24-student class into two groups of 12 and met with each one. "I wanted something more and different from my classroom experience," Duberman recalled. "I felt that most students did also."[4]

Duberman's account captures many of the central themes in the experimentation that seized American colleges and universities during these years. To be sure, the vast majority of instruction continued in much the same way as it had before: large lectures by a professor, sometimes interspersed with TA-led discussion sections. Nor did every new experiment dispense so radically with the standard features of traditional classes, like assignments and grades.

But a new spirit of change and innovation captured many college classrooms, marked by the same somewhat contradictory features that Duberman celebrated: individual freedom and interpersonal exchange. Much of it was sponsored by younger professors (Duberman was 36) who had participated in—or were inspired by—student protest movements, which likewise emphasized personal liberation and communication. But it also found favor among some older faculty members, who praised the new trends as an antidote to their own rigid, traditional instruction. Azusa Pacific College professor Mildred Magruder recalled that when she started teaching in the 1940s, she was the sole authority in class: she lectured, the students took notes, and she tested them on what she said. But the new generation of students rejected that pattern and taught her a new way to teach. "We must maintain a fierce democracy, with no one dominating," Magruder wrote in 1973. "So I must not impose myself as Light-bearer to rows of passive students; I must free them to talk to each other in small groups. I must be a sharer and an inquirer along with the students, not claim to have the answers. I must be willing to be vulnerable, and to allow the ambiguity and paradox of experience to go unresolved." After mostly lecturing to his classes at Cornell for nearly 50 years, historian Frederick Marcham retired and then served as an unpaid TA—at the age of 73—in a colleague's course. Meeting with students in groups ranging from two to eight in size, Marcham discovered "a new kind of teaching," as he wrote. "The students interrupt me, question me, challenge me," Marcham added. "I could live out the rest of my life in a succession of days of class discussions and informal meetings with individual students." And so he did, for the next two decades, until two months before he died. He was 94.[5]

Like Martin Duberman, other professors drew directly on the language and techniques of psychotherapy. "My students have helped me to recreate myself, to break down the psychic and social boundaries of the tranquilized Fifties," an English professor at SUNY Buffalo wrote in 1971. His seminar, entitled "The Literature of Mental Crisis and Madness," was "hovering between a 'class' and an Encounter Group," he added, which was exactly what he wanted. A similarly oriented colleague began each class with feelings rather than words—not the feelings of the author being discussed, he noted, but "the feelings of the students, the teacher, and the relationship between the two." Too many professors tried to avoid emotions in class, he added, on the specious grounds that they were not "trained psychologists." Actually, the university's student counseling center had offered the services of one of its therapists "to help us deal more effectively with some of the problems that often inhibit group discussions," a third SUNY Buffalo professor reported. At UC Santa Cruz, meanwhile, the founding provost of one of its colleges invited Carl Rogers himself to conduct a series of workshops with faculty on T-groups, Rogers's signature method for generating emotional honesty and understanding. The provost subsequently decided that he and many others had not been teaching students at all, but simply talking at them. He spent the next two summers in "personal growth exercises" at the National Training Laboratories in Bethel, Maine, a kind of mecca for the T-group philosophy. Another UC Santa Cruz professor visited Hampshire College and resolved to adopt the T-groups he had witnessed there.[6]

UC Santa Cruz and Hampshire College were part of a wave of roughly 40 experimental colleges that burst across American higher education during these years, often aiming to inscribe small-group discussion and exploration at an institutional scale. Most of them began as branches of existing schools, like the Tussman Experimental College at UC Berkeley and Livingston College at Rutgers; others were freshly created and freestanding institutions, ranging from small liberal arts colleges (Hampshire, Pitzer) to public universities (UC Santa Cruz, Evergreen, SUNY Westbury). Inspired by Alexander Meiklejohn's fleeting interwar Experimental College at the University of Wisconsin, some of the new schools emphasized a shared "great books" curriculum; more commonly, they let students design their own paths. What bound them together was a "revolt against assembly-line academics"—as one journalist observed in 1966—and an emphasis on small-group learning, which would replace the "impersonality of the 'multiversity'" with more friendly, informal settings. The term "multiversity" had been coined by University of California president Clark Kerr, who celebrated the expansion and pluralistic purposes of large universities but acknowledged their central drawback: a diminished attention to undergraduate teaching. Kerr imagined UC Santa Cruz as a corrective to the impersonal, factory-like instruction that marked so many other UC campuses. It was built around a set of residential colleges, where students and faculty would experiment with new kinds of living and learning. At most universities, one enthusiastic observer wrote, human beings are "removed from the possibility of meaningful community." The experimental schools would forge new ones, replacing alienation with intimacy and despotism with liberty.[7]

Most of all, as UC Santa Cruz founding chancellor Dean McHenry predicted, they would bridge the "chasm" between teachers and students. McHenry was an avid reader and collector of literature about utopias, from

Edward Bellamy's *Looking Backwards* to more recent works about Israeli kibbutzim. In the utopian vision that stirred UC Santa Cruz, as in so many other experiments of the era, older structures of power and authority melted away. "Small group process is employed to establish a more intimate setting," a visitor to a sociology course at UC Santa Cruz recorded. "There is an attempt to connect exploration of a theme with personal experience, simultaneously encouraging expressions of feeling. The faculty member minimizes her role as an authority and presents herself as a facilitative member of the group who shares life material with them as a near equal." A co-taught course entitled "Our Human Environment" in 1974–75 included weekly T-groups to reflect on the interpersonal dynamics of the class. "This course offers a new definition of education, the relationship between teacher and student, and the processes of learning," one student gushed in a course evaluation. "We all teach each other." As the praise for the course's novelty suggested—and as other course evaluations confirmed—many UC Santa Cruz classes failed to meet this pedagogical ideal: one professor ridiculed students for allegedly stupid questions, another posed his own tough queries in what scared students called "Gestapo interrogations," a third insisted that students call him "Dr." rather than by his first name, and many teachers continued to weary students with dry or unintelligible lectures. Even mathematician and renowned political satirist Tom Lehrer got low marks for his "terribly boring" classes; as one student quipped, drawing on one of the professor's famous songs, "Mr. Lehrer could have spent his time more effectively poisoning pigeons in the park." Blasting faculty for deviating from UC Santa Cruz's norms of "non-competitive" classrooms and student-teacher equality, these critiques also demonstrated the overwhelming support for the norms themselves. A new definition of teaching had arisen, and teachers who failed to abide by it would hear about it from their students.[8]

At the State University of New York at Westbury, meanwhile, students and faculty joined hands to determine the entire structure of the institution. It began with a set of planning sessions attended by invited students from notably experimental schools, including Antioch and Goddard, who mostly favored A. S. Neill's "'do your own thing' style of education" over the great books model, as one participant wrote. They also demanded "full partnership" for students in all future policy making, which was written into the university's master plan. The same spirit permeated the first classes at Old Westbury, which opened with 84 students in 1968. One faculty member met his class under a table, so everyone could be on the same level; another turned his course into a "marathon encounter group," likewise designed to obliterate any distinctions of hierarchy or authority. When faculty deviated from this model, moreover, students were not shy about letting them know. "You're not teaching me, tonight; you're just talking at me," one student told her professor during a discussion of *Antigone*, after he "tried to impose his expertise" and "lay down just what *Antigone* was all about." The class then took up the question of egalitarianism in the classroom, the student recalled, and the professor "bounced back, one semester later, [as] a better teacher." Professors needing further assistance could also call on Old Westbury's administrative director, who attended a "sensory awakening" class at the Esalen Institute in Big Sur, California, and returned with a new commitment to emotional dialogue and exchange in the classroom and beyond it. The same emphasis seeped into every part of Old Westbury's academic culture, including faculty hiring. "What do you *feel*?" students asked a job candidate, frustrated by his attention to intellectual matters rather than emotional ones. "You know, just feel."[9]

Emotionality in the classroom did not lend itself easily to grading, which also challenged the ethos of faculty-student equality: in a truly nonhierarchical environment, how could professors evaluate students at all? Not surprisingly, then, many experimental colleges—and also some more traditional ones—explored new modes of grading and assessment during these years. UC Santa Cruz required professors to submit narrative evaluations along with a "pass" grade indicating satisfactory work; students who did not pass received a mark of "no record" rather than failure, although they were required to pass a minimum total of courses per year to remain in good standing. Other schools began to experiment with pass-fail systems, which allowed students to receive a "P" or "F"—rather than a regular letter grade—in a limited number of courses. That would encourage students to try classes outside of their own fields, allowing a physics major to take a poetry course "without the risk of marring his record with a low grade," as one journalist observed; inside the classroom, as a UC Irvine student noted, the P/F option let students ask "possibly stupid questions" and not worry about their grades. Around the country, meanwhile, a handful of professors experimented with self-grading systems that let students determine their own marks; still others refused to give grades at all, which got several radical young faculty members fired. When a sociologist at the University of Wisconsin announced he would not submit grades, senior colleagues took over his class and decided not to renew his contract; at Temple, meanwhile, education professor Sidney Simon was dismissed after submitting an "A" for all of his students. Officials did not care that he also provided a written evaluation of each one. Simon's dismissal led to student protests and a teach-in featuring Paul Goodman, author of *Growing Up Absurd* and one of the authors who had inspired Martin Duberman's ungraded seminar. But unlike Duberman, who received permission not to grade, Simon proceeded on his own. And as Temple officials insisted, the system could not work if everyone made their own rules.[10]

Experimentation under Fire

The experimental movement in college teaching generated opposition from the very beginning. The most predictable criticism came from traditionally minded faculty members, who derided the new emphasis on interpersonal relations as both anti-intellectual and self-defeating. Denouncing courses that descended into "therapy for credit" and "feelies"—academic shorthand for "touchy-feely"—an Oregon State philosopher noted how little real disciplinary learning took place within them: students got to know other members of the group, to be sure, but they rarely learned much about the subject matter at hand. That was especially true for lower-middle-class and minority students, who regarded college as a privilege and valued hard work over "identity play" and other frivolities, as a University of Pittsburgh biologist observed. "If it's psychotherapy you want, come to the University of Pittsburgh," he quipped. "If you desire an education of the traditional kind, go elsewhere." In a 1972 forum, several award-winning college teachers acknowledged that change was in the air: although he was still "teaching by the old model," Amherst professor Benjamin DeMott admitted, his students were clamoring to "split into three little groups." That left little room for him to exert his own knowledge and expertise, which were devalued by the radical egalitarianism of the modern-day classroom. The most searing critique came from sociologists Gerald Grant and David Riesman, who noted that "the imperative to be inclusive and reinforcing may be at odds with the cultivation of excellence." The more that teachers emphasized "feeling and process," Grant and Riesman wrote, the less they could demand rigor and erudition.[11]

Here faculty critics often found common cause with students, who echoed many of the same frustrations with the new approaches. Especially at experimental colleges, to be sure, many students embraced the philosophies of independent learning and intergroup exchange (or they simply liked the minimal study requirements: at a UC Santa Cruz commencement, for example, one student openly declared that she was "not much into academics" and had spent most of college hanging out "on the boardwalk" or at parties). But at institutions of every kind, other students bridled at the banality of T-groups and other ostensibly "student-centered" methods. "The professor seems to be playing games with the course, trying to project a 'super-sympathetic' (I understand my students) role," one skeptical student wrote, describing an anthropology course with no mandatory examinations and only one required book. "It's nice, but is it teaching?" Across the country, many students gave a tart reply: no. "I am sick and tired of those classes where the teacher comes in and says, 'Well, what's the structure going to be this year?'" one student wrote. Students at Hampshire College complained that courses sometimes proceeded for weeks before the professor clarified so much as the subject matter of the class, let alone its structure. Even at more traditional institutions, however, course evaluations skewered professors who ceded too much authority—and airtime—to students. At George Washington, one professor was notorious for leading "unorganized rap sessions," another let the class get "bogged down in 'personal questions,'" and a third "seemed to be trying too hard to come down to the level of the student, without maintaining some semblance of the instructor that he was." Indeed, as a Columbia student argued, so-called "in" or "groovy" professors actually forsook their duties to the young minds in their charge. If he wanted more bull sessions, the student added, he could just stay in his dormitory.[12]

But the harshest epitaphs for experimental courses frequently came from the same faculty members who had taught them. They began these classes with romantic hopes, pledging to revolutionize teaching and learning. But they ended like jaded lovers, often casting blame on the very people whom they had pledged to liberate: their students. At Yale, two professors who reorganized their psychology class into small "work groups"—which researched a topic, reported about it to the class, and graded their own performance—discovered that students did not *want* to direct their own learning; socialized from their earliest years to rely on "external incentives," they were "not ready to use effectively intellectual freedom which demands self-control." Meanwhile, a University of Missouri instructor who tried to "break the mold" in his English class found his own spirit broken instead. At the start, he wrote, students eagerly embraced his proposal that they write papers on any subject they chose and spend class time discussing "the burning issues of the day." But "things went from initial ecstasy to final catastrophe," and much faster than he had imagined: rebelling at the full rein he gave them, the students eventually forced him to take it back. "You had the opportunity to be free—free from the usual absurdities of a composition class where topics are assigned, thesis statements are submitted and so on," he wrote, in a bitter 1971 farewell note to the class, "and you succeeded in proving to me and to yourselves that freedom is slavery, a line from 1984." Nor was he willing to write off their reticence to prior conditioning, like the two Yale professors did; rats and dogs were conditioned, he wrote, but human beings had the power to break free from prior patterns. The question was whether they could do so as young adults, or whether it was already too late. When students in his own experimental class at Princeton resisted choosing their own readings, Martin Duberman wondered if "freedom" was something of a chimera in higher education. Students "hope that someone else would, as always, 'do it for them,'" a gloomy Duberman wrote. "In short, they preferred dependency to active exertion in their own behalf."[13]

Other students actually preferred experimental courses, their professors found, but only because these classes were easy. From this perspective, students had *too* much choice, and they were exerting it in all the wrong ways. An Old Westbury art professor was "reluctant to tell students what he wanted them to do," one journalist wrote, so "they often did nothing." Here they received support or even encouragement from college officials, who did not want to be seen as restraining student freedom in any way. One faculty member was asked not to schedule his course at 9:00 a.m., because "students did not like to get up that early"; another was urged to remove an 80-page writing requirement from a course description for his fiction workshop, which might "discourage" students from taking it. Sure enough, when another professor assigned 90 pages of reading per week for his sociology course, enrollment fell promptly from 15 to 3. In a 1969 conference paper, Westbury philosophy professor Lawrence Resnick charged the school with "pandering" to students' inertia and laziness rather than challenging it head-on. Resnick was also the likely author of an anonymous satire of Old Westbury, "Progressive Education at Winterhole," which cleverly captured the dependence that independence could foster. "Here in the murmuring pines, 10,000 babies crawl around educating themselves at their own pace," the satire began. "Director A. S. Schlemiel fondly recalls the story of Freddy, who at 13 had not yet decided to learn to control his sphincter muscles. In fact, at this writing, Freddy is 21 and has not made the inner commitment. Proud, but soiled, Freddy crawls through life (he has not yet decided to learn to walk either) a truly free man."[14]

Written for levity more than accuracy, "Progressive Education at Winterhole" understated how students could also exert their freedom and autonomy by *resisting* experimental education. To jaded romantics like Martin Duberman, opposition to T-groups, self-grading, and optional reading reflected students' reflexive adherence to professorial wisdom and wishes. "I remain something of an authority figure, no matter how I try not to be," Duberman told a student. "I'm the guy with the credentials, the status, and older. . . . That really does impede the process of learning." But his students insisted he was wrong, and they were probably right. Around the country, students rebelled against the antiauthoritarian spirit of experimental teaching by demanding that their teachers exert more authority. In a 1967 survey at Yale, for example, students reported that they learned more when professors exerted more classroom control, via lectures and feedback to the class; by the same token, they learned less when professors assumed a less central role. "Although students may clamor for the *general concept* of greater autonomy, when it comes down to confronting *specific instructor behaviors* which would provide greater autonomy, their enthusiasm diminishes," the survey's author underlined. "So if the opportunity were presented tomorrow, I'm not sure how many students would really want increased influence in their courses." Besides, as another observer noted, the deep interpersonal exchange that experimental education envisioned was only feasible in small-group settings that most institutions could not afford to establish. Nor would students be pleased if those added costs were passed on to them in the form of tuition hikes. What students really wanted was a system that was structured enough to help them master material but sufficiently flexible to let them move through it at their own pace. At Old Westbury, for example, a chemistry professor redesigned his course as a set of modules that students could complete when they were ready to do so. That was a "personal" approach too, but it was radically different from the one envisioned by the champions of T-groups and interpersonal exchange. It placed the self-directed individual—not the group—at the heart of experimental education.[15]

From Programmed to Personalized Learning

In 1971, Fitchburg State College biology professor Neal Anderson caught a glimpse of a glorious future for college teaching. "After attending the Keller Plan [conference] at MIT this weekend it is difficult to resist standing in the courtyard singing 'Hosanna,'" Anderson wrote. "I feel radicalized." But there was nothing truly radical about the PSI devised by Fred S. Keller, who drew on a long history of theory and practice in behavioral psychology. Going back to John B. Watson in the early twentieth century, behaviorists had imagined education as a set of stimuli and responses that teachers could influence by proper reinforcement. According to Keller's memoir, a chance encounter with a Watson textbook at the Old Corner Bookstore in Boston led him to behaviorism and—ultimately—to PSI. A desultory undergraduate student, Keller had dropped out of Tufts because he could not follow lectures: he never knew what to write down during class, when any "disarray of the instructor's clothing" or errant sound could send his mind wandering. But reading Watson inspired him to complete his degree and then enter the PhD program in psychology at Harvard, where B. F. Skinner was a fellow graduate student. Keller was entranced by Skinner's experiments with rats—and, later, with human beings—but did not initially apply them to his own classroom: at Colgate and Columbia, where he taught after graduate school, he stood on a platform and lectured like most of his colleagues. But he also felt like a failure, and his students felt like they were failing as well. They retained only a tiny fraction of what he said and were rewarded—such as it was—with Cs and Bs for whatever they could recount on his tests. He also realized that he was somewhat of an "outsider" among college professors, who relished debate and discussion. But he was happiest in situations where there was a single right answer, which he could find out for himself and—in the ideal—share with others.[16]

By the 1950s, Fred Keller had grown deeply disillusioned with college teaching. Then he rediscovered Skinner, who had developed teaching machines—known also as "programmed learning"—at Harvard. Skinner divided subject matter into small units or "frames," presented as questions; when students responded, they received immediate feedback on their answers. Programmed learning enjoyed a brief burst of growth around the country in the early 1960s, especially at community colleges. Some of them used Skinner-like machines such as "Tutorfilm," a microfilm reader that Bronx Community College employed to teach an electricity course to engineering students; featuring about 10,000 frames, it also recorded students' replies to multiple-choice questions. Cerritos Junior College in California purchased two "Autotutors," which offered programming in several subjects; Los Angeles Valley College employed a gadget that looked like an adding machine, which—following Skinner—rewarded the user for being right. "It couldn't be simpler," one observer wrote. "The more often a person is right and the quicker he knows it, the faster and better he learns." Other schools replaced the often unwieldy machines with programmed books, which operated on the same principle: students placed a "shield" over a response column, answered a question, and then lifted the shield to see whether they were correct. By 1963, over 800 students at Delta College in Michigan had completed "fully programmed" courses, which one

official called "education's counterpart of the industrial revolution." With more
and more students flooding into junior colleges, he added, "ineffective and
time-consuming methods of education" would no longer suffice. "Democracy
will be more secure if the great majority of the citizens in the United States are
well educated, well trained, and well informed," he concluded, connecting programmed learning to the fate of the republic itself.[17]

Yet some Delta students also bristled at the "impersonal atmosphere" of
programmed learning, which worried observers like Fred Keller. Praising
these new projects for "teaching the *individual* student, rather than the group,"
Keller aimed to retain the individualized character of programmed instruction
without separating individuals from each other. Enter PSI, which Keller devised in 1963 and 1964 during a consultancy at the new University of Brasilia
in Brazil. Like the programmed-learning efforts already underway, PSI let students proceed through material at their own pace. But their mastery of it
would be tested by a set of student proctors, who provided the human "reinforcement"—to borrow the Skinnerian term—that earlier systems lacked. According to Keller, the real precursor to PSI was the Lancasterian system in
urban schools of the early nineteenth century, when vast numbers of students
were taught via "monitors" who were barely older than themselves. Keller instituted PSI for the first time in a psychology class in 1965 at Arizona State
University, where he selected 10 proctors from students who had already successfully passed the course. Each one monitored about 10 students through
20 units, administering paper-and-pencil tests to students on each unit; failing students would review their answers with the proctors and then retake the
test until they passed it. Keller restricted his tests mostly to true-false questions, to avoid situations that might get the proctors into "arguments"; he
was also on hand to answer questions himself and to give the occasional lecture (where attendance was always optional). But the most important teacher
was the proctor, who "personalizes the course wonderfully," Keller wrote.
"When you get a firm, friendly, helpful hand from your proctor, it really means
something," he added. Jettisoning the hated grade curve, the course promised
an "A" to any student who mastered its content. That also enhanced social relations, as proctors aimed to assist all the students instead of trying to rank
them in order of performance.[18]

Indeed, Keller insisted, virtually anyone could learn and achieve—at the
highest levels—in any PSI course. "I am taking John Watson more seriously
than I used to, even when I supported his position about Give me a healthy
child," Keller told a former Columbia colleague, amid his first PSI course at

Arizona State. Here he referred to John B. Watson's famous boast that he could turn any healthy infant into a doctor or a lawyer—or, Watson warned, into a beggar or a thief—with the proper conditioning. Many of Keller's fellow professors had "a vested interest in showing that students, especially Arizona students, are of an inferior race," he wrote; working at a second-tier university, they also "secretly think of themselves as inferior." But Keller had boundless faith in his students and—especially—in his system. Conventional education was "elitist," he wrote, insofar as it reinforced the inequalities and failures of society; PSI was democratic, by contrast, because it allowed everyone to succeed. "Your principal aim is not to separate the sheep from the goats, in the interests of some using agency—J.C. Penny, IBM, General Motors, or whatever," Keller told his hosts in Brazil, while designing PSI. "Nor is it to measure the IQ of your pupils. It is simply to teach them what you, as the expert, think they ought to know." Just as the rat was always right in the laboratory, Keller wrote, the student would always be right "if we provide the right contingencies of reinforcement." That would require a reconceptualization of the teacher as an "educational engineer" and "contingency manager," not as a "classroom entertainer, expositor, critic, and debater." More than that, though, PSI also implied an entirely new way of looking at human potential and achievement. "PSI is a model for all social systems," Keller told his Georgetown University collaborator J. Gilmour Sherman in 1972. "I, too, see it as important in forming a better world for all. In fact, I think there will be chaos without it."[19]

The following year, with support from the Carnegie Corporation, Sherman and Keller formed the Center for Personalized Instruction. Located at Georgetown, it served as a clearinghouse for information and as a sponsor of conferences like the Massachusetts Institute for Technology gathering that had thrilled Fitchburg State's Neal Anderson. Most of all, Keller hoped, the CPI would help spread the good word to people who had not yet received it. "Every user of PSI . . . becomes a missionary," Keller told a colleague. "I suppose it's because we know a good thing when we find it and want to tell the world about it!" By 1973, Gilmour estimated, roughly 2,000 professors at hundreds of institutions in the United States taught courses via PSI. At Temple Buell College in Colorado, fully half of all classes used the method; three years later, a quarter of faculty at East Stroudsburg State College in Pennsylvania taught a "PSI course." Unlike earlier initiatives for programmed learning, meanwhile, PSI also made inroads at elite colleges and universities. At MIT, professors offered eight PSI courses and also secured a National Science Foundation grant to train 20 other selected faculty members around the country in the method; Rice used PSI to teach astronomy, physics, and English composition; Drake University offered a PSI religion course on the New Testament; nearly 120 students registered for a PSI-taught course in psychology at Barnard, where only two dropped out; and at Lafayette, the psychology department doubled its majors after introducing PSI in several classes. "There is no turning back, as you must know," a Lafayette faculty member told Keller. "We would simply have a student riot if we reverted to the old lecture system for our course. We may even get a small riot when we curtail enrollments next year."[20]

Meanwhile, dozens of other institutions offered "self-paced" courses that drew on the same spirit—if not the exact specifications—of PSI. After the City University of New York declared open admissions, which brought in large numbers of poorly prepared students, several colleges in the system offered remedial courses on the "learn-as-you-go" plan, as one reporter called it. Student "coaches" (the equivalent of Keller's proctors) administered questions that appeared at the end of each textbook chapter, allowing students to proceed to the next one if they passed; it also allowed the cash-strapped CUNY schools to serve their growing hordes of students "using less teachers and space (and therefore less money)," as one observer wrote. Some institutions described this approach as "modularization," because students had to complete sequential lesson modules; others called it "Mastery Learning," which became an educational buzzword in the 1970s. (One enthusiast described PSI as "Mastery Learning with the Personal Touch," because it required constant interaction between students and proctors.) Outside of PSI itself, the best-known self-paced approach in the United States was the audio-tutorial (A-T) system developed at Purdue University by botanist Sam Postlethwait. Frustrated at the inability of his audience to keep up with his lectures, Postlethwait taped them so they could be viewed—and paused—at any time; then, he rewrote his course's laboratory manual to correspond with the lectures and added questions to them, which students could answer as they listened along in specially equipped study carrels. The A-T system spread to nearby Ohio State, where 4,500 students used it in a biology course; when the new Permian Basin campus of the University of Texas opened, officials forecast that its entire undergraduate upper division would be taught via the A-T system. Besides letting students learn at their own pace, Postlethwait noted, the A-T system enhanced their ability to concentrate on their studies. "The earphones shut out the garbage collecting and the carrel's three walls shut out the pretty girls," he quipped.[21]

Critiques of Personalized Learning

On the whole, however, students proved much less enthusiastic about personalized learning than its tribunes imagined. Many found PSI highly *impersonal*, despite Keller's claim that it would build in the social dimensions that programmed learning had neglected. The routinized, mechanical rhythm of unit tests did not promote much substantive dialogue between students and proctors. Nor did students interact with their professors, who stood mostly behind the curtain—like the Wizard of Oz—and rarely left much of an imprint on the class. "The course was individualized, but ironically lacked a personal touch," one PSI evaluator surmised. Students in a PSI-taught chemistry class at UC Santa Cruz described their professor as a "grading machine," since she limited her role to correcting tests; she obviously knew a great deal, yet they did not know her. Sensing that his own students felt alienated from him—and, by extension, from his course—a PSI instructor at the University of Texas made a conscious effort to chat with them (about the latest football game, where they grew up, and so on) and found that their average test scores rose. "The presence of the teacher matters," he told Keller. "I can not help but feel that learning is a social act and that humans like humans, at least in a less than perfect world." To create more faculty-student interaction, some PSI professors began to conduct their own recitation-style "group quizzes"; others awarded points for attendance at lecture or at discussions with faculty about their research. "Somehow a course where the students never get a chance to even see the person who has designed it is missing something," Barnard psychologist Edward Cobb told Keller, who had been his undergraduate professor at Columbia. Without in-person lectures, Cobb added, he would not have encountered Keller or been inspired to pursue psychology further. The course would have been a forgettable exercise "to fulfill a science requirement," Cobb noted, "and that would have been that."[22]

Even when the professor was more present, students reported that they learned less in self-paced classes than in traditionally taught ones. Younger students, especially, had a difficult time mustering the motivation—and the maturity—that PSI demanded; meanwhile, working-class and first-generation students often lacked basic skills that self-paced courses assumed they already had. Fully half of the students enrolled in PSI classes at Cal State University in Bakersfield in 1972–73 did not finish them, receiving incomplete grades, and nearly half of that group did not complete their work by the following semester, putting them in jeopardy of failing the course. At California State University,

Dominguez Hills, meanwhile, not a single one of 20 students who signed up for a self-paced course entitled "Individual Differences and the Exceptional Person" completed the course by the end of the quarter; apparently, as one observer wrote, many of them thought that "self-pacing" simply meant "going slower than normal." To be sure, plenty of students around the country enjoyed PSI courses and continued to register for them. "Hurray for behavior modification," one student wrote, in praise of PSI. "For the first time in any college course, I felt responsible for what I learned—and was treated like a responsible individual." But as research about PSI courses at Drake University confirmed, "the less apt student profits least" from self-paced instruction: stronger students moved quickly through the courses, while weaker students often dropped out of them. In an effort to reach every individual, indeed, self-paced courses tended to ignore the differences *between* individuals. "As you will no doubt figure out by my test scores, I believe this course was a total flop," one Cal State student wrote, after taking an A-T art class. "I hope to repeat this course under a human, not a cassette player."[23]

Personalized learning also sparked opposition among graduate students, who saw it as a way to replace TAs with inexpensive undergraduate proctors. "If it were really true that undergraduates . . . are better tutors, graduate school would be quite superfluous (except to provide cheap labor for research projects)," a physics TA at UC San Diego wrote, denouncing an advertisement in the campus press seeking PSI proctors for his department. "We could probably even devise a system whereby all professors could be replaced by undergraduates who had just completed the courses." Indeed, he added, the department's claim that "the Keller Plan works better than regular lectures" spoke volumes about the low expectations for faculty in regular classrooms. "It is clear that human communication is the ultimate in learning (the brain is not a machine that simply needs programming!)," he wrote. "Lectures, even if they are large, can motivate students and communicate ideas far more effectively than any book ever could." Here the TA was echoed by many faculty members, both at UC San Diego and beyond, who blasted what one Bucknell professor called the "de-humanizing" dimensions of PSI: if any course could be reduced to a set of standardized questions and answers, they argued, professors became irrelevant and disposable. Actually, as a Rice professor noted, most PSI courses could not be easily transferred from one teacher to another; professors were too idiosyncratic for that, often preferring to substitute their own units. "Sharing materials is the obvious solution but, as yet, it is not usually feasible," he observed. "PSI is <u>very</u> personal." Yet what Fred Keller derided as

"Skinnerphobia"—the fear that behavioral systems would eliminate human will and choice—turned many academicians against PSI. Keller was worried enough about that negative association that he kept his distance from Skinner himself, turning down an invitation from his graduate school friend to speak at a symposium on behaviorism. Too many professors already thought that PSI would reduce people to rats or machines, which was the most frequent refrain of Skinnerphobia. Appearing in public alongside Skinner would only give them further ammunition, Keller concluded.[24]

But the harshest critics of PSI were college and university administrators, who would eventually deal a lethal blow to Fred Keller's dream. From the start, officials worried that PSI's system of evaluation, in which everyone mastering the material gets an A, would award too many of them. Keller's first course at Arizona State gave out 41 As, 13 Bs, 1 D, and 3 Fs, which raised eyebrows immediately. So did a popular PSI course at Hunter College, as a professor there explained. "The very success of the method creates intractable problems in the educational establishment," he told Keller. "At Hunter we succeeded in increasing the proportion of A's earned by students, and we are now dealing with the accusation that we must have lowered our standards." Other officials worried that PSI would depress enrollments, because students chose courses—and majors—when they were attracted to a "charismatic professor" in the field, as one observer wrote. Still others argued that students expected—and deserved—a live performance by the professor, whether charismatic or not. That was the argument that forced out Keller disciple J. Gilmour Sherman from Georgetown University, where several students reportedly demanded refunds after taking PSI courses. As a selective institution, Georgetown "promises pedagogy of the highest order, and defends both its high costs and its high selectivity partly, if not principally, on the basis of an expensive faculty at the cutting edge of the learned professions," Sherman's department chair wrote. "And a <u>Georgetown</u> education promises students <u>far</u> more than supervision by fellow-undergraduates." Like a correspondence course teacher, the chair continued, a PSI professor could live in Alaska and still "teach" a course, via tests and student monitors. But that was not a legitimate form of teaching, as Georgetown—and most other institutions—understood it.[25]

By the time J. Gilmour Sherman took a buyout and retired, in 1990, PSI was all but gone. The Carnegie Corporation and the federal Fund for the Improvement of Postsecondary Education declined to renew their grants to the Center for Personalized Instruction, which closed its doors in 1978. In 1985, looking back on the "lightning bolt" of PSI, Fred S. Keller pronounced it a "flash in the pan" instead. The biggest obstacles were professors, of course, who were "pining for the podium" and refusing to relinquish their role as lecturers. Another problem was the bias toward research in the modern university, which discouraged faculty from the large investment of planning that PSI required; a third was the system of student evaluations, which rated professors on their "performance" in class rather than on how much students learned. Finally, Keller wondered whether he had actually misinterpreted human nature by trying to eliminate competition from education; the world was "dog-eat-dog," he conceded, and "coddling" students would not prepare them for it. "I thought I saw the second Renaissance ahead, but I was living in a dream," Keller concluded. "The system was unrealistic and involved too many people; it was too expensive . . . and, in the last analysis, it was unnecessary. Some well-selected teachers and some well-selected students can look after all that we require in higher education. What we really need today is the early separation of the sheep from the goats." Perhaps, then, the idea of success for all in college was just a chimera. Writing from Ann Arbor, Keller's fellow psychologist Wilbert J. McKeachie tried to cheer him up. In his long career, McKeachie wrote, he had seen several trends "fade from popularity" and then rise up again; within the next decade, he predicted, "someone will come up with PSI, perhaps under a new name." Meanwhile, McKeachie and other reformers were turning their attention to other perennial problems in college instruction: how to select the best teachers, and how best to prepare, evaluate, and reward them—in other words, the separation of the sheep from the goats.[26]

Improving Teaching
Faculty Development

The 1960s and 1970s were years of improvement—not just of experimentation—in college teaching. The difference was neatly captured in a 1977 address by Wilbert McKeachie, who questioned the quest for a "Messiah" that would radically alter undergraduate instruction. "Nice as it would be to save higher education, I suspect that many of our faculty and students don't need us," he declared. "They are inheritors of hundreds of years of accumulated wisdom about teaching and learning. . . . What we have to work on is improving the effectiveness of the many teachers who are doing less well than they are potentially capable of doing." McKeachie had been doing that since the 1940s, working quietly but steadily for more organized lectures, more engaged classroom discussion, and more sophisticated teacher evaluations. The campaign for improvement stepped up in the 1960s, spurred by the same force that had motivated experimentation: student protest and dissent. From one perspective, campus protest signaled the need for radical change; anything less would unleash yet more violence and—ultimately—a "revolution in our country," as one speaker warned a 1970 UC Santa Cruz conference on innovation and experimentation in higher education. But others argued for a more deliberate and incremental approach, based on a growing body of knowledge about the habits and practices of effective instruction. "'New' is the 'in' word in education," a skeptical McKeachie wrote in 1966, at the dawn of the experimental era. "If we fail to get with it and adopt the latest 'new' fad, we're obviously moss-backed old fuddy-duddies who are opposed to the improvement of education." But it did not require a revolution to improve college teaching, he added. It simply demanded that teachers attend to what was already known.[27]

McKeachie became a central figure in "faculty development," a term that entered the academic lexicon during these same years. In 1976, 60 percent of responding colleges and universities reported that they had instituted some kind of faculty development program; that same year, one scholar called faculty development "a national pastime in higher education." Fifteen years after McKeachie started the first university-based teaching center, over 200 institutions had done the same. Most of the centers offered individual consultation to professors, often videotaping their classes so the professor could analyze her or his teaching alongside the consultant; others conducted seminars on instructional improvement for faculty and TAs; still others provided grants for professors to develop new courses or methodologies. Like efforts to upgrade teaching in the Cold War, faculty development projects also received enormous assistance from the foundation world. Established by the family behind the world's largest pet food company, Ralston Purina, the Danforth Foundation plowed millions into teaching centers, prizes, and other improvement efforts. So did the Carnegie Corporation, which funded the nationwide Project to Improve College Teaching between 1969 and 1971. It was directed by University of Utah English professor Kenneth Eble, who visited 70 institutions in 40 states to gather information about college teaching and—most of all—to spread the word about effective practices. Eble's first two "special reports" on teaching were sent to all 90,000 members of the American Association of University Professors, which cosponsored the project; he also published a regular column in the *Chronicle of Higher Education*, which reported at length on his activities. So did the mainstream press, where the formerly obscure scholar of F. Scott Fitzgerald became one of the two or three most frequently cited academicians of his era. "No passably effective teacher could succeed without some sense of the good or bad of what he is doing," Eble declared in 1971, in a much-quoted comment. "There is a wide agreement on the particulars of effective teaching."[28]

That consensus was neatly summarized the previous year by Samuel P. Kelly, director of the teaching center at Western Washington State College. The center had sponsored a series of talks by eight different professors from around the Pacific Northwest, all known as excellent teachers, who were asked to speak on the subject of "Methods and Techniques of College Teaching I Have Found Effective." Significantly, none of them gave much attention to headline-grabbing experimental approaches like "buzz groups, committee assignments, classroom democracy, T-groups, sensitivity, etc.," Kelly observed. Instead, he wrote, they coalesced around a series of practices that had always marked the best teachers: "continual specification of just what was and was not expected, continual feedback to the student, and constant opportunity for challenge and questioning by the student of the instructor." Good teachers started every class with a statement of what they expected to happen in it; they elicited and welcomed questions and comments throughout the lesson; they had "no hang-ups over using lecture appropriately," but they did not overdo it; and if they did lecture, they told students when—and how—to take notes. Most of all, they were interested in what the students had to say. "They like the give and take of discussion," Kelly wrote. "A question brings the undivided attention of the instructor to the questioner and his query." Many of the Western Washington presenters were reluctant to discuss these traits for fear of sounding "trite" and "old hat," Kelly wrote. But that was precisely the point, as well as the problem. In their bones, most American professors knew what good teaching was. They just did not know how to talk about it or—in too many cases—how to do it.[29]

So faculty development would show them. To be sure, as Bucknell professor John Anderson observed, faculty had always helped each other with teaching. But that discussion typically took place around the proverbial water cooler or in other informal settings. Just as the British Royal Society was originally named "The Invisible College," Anderson noted, most faculty development happened out of sight. People like Kenneth Eble and Samuel Kelly sought to make it visible, especially via conferences and workshops. With the assistance of the Lilly Foundation, Ball State University provided workshops on course design, lecturing and discussion techniques, and many other aspects of classroom instruction; at the University of Vermont, a Ford Foundation grant funded a campus-wide "instructional improvement program," including training for all teaching staff; the federal Fund for the Improvement of Postsecondary Education (FIPSE) designated Bucknell as one of 11 institutional "Associates," which hosted seminars and workshops aimed at "elevating the importance of teaching"; and at Beaver College in Pennsylvania, FIPSE funded workshops to help faculty infuse problem-solving and critical thinking into their instruction. As their evaluations illustrate, many faculty who attended these events found them useful or even inspirational. "The workshop encouraged me to strive for more student involvement in my classes by asking directed questions to my students rather than straight lecturing only," one Ball State participant wrote. To another, the best outcome was the simple reminder that instruction could be changed at all. "It has proved in a way that some thought impossible that teaching itself is an art that can be learned, improved, or renewed," the professor wrote.[30]

But other faculty members were much more skeptical about faculty development. Some Ball State participants dismissed the workshops as window dressing by an administration bent on crowding ever more students into their classes, which would prevent faculty from implementing any of the methods they had learned. Others wondered why they should invest in improving their teaching when it would not—in most cases—improve their chances of tenure and promotion; indeed, several junior faculty members feared that their faculty development activities had put their academic futures at risk by making senior colleagues question their dedication to research. Others asked whether a seminar or two would actually upgrade their instructional skills, which many professors continued to regard as inbred and—by extension—impervious to modification. So while thousands of American faculty members engaged in these activities in the 1960s and 1970s, a much larger number took a pass. "I might start with a very simple question which I imagine everyone here has asked himself: why are so few of us here?" UC Santa Barbara historian Albert Lindemann asked, beginning his remarks at a 1974 teaching conference. "I feel as if I am in the crypts of ancient Rome with a few left." The meeting was held on a Friday, Lindemann joked, which was the hardest time to get faculty to show up for anything. But there was a deeper reason, of course. "The faculty don't think it's worth a damn," he stated flatly. "They don't think it's worthwhile. They think it's a waste of time." Indeed, Lindemann himself entertained "serious doubts" about the usefulness of the conference and of faculty development in general. When he served on UC Santa Barbara's "Effective Teaching Committee," Lindemann added, he read the literature on the subject and found it full of "platitudes." Samuel Kelly was correct: most commentary on best practices in teaching was fairly obvious. But to Albert Lindemann, that was also the best reason to ignore it.[31]

It also helps explain the bias in these projects toward experimental teaching, which was as popular in faculty development circles as it was in certain quarters of the student movement. But the reasons were different. Socialized to value research, which advanced via fresh and original contributions to a field, professors were far more interested in exploring programmed learning, computer-assisted instruction, or some other novel method than in improving the quotidian, day-to-day practice in their classrooms. So when the University of California inaugurated a journal about teaching, which school officials advertised as a way to revive the status of undergraduate instruction, its title—*Experiment and Innovation*—downplayed the day-to-day in favor of the up-to-date. Likewise, teaching-related grants awarded to faculty in the California State University system mostly funded self-paced learning, independent study, and other ostensibly pioneering methods. Here, too, the name of the Cal State program was instructive—"Innovation and Improvement"—as was the teaching journal it started in the 1970s: *Future Talk: Educating for the '80s*. But as one California State University, Los Angeles, mathematician noted, criticizing the cult of innovation, some students in his Intermediate Algebra class could not even do basic arithmetic. The "educational fads and fancies" favored by faculty development promised "learning without tears," he wrote, but what his students really needed was some good old-fashioned (and rigorous) teaching. Likewise, a UCLA official wondered whether innovation was the best target for faculty development. "The most numerous opportunities for improvement of teaching exist simply in doing better the customary work of instruction," he wrote. "Measures of this kind lack the romance of 'challenge' to the establishment but they do tend to improve its functioning." By throwing in their lot with "experimentation," he added, university faculty and administrators could signal "preference for the fashionable, the chic, the 'in thing' of the moment." But he doubted that that would improve college teaching in the long run.[32]

The lone exceptions to the bias toward innovation were the rare faculty development opportunities for teachers at historically black colleges and universities, which tended to focus on the nuts and bolts of daily instruction. The Carnegie Corporation sponsored several summer institutes for "Negro College Faculty" in the 1960s, aimed at upgrading content-area knowledge and, especially, at weaning African Americans off their allegedly rote, textbook-driven pedagogy. One institute used the laboratory-based, hands-on Physical Science Study Committee curriculum developed by MIT physicist Jerrold Zacharias, who wrote that the typical black faculty member was "the servant of his books rather than his master"; following a summer institute for black history faculty, likewise, Carnegie Mellon historian Edwin Fenton—famous for promoting critical approaches to the discipline in the classroom—complained that black history teachers "have been slaves to the old concept of 'coverage'—x number of pages a day to memorize." As the loaded language of masters and slaves suggests, white organizers of these institutes showed little awareness that their assumptions might have condescended to the same faculty members they aimed to assist. At the 1964 institute for black English professors, a Howard University evaluator noted that participants "objected strongly to what they considered to be a patronizing manner" among the institute's directors and staff. After his own visit to an institute, similarly, sociologist David Riesman warned that the white organizers had failed to understand or appreciate the conservative cultural milieu of black faculty. "The Negro who has made sacrifices of immediate hedonism in order to get a college education will be harsher on his own students than a white teacher would be," Riesman wrote. "To tell a Negro high school or college teacher who just managed to raise himself from the Negro lower class . . . that he should be relaxed and permissive and exploratory in his teaching may be taken by such a teacher as a threat to send him back where he came from!"[33]

Selecting and Preparing New Faculty

To other observers, meanwhile, the only real chance for improving college teaching lay not in the starry future of "experimentation" but in selecting—and training—a better generation of future instructors. That was a dream going back at least to the 1920s, when critics claimed that the professoriate was not attracting the "right" kind of person to instruct the teeming masses who were flooding into American classrooms. The concern continued into the 1960s and early 1970s, when a report produced by Kenneth Eble for the Project to Improve College Teaching worried that "the supply of handcrafted, fully energized, extended-range, stereophonic, fine-tuned, living color professors simply falls short of the apparent demand." The quip referred to television, of course: in the era of electronic mass media, how could colleges attract people with the charisma to compete with the living-room screen? One solution was to harness television itself. Starting in 1962, ABC aired a series called "Meet the Professor" that portrayed college teachers "at work in the classroom, laboratory, and office." Its aim was to show how professors "stimulate the curiosity and creativity of their students"; they are "a vital part of the American fabric, not just musty features on the campus," a news release proclaimed. Promoting that view was a tall order, Northwestern scholar David Epperson told Eble's research team in 1970. "Seldom do the mass media portray a professor who gives much evidence of either personal warmth or common sense," Epperson wrote. "He is usually coldly rational, forgetful, humorless, and nearsighted, or more recently a bearded supporter of radical student disruption." Since the 1940s, he noted, American audiences had laughed at comedian Irwin Corey's "professor" routine, in which Corey played a bumbling blowhard who spouted nonsense while proclaiming himself "The World's Foremost Authority." The only way to fight that image was by creating new ones, using all of the tools at hand. "Mark Hopkins did not live in the Age of McLuhan," Epperson emphasized. If the medium was the message, as per Marshall McLuhan's famous aphorism, the professoriate needed to manipulate both of them to its own ends.[34]

As in the Cold War, foundations continued to provide material incentives to enter college teaching. The most important player was the Danforth Foundation, which provided grants to college seniors and recent graduates who envisioned careers as college teachers. Unlike the Woodrow Wilson Fellowship, which gave support for only the first year of graduate study, the Danforth Fellowship was renewable for up to four years. It also placed an emphasis on personal character and faith, reflecting the foundation's religious history and orientation: as a Danforth leaflet explained in 1965, it sought candidates demonstrating "concerns which range beyond self-interest" and "which take seriously the questions with which religious expressions attempt to deal." As applications to the fellowship confirm, it attracted undergraduates who shared the foundation's emphasis on teaching as a moral and spiritual enterprise. At Carleton, one student applicant described college teaching as "a unique opportunity for service and for growth through interpersonal relationships," while another tied his interest in the profession to theologian Paul Tillich's quest for meaning in life. By 1979, the foundation had awarded graduate fellowships to 3,600 people; 94 percent of them received doctorates, and 85 percent became college teachers. They included a physicist who went on to author an acclaimed textbook—and to endow a national teaching prize—and a philosopher who was ordained as an Episcopal priest. That made him a better professor, he wrote, and "the reverse is also true": being a professor made him a more empathetic and effective priest.[35]

But the Danforth fellowship did not actually train people to become college teachers, as recipient Jane Tompkins remembered. All it did was pay for her to go to graduate school, where she and her fellow PhDs "were let loose in the classroom with virtually no preparation for what we would encounter." That was a perennial problem, which took on new urgency in the 1960s and 1970s as more and more undergraduates were taught by TAs. Around the country, institutions slowly established formal training programs for TAs. But the process proceeded in fits and starts, hamstrung by the lower overall priority that the professoriate gave to teaching in general. At UC Berkeley, a Ford Foundation grant freed mathematics TAs from half of their usual teaching duties so they could participate in a seminar. But the department had a difficult time finding a professor to supervise the course, which died after a few semesters; so did a similar seminar at Stanford, where "the 'training' . . . consists of handing the T.A. the text and telling him, 'go teach,'" as one faculty member admitted. Likewise, a mathematics TA seminar at UC Davis could find only one professor willing to sponsor it, "and even he grudgingly." When TA training was implemented on a university-wide basis, as at UCLA, it was so diffuse and amorphous that nobody could tell what—if anything—it did to improve teaching. "Like motherhood," one professor quipped, "we must assume that undergraduate education is better off with these programs than without them." To be sure, scattered departments at institutions around the country provided careful training and supervision of their TAs. But the big picture was not a pretty one. If "the brightest hope is to provide a more balanced background for the professor of tomorrow," as University of Virginia professor Frank Finger suggested, most PhD programs were unlikely to provide it.[36]

So some reformers looked to new college teaching degrees, reviving yet another dream from the Cold War years. They focused on the doctor of arts (DA), which—like earlier alternative degrees—required coursework and a supervised teaching internship but no lengthy research-based doctoral thesis; instead, candidates would write shorter treatises about a specific problem in teaching. Carnegie Mellon awarded the first DA degree in 1968, which caught the eye of Carnegie Corporation official E. Alden Dunham. "I am absolutely convinced that an alternative to the Ph.D. degree is essential as this country moves toward what is generally called universal higher education," wrote Dunham, who was completing a book on state colleges and regional universities called—significantly—*Colleges of the Forgotten Americans*. Dunham also cited the recent book by Christopher Jencks and David Riesman, *The Academic*

Revolution, which showed how nearly every kind of school was attempting to become a "research" institution. Like Jencks and Riesman, Dunham thought it was impossible to make PhD programs take teaching seriously; instead, America needed a serious college teaching degree. Lest anyone dismiss it as a fad conjured by the much-maligned schools of education, Dunham emphasized that the DA—like the PhD—would be located in academic departments. "This is a subject matter degree, not an education degree," he underscored. "It is not a consolation prize for losers on route to the Ph.D." Two years later, the Carnegie Corporation donated $1 million in planning grants to 10 institutions considering establishing the DA; eventually, it would give out $4 million in support of the degree. The DA was even backed by "that Holy of Holies," the Council of Graduate Schools, as another advocate triumphantly noted in the Carnegie Corporation's journal. "The highly specialized research required for the Ph.D. is simply not appropriate training for much of undergraduate teaching," Carnegie president Alan Pifer argued. From his perch atop the Carnegie Corporation's Commission on Higher Education, where he moved after leaving the University of California presidency, Clark Kerr agreed. The DA, he declared, should become "the standard degree for college teaching in the United States."[37]

That never happened, of course. Twenty different institutions offered the DA in 1972, up from three in 1970, but only three more started after that. The dream of the DA crashed almost as quickly as it arose, thanks to an unexpected development: a glut of PhDs. An economic downturn slowed job growth at college and universities, while a sudden oversupply of doctorates gave them the pick of the litter. And when faced with a choice between a PhD and a DA, hiring committees inevitably chose the former. Seeing the writing on the wall, Dartmouth and MIT returned their Carnegie DA grants in 1972. The UC Berkeley faculty voted against creating the degree, and Brown decided to eliminate its own DA program five years after it had begun. "It is a fine idea but came too late," one graduate school dean said in 1974, pronouncing an epitaph for the DA; it was a "second-class degree," another dean added, which could never compete with the PhD in a tight job market. Some of the DA programs that held on taught a block of education courses resembling secondary and elementary teacher preparation, which simply reinforced the low status of the degree; others ignored teaching altogether, exactly like the PhD programs they had hoped to replace. In 1971, just three years after he heralded the DA as the harbinger of the future, a glum Alden Dunham conceded that the PhD octopus—as William James had called it, 70 years earlier—was simply too strong to overcome. So long as research continued to be valued more highly than teaching, he concluded, nothing would really change.[38]

New Incentives

Finally, these same years also witnessed several direct efforts to challenge the same bias that led to the demise of the DA: the low status of undergraduate instruction at American colleges and universities. In the 1930s and 1940s, a handful of schools had initiated awards to recognize outstanding teachers on their faculties. Such prizes became ubiquitous in the 1960s, starting at the University of Pennsylvania and then spreading like wildfire across the country. Press accounts of the Penn award (which actually began in 1959) left little doubt about its purpose: since the successful researcher had long been the "Prince Charming of the faculty," one observer wrote, the new prize was a "reverse gesture" designed to enthrone good instruction as well. Ten years later, in 1969, 360 institutions gave teaching prizes; so did several nonprofits, such as the Danforth Foundation, which recognized five or six professors around the country each year for their outstanding instruction. Institutional prizes ranged from $100 to $4,000, with the median at about $1,000; some schools also provided medals, gold watches, plaques, or scrolls. Perhaps the most coveted (and surely the most ironic) prize was a year's leave, meaning that the winner of the award for teaching was released from it. There was also wide variation in the selection systems for the awards: some were chosen via alumni or student polls, while others were selected by a committee composed of faculty, students, or both. Regardless of the details, however, the goal of the prizes was always the same. "We want to encourage teaching as opposed to highly prized researchers, who rarely see students," a Danforth official explained in 1969. "The researcher has his place, but the teacher-scholar too often goes without recognition, both professionally and financially."[39]

But teaching awards also sparked considerable controversy and opposition among the same population they were designed to recognize: college teachers. Some critics mocked the idea that a modest monetary award could actually serve to elevate or incentivize teaching; as one Ohio professor wrote, borrowing from the language of behaviorism, "the pay-off is too remote to serve as an 'operant conditioner.'" Others worried that teaching prizes would foster competition—and, for the losers, jealousy—among colleagues: at Carleton, for example, a teaching award was discontinued for its "divisive influence on the faculty." When professors selected the award recipient, one observer noted, they tended to favor the same kind of "innovations" that faculty development efforts emphasized rather than "devotion in reading student papers" and other day-to-day activities. But if students or alumni chose the winner, other critics charged, the prize would inevitably go to the most popular teacher rather than the best one. "It is not unknown to have a professor carry on his own campaign among his students to win the accolade of 'Great Teacher,'" a New York University education scholar warned. "This, of course, makes a 'Miss Rheingold' contest of what is supposed to be serious business." The most bitter dispute occurred in Oregon, where the state legislature authorized $500,000 for teaching prizes at state universities on the stipulation that students were involved in deciding who would receive them. Oregon State University held a student vote, which drew nearly 6,000 ballots; based on the results, 47 professors received $1,000 "merit awards" for teaching. But two campuses in the state declined to participate, denouncing the legislature for interfering with faculty governance and for basing the prize on student opinion. "Are all students really equipped or blessed with sufficient maturity, knowledge, and high-mindedness to soundly judge their teachers?" Oregon College of Education professor E. K. Dortmund asked. "Is it not a bad thing to have [a] doctor's career partially determined by the ill-informed opinions of his patients?"[40]

Most of all, faculty members questioned whether the medicinal magic of a teaching award could help cure the research/teaching imbalance that ailed American universities. Like many faculty development projects, critics said, the teaching award was a way for college administrators to demonstrate a rhetorical commitment to undergraduate instruction without doing anything real to improve it. And when the rubber hit the road, research would still come out on top. Everyone knew that faculty could earn more by publishing another book or article—and winning the higher base pay that came with promotion— than by winning a one-off, single-year teaching award. In several well-publicized cases, moreover, faculty members who won teaching prizes were denied tenure soon thereafter. These unfortunates were "distinguished, then extinguished," one UC Santa Barbara professor noted, quoting Cicero's aphorism; continuing the ancient history motif, he compared them to slaves who were made king for two weeks during the Saturnalia in Rome and then beheaded afterward. ("This did not inspire many slaves to kingship," he dryly added.) Three consecutive prizewinners at Stanford in the 1970s failed to receive tenure; at Penn, three of six winners in the early 1980s suffered the same fate. "When it comes right down to it, the University doesn't pay as much attention to teaching as it does to other considerations," one rejected (and dejected) teaching award winner at Penn declared. Created to enhance the lowly status of undergraduate instruction, teaching prizes ultimately confirmed it. "At present the universities are as uncongenial to teaching as the Mojave Desert to a clutch of Druid priests," classicist William Arrowsmith told the American Council on Education, in a much-quoted 1966 address. "If you want to restore a Druid priesthood, you cannot do it by offering prizes for Druid-of-the-year. If you want Druids, you must grow forests. There is no other way of setting about it."[41]

Actually, during these same years, many institutions were also making broader efforts to incentivize teaching and to challenge—if not reverse—the primacy of research. In 1969, most prominently, University of California president Charles J. Hitch declared that all recommendations for promotion must include "clear documentation of ability and diligence in the teaching role." Sent to the nine chancellors in the UC system, the "Hitch Memo"—as it became known—said that tenure and promotion committees "should consider such points as the following":

> the candidate's command of his subject; his continuous growth in his field; his ability to organize his material to present it with force and logic; his capacity to awaken in students an awareness of the relationship of his subject to other fields of knowledge; his grasp of general objectives; the spirit and enthusiasm which vitalize his learning and teaching; his ability to arouse curiosity in beginning students and to stimulate advanced students to creative work; his personal attributes as they affect his teaching and his students; the extent and skill of his participation in the general guidance and advising of students.

The following year, Hitch ordered UC universities to submit "plans of action" for strengthening undergraduate teaching. The plans were to specify how schools intended to evaluate professors' instruction, Hitch noted, which could include student ratings or assessments by fellow faculty members. Blasting universities for hiring research stars who rarely if ever taught undergraduates, Hitch decreed that "faculty members of all ranks" should teach "at all levels." That included freshmen classes, he pointedly added: each academic year, every first-year student should have the chance to enroll in a small-group class taught by a full-fledged faculty member. As Hitch told a 1970 press conference, most lower-division undergraduates saw too much of TAs and too little of professors, except in huge lecture classes. His proposal took direct aim at that trend, instructing universities to alter the allocation of faculty teaching even as they improved its overall status in promotion and salary.[42]

Hundreds of other institutions promulgated similar policies during these years, declaring that teaching should assume a larger role in both the work lives of faculty and their career trajectories. So did a national task force convened by the federal Department of Health, Education, and Welfare, which proclaimed that "our colleges and universities must be less concerned with academic prestige and more concerned with becoming centers of effective learning." Most faculty members agreed, at least in theory: in a nationwide 1971 faculty survey commissioned by the Project to Improve College Teaching, 92 percent of respondents said that the "effectiveness of a teacher" should be "quite" or "very" important in determining salary and promotion. But only 39 percent said that it actually *was* important where they worked, and most of those professors were at smaller liberal arts schools or junior colleges. At larger universities, the new statements about teaching were greeted with a mix of skepticism and ennui. "The jury is still out on this one and a common reaction is 'I'll believe it when I see it,'" UCLA associate dean of public health Daniel Wilner told his faculty in 1970, following Charles Hitch's announcements. To be sure, universities bore a "contractual (and moral?) obligation" to "juice-up our teaching," Wilner acknowledged. But as his question mark also suggested, he wondered whether that could happen so long as universities continued to demand research productivity as a precondition for promotion. "Since faculty time is a zero-sum concept, it is clear that something else must give if <u>more time</u> is to be devoted to students," he underlined. "<u>We have many conflicting signals</u>."[43]

Most faculty members had no problem deciphering these signals, of course. At Yale, where administrators proudly proclaimed the school's renewed commitment to teaching, hiring and promotion committees continued to look almost exclusively at publications and letters from outside scholars; although Yale required a statement on the candidate's teaching, one department chair privately admitted, it was "pro forma" and went mostly unnoticed. "We try to pretend that teaching ability plays a role in departmental decisions," another chair confessed. "We sincerely hope this will be really true in the future." For the present, however, it was usually false. "Oh, yes, a number of colleges are now . . . stressing the importance of teaching," UCLA education scholar W. James Popham told a conference on the subject in 1974. "But in all too many of our universities this emphasis is rhetorical rather than real." Reward structures remained largely unchanged, Popham noted, and requiring star faculty to teach undergraduates—the other strand of Charles Hitch's reform plan— would not necessarily improve the outcome. "From a number of reports I have heard, the students may have been better off with the teaching assistants," Popham wrote. "Not all Nobel Prizewinners can whomp up a winning lecture." Nor could most large universities afford Hitch's envisioned professor-led freshman seminars, critics said, which would merely force them to cut back elsewhere. "For us to guarantee a small group class for freshmen would simply mean destroying the senior seminar program or the graduate teaching," a UC San Diego professor wrote. "Is there any possible educational justification for giving raw freshmen the preference over department majors?"[44]

Finally, as many professors correctly noted, none of the new incentives or projects to improve college teaching could work unless universities developed dependable and consistent systems for evaluating it. But most institutions lacked any such mechanism, or even an agreement about the need for one. "If you asked ten different members of our Department about the evaluation of teaching, you would get ten different opinions," a Yale department chair wrote in 1970, "and I defy anyone to get a consensus." Insofar as departments made efforts to assess teaching, another chair wrote, it proceeded mostly on the basis of hearsay or gossip. "Evaluation of teaching comes largely through osmosis," he admitted. "We are not yet expert enough to know how to do it well." Many chairs were still reluctant to visit classes taught by faculty, who were likewise loath to be observed. So officials increasingly fell back on "the judgment of the ultimate consumer of instruction, the student," as one California scholar observed in 1972. By the late 1970s, most institutions had settled on student evaluations as the major—if not the only—institutional arbiter of faculty teaching. "It has become almost as common in colleges and universities for students to grade professors as for professors to grade students," a *New York Times* reporter quipped in 1978.[45]

Dating back to student protests in the 1920s and 1930s, some evaluations were still run by irreverent campus journalists who poked fun at poor teachers and hapless administrators. But most evaluations were taken over by those same administrators, who used them not just to keep tabs on faculty but—just as important—to keep students happy. Evaluations "have become an integral part of consumer politics and a staple in the public relations 'concern for students' approach to potential students and their families," an Oregon State University professor wrote in 1978. The consumer revolution spread to smaller colleges too, as a Hartwick College professor reported five years after that. "A bad sign around the campus these days is that students are too often referred to or thought of as customers," English professor David Baldwin wrote despairingly in 1983, condemning the school's rising dependence on student evaluations. "This is a stupefying and craven idea, craven because it would turn the College into a commercial venture. If students are customers, then of course, following the good old American adage, the customer is always right." The customer might not always have been right, but Baldwin was. Over the next three decades, college teaching would become a consumer good just like anything else. Whether that benefitted the seller or the buyer—or both, or neither—was a more difficult matter to evaluate.[46]

The Decade of the Undergraduate?

College Teaching in the 1990s and Beyond

In 1993, Georgetown English professor Randall Bass published a brief article decrying the mismatch between the way faculty members were prepared for their jobs and the duties they would actually perform. Graduate training was devoted almost entirely to making future professors into "competent and original scholars," Bass wrote, which neglected or ignored their function as teachers. It would not do just to add a course about pedagogy to students' scholarly training, Bass warned; instead; universities needed to reimagine teaching as a legitimate form of scholarship in its own right. Here he echoed the much-publicized 1990 report by Ernest Boyer, president of the Carnegie Foundation for the Advancement of Teaching. Boyer called upon colleges and universities to recognize and reward the intellectual activity of undergraduate instruction, which was every bit as knotty and complex as the problems faculty addressed in their research. His report kicked off a series of national studies and statements about college teaching in the 1990s, which "may well come to be remembered as the decade of the undergraduate in American higher education," Boyer predicted. What was needed was a culture shift, Bass and Boyer agreed, whereby universities gave teaching the same professional attention and status that research received. Otherwise, Randall Bass warned, the college classroom would continue as "Higher Education's Amateur Hour," to quote the title of his article.[1]

And amateur it remains, which is why I borrowed from Bass's title for my own. There was nothing new about his plea for graduate schools to take teaching seriously, which dated back to the first decades of the twentieth century. Ditto for most of the other college teaching reforms in the 1990s and thereafter, which focused on promoting intellectual engagement in the classroom; repackaged as "active learning," it was generally old wine in new bottles. To be sure, there were also significant changes. Between 1992 and 2011, most notably, the fraction of graduate students who received at least some teacher training as part of their PhD programs doubled. That movement was fueled by yet another infusion of foundation dollars, especially to the nationwide Preparing

Future Faculty program: pairing graduate students at PhD-granting universities with liberal arts and community colleges, it gave the students real-life teaching experience and mentorship at the types of institutions where they would most likely spend their careers. These years also witnessed a surge of mass media attention to the problem of college teaching, spurred by political forces outside of the university and several high-profile mea culpas within it. State legislatures appropriated funds for teaching prizes and faculty development while also passing measures requiring minimum instructional commitments from professors, which one Louisiana lawmaker characterized as "teach or terminate": if the carrot of more money did not work, maybe the threatened stick of dismissal would. Meanwhile, university leaders denounced the neglect of undergraduate instruction with unprecedented candor and intensity. The loudest note was struck by Stanford president Donald Kennedy, who made national headlines—and shocked his own faculty—by charging that they had forsaken their responsibilities as teachers. He announced a $7 million initiative to fund teaching prizes, new course development, and the expansion of computer technologies in instruction. As one local professor wrote, borrowing a metaphor from the earthquake-prone Bay Area, Kennedy's project struck with a force "measuring 8.5 on the academic Richter scale."[2]

But Stanford had heard this particular rumbling several times before, as another observer cautioned. In the 1970s, students protesting the denial of tenure to a popular professor had formed a task force to examine the low priority of teaching on the campus; ironically, one of its members was a biology professor named Donald Kennedy. The university had accepted many of the panel's recommendations, including teaching awards and mandatory student evaluations. Like other campuses, it had also instituted a range of new faculty development programs aimed at replacing lectures with more active, participatory strategies. Lecturing had been the *bête noire* of reformers since the 1920s, of course, decried alternately as authoritarian—and hence anathema to democracy—or simply as dull. Yet it probably came under its harshest fire in the 1990s and early 2000s, when a dynamic new machine—the personal computer—seemed poised to obviate it forever. Now that information was freely available on the World Wide Web, a *New York Times* article asked in 2002, why should professors dispense it in class? The article quoted former Rollins College president Hamilton Holt, pioneer of the school's illustrious "conference" system, who had famously denounced lecturing as "the worst scheme ever devised for imparting knowledge." In the age of the computer, it was also unnecessary. "In the next 10 years, there will be much more flexibility in teaching modalities,"

University of Pennsylvania president Judith Rodin told the *Times*. "The standard college lecture will be pretty much a thing of the past. The teacher of the future will be more of a mentor and less of a didactic lecturer." The last great technological innovation, television, had merely changed the medium of the lecture. The computer would help eliminate it altogether.[3]

Yet reports of the demise of the lecture were premature, just as they had been in the days of Hamilton Holt. (The *Times* neglected to report that Holt's faculty eventually rejected his conference plan and returned to traditional lecture classes.) As several studies confirmed, American professors lectured less often than they had before; they also reported using more interactive and student-centered techniques, which sociologist Steven Brint labeled "The New Progressivism." But lectures lived on. Some professors developed "hybrid" models, punctuating their lectures with discussion and other activities; many others just delivered a monologue, albeit accompanied by PowerPoint slides. One big reason, as before, was money: lecturing might not have been the best method of college instruction, but it was always the cheapest. Often starved by their state legislatures, large public universities felt the economic pressure most acutely. At the University of California, Santa Cruz, which was started in the 1960s to counter the anomie of big lecture classes, professors were increasingly called upon to teach them. "If you get 150 people, it's three midterms and a final and that's it," chemistry professor Frank Andrews noted. Nor could he possibly provide narrative evaluations instead of letter grades for each student, Andrews added, a practice that most UC Santa Cruz professors abandoned when class sizes rose. Andrews had left a prior job at the University of Wisconsin, which seemed "like a factory," but now UC Santa Cruz felt like one as well. At the University of California, Irvine, similarly, state budget cuts forced the school to increase class sizes and cut the number of teaching assistants. Saddled with classes of 100 students or more, even faculty who were not disposed to lecture had little choice but to do so.[4]

But other professors held on to the lecture for philosophical reasons, not just for economic ones. Many of them perceived—correctly—that the New Progressivism was not delivering on the expanded learning that it promised. If coupled with rigorous assignments and close faculty direction, research showed, student-centered classes could indeed yield deeper knowledge and understanding. Like encounter-group classes in the 1960s, however, active-learning strategies often generated lively exercises that taught very little; students were "engaged" by the new approach, to quote a favorite New Progressive metaphor, but they were not necessarily educated by it. That was especially the case among less privileged students, who frequently lacked both the basic knowledge and self-direction that these methods presumed. "The students, like squirrels, are expected to gather information as though foraging for nuts and berries, out of which material they are to construct knowledge, while the instructor stands by idly," one skeptical community college English professor wrote, denouncing the new paradigm. "Learning is somehow whipped up out of some ether in the classroom." Other professors argued that active-learning methods might be appropriate for the humanities but not for the natural sciences, where there was often only one right answer; as a physicist at Holy Cross told his colleagues, the interpretation of a painting changes every five years, but the law of gravity does not. "I don't think that all courses should be taught the same," he added. "I would just like the community to see that some traditional types of teaching are very appropriate in certain situations." Most of all, critics worried that the "student-centered" approach actually harmed students by "implicitly teaching them that anything goes," as one scholar noted. The most devastating critique was delivered by journalist Janet Malcolm, who denounced "the democratizing discussion class" as a pseudoegalitarian sham. "Modern American pedagogy is poised on the fiction that there is no 'greater man' or 'lesser man' in the teacher/student dyad," Malcolm wrote. "Here any idiotic thing the student says is listened to as if it was brilliant, and here our national vice of talking for the sake of hearing ourselves talk is cultivated as if it was a virtue."[5]

Professors also liked to hear themselves talk, of course, which was another reason that the lecture continued. So did bitter student complaints about poor lecturers, which were as long-standing a tradition as the lecture itself. Students still reported that professors simply repeated what the textbook said; some faculty even read aloud from books they had authored, which "literally joins teaching with research," as one annoyed observer quipped. As in the past, meanwhile, students seemed to compete to find different (and snarky) ways to say the same thing: the lecture was dull. At Yale, one student described a chemistry professor as an "anesthetic"; in a physics class, another said that the best part of the course was "waking up and realizing the lecture was over." But other students described their lecturing professors in sacred and superhuman terms, echoing the hero worship that had surrounded selected teachers since the dawn of the university. "Wisdom drips out of every orifice of his body," a student wrote, in praise of Yale religion professor Louis Dupre. "I felt like I was in the presence of greatness." So did an undergraduate taking a history class with historian Jon Butler, saying that he would gladly wash Butler's feet; in a course with a second Yale historian, John Demos, another student declared that Demos "has been touched by the hand of God." Such metaphors recur across student memoirs and evaluations, from the early twentieth century into the present, reminding us about the love and power that a single charismatic personality can generate in a room of students. "Literature was living, breathing, walking all around me, and I could barely contain the excitement," a student at Pomona College wrote, describing the large lecture class taught in the 1990s by English professor Brian Stonehill. "My roommate and friends laughed at my new obsession, but couldn't deny the facts. Something was going on, and we all knew Stonehill himself had everything to do with it."[6]

But nobody could say exactly what it was, of course, which was another hallmark of charisma. In Stonehill's case, it was also enhanced by his tragic death in an auto accident at the age of 43. "Nothing is more difficult, I think, than to convey any idea of what it is that makes a great teacher great: it cannot be reduced to a method," Stonehill's department chair wrote, in a posthumous tribute to him. "So, except in the most superficial ways, I can't tell you what it was that Brian did." All he knew, the chair added, was that Stonehill possessed a "special magic" in the classroom. Reflecting back on their own education, other professors in the 1990s used similar language to describe the "great teachers" of their youth: they possessed a kind of mysterious presence in the classroom, which was so indescribable that it made them greater still. "The lecture has a quasi-religious character about it, since exalted speech partakes of the sacred," historian Page Smith wrote. Like Mass or any other religious ceremony, a lecture was a dramatic act; the professor did not simply "say" the words but infused them with meaning via gestures, cadences, and intonations. Sociologist Robert Nisbet likewise praised the great lecturers of his undergraduate years at UC Berkeley in the 1930s, when theatrical performers like historian Henry Morse Stephens strode the stage. Sixty years later, Nisbet could still conjure the "expression and dramatic intensity" that Stephens evoked when holding forth on the Jacobins, the Terror, and the rise of Napoleon. Stephens entered the lecture hall puffing a cigar and relighted it immediately after class, announcing that "no gentleman . . . could be away from his cigar for more than 50 minutes." The charismatic lecturer was a "character" as well as a spellbinder, as eccentric off the podium as he was entertaining on it. Most freshmen were "hero-worshippers," Nisbet recalled. They fell hard for the "teacher-heroes" of Berkeley, he added.[7]

But as Nisbet also observed, writing glumly in 1992, the large lecture course "is not as charismatic as it once was." The leading figures on campus no longer taught undergraduate courses and certainly not introductory ones, which were sloughed off on junior faculty and TAs. But the conventional wisdom on teaching had changed too: in the era of the New Progressivism, so-called active learning was "in" and the lecture was "out." It is tempting to dismiss glowing accounts of big-class lecturers—almost all white, almost all male—as reactionary nostalgia for an older America, where expertise was carefully bounded by race and gender; indeed, advocates for the student-centered approach often framed it as particularly appropriate for women and minorities, whose teaching styles were supposedly more "democratic" and less "authoritarian." But female and minority professors were also powerful lecturers in their own right, often drawing on the verbal traditions of the feminist and civil rights movements. Arriving at Berkeley to teach Afro-American studies in 1971, black psychologist William Banks took the classroom by storm. Asked in a 2004 interview about the secret to his teaching success, Banks said it had less to do with any specific method than with the spirit he exuded. "How important it is to introduce charisma to the class," Banks explained. "That's not a popular thing to say, but in my classes I give students somebody—a real person—to interact with, as opposed to just ideas. . . . I employ irony, and just sort of bring myself into the situation to give people something to react to other than just the material." To Banks, that approach— the teacher in front of the room, riffing with the students but still very much in charge—reflected his own African American roots. "It's part of black culture, that kind of expressive culture that argues back and forth," he observed. Banks often deliberated with himself as he lectured, taking one position and then the opposite one. That gave students a model for entering the dialogue with him, when they felt ready to do so.[8]

Banks's apologetic aside about charisma in class—"that's not a popular thing to say"—spoke to the ongoing suspicion of it in American college teaching. Since the early twentieth century, students had raved about theatrical display in the lecture hall and professors had reviled it; skill at the podium marked the popular teacher as a "mere entertainer," the most dismissive label that an academic could receive. English professor and longtime University of Washington department chair Robert Heilman went even further in a 1991 essay entitled "The Great-Teacher Myth," which cast charismatic professors as flat-out frauds. Heilman likened them to the figure of John Keating in the 1989 hit movie *Dead Poets Society*, where we never see Keating—a prep school teacher played by Robin Williams—actually teach any content; he instead runs a "special classroom show," which is all the more injurious to students because it is intoxicating to them. "It is a rare university that does not have its own resident Keating," Heilman wrote. "He tends to become the local Great Teacher, a resonant voice that beguiles its publics (undergraduates and off-campus auditors) while leaving colleagues unmoved. . . . It is immoral when the teacher becomes greater than the thing taught, living in the adulation of innocent youngsters." A recent book about efforts to reform college teaching concludes with a plea to educate the public about quality college instruction, which involves student activity rather than professorial performance. "The challenge these days is getting beyond the cult of personality, which leads to good teaching being equated with an engaging TED talk and entertainment trumping substance," the authors conclude. A popular teacher may not be a good one, they argued, and Americans needed to learn the difference.[9]

But popularity is still the coin of the realm in college teaching, precisely because instruction has never been professionalized. Nobody would think of judging a faculty member's research by polling students about it. But the vast majority of higher-education institutions appraise teaching primarily—or even exclusively—via student evaluations, which shifted from informal student-run publications in the 1960s to official administrative mechanisms in the 1980s and 1990s. Evaluations were no longer just a way for students to share information about which professors were interesting or boring (or easy or hard); instead, the evaluations became part of the way that institutions determined tenure, rank, and salary. A 1983 survey of liberal arts deans showed that most of them hinged tenure and promotion at least in part on "classroom performance," usually judged via student ratings, but only 11 percent of the deans said they had conducted research to see whether those scores reflected classroom *effectiveness.* Had they done so, they would have discovered that course evaluations embody deep cultural biases: highly rated professors are more likely to be male, white, good-looking, and easy, yet there is scant evidence that their students actually learn more. But even as increasing numbers of schools declared themselves research institutions, they mostly ignored the research about teaching evaluations. "In university settings where the scientific method is sacrosanct and objectivity is the valued norm, student ratings of professors are neither scientific nor objective," one Texas junior college professor wrote in 1983. "Fugitives from Pflugerville football and the Farmersville F.F.A [Future Farmers of America] are to be a jury on your professional competence. What are their qualifications for this serious business? Well, they paid tuition." It was a consumerist institution now, and the customer always came first.[10]

By the 1990s, student evaluations were ubiquitous. Whether or not the nineties were "the decade of the undergraduate," as Ernest Boyer had hoped, they were certainly the decade of the undergraduate evaluation. Faculty members sensed, correctly, that an important shift was underway: formerly the rulers of their classrooms, they were now subject to the whims of students who did not even reveal their names. "As we know, the only proper place for anonymous letters is the wastebasket," University of Michigan English professor Cecil Eby complained to his dean. "They might amuse, but no responsible administrator this side of the Kremlin would formulate a policy based on them." Yet most institutions had done exactly that, requiring every professor to submit to the humiliation of student evaluations and hinging pay, promotions, and prizes on the result. "Always I feel like some cheap charlatan when I convert the fifteen minute segment of the final class period into some sort of Nielsen-Rating System. 'Here's Johnny!,'" Eby quipped, referring to late-night talk show host Johnny Carson, "but unfortunately without Johnny's stable of gag-writers." Eby then had to select a student to carry the evaluations to the department office, lest he alter or fabricate them if they were left in his possession. "I find this unconscionable and insulting," Eby declared. "In effect, I am telling the class that I am not a professional but a potential sneak." Some students cut his class for the entire semester but showed up at the end to fill out a course survey; while he welcomed feedback from "committed students," Eby wrote, "why should we care about the random pickings of some sleepy, back-row bench-warmer?" Ignoring the obvious differences between students, evaluations also made a mockery of the expert authority that he brought to the classroom.[11]

But when it came to teaching, few faculty members *were* experts; they were amateurs, working according to folkloric traditions rather than codified ones. And they resisted most attempts to make their teaching truly professional, which would have required them to submit to the judgment of each other. That's what they do as researchers, of course, where peer review is a near-universal practice. But most efforts to promote peer review of college teaching have come to naught, because faculty have not signed on to them. Several foundations provided major support for the "portfolio assessment" movement in the 1990s, whereby faculty submitted documents—syllabi, class handouts, teaching philosophies, and so on—that peers would evaluate, as they do with scholarship. But many professors simply did not trust each other to render informed judgments about the portfolios, while others questioned whether the collected materials reflected teaching quality any better than student evaluations did. "What good is the effective documentation of marginally important information?" a professor at Louisiana State University asked. "Has improvement in teaching efficacy been reliably, scientifically established as attributable to the TP [teaching portfolio] method?" Observing portfolio reviews at Manhattanville College, one participant warned that "the definition of excellence varies from committee to committee." Skilled insiders could therefore turn TP into a "massive bureaucratic game," a University of Maryland professor worried, using the right words to get what they wanted. Ultimately, TP fell victim to the same amateur culture it was aiming to uproot: without shared professional standards of good teaching, faculty members were understandably suspicious about new ones being imposed on them. Asked to comment on a survey about the "challenges" of teaching portfolios and peer review, one anonymous professor replied in verse (and in all caps):

JUST THE USUAL STUFF
BEING ALL THAT STUFF,
THAT WE ARE SUPPOSED TO DO, TEACH, RESEARCH, ADMINISTER,
    RAISE FAMILIES . . .
AND NOW YOU TELL US TO LEARN NEW TRICKS OURSELVES
YOU ARE WITHOUT MERCY.[12]

Other faculty critics associated the portfolio movement—and not always fairly—with the outcomes-based assessments that state legislatures instituted during these years, which sought to evaluate colleges based on students' academic progress. Institutions were allowed to set their own targets, as well as their own measures for meeting them, which really did become a massive bureaucratic game: defining "progress" to include factors such as graduation rates and job placements, schools could claim they had improved teaching without actually doing anything to change it. It was left to true believers like Temple classicist Daniel Tompkins to "spread the peer review gospel," as he wrote. Appointed to serve as a "Faculty Fellow for Learning Communities" at his institution, Tompkins found that most departments were suspicious or hostile toward peer review. "They envision thought police from higher up, the heightening of intra-departmental tensions (already often quite elevated), increased work," Tompkins wrote. "I'm not sure that we're winning over the audience that we seek." Perhaps the term might be changed to "peer collaboration," he suggested, which somehow sounded less threatening. "My model is not quite the Jesuits in China, who sold Christianity by presenting it as just another form of ancestor worship, omitting confusing trivia like the role of the virgin Mary," Tompkins added, striking a jocular tone. But advocates for peer review did need to simplify their sales pitch if they wanted anyone to buy the new faith, he emphasized. Otherwise, universities would continue to "fine-tune" student evaluation questions, Tompkins concluded, "when the real need is to supplement that instrument with better assessment measures."[13]

Part of that fine-tuning involved new questions about professors' behavior and attitude around race and gender, highlighting yet another challenge to their classroom authority during these years. In 1981, a faculty committee at the University of Colorado rejected a proposal to add an item about sexual and racial discrimination to the school's course questionnaire; although the topic was "important," the committee chair wrote, the course evaluation form was "an improper means" of addressing it. But eight years later, at the dawn of the decade of the undergraduate, Colorado added two new fill-in-the-blank items: "The instructor's treatment of ethnic/gender/minority students was _____ " and "How the course addressed ethnic/gender/minority issues/information was _____." The impetus for these kinds of additions often came from female faculty members, who argued that earlier evaluation forms were biased against them: asking about professors' lectures and command of the subject matter, they ignored the interpersonal skills that women often brought to the classroom. But the gender and race questions also created new constraints, causing professors to avoid themes and topics that might offend students. Evaluations were not the only factor in this dynamic, to be sure, which involved broader trends surrounding race and gender in the 1990s. But the course questionnaires surely made faculty more cautious, adding to an overall spirit of anxiety and self-censorship in the classroom. "We, as professors, have to be role models, and encourage our students to voice their opinions no matter how objectionable we find them," pollster Frank Luntz complained, during his adjunct teaching stint at the University of Pennsylvania in 1994. "If we reward cowardice in a university setting, we will be producing cowardly adults—they'll say what they think is socially acceptable, rather than what they truly believe."[14]

Luntz's remarks earned a sharp rejoinder from English professor Houston Baker, director of Penn's Center for the Study of Black Literature and Culture, who argued that some faculty speech *should* be curtailed. "No professors should be empowered to harass or diminish students in the classroom, and that includes a professor's verbal behavior," Baker argued. Such debates have a familiar ring today, conjuring recent controversies over race, gender, and free speech at the university. Yet we tend to forget that these issues date to the 1990s, when faculty members started to complain about a new pall of censorship that was descending on their classrooms. In 1995, for example, a junior college professor in California barred students from taping his class lest his words be used against him later. "With the controversial issue of being politically correct nowadays, it is just too much to worry about," he told his class. "You can call me paranoid." They certainly had the power to call him that—or anything else—in their end-of-semester evaluations, which made some of their teachers gun-shy. "The constraint exerted by the course evaluation is both a good and bad thing," three scholars observed in 2008, reviewing developments over the previous decade. "It is good in forcing professors to attend seriously to their teaching duties. It has less desirable consequences insofar as it may induce professors to be overly cautious and to steer clear of controversy lest they offend students." Professors also had to worry about insulting political conservatives, who mobilized in the 1990s and early 2000s to monitor classes for signs of left-leaning bias. At UCLA, most notoriously, a right-wing group offered students cash in exchange for class handouts or recorded lectures showing that professors were "proselytizing their extreme view in the classroom." For most of the twentieth century, with the important exception of the McCarthy years, American faculty members had enjoyed a great deal of autonomy in their own classrooms. For good or ill, that leeway would narrow in the 1990s and thereafter.[15]

Student evaluations also contributed to grade inflation, which continued to soar even as assigned classwork plummeted. About 43 percent of college letter grades in 2011 were As, up from 31 percent in 1988 and 15 percent in 1960. Over roughly the same span, the average amount of studying by people in college declined by almost 50 percent, from 25 to 13 hours per week. In a recent survey of undergraduates at 24 widely varying institutions, half the respondents said they were not taking a single course requiring a total of 20 pages of writing. Again, we cannot lay the entire blame for these problems at the feet of student evaluations. But surely evaluations encouraged faculty to decrease their demands on students, as several professors frankly acknowledged. After losing one teaching job because of poor evaluations, SUNY Oswego professor Robert Owen relaxed his course requirements by substituting a literature review for a research paper and multiple-choice tests for essay exams. His evaluations went up after that, for reasons that Owen—a professor of marketing—understood all too well. "The student in college is being treated as a customer in a retail environment, and I have to worry about customer complaints," he admitted. Gary Trudeau captured the spirit of this dynamic in a hilarious 1993

cartoon, featuring a mathematics professor ("Deadman") and his college president. Deadman is being sued for giving a low grade to a member of the
"Greco-American Athletic Community," Trudeau's wry shorthand for
fraternities.

> PRESIDENT. Well, Deadman, your department made itself vulnerable with all
> the grade inflation. How could that happen with math, anyway?
> DEADMAN. We dumbed down the tests, sir. Under student pressure, we traded
> learning for "success." At least some of us did!
> PRESIDENT. Well, the customer is always right, eh, Deadman?
> DEADMAN. Words to teach by, sir.
> PRESIDENT. It's a different world, professor. Adapt or die.[16]

The pressure was probably greatest on the growing corps of contingent and
adjunct faculty, whose livelihoods often rested entirely on keeping the customer satisfied. Recent exposés about the "adjunctification" of the professoriate often fail to note that this problem also has roots in the 1980s and 1990s,
when tenure-track hires slowed. By the mid-1990s, 40 percent of college faculty were already part-timers. So the decade of the undergraduate was also
the decade of the adjunct, described alternately as a gypsy, a nomad, or—most
often—as a "freeway flyer." In 1995, the *New York Times* profiled an adjunct
English instructor who drove 100 miles each day to teach 100 students at three
different California campuses. "I feel like this information machine, sort of
Teach 'R' Us," she said. "What are we doing in our cars, all these Ph.D.'s on the
freeways, listening to talk radio?" When they got to campus, moreover, adjuncts often discovered that they lacked basic amenities like an office, phone,
or mailbox; one instructor's mail was collected in a discarded snack-food box,
a grim symbol of adjuncts' lowly status in higher education. Not surprisingly,
as a 1994 study confirmed, adjunct instructors spent less time interacting with
students than regular professors did; they were also more likely to use multiple-
choice tests, less likely to assign papers, and less likely to require multiple
drafts of them. They were too busy driving to multiple campuses and shoul-
dering the classes that nobody else wanted to teach, especially those in the
early mornings and late evenings. "University life is like the Civil War, when
the rich hired the poor to fight their battles," one California professor admitted in 1990. "In the contemporary groves-of-academe version, temporary lecturers are the conscripts on the firing line." They were also at the greatest risk
of getting shot down via student evaluations. As an Illinois professor noted,
several years earlier, administrators could fire adjuncts merely on the grounds

of a poor evaluation or a "high flunk rate" in their classes. Nothing else was needed.[17]

By the mid-1990s, other officials were imagining replacing adjuncts—indeed, classroom professors of every kind—with online courses. As computer technologies became more widely available, colleges encouraged the use of "Digital Chalk"—as a 1994 faculty development seminar called it—to improve regular classes. Teachers beamed lecture notes from their laptops and shared them online; others posted material for students to read before discussing it in class, prefiguring today's "flipped classroom." But other institutions were already promoting classes that could be taught entirely online, offering professors stipends to "convert" their courses into online formats but "no incentives to use computers to improve learning in traditional, face-to-face courses," as one faculty critic complained. Students sensed the difference too, worrying that online classes advertised as "personalized"—because each individual could take them at their own pace, and in their own space—would actually remove the personal element from education, just as televised classes and programmed learning had done. "A university is a place where the knowledge of one generation is passed on to the next, and this cannot be done by machine," the Louisiana State University student newspaper warned in 1993. "Information can be found in a computer, but only by the human touch is the knowledge of generations transmitted." Here the paper echoed a long tradition of student anxiety about impersonal and faceless instruction, warning that students would not learn from someone they did not know. "As we head toward a time when our classrooms are defined by cyberspace, we should first examine our literal classroom experiences," the University of Pennsylvania student paper urged in 1998. It knew which way the wind was blowing, but it also believed that careful student evaluation would underscore the ongoing importance of face-to-face instruction.[18]

Like their professors, however, other students voiced deep skepticism about student evaluations. In earlier eras, they had rallied around course ratings in order to hold professors accountable for teaching—and, ideally, to help them improve. By the 1990s, however, many students saw evaluations as an empty organizational ritual with little connection to their classrooms or lives. Asked how they thought teaching evaluations were used at Louisiana State University, one student replied "as scratch paper"; another said they were "put in a file that no one uses"; and a third simply replied, "Who knows, man?" Professors routinely received poor evaluations but continued teaching the same classes in the same way, suggesting that the institution paid little mind to the exercise. Predictably, then, students often followed their lead. "Most students don't take evaluations seriously and just write down anything," one student admitted. Others wondered why they should bother to attend class at all, now that many professors were posting their lecture notes online. But students also recognized that they were being cheated, especially as tuition costs continued to rise. "We pay for an education—I'd like to receive one," an LSU student flatly proclaimed. A second student was even more pointed, noting the low priority that undergraduate teaching continued to receive. "If an instructor is doing consistently poorly then he should be consulted on how to improve his teaching ability," the student wrote. "I'm paying for an education not for someone to talk down to me, treat me like dirt, nor for this person to busy himself in his research. This is an institution first and foremost for EDUCATION."[19]

Was it? And who really wanted education, if it involved more effort? When professors tried to improve their teaching, especially by adding more problem-solving activities in class, they often faced resistance—and, of course, low evaluations—from students who preferred to listen to a lecture, take a few notes, and spit them back on an exam. Critical thinking was "new and possibly painful or threatening," a Kansas professor privately wrote, and many people did not want to do it: on his own evaluations, students pleaded with him to just to give them the "right answers" instead of asking them to come up with their own. Despite the new rhetorical emphasis on teaching in the 1990s, meanwhile, research remained the key to academic promotion and success. The students knew it—hence their digs at teachers who snubbed them for research—and their professors knew it best of all. Most faculty members described research as their "work" and teaching as their "load," which spoke volumes about academic priorities. And that held constant across different kinds of institutions, where poor student evaluations could sink you only if your research had not risen to the top. The refreshingly blunt Harvard president Lawrence Summers admitted as much in 2004, telling a student who complained about the dismissal of a renowned teacher that Harvard hired and promoted based on scholarship alone. "If you wanted somewhere that focused on undergraduate teaching, you should go to a place like Amherst or Swarthmore," Summers said. But even small liberal arts colleges were placing more emphasis on research, as their own efforts to upgrade teaching indirectly—and ironically—illustrated. "A Center for Teaching?" an emeritus professor at Colby asked incredulously in 1992, after the college had established one. "I thought that's what the whole college was."[20]

It was not, of course, which is why Colby—like hundreds of other institutions—felt the need to designate an arm of the school that was devoted specifically to instruction. Yet there is also considerable evidence that college teaching has improved over the past few decades, in part because of the new institutional focus on learning theory and best practices. More and more professors leavened lectures with in-class activities or dispensed with the lecture altogether, substituting discussions, role-playing games, or group projects. In the hands of a skilled teacher, this kind of instruction increased retention of information and promoted higher-order skills like problem-solving and critical thinking. Other professors provided frequent quizzes via iClickers or other new devices, drawing on a solid body of evidence that students learned more when they were forced to answer questions. These trends were spearheaded by campus-wide initiatives like the Course Transformation Project at the University of Texas—which helped professors infuse student interaction into introductory classes—and the Structured, Active, In-Class Learning program at the University of Pennsylvania, where I taught while writing this book. But many faculty members—probably most faculty members—around the country remained blissfully unaware of these reforms; others tried to implement them without any substantial guidance or training, which was a formula for chaos and confusion. Preparation for college teaching remained the "missing course" of American higher education, as teaching expert David Gooblar plaintively noted in his 2019 book of that title. The explosion of knowledge about learning did not spark a commensurate revolution in the classroom, where too much instruction went on much as before. With no real incentive to change, most professors stayed the same.[21]

Indeed, the lack of tangible career-related returns on teaching remains the central barrier to improving it. As a Penn professor quipped in 1990, on the eve of the so-called decade of the undergraduate, college teaching was "a famously idiosyncratic activity that is not famously rewarded."[22] Over the past century, that idiosyncrasy has been both the Achilles heel and the saving grace of undergraduate instruction. On the one hand, it has prevented colleges and universities from establishing professional norms that would systematically elevate and enhance teaching; on the other hand, it has given American college teachers the space to display their individual preferences and personalities. As a small set of colleges evolved into a gigantic higher-education industry, patronized by nearly three-quarters of the citizens in our country, the amateur nature of college teaching yielded some truly appalling and unjust outcomes: dull instruction, disengaged students, and limited learning. I cannot defend that, nor will I try, and I applaud the many people in these pages who have struggled to make it better.

But I also believe that teaching is a deeply personal and even spiritual act that defies rational organization, which accounts for much of its magic as well as its miseries. Even the best-prepared teachers cannot predict or control what happens in class; there's always an element of suspense and surprise, reflecting the configuration of students in the room and the happenstance of their mood and temperament at that particular time. The charisma of the professor also varies, of course, across different moments and—especially—across different individuals. Some great teachers dominate the classroom with the dramatic force of their personalities; others assume a quieter demeanor, creating an atmosphere of close but calm attention. But every effective teacher establishes a distinctive rapport with their students, a kind of mystical presence that cannot always be defined but also cannot be denied.[23] I do not believe that this face-to-face energy can be communicated via computer modems, which connect our minds but not our bodies or our souls. One hundred years ago, Max Weber warned that the iron cage of bureaucracy would squeeze the charismatic spirit out of modern life. Even as we work for systemic change in college teaching, which has languished for too long under the dead hand of tradition, we also need to keep alive the mystique—and the charisma—that drew so many of us to it in the first place.

Archives of College Teaching

College and University Archives

Amherst: Archives and Special Collections, Amherst College, Amherst, Massachusetts

Bennett: Archives and Special Collections, Bennett College, Greensboro, North Carolina

Bowdoin: Special Collections and Archives, Bowdoin College, Brunswick, Maine

Bryn Mawr: College Archives, Bryn Mawr College, Bryn Mawr, Pennsylvania

Bucknell: Special Collections / University Archives, Bucknell University, Lewisburg, Pennsylvania

California State University, Dominguez Hills: Donald R. and Beverly J. Gerth Archives and Special Collections, California State University, Dominguez Hills, Carson, California

Carleton: College Archives, Carleton College, Northfield, Minnesota

Claremont: Special Collections, The Claremont Colleges, Claremont, California

Colby: Special Collections, Colby College, Waterville, Maine

Columbia: Rare Book and Manuscript Library, Columbia University, New York, New York

Dartmouth: Rauner Special Collections Library, Dartmouth College, Hanover, New Hampshire

George Washington: Special Collections Research Center, George Washington University, Washington, DC

Harvard: Harvard University Archives, Harvard University, Cambridge, Massachusetts

Holy Cross: Archives and Special Collections, College of the Holy Cross, Worcester, Massachusetts

Johns Hopkins: Ferdinand Hamburger University Archives, Johns Hopkins University, Baltimore, Maryland

Louisiana State University: University Archives, Louisiana State University, Baton Rouge, Louisiana

New York University: University Archives, New York University, New York, New York

Northwestern University: University Archives, Northwestern University, Evanston, Illinois

Oberlin: College Archives, Oberlin College, Oberlin, Ohio

Oregon State University: Special Collections and Archives Research Center, Oregon State University, Corvallis, Oregon

Penn State: Special Collections Library, Pennsylvania State University, State College, Pennsylvania

Pepperdine: Boone Special Collections and Archives, Pepperdine University, Malibu, California

Princeton, I: Rare Books and Special Collections, Firestone Library, Princeton University, Princeton, New Jersey

Princeton, II: Seeley G. Mudd Manuscript Library, Princeton University, Princeton, New Jersey

Rice: University Archives, Rice University, Houston, Texas

Rollins: Archives and Special Collections, Rollins College, Winter Park, Florida

Stanford: Special Collections and University Archives, Stanford University, Stanford, California

Swarthmore: Swarthmore College Archives, Friends Historical Library, Swarthmore College, Swarthmore, Pennsylvania

Temple: Urban Archives, Temple University, Philadelphia, Pennsylvania

Tufts: Digital Collections and Archives, Tufts University, Medford, Massachusetts

University of Arizona: Special Collections, University of Arizona, Tucson, Arizona

University of Buffalo: University Archives, University of Buffalo, Buffalo, New York

University of California, Berkeley: Bancroft Library, University of California, Berkeley, Berkeley, California

University of California, Irvine: Special Collections and Archives, University of California, Irvine, Irvine, California

University of California, Los Angeles: Charles E. Young Research Library, University of California, Los Angeles, Los Angeles, California

University of California, San Diego: Special Collections and Archives, University of California, San Diego, La Jolla, California

University of California, Santa Barbara: Special Research Collections, University of California, Santa Barbara, Santa Barbara, California

University of California, Santa Cruz: Special Collections and Archives, University of California, Santa Cruz, Santa Cruz, California

University of Chicago: Special Collections Research Center, University of Chicago, Chicago, Illinois

University of Colorado: Special Collections, Archives, and Preservation, University of Colorado, Boulder, Colorado

University of Georgia: Hargrett Rare Book and Manuscript Library, University of Georgia, Athens, Georgia

University of Maryland: Special Collections and University Archives, University of Maryland, College Park, Maryland

University of Michigan: Bentley Historical Library, University of Michigan, Ann Arbor, Michigan

University of Minnesota: Archives and Special Collections, University of Minnesota, Minneapolis, Minnesota

University of Missouri–St. Louis: University Archives, University of Missouri–St. Louis, St. Louis, Missouri

University of Nevada: Special Collections and University Archives, University of Nevada, Reno, Nevada

University of New Hampshire: Special Collections, University Archives and Museum, University of New Hampshire, Durham, New Hampshire

University of Pennsylvania: University Archives and Records Center, University of Pennsylvania, Philadelphia, Pennsylvania

University of Texas: Briscoe Center for American History, University of Texas, Austin, Texas

University of Utah: University Archives and Records Management, University of Utah, Salt Lake City, Utah

University of Vermont: Special Collections Library, University of Vermont, Burlington, Vermont

University of Virginia: Albert and Shirley Small Special Collections Library, University of Virginia, Charlottesville, Virginia

University of Washington: Special Collections, University of Washington, Seattle, Washington

Wellesley: College Archives, Wellesley College, Wellesley, Massachusetts

Wesleyan: Special Collections and Archives, Wesleyan University, Middletown, Connecticut

Western Washington: University Archives and Records Center, Western Washington University, Bellingham, Washington
Williams: Archives and Special Collections, Williams College, Williamstown, Massachusetts
Xavier University: Archives and Special Collections, Xavier University, New Orleans, Louisiana
Yale: Beinecke Rare Book and Manuscript Library, Yale University, New Haven, Connecticut

Other Archives

American Philosophical Society, Philadelphia, Pennsylvania
Hoover Institution Library and Archives, Stanford, California
Library of Congress, Washington, DC
Tamiment Library and Robert F. Wagner Labor Archives, New York University, New York, New York

Introduction · Personality over Bureaucracy: The Paradox of College Teaching in America

1. Max Weber, "American and German Universities" (1911), in *Max Weber on Universities*, ed. Edward Shils (Chicago: University of Chicago Press, 1974), 29–30; Max Weber, "Science as a Vocation" (1919), in Shils, *Max Weber on Universities*, 57–58.

2. Weber, "Science as a Vocation," 57–58, 55.

3. Samuel P. Capen, "The Supervision of College Teaching," *Pedagogical Seminary* 18, no. 4 (December 1911): 545–46.

4. Capen, "Supervision of College Teaching," 546; Clyde Furst, "Tests of College Efficiency," *School Review* 20, no. 5 (May 1912): 326; Maude Weidner, "The College of Tomorrow," in *The Students Speak Out! A Symposium from Twenty-Two Colleges* (New York: New Republic, 1929), 251; Gus E. Snavely, "Who Is a Great Teacher?," *Association of American Colleges Bulletin* 15, no. 1 (March 1929): 68–69.

5. Max Weber, *Economy and Society: An Outline of Interpretive Sociology* (New York: Bedminster, 1968), 215; William Clark, *Academic Charisma and the Origins of the Research University* (Chicago: University of Chicago Press, 2006), 3; Jackson J. Spielvogel, "The Art and Craft of Teaching," in *The Penn State Teacher: A Collection of Readings and Practical Advice for Beginning Teachers*, ed. Diane M. Enerson and Kathryn M. Plank (State College: Penn State University, 1993), 28. On Weber and the fate of charisma in modern academic life, see also Mark R. Schwehn, *Exiles from Eden: Religion and the Academic Vocation in America* (New York: Oxford University Press, 1993), esp. 3–21.

6. Alvin Kernan, *In Plato's Cave* (New Haven, CT: Yale University Press, 1999), 120; Brooks Mather Kelley, *Yale: A History* (New Haven, CT: Yale University Press, 1974), 282; Bliss Perry, *And Gladly Teach* (New York: Houghton Mifflin, 1935), 269; Joan Shelley Rubin, "'Information, Please!': Culture and Experience in the Interwar Period," *American Quarterly* 35, no. 5 (Winter 1983): 504.

7. Christopher P. Loss, *Between Citizens and the State: The Politics of American Higher Education in the 20th Century* (Princeton, NJ: Princeton University Press, 2012), 19–52; J. Douglas Brown, "Comments on Questionnaire" (MS, 1954), enclosed with J. Douglas Brown to Richard L. Park, 18 August 1954, folder 33, box 3, series I, Clark Kerr Personal and Professional Papers, Bancroft Library, University of California, Berkeley; Jeffrey L. Sammons to Robert L. Herbert, 15 December 1970, folder 6, box 9, Records of the Dean of Yale College, Beinecke Rare Book and Manuscript Library, Yale University (hereafter "BRBML—Yale").

8. Nicholas Murray Butler, "Methods of University Teaching," *Journal of Education* 67, no. 12 (19 March 1908): 313–14; George E. Carrothers, *Rollins Plan of College Instruction* (Winter Park, FL: Rollins College, [1927?]), 20; Edward Safford Jones, *Comprehensive Examinations in American Colleges* (New York: Macmillan, 1933), 179; John Palmer Gavit, *College* (New York: Harcourt Brace, 1925), 94.

9. I. J. Sandorf to American Association of University Professors, 11 November 1968, "General Educational Television 1965–1968," folder, box 6, Committee C series, American Association of University Professors Papers (hereafter "AAUP Papers"), Special Collections Research Center, George Washington University; Richard L. Evans, *Resistance to Innovation in Higher Education: A Social Psychological Exploration Focused on Television and the Establishment* (San Francisco: Jossey-Bass, 1967), 75.

10. David Riesman, *On Higher Education: The Academic Enterprise in an Era of Rising Student Consumerism* (San Francisco: Jossey-Bass, 1980), 256, 255; Andrew Delbanco, "MOOCs of Hazard," *New Republic*, 31 March 2013, https://newrepublic.com/article/112731 /moocs-will-online-education-ruin-university-experience; Mark Clayton, "Give Me an 'A,' Professor—I'll Give You One, Too," *Christian Science Monitor*, 17 March 1998, B6.

11. Jordan J. Titus, "Pedagogy on Trial: When Academic Freedom and Education Consumerism Collide," *Journal of College and University Law* 38 (2011–12): 161–64; "'Opening Up' Faculty Evaluation," *Regional Spotlight* (Southern Regional Education Board) 10, no. 1 (September 1975): 7; "Comm. C—Evaluation of Faculty," folder, box 1, Committee C series, AAUP Papers; Robert C. Wood, "Why Improve University Teaching Now?," in *Reform, Renewal, Reward*, ed. Dwight W. Allen, Michael A. Melnik, and Carolyn C. Peele (Amherst: Clinic to Improve University Teaching, University of Massachusetts at Amherst, 1975), 21–22; Arthur M. Cohen and Florence B. Brawer, *The Two-Year College Instructor Today* (New York: Praeger, 1977), 102; Sherrill Cleland, "Internships Are Second Best," *Liberal Education* 55, no. 3 (October 1969): 424.

12. Malcolm W. Willey to J. L. Morrill, 9 April 1957, "Conference on College Teaching. 1957–March 1958" folder, box 85, President's Office Papers, Archives and Special Collections, University of Minnesota, Minneapolis, MN; *Update 1976. Undergraduate Policies Digest and Teacher Evaluations* (Associated Students of the University of California at Los Angeles, 1976), 22, "Undergraduate Policies Digest and Teacher Evaluations" folder, box 60, Associated Students Subject Files, Special Research Collections, University of California, Santa Barbara.

13. James S. Fairweather, "Faculty Reward Structures: Toward Institutional and Professional Homogenization," *Research in Higher Education* 34, no. 5 (1993): 603–23; Michael S. Sherry, "We Value Teaching Despite—and Because—of Its Low Status," *Journal of American History* 81, no. 3 (December 1994): 1054; James R. Angell to Fernandus Payne, 17 May 1932, folder 133, box 12, James Rowland Angell Presidential Records, BRBML—Yale; William Lyon Phelps, *Teaching in School and College* (New York: Macmillan, 1912), 2; "Report of the Field Director to the Committee. Part II—Section B: Summary of Reports and Letters Resulting from Visits Made by Members of the Committee" (MS, 2 October 1932), 86, folder 134, box 12, Angell Presidential Records.

14. Mary Wortham, "The Case for a Doctor of Arts Degree: A View from the Junior College Faculty," *Bulletin of the AAUP* 53, no. 4 (December 1967): 375; Alan N. Schoonmaker, *A Students' Survival Manual; or, How to Get an Education, Despite It All* (New York: Harper & Row, 1971), 55; Weber, "Science as a Vocation," 58.

15. Henry Adams, *The Education of Henry Adams* (1918; repr., New York: Oxford University Press, 1999); Kenneth E. Eble, *Professors as Teachers* (San Francisco: Jossey-Bass, 1972), 18. Adams printed his memoir privately in 1907, but it was not published by a commercial press until shortly after his death in 1918.

16. Henry Adams, "Harvard College, 1786–1787" (1872), in *Historical Essays* (1891; repr., New York: Georg Olms Verlag, 1973), 80–82.

17. "Interview with Regina M. Edmonds" (MS, 28 October 2012), 34, Worcester Women's Oral History Project, https://www.wwohp.org/interview-list/regina-edmonds.

18. See, e.g., Andrew Hacker and Claudia Dreifus, *Higher Education? How Colleges Are Wasting Our Money and Failing Our Kids—and What We Can Do about It* (New York: Times

Books, 2010); Richard Arum and Josipa Roksa, *Academically Adrift: Limited Learning on College Campuses* (Chicago: University of Chicago Press, 2011); Susan Blum, *"I Love Learning; I Hate School": An Anthropology of College* (Ithaca, NY: Cornell University Press, 2016); Jacques Berlinerblau, *How College Works, or Doesn't, for Professors, Parents, and Students* (New York: Melville, 2017); and Jason Brennan and Phillip Magness, *Cracks in the Ivory Tower: The Moral Mess of Higher Education* (New York: Oxford University Press, 2019).

19. See, e.g., Peter C. Brown, *Making It Stick: The Science of Successful Learning* (Cambridge, MA: Harvard University Press, 2014); Benedict Carey, *How We Learn: The Surprising Truth about When, Where, and Why It Happens* (New York: Random House, 2014); James M. Lang, *Small Teaching: Everyday Lessons from the Science of Learning* (San Francisco: Jossey-Bass, 2016); Joshua R. Eyler, *How Humans Learn: The Science and Stories behind Effective College Teaching* (Morgantown: West Virginia University Press, 2018).

20. Although there is still no comprehensive history of American college teaching, there are many outstanding histories of American higher education writ large. None of them take teaching as their main subject, but many of them include important material and analysis about it. See, e.g., Laurence R. Veysey, *The Emergence of the American University* (Chicago: University of Chicago Press, 1965), esp. 221–33; Julie A. Reuben, *The Making of the Modern University: Intellectual Transformation and the Marginalization of Morality* (Chicago: University of Chicago Press, 1996), esp. 230–65; Loss, *Between Citizens and the State*, esp. 147–56; John R. Thelin, *Going to College in the Sixties* (Baltimore: Johns Hopkins University Press, 2018), esp. 116–36; John R. Thelin, *A History of American Higher Education*, 2nd ed. (Baltimore: Johns Hopkins University Press, 2011); Roger L. Geiger, *American Higher Education since World War II: A History* (Princeton, NJ: Princeton University Press, 2019), esp. 338–45; Roger L. Geiger, *The History of American Higher Education: Learning and Culture from the Founding to World War II* (Princeton, NJ: Princeton University Press, 2015); Andrew Jewett, *Science, Democracy, and the American University: From the Civil War to the Cold War* (Cambridge: Cambridge University Press, 2012), esp. 28–54 and 196–224; and Charles Dorn, *For the Common Good: A New History of Higher Education in America* (Ithaca, NY: Cornell University Press, 2017). I have also drawn from several excellent histories of specific institutions, especially James Axtell, *The Making of Princeton University: From Woodrow Wilson to the Present* (Princeton, NJ: Princeton University Press, 2006); Robert A. McCaughey, *Stand, Columbia: A History of Columbia University in the City of New York, 1754–2004* (New York: Columbia University Press, 2003); Morton Keller and Phyllis Keller, *Making Harvard Modern: The Rise of America's University* (New York: Oxford University Press, 2001); John L. Puckett and Mark Frazier Lloyd, *Becoming Penn: The Pragmatic American University, 1950–2000* (Philadelphia: University of Pennsylvania Press, 2015); Rebecca Lowen, *Creating the Cold War University: The Transformation of Stanford* (Berkeley: University of California Press, 1997); John Aubrey Douglass, *The California Idea and American Higher Education: 1850 to the 1960 Master Plan* (Stanford, CA: Stanford University Press, 2000); David B. Potts, *Wesleyan University, 1831–1910: Collegiate Enterprise in New England* (Middletown, CT: Wesleyan University Press, 1999); David B. Potts, *Wesleyan University, 1910–1970: Academic Ambition and Middle-Class America* (Middletown, CT: Wesleyan University Press, 2015). Two important works that focus specifically on college teaching are Hugh Hawkins, "University Identity: The Teaching and Research Function," in *The Organization of Knowledge in Modern America, 1860–1920*, ed. Alexandra Oleson and John Voss (Baltimore: Johns Hopkins University Press, 1979), 285–312; and Larry Cuban, *How Scholars Trumped Teachers: Change without Reform in University Teaching and Research, 1890–1990* (New York: Teachers College Press, 1999).

21. On the complex meanings of "amateurism" in American life and letters, see Wayne Booth, *For the Love of It: Amateuring and Its Rivals* (Chicago: University of Chicago Press, 1999); Marjorie Garber, *Academic Instincts* (Princeton, NJ: Princeton University Press, 2001), 3–51.

22. On the growth of professional knowledge about teaching—and the reluctance of most college professors to learn about it, or to apply its lessons—see David Gooblar, *The Missing Course: Everything They Never Taught You about College Teaching* (Cambridge, MA: Harvard University Press, 2019); Aaron M. Pallas and Anna Neumann, *Convergent Teaching: Tools to Spark Deeper Learning in College* (Baltimore: Johns Hopkins University Press, 2019), esp. 3–5.

23. *The Penn State Teacher II: Learning to Teach, Teaching to Learn* (University Park: Penn State University, July 1997), 8; Arthur G. Powell, "The Education of Educators at Harvard, 1891–1912," in *Social Sciences at Harvard, 1860–1920: From Inculcation to the Open Mind* (Cambridge, MA: Harvard University Press, 1965), 226. A list of the university archives consulted for this book appears in the appendix.

Chapter 1 · *Between the Two Ends of the Log: Teaching and Learning in the Nineteenth Century*

1. Ralph Keyes, *The Quote Verifier: Who Said What, Where, and When* (New York: St. Martin's, 2007), 130–31. According to *Yale Book of Quotations* editor Fred Shapiro, the first published reference to Garfield's speech—appearing eight years after the Delmonico's dinner—was slightly different: "Take a log cabin in the West, put a wooden bench in it, with Mark Hopkins on one end and a student on the other, and you have a college." Fred R. Shapiro, "Quotable Williams," *Williams Alumni Review*, September 2008, 12, https://magazine.williams.edu/files/archive/2008-fall.pdf.

2. B. B. McClellan to Rev. Mark Hopkins, DD, 2 January 1885, folder 1, box 8, Hopkins Family Papers, Archives and Special Collections, Williams College, Williamstown, MA; Bliss Perry, *And Gladly Teach* (New York: Houghton Mifflin, 1935), 61; Leverett Wilson Spring, *Mark Hopkins, Teacher* (New York: Industrial Education Association, 1888), 24; Frederick Rudolph, *Mark Hopkins and the Log: Williams College, 1836–1872* (New Haven, CT: Yale University Press, 1956), 49.

3. Leverett Wilson Spring, "Socratic Yankee," in *Great Teachers Portrayed by Those Who Studied under Them*, ed. Houston Peterson (New Brunswick, NJ: Rutgers University Press, 1946), 76; Rudolph, *Mark Hopkins and the Log*, 51.

4. James McMurtry Longo, *From Classroom to White House: The Presidents and First Ladies as Students and Teachers* (Jefferson, NC: McFarland, 2011), 85, 80; Jonathan Zimmerman, *Small Wonder: The Little Red Schoolhouse in History and Memory* (New Haven, CT: Yale University Press, 2009), 29.

5. Leon Burr Richardson, *History of Dartmouth College* (Hanover, NH: Dartmouth College, 1932), 2:456–57; Thomas Le Duc, *Piety and Intellect at Amherst College, 1865–1912* (New York: Columbia University Press, 1946), 49; Rudolph, *Mark Hopkins and the Log*, 53; David B. Potts, *Wesleyan University, 1831–1910: Collegiate Enterprise in New England* (Middletown, CT: Wesleyan University Press, 1999), 35; W. H. Cowley, "College and University Teaching, 1858–1958," in *The Two Ends of the Log: Learning and Teaching in Today's College*, ed. Russell M. Cooper (Minneapolis: University of Minnesota Press, 1958), 114; Perry, *And Gladly Teach*, 42, 51.

6. Burton J. Bledstein, *The Culture of Professionalism: The Middle Class and the Development of Higher Education in America* (New York: Norton, 1976), 238; John S. Brubacher and Willis Rudy, *Higher Education in Transition: A History of American Colleges and Universities*, 3rd ed. (New York: Harper & Row, 1976), 85; Linda Armstrong Chisholm, "The Art of Undergraduate Teaching in the Age of the Emerging University" (PhD diss., Columbia University, 1982), 32–33; William Lyon Phelps, *Teaching in School and College* (New York: Macmillan, 1912), 101; Richardson, *History of Dartmouth College*, 438.

7. Perry, *And Gladly Teach*, 43; William Gardiner Hammond, *Remembrance of Amherst: An Undergraduate's Diary, 1846–1848*, ed. George F. Whicher (New York: Columbia University

Press, 1946), 165; Andrew D. White, *Autobiography of Andrew D. White* (New York: Century, 1905), 1:68, 27; Brubacher and Rudy, *Higher Education in Transition*, 87.

8. Chisholm, "Art of Undergraduate Teaching," 34–37; Henry Johnson, *The Other Side of Main Street: A History Teacher from Sauk Centre* (New York: Columbia University Press, 1943), 56; Potts, *Wesleyan University, 1831–1910*, 39; Rudolph, *Mark Hopkins and the Log*, 221.

9. Carl Albert Hangartner, SJ, "Movements to Change American College Teaching, 1700–1830" (PhD diss., Yale University, 1955), 322; Potts, *Wesleyan University, 1831–1910*, 39; Louise L. Stevenson, "Preparing for Public Life: The Collegiate Students at New York University, 1832–1881," in *The University and the City: From Medieval Origins to the Present*, ed. Thomas Bender (New York: Oxford University Press, 1988), 161.

10. Mark Garrett Longaker, *Rhetoric and the Republic: Politics, Civic Discourse, and Education in Early America* (Tuscaloosa: University of Alabama Press, 2007), 131; Hammond, *Remembrance of Amherst*, 58, 64, 187.

11. Longaker, *Rhetoric and the Republic*, 43; Longo, *From Classroom to White House*, 32; Roger Geiger, *The History of American Higher Education: Learning and Culture from the Founding to World War II* (Princeton, NJ: Princeton University Press, 2015), 256; Brooks Mather Kelley, *Yale: A History* (New Haven, CT: Yale University Press, 1974), 157–58; Robert F. Pace, *Halls of Honor: College Men in the Old South* (Baton Rouge: Louisiana State University Press, 2004), 23; Hangartner, "Movements to Change American College Teaching," 342.

12. Burgess Johnson, *Campus versus Classroom: A Candid Appraisal of the American College* (New York: Ives Washburn, 1946), 13; Geiger, *History of American Higher Education*, 322; Le Duc, *Piety and Intellect at Amherst College*, 52; W. Bruce Leslie, *Gentlemen and Scholars: College and Community in the "Age of the University," 1865–1917* (University Park: Penn State University Press, 1992), 85, 79.

13. W. E. B. Du Bois, *The Autobiography of W. E. B. Du Bois* (New York: International, 1971), 163; A. B. Hart, "Methods of Teaching American History," in *Methods of Teaching History*, ed. G. Stanley Hall (Boston: D. C. Heath, 1884), 5; Chisholm, "Art of Undergraduate Teaching," 108; Leon B. Richardson, *A Study of the Liberal College* (Hanover, NH: Dartmouth College, 1924), 185.

14. Hangartner, "Movements to Change American College Teaching," 316; Chisholm, "Art of Undergraduate Teaching," 68, 90–91; Lane Cooper, *Two Views of Education* (New Haven, CT: Yale University Press, 1922), 223; Ephraim Emerton, "The Practical Method in Higher Historical Instruction," in Hall, *Methods of Teaching History*, 32.

15. John D. Hicks, "Why Lecture?," *Teacher on the Hill* (University of California at Santa Cruz), no. 5 (March 1978): 5; Hugh Hawkins, *Pioneer: A History of the Johns Hopkins University, 1874–1889* (Ithaca, NY: Cornell University Press, 1960), 218–20; *Address at the Inauguration of Charles William Eliot as President of Harvard College* (Cambridge, MA: Sever & Francis, 1869), 42; *Report of the President and Treasurer of Harvard College, 1879–1880* (Cambridge, MA: John Wilson & Son, 1880), 15–16.

16. Horace W. Hewlett, "An Interview with George William Bain. Samuel A. Hitchcock Professor of Mineralogy and Geology, Emeritus" (MS, 22 December 1977), 10–11, folder 3, box 1, Amherst College Oral History Project, Archives and Special Collections, Amherst College, Amherst, MA; Margaret Sumner, *Collegiate Republic: Cultivating an Ideal Society in Early America* (Charlottesville: University of Virginia Press, 2014), 138–40; Hawkins, *Pioneer*, 220; A. J. Angulo, *William Barton Rogers and the Idea of MIT* (Baltimore: Johns Hopkins University Press, 2009), 114; Henry Adams, *The Education of Henry Adams* (1918; repr., New York: Oxford University Press, 1999), 55.

17. Geiger, *History of American Higher Education*, 126–28, 224–26, 366–67.

18. Kelley, *Yale*, 269; Adams, *Education of Henry Adams*, 54–55, 50; Andrew Delbanco, *College: What It Was, Is, and Should Be* (Princeton, NJ: Princeton University Press, 2012), 69–70.

19. Richardson, *History of Dartmouth College*, 460, 469; Henry Holt, *Garrulities of an Octogenarian Editor* (New York: Houghton Mifflin, 1923), 17; Samuel Eliot Morison, *Three Centuries at Harvard* (Cambridge, MA: Harvard University Press, 1936), 260; Holt and Morison both quoted in Cowley, "College and University Teaching," 106.

20. Frederick Rudolph, *The American College and University* (1962; repr., Athens: University of Georgia Press, 1990), 164; Bledstein, *Culture of Professionalism*, 238; Carroll Perry, *A Professor Life: A Sketch of Arthur Latham Perry of Williams College* (Boston: Houghton Mifflin, 1923), 80–81; Benjamin Horner Hall, *A Collection of College Words and Customs* (Cambridge, MA: Metcalf, 1851), 245; Richardson, *History of Dartmouth College*, 489; Joseph F. Kett, *Merit: The History of a Founding Ideal from the American Revolution to the 21st Century* (Ithaca, NY: Cornell University Press, 2013), 76; Hammond, *Remembrance of Amherst*, 163.

21. Hammond, *Remembrance of Amherst*, 163; Adams, *Education of Henry Adams*, 302; Laura Dassow Walls, *Henry David Thoreau: A Life* (Chicago: University of Chicago Press, 2017), 67–68; Bruce Kimball, *Orators and Philosophers: A History of the Idea of Liberal Education* (New York: Teachers College Press, 1986), 251.

22. Kimball, *Orators and Philosophers*, 251; Rudolph, *Mark Hopkins and the Log*, 221; Richardson, *History of Dartmouth College*, 432; Pace, *Halls of Honor*, 23.

23. Richardson, *History of Dartmouth College*, 435; Mary Lovett Smallwood, *An Historical Study of Examinations and Grading Systems in Early American Universities* (Cambridge, MA: Harvard University Press, 1935), 36, 29; Barbara Solomon, *In the Company of Educated Women* (New Haven, CT: Yale University Press, 1985), 96.

24. Hammond, *Remembrance of Amherst*, 51; Cowley, "College and University Teaching," 108; Rudolph, *Mark Hopkins and the Log*, 221; Kett, *Merit*, 86; Longo, *From Classroom to White House*, 62, 105–7; Pace, *Halls of Honor*, 23–24; Bledstein, *Culture of Professionalism*, 237; Harry R. Lewis, *Excellence without a Soul: How a Great University Forgot Education* (New York: Public Affairs, 2006), 38.

25. Cowley, "College and University Teaching," 108; Peggy Aldrich Kidwell, Amy Acerberg-Hastings, and David Lindsay Roberts, *Tools of American Mathematics Teaching, 1800–2000* (Baltimore: Johns Hopkins University Press, 2008), 25; Rudolph, *Mark Hopkins and the Log*, 222; Richardson, *History of Dartmouth College*, 485–89; Pace, *Halls of Honor*, 26; James Axtell, *The Making of Princeton University: From Woodrow Wilson to the Present* (Princeton, NJ: Princeton University Press, 2006), 40–41.

26. Pace, *Halls of Honor*, 27; Chisholm, "Art of Undergraduate Teaching," 62–64; Lyman H. Bagg, *Four Years at Yale: By a Graduate of '69* (New Haven, CT: Charles Chatfield, 1871), 620–27, 554; Hangartner, "Movements to Change American College Teaching," 348.

27. Ralph Waldo Emerson, *Selected Writings of Ralph Waldo Emerson*, ed. William H. Gilman (New York: Penguin, 2011), 117; Nancy Barton Bush, "The Student and His Professor: Colonial Times to Twentieth Century," *Journal of Higher Education* 40, no. 8 (November 1969): 600; Le Duc, *Piety and Intellect at Amherst College*, 48–49.

28. Wilson Smith, "Apologia pro Alma Mater: The College as Community in Antebellum America," in *The Hofstadter Aegis: A Memorial*, ed. Stanley Elkins and Eric McKitrick (New York: Knopf, 1974), 142n34; Leslie, *Gentlemen and Scholars*, 70–72; Morison, *Three Centuries at Harvard*, 347.

29. Spring, *Mark Hopkins, Teacher*, 4, 18.

Chapter 2 · Scholarship and Its Discontents: Teaching and Learning in the Progressive Era

1. "The Decline of Teaching," *Nation*, 8 March 1900, 180–81.

2. George Herbert Palmer, "Necessary Limitations of the Elective System," in George Herbert Palmer and Alice Freeman Palmer, *The Teacher: Essays and Addresses on Education* (Boston: Houghton Mifflin, 1908), 264.

3. These themes were dominant during the Progressive Era, but they also generated detractors. On resistance to "efficiency," see esp. Jonathan Zimmerman, "Simplified Spelling and the Cult of Efficiency in the 'Progressiv' Era," *Journal of the Gilded Age and Progressive Era* 9, no. 3 (July 2010): 365–94.

4. Larry Cuban, *How Scholars Trumped Teachers: Change without Reform in University Curriculum, Teaching, and Research, 1890–1990* (New York: Teachers College Press, 1999), 108.

5. Claude Charleton Bowman, *The College Professor in America: An Analysis of Articles Published in General Magazines, 1890–1939* (1938; repr., New York: Arno, 1977), 129; Edwin E. Slosson, *Great American Universities* (New York: Macmillan, 1910), 17–18, 76.

6. William James, "The Ph.D. Octopus," *Educational Review* 55 (February 1918): 153, 155.

7. John Harrington Cox, "What Is the Best Preparation for the College Teacher of English?," *English Journal* 2, no. 4 (April 1913): 208; William De Witt Hyde, "The Place of College in the Social System," *School Review* 12, no. 10 (December 1904): 786; Frederick P. Keppel, *The Undergraduate and His College* (Boston: Houghton Mifflin, 1917), 306; William H. Allen, *Self-Surveys by Colleges and Universities* (Yonkers-on-Hudson, NY: World Book, 1917), 326.

8. David S. Jordan, "The Care and Culture of Freshmen," *North American Review*, April 1910, 441–42, quoted in Edward A. Gallagher, "Jordan and Lange: The California Junior College's Role as Protector of Teaching," *Michigan Academician* 27 (1994): 2; Frank P. Graves to Samuel P. Capen, 19 October 1910, folder 1, box 1, Samuel P. Capen Papers, University Archives, University of Buffalo; Abraham Flexner, "The Problem of College Pedagogy," *Atlantic Monthly* 103 (June 1909): 844.

9. Julie R. Reuben, *The Making of the Modern University: Intellectual Transformation and the Marginalization of Morality* (Chicago: University of Chicago Press, 1996), 68; Cox, "What Is the Best Preparation," 212; Thorstein Veblen, *The Higher Learning in America: A Memorandum on the Conduct of Universities by Business Men* (New York: B. W. Huebsch, 1918), 16–17. On Veblen as a poor teacher, see Joseph Dorfman, *Thorstein Veblen and His America* (1934; repr., New York: Augustus M. Kelley, 1966), 119–20, 247–50, 273–74, 307–8, 315.

10. Robert J. Connors, *Composition-Rhetoric: Backgrounds, Theory, and Pedagogy* (Pittsburgh: University of Pittsburgh Press, 1997), 191–92, 196; Lane Cooper, "The Correction of Papers," *English Journal* 3 (1914), in *The Origins of Composition Studies in the American College, 1875–1925: A Documentary History*, ed. John C. Brereton (Pittsburgh: University of Pittsburgh Press, 1995), 297; John Wells Morse, "The Section Meetings of Economics A" (MS, February 1914), 1–2, "Investigation of the Department by the School of Education" folder, box 16, Harvard Department of Economics General Office Files, Harvard University Archives (hereafter "HUA"), Harvard University, Cambridge, MA; *The Teaching of Economics at Harvard University: A Report Presented by the Division of Education at the Request of the Department of Economics* (Cambridge, MA: Harvard University Press, 1917), 137–38.

11. George E. Vincent to Samuel P. Capen, 31 October 1910, folder 2, box 1, Capen Papers; E. A. Birge, "How Many Hours a Week Should Be Required of Teachers in a University?," *Transactions and Proceedings of the National Association of State Universities in the United States of America* 14 (1916): 74–75.

12. John Bovington, "Can We Improve upon the College Lecture System?," *School and Society* 4 (9 September 1916): 393; Edward L. Thorndike, "Collegiate Instruction," *Science* 31

(18 March 1910): 429; John Erskine, *My Life as a Teacher* (Philadelphia: J. B. Lippincott, 1948), 33; Nicholas Murray Butler, "Methods of University Teaching," *Journal of Education* 67, no. 12 (19 March 1908): 313–14.

13. Butler, "Methods of University Teaching," 313; Frederick H. Pratt, "The Dangers and Uses of the Lecture," *Educational Review* 24 (December 1902): 486–89.

14. A. K. Rogers, review of *A Beginner's History of Philosophy*, vol. 1, by Herbert Ernest Cushman, *Philosophical Review* 20, no. 2 (March 1911): 212; Laurence R. Veysey, *The Emergence of the American University* (Chicago: University of Chicago Press, 1965), 144; Lloyd Osborn Coulter to Athern P. Daggett, 6 February 1955, "Alumni Letters A–C" folder, box 3, Self-Study Reports Collection, Special Collections and Archives (hereafter "SCA—Bowdoin"), Bowdoin College, Brunswick, ME; Slosson, *Great American Universities*, 517; William Lyon Phelps, *Teaching in School and College* (New York: Macmillan, 1912), 16.

15. John D. Hicks, *My Life with History: An Autobiography* (Lincoln: University of Nebraska Press, 1968), 66–67, 85; Irwin Edman, *Philosopher's Holiday* (New York: Viking, 1938), 130–32; Alfred Pearce Dennis, "Princeton Schoolmaster," in *Great Teachers Portrayed by Those Who Studied under Them*, ed. Houston Peterson (New Brunswick, NJ: Rutgers University Press, 1946), 134; David Levering Lewis, *W. E. B. Du Bois: Biography of a Race, 1868–1919* (New York: Henry Holt, 1993), 215.

16. Charles A. Ellwood, "How Should Sociology Be Taught as a College or University Subject?," *American Journal of Sociology* 12, no. 5 (March 1907): 593; O. F. Boucke, "Lecture or Recitation in Colleges?," *Educational Review* 52 (May 1917): 499; "The Meeting of the American Historical Association at Baltimore," *American Historical Review* 11, no. 3 (April 1906): 502; A. L. Bouton, "Reminisces from 1892" (MS, 14 January 1915), folder 9, box 17, Records of the Office of the Dean, University College of Arts and Sciences, University Archives, New York University.

17. Willis Milham to Harry A. Garfield, 12 March 1910, folder 2; S. J. Clarke to Garfield, 15 March 1910, folder 3; Karl Weston to Garfield, 12 March 1910, folder 2; W. E. McElfresh to Garfield, folder 3, all in box 51, President's Papers—Harry A. Garfield (hereafter "Garfield Papers"), Archives and Special Collections, Williams College, Williamstown, MA.

18. "Present Problems of Instruction in the University of Chicago," *University of Chicago Magazine* 3, no. 2 (December 1910): 64–65; L. C. Marshall, R. C. Chapin, and F. R. Fairchild, "The Teaching of Economics in the United States," *Journal of Political Economy* 19, no. 9 (November 1911): 771; Carol F. Baird, "Albert Bushnell Hart: The Rise of the Professional Historian," in *Social Sciences at Harvard, 1860–1920: From Inculcation to the Open Mind*, ed. Paul Buck (Cambridge, MA: Harvard University Press, 1965), 160; Morse, "Section Meetings of Economics A," 2–3.

19. Marshall, Chapin, and Fairchild, "Teaching of Economics," 771; Frank Goodrich to Harry A. Garfield, 11 March 1910; and Theodore Clark Smith to Garfield, 11 March 1910, both in folder 2, box 51, Garfield Papers; Cornelius Howard Patton and Walter Taylor Field, *Eight O'Clock Chapel: A Study of New England College Life in the Eighties* (Boston: Houghton Mifflin, 1927), 124; William Graham Sumner, "Discussion," in Ellwood, "How Should Sociology be Taught," 599.

20. Reuben, *Making of the Modern University*, 72; Henry Seidel Canby, *Alma Mater: The Gothic Age of the American College* (New York: Farrar & Rinehart, 1936), 64, 83; Patton and Field, *Eight O'Clock Chapel*, 124; Dorothy Cowser Yancey, "William Edward Burghardt Du Bois' Atlanta Years: The Human Side—a Study Based upon Oral Sources," *Journal of Negro History* 63, no. 1 (January 1978): 61–62; Lewis, *W. E. B. Du Bois*, 216; George Wilson Pierson, *Yale College: An Educational History, 1871–1921* (New Haven, CT: Yale University Press, 1952), 285. "Durfee and South" were classroom buildings at Yale.

21. Phelps, *Teaching in School and College*, 103–4; Morse, "Section Meetings of Economics A," 5–6; Rogers, review of *A Beginner's History of Philosophy*, 212; "Is Our Teaching All

Wrong? Princeton's President Says the Recitation Method Won't Do in College," *Kansas City Star*, 17 December 1903.

22. "Meeting of the American Historical Association at Baltimore," 500; "Bowdoin: Trial of a Scheme of Tutorial Assistance," *New York Tribune*, 25 September 1899, 5; William De Witt Hyde, "The New Standard in College Teaching," *Nation* 90 (3 February 1910): 107–8; William De Witt Hyde, "The Bowdoin Revolution in Teaching" (MS, n.d.), folder 6, box 7, William De Witt Hyde Collection, SCA—Bowdoin.

23. Hyde, "New Standard in College Teaching," 108; Ralph Barton Perry, "The Preceptorial or Tutorial System: Report by Committee G," *Bulletin of the AAUP* 10, no. 7 (November 1924): 40; James Axtell, *The Making of Princeton University: From Woodrow Wilson to the Present* (Princeton, NJ: Princeton University Press, 2006), 63–64; Ray Stannard Baker, *Woodrow Wilson: Life and Letters* (Garden City, NY: Doubleday, 1927), 2:162, 165; "A Brief Sketch of the Development of the Princeton Plan of Undergraduate Instruction," (MS, [1971?]), 10, folder 6, box 1, Commission on the Future of the College Collection, Seeley G. Mudd Manuscript Library, Princeton University; Harold T. Shapiro, *Teaching at Princeton. Report of the President, 1991* (Princeton, NJ: Princeton University Printing Services, 1991), 3, "Teaching Assessment" folder, box 2, Committee C series, American Association of University Professors Papers, Special Collections Research Center, George Washington University.

24. Axtell, *Making of Princeton University*, 68–70; *The Preceptorial Method of Instruction: Report of the Committee of Eight* (Princeton, NJ, 1913), 26–27, 33.

25. "Preceptors," *Daily Princetonian* 38, no. 153 (12 January 1915); Wilson M. Hudson, "F. Scott Fitzgerald and a Princeton Preceptor" (MS, [1955?]), 1–4; and A. R. Towers to Wilson M. Hudson, 11 August 1952, both in folder 31, box 13, sec. VII.F, F. Scott Fitzgerald Additional Papers, Rare Books and Special Collections, Firestone Library, Princeton University.

26. Nancy P. Van Arsdale, "Princeton as Modernist's Hermeneutics: Rereading *This Side of Paradise*," in *F. Scott Fitzgerald: New Perspectives*, ed. Jackson R. Bryer, Alan Margolies, and Ruth Prigozy (Athens: University of Georgia Press, 2012), 40–43; Arthur Mizener to Wilson M. Hudson, 8 January 1952, folder 31, box 13, sec. VII.F, F. Scott Fitzgerald Additional Papers.

27. Samuel P. Capen, "The Supervision of College Teaching," *Pedagogical Seminary* 18, no. 4 (December 1911): 543–50.

28. William W. Warren to Samuel P. Capen, 19 October 1910, folder 1; William De Witt Hyde to Capen, 17 October 1910, folder 1; Frank [?] (unintelligible) to Capen, 17 October 1910, folder 1; Flavel S. Luther to Capen, 24 October 1910, folder 2; A. J. Roberts to Capen, 18 October 1910, folder 1, all in box 1, Capen Papers.

29. William F. Slocum to Samuel P. Capen, 18 October 1910, folder 1; George Edward Reed to Capen, 17 October 1910, folder 1; Isaac Sharpless to Capen, 17 October 1910, folder 1; David C. Barrow to Capen, 2 November 1910, folder 2; A. Ross Hill to Capen, 20 October 1910, folder 1; Henry King to Capen, 20 October 1910, folder 2; George E. Vincent to Capen, 31 October 1910, folder 1, all in box 1, Capen Papers; Capen, "Supervision of College Teaching," 543; Alexander Meiklejohn to Capen, folder 1, box 1, Capen Papers.

30. Flavel S. Luther to Samuel P. Capen, 24 October 1910, folder 2; George E. Vincent to Capen, 31 October 1910, folder 1; Henry King to Capen, 20 October 1910, folder 2; John F. Downey to Capen, 18 October 1910, folder 1, all in box 1, Capen Papers.

31. Keppel, *Undergraduate and His College*, 319; Edwin E. Slosson, "Grading Professors," *Independent* 70 (20 April 1911): 836–39.

32. Charles S. Howe to Samuel P. Capen, 13 October 1920, folder 1; and Gardner C. Anthony to Capen, 18 November 1910, folder 2, both in box 1, Capen Papers; Axtell, *Making of Princeton University*, 39–41, 53–56; Henry Wilkinson Bragdon, *Woodrow Wilson: The Academic Years* (Cambridge, MA: Harvard University Press, 1967), 295; John M. Mulder, *Woodrow Wilson: The Years of Preparation* (Princeton, NJ: Princeton University Press, 1978), 162.

33. Charles F. Emerson to Samuel P. Capen, 18 October 1910, folder 1; and James N. Anderson to Capen, 20 November 1910, folder 2, both in box 1, Capen Papers.

34. Ruth Bordin, *Women at Michigan* (Ann Arbor: University of Michigan Press, 1999), 20, 31; Hans-Joerg Tiede, *University Reform: The Founding of the American Association of University Professors* (Baltimore: Johns Hopkins University Press, 2015), 13; Winterton C. Curtis, "Recruiting of Teachers for the Colleges," *School and Society* 11 (3 January 1920), 16; Andrew Jewett, *Science, Democracy, and the American University: From the Civil War to the Cold War* (New York: Cambridge University Press, 2012), 45; "The Teacher," *Cornell Daily Sun*, 12 March 1907, 4; J. M. Thomas, "Training for Teaching Composition in Colleges," *English Journal* 5, no. 7 (September 1916): 449–50; Charles F. Richardson, "The Problem of Waste in the College Lecture," *School Review* 21, no. 5 (May 1913): 343.

35. Allen, *Self-Surveys by Colleges and Universities*, 274; Capen, "Supervision of College Teaching," 545–56.

36. H. H. Horne, "The Study of Education by Prospective College Instructors: The Views of Some College Presidents," *School Review* 16, no. 3 (March 1908): 162–64; Bouton, "Reminisces from 1892," 13; Phelps, *Teaching in School and College*, 2–3.

37. Phelps, *Teaching in School and College*, 97; Sinclair Lewis, "William Lyon Phelps," in *The Teacher's Treasure Chest*, ed. Leo Deuel (Englewood Cliffs, NJ: Prentice Hall, 1956), 162–63; Alvin Kernan, *In Plato's Cave* (New Haven, CT: Yale University Press, 1999), 120; Alfred Putnam to Paul Hollister, 18 July 1957, "Letters to Donald Adams and Paul Hollister about Copeland #1" folder, box 1, Charles Townsend Copeland Papers, HUA.

38. Alfred Putnam to Paul Hollister, 18 July 1957, "Letters to Donald Adams and Paul Hollister about Copeland #1" folder; and Samuel T. Williamson to Donald Adams, 26 July 1957; "Professor Copeland" (MS, [1957?]), both in "Letters to Donald Adams and Paul Hollister about Copeland #2" folder, all in box 1, Copeland Papers; J. Donald Adams, *Copey of Harvard: A Biography of Charles Townsend Copeland* (Boston: Houghton Mifflin, 1960), 150, 171–72.

39. Adams, *Copey of Harvard*, 46; "Professor Copeland"; John R. Tunis, *A Measure of Independence* (New York: Atheneum, 1964), 99; Alfred Putnam to Paul Hollister, 18 July 1957, "Letters to Donald Adams and Paul Hollister about Copeland #1" folder, box 1, Copeland Papers.

Chapter 3 · The Curse of Gigantism: Mass-Produced Education and Its Critics in Interwar America

1. *The Report on Undergraduate Education of the Dartmouth College Senior Committee* (Hanover, NH, 15 May 1924), 20–22, Rauner Special Collections Library, Dartmouth College, Hanover, NH; Edward Duffy, "A Critical Survey of the Dartmouth Report," *Intercollegiate World*, March 1926, 36 (enclosed with *Report on Undergraduate Education*); "A Study in the Nude," *Dartmouth*, 16 April 1924, folder 24-2, box 1, series I-B, William H. Cowley Papers, Special Collections and University Archives, Stanford University.

2. David O. Levine, *The American College and the Culture of Aspiration* (Ithaca, NY: Cornell University Press, 1986), 42; Frederick J. Kelly, *The American Arts College: A Limited Survey* (New York: Macmillan, 1925), 86; Lane Cooper, *Two Views of Education* (New Haven, CT: Yale University Press, 1922), 225; "Students Resent Fordized Education," *New Student* 4, no. 26 (11 April 1925): 1.

3. "Plenty of Rope at Dartmouth," *Boston Globe* [1924?], folder 24-4, box 1, series I-B, Cowley Papers; "Student Parley Debates on Value of Colleges, as Now Conducted," *Boston Daily Globe*, 13 December 1925, B4.

4. "Passing the Buck," *Argus* (Illinois Wesleyan University), 13 January 1932, 4.

5. Oswald F. Boucke, "My Creed as a College Teacher" (MS, October 1924), 1, Oswald Frederick Boucke Essay and Letters Collection, Special Collections Library, Pennsylvania State

University, State College, PA; John R. Thelin, *A History of American Higher Education*, 2nd ed. (Baltimore: Johns Hopkins University Press, 2011), 205; David Gold, *Rhetoric at the Margins: Revising the History of Writing Instruction in American Colleges, 1873–1947* (Carbondale: Southern Illinois University Press, 2008), ix; Nicholas Murray Butler, introduction to *College Teaching: Studies in Methods of Teaching in the College* (Yonkers-on-Hudson, NY: World Book, 1920), xiv; Hayward Keniston, "The Training of College Teachers" (MS, February 1939), 1, folder 3, box 2, Committee on the Preparation of Teachers Collection, Special Collections Research Center, University of Chicago (hereafter "SCRC—Chicago").

6. Edward N. Doan, "Faculty Responsibility for Student Opinion," *Bulletin of the AAUP* 24, no. 7 (December 1938): 612; James M. Todd, ed., *The College Conundrum* (New York: Round Table, 1935), 100; "Guinea Pigs Revolt against Milk Died and Dry Excelsior," *Argus* (Wesleyan University), 11 December 1924, folder 24-10, box 1, series I-B, Cowley Papers; M. M. Pinckney et al., "A Report to Be Rendered to G.O. Ferguson, by the O.D.K. Fraternity" (MS, 9 February 1927), box 1, Papers of Omicron Delta Kappa, Albert and Shirley Small Special Collections Library, University of Virginia (hereafter "SCL—UVA"), Charlottesville, VA.

7. John S. P. Tatlock, "The Intellectual Interests of Undergraduates," *Bulletin of the AAUP* 8, no. 5 (May 1922): 23; William B. Munro, "College Teaching," *Bulletin of the AAUP* 22, no. 2 (February 1936): 144.

8. Todd, *College Conundrum*, 115; Stuart D. Brewer to Athern B. Daggett, 5 February 1956, "Alumni Letters A–C" folder, box 3, Self-Study Reports Collection, Special Collections and Archives, Bowdoin College, Brunswick, ME; "Social Survey of Undergraduates at the University of Chicago" (MS, [1920?]), 20, folder 1, box 78, Office of the President, Harper, Judson and Burton Administrations, Records, SCRC—Chicago; student survey [1929?], folder 10, box 68, Hamilton Holt Papers, Archives and Special Collections, Rollins College, Winter Park, FL; William Allen White, "Why Students Are Stupid," *New Student* 3, no. 7 (5 January 1924): 1.

9. *La Critique* 1, no. 1 (March 1923): 1–3, folder 24-1A, box 1, series I-B, Cowley Papers; "Undergraduate Report: An Estimate of the Intellectual Activity within the University of Oregon. Suggested Changes in Administrative Policies," *University of Oregon Bulletin* 25, no. 5 (May 1926), "Instruction Com.–Curriculum Com." folder, box 38, Frank Aydelotte Papers, Swarthmore College Archives, Friends Historical Library, Swarthmore, PA; Levine, *American College*, 120.

10. Martin J. Finkelstein, *The American Academic Profession: A Synthesis of Social Scientific Inquiry since World War II* (Columbus: Ohio State University Press, 1984), 25; John Palmer Gavit, *College* (New York: Harcourt Brace, 1925), 98; Benjamin B. Kendrick, "Research by Southern Social Science Teachers," *Social Forces* 9, no. 30 (May 1931): 367; "Gigantism and the University," *New Student* 4, no. 15 (24 January 1925): 7; John W. Boyer, *The University of Chicago: A History* (Chicago: University of Chicago Press, 2015), 198; "Report of the Committee on College and University Teaching," *Bulletin of the AAUP* 19, no. 5 (May 1933): 41; Horace W. Hewlett, "An Interview with Willard L. Thorp Professor Economics, Emeritus. March 23–28, 1978" (MS, 1978), 2, Amherst College Oral History Project Collection, Archives and Special Collections, Amherst College, Amherst, MA.

11. Fredson Bowers, untitled manuscript (11 March 1958), 30–33, folder 4, box 1, Bernard R. Berelson Study of Graduate Education Records, SCRC—Chicago; Fernandus Payne and Evelyn Wilkinson Spieth, *An Open Letter to College Teachers* (Bloomington, IN: Principia, 1935), 58; "The 'Ph.D. disease,'" *New Student* 6, no. 5 (27 October 1926): 1; Leona Friedman, "Disillusioned," *New Student* 6, no. 14 (12 January 1927): 2; "Charles River Anthology," *New Student* 8, no. 6 (March 1929): 11.

12. R. H. Edwards, J. M. Artman, and Galen M. Fisher, *Undergraduates: A Study of Morale in Twenty-Three American Colleges and Universities* (Garden City, NY: Doubleday, 1928), 311;

James L. McConaughy to Ernest Wilkins, 4 December 1928, "Correspondence with Commission (1928)" folder, box 92, Ernest Wilkins Presidential Papers, Oberlin College Archives, Oberlin College, Oberlin, OH; J. D. A. Ogilvy, "Our Intellectual Treadmills," *American Scholar* 3, no. 3 (Summer 1934): 277; "Gifts to Columbia Drop to $1,990,364," *New York Times*, 18 December 1938, 27.

13. "From Mr. Ullman, Department of Latin" (MS, [1930?]), enclosed with Harlan H. Barrows to Frederic Woodward, 25 June 1930; and Robert M. Hutchins, "Memorandum on Graduate Study" (MS, 9 December 1929), both in folder 2, box 96, Office of the President, Hutchins Administration, Records, SCRC—Chicago; Boyer, *University of Chicago*, 284; Homer L. Dodge, "The Improvement of College Teaching," *Journal of Higher Education* 3, no. 9 (December 1932): 559; Albert Britt to Ernest Wilkins, 21 May 1930, "Correspondence with Commission (1930)" folder, box 92, Wilkins Papers.

14. S. Stephenson Smith, "The Lecture System, I. Improving Its Technique," *New Student* 7, no. 15 (11 January 1928): 3; Leon B. Richardson, *A Study of the Liberal College* (Hanover, NH: Dartmouth College, 1924), 193; "Notes on Higher Culture at Indiana University," *Vagabond* 2, no. 3 (March 1925): 26–27.

15. Max McConn, *College or Kindergarten?* (New York: New Republic, 1928), 140; untitled editorial, *New Student* 5, no. 4 (28 October 1925): 2; Harry Lloyd Miller, *Creative Learning and Teaching* (New York: Charles Scribner's & Sons, 1927), 120; Mortimer J. Adler, *How to Read a Book: The Art of Getting a Liberal Education* (New York: Simon & Schuster, 1940), 51.

16. James Axtell, *The Making of Princeton University: From Woodrow Wilson to the Present* (Princeton, NJ: Princeton University Press, 2006), 181; "Bootlegging Notes," *Dartmouth*, 11 January 1924, folder 24-2, box 1, series I-B, Cowley Papers; Franz Schneider, "The Student-Faculty Reaction Sheet and Its Dean of Instruction" (MS, [1940?]), 12; and "Bored '38," "'Canned' Lectures," *Daily Californian*, 25 April 1938, both in "Writings (3 of 3)" folder, carton 2, Franz Schneider Papers, Bancroft Library, University of California, Berkeley.

17. *The Students Speak Out! A Symposium from 22 Colleges* (New York: New Republic, 1929), 115; Claude Charleton Bowman, *The College Professor in America: An Analysis of Articles Published in the General Magazines, 1890–1939* (1938; repr., New York: Arno, 1977), 20; "Are Our Teachers Teaching Us?," *New Student* 4, no. 29 (2 May 1925): 1; David E. Berg, *Personality Culture by College Faculties* (New York: Institute for Public Service, 1920), 43; F. G. Davis, "Methods in College Teaching," *Educational Administration* 14 (October 1928): 476.

18. Thomas B. Bailey, *The American Pageant Revisited: Recollections of a Stanford Historian* (Stanford, CA: Hoover Institute Press, 1982), 28; Robert Nisbet, "Teggart of Berkeley," in *Masters: Portraits of Great Teachers*, ed. Joseph Epstein (New York: Basic, 1981), 73, 70; Fred S. Keller, *Pedagogue's Progress* (Lawrence, KS: TRI, 1982), 11; "Gleanings," *NFSA News Service* 5, no. 30 (19 May 1934): 4, "News Service 1934" folder, box 1, series II, Archives of the National Student Federation, Special Collections and University Archives, University of Maryland, College Park, MD.

19. Barnet Baskerville, *The People's Voice: The Orator in American Society* (Lexington: University Press of Kentucky, 1979), 146, 188–89; "Articles in the News," *Daily Pennsylvanian* (University of Pennsylvania) 55, no. 131 (1 May 1939): 2; Bliss Perry, *And Gladly Teach* (New York: Houghton Mifflin, 1935), 269–70; "Song of the Popular Professor," *New Student* 5, no. 29 (28 April 1926): 2.

20. "Albert G. Keller, '96, Retires after Fifty Years at Yale," *Yale Daily News*, 17 January 1942, 3; Todd, *College Conundrum*, 172; R. M. Hughes to Ernest Wilkins, 5 December 1928, "Correspondence with Commission (1928)" folder, box 92, Wilkins Papers; "Starvation Courses," *New Student* 7, no. 16 (18 January 1928): 8; David R. Holmes, *Stalking the Academic Communist: Intellectual Freedom and the Firing of Alex Novikoff* (Hanover, NH: University

Press of New England, 1989), 21; Elston D. "El" Harron, "Campus Inactivities," *Daily Illini* (University of Illinois) 61 (20 March 1932): 2.

21. Berg, *Personality Culture by College Faculties*, 72; Smith, "Lecture System," 3; Duffy, "Critical Survey of the Dartmouth Report," 38; Charles H. Judd, "The Psychology of the Learning Process at the Higher Levels," *Bulletin of the AAUP* 18, no. 2 (February 1932): 113.

22. Richardson, *Study of the Liberal College*, 198; "Robert Frost," *Daily Illini* 55 (25 December 1925): 4; Patricia Ann Palmieri, *In Adamless Eden: The Community of Women Faculty at Wellesley* (New Haven, CT: Yale University Press, 1995), 164; "Dear Sir" (MS, [1940?]); untitled manuscript (MS, [1940?]); "The Revelation" (MS, [1940?]), all in folder 4, box 125, Kimon Friar Papers, Rare Books and Special Collections, Firestone Library, Princeton University.

23. Bob Heege to "Mr. Friar," 14 February 1940; "How Do You Think We Could Improve Our English Class" (MS, [1940?]); "What I Thought of the English Course Last Semester" (MS, [1940?]); "My Comment on the English Class" (MS, [1940?]); Eleanor Waite, "Teaching Methods" (MS, 14 February 1940), all in folder 4, box 125, Friar Papers.

24. H. H. Horne, "University Students and the Discussion Method," *School and Society* 16 (19 August 1922): 220; "Comments Made by Students on Evaluation Questionnaires March 11 and May 25, 1938" (MS, 1938), 3, folder 11, box 9, Dean of the College Records, SCRC—Chicago; Douglas Carmichael to "Gentlemen," 6 February 1955, "Alumni Letters A–C" folder, box 3, Self-Study Reports Collection, Bowdoin College; D. Maurice Allan, "Report of a Study," in *Report of Committee on What Constitutes Good Teaching in College from the College Students' Point of View* (1939), 45, General Collection, SCL—UVA.

25. "Emasculating the Professor," *Vagabond* 2, no. 3 (March 1925): 48; "A Professor Is Fired," *NFSA News Service* 6, no. 27 (19 April 1935): 4, "News Service 1935" folder, box 1, series II, Archives of the National Student Federation; Timothy Reese Cain, *Establishing Academic Freedom: Politics, Principles, and the Development of Core Values* (New York: Palgrave Macmillan, 2012), 89; Bowman, *College Professor in America*, 106; Irwin Edman, "Flower for a Professor's Garden of Verses" (1942), in *The Teacher's Treasure Chest*, ed. Leo Deuel (Englewood Cliffs, NJ: Prentice Hall, 1956), 307–8.

26. "The Student Conference at Hartsdale. Held under Auspices of the National Student Forum," *New Student* supplement, 13 January 1923, 4; "What the Undergraduate Wants," *New Republic*, 30 July 1924, folder 24-4, box 1, series 1-B, Cowley Papers; Alvin W. Rohrbach, "How College Teaching Could Be Made More Interesting, as Viewed by the Student," in *Studies in Education*, Yearbook XVI (Chicago: University of Chicago Press, 1928), 20.

27. "Bell-Hop to the World," *Time*, 4 August 1924, folder 24-4, box 1, series I-B, Cowley Papers; "Undergraduate Report: An Estimate of the Intellectual Activity within the University of Oregon," 7, 11; Nathan M. Sorber and Jordan R. Humphrey, "The Era of Student Bureaucracy and the Contested Road to the *Harvard Redbook*, 1925–1945," *Higher Education Review* 8 (2001): 24; The Gentleman from Zero, "Dear Teacher," *Vagabond* 6, no. 2 (December 1929): 49; W. H. Cowley, *Presidents, Professors, and Trustees* (San Francisco: Jossey-Bass, 1980), 114; Student Curriculum Committee, "General Report" (MS, [1930?]), 1, 8, "Com. on Instruction" folder, box 19, Aydelotte Papers; W. H. Cowley, "College Teaching" (MS, 30 May 1923), 1, folder 23-5, box 1, series I-B, Cowley Papers.

28. George Bernard Shaw, "Dictatorship by the Learner," *New Student* 5, no. 26 (7 April 1926): 1; *La Critique*, 3; "From Our Colleges," *New Student* 2, no. 17 (19 May 1923): 3.

29. "Students Debunk College Catalogue," *New Student* 5, no. 1 (3 October 1925): 1, 3; "Guides to the Curriculum," *New Student* 5, no. 16 (27 January 1926): 1; *Confidential Guide to Freshman Courses* (Cambridge, MA: Harvard Crimson, 1934), 5, in box 1, Confidential Guide to Courses / Harvard Crimson Collection (hereafter "Confy—HUA"), Harvard University Archives.

30. "Students Judge Their Teachers," *Boston Daily Globe*, 12 April 1925; *Division of Social Sciences: A Self Study* (Greensboro, NC: Bennett College, 1968), 34, box 1, Self-Study Collection, Bennett College Archives, Greensboro, NC; "Report of the Committee on College and University Teaching," 36–37; Frederick J. Kelly, "Improving Instruction in the University of Idaho," in *The Training of College Teachers*, ed. William S. Gray (Chicago: University of Chicago Press, 1930), 174.

31. E. R. Guthrie, "The Faculty Questionnaire," *University of Washington Record* 2, no. 10 (June 1950), 7, folder 5, box 3, Edwin R. Guthrie Papers, Special Collections, University of Washington, Seattle, WA; Oberlin College, *The Report of the Committee on Bases of Promotion* (November 1930), enclosed with Ernest H. Wilkins to William B. Munro, 25 March 1931, folder 3, box 42, series IIIA, Carnegie Corporation of New York Records, Rare Book and Manuscript Library, Columbia University; AAUP Survey of College and University Teaching, "Report of the Field Director to the Committee" (MS, 1 October 1932), 34, folder 134, box 12, James Rowland Angell Presidential Records, Beinecke Rare Book and Manuscript Library, Yale University; "Report of the Committee on College and University Teaching," 59–60; Franz Schneider to "Miss Robb," 11 November 1939, "Correspondence 1939" folder, Carton 1, Schneider Papers.

32. Franz Schneider to W. R. Dennes, [1940?], "Correspondence 1940" folder, carton 1, Schneider Papers; "Reaction Over Prof [*sic*] Evaluation," *Daily Californian*, 17 March 1966; and "Roadblocks on the Way to Student Evaluation of Faculty," *Daily Californian*, 24 February 1965, both in "Franz Schneider" folder, box 60, Kenneth Eugene Eble Papers, University Archives and Records Management, University of Utah, Salt Lake City; Franz Schneider, *Students Examine Their Professors: A Student-Reaction Plan at Work* (Berkeley, CA: Pestalozzi, 1939), 16, 31; Robert Nisbet, *Teachers and Scholars: A Memoir of Berkeley in Depression and War* (New Brunswick, NJ: Transaction, 1992), 127; Franz Schneider to Virginia Hill, 9 December 1940, "Correspondence 1940" folder, carton 1, Schneider Papers.

33. "Kick Coming," *Daily Californian*, 17 March 1938, "Writings (3 of 3)" folder; and Franz Schneider, "The Student-Faculty Reaction Sheet and Its Dean of Instruction" (MS, [1946?]), 9–10, "Manuscripts (3 of 3)" folder, both in carton 2, Schneider Papers; Henry C. Morrison, "The Supervision of College Teaching" (MS, [1930?]), 7, "Training of Young Teachers" folder, box 92, Wilkins Papers; *Confidential Guide to Freshman Courses* (1934), 12; *Crimson Confidential Guide to Freshman Courses, 1940* (Cambridge, MA: Harvard Crimson, 1940), 29; *Crimson Confidential Guide to Freshman Courses, 1941* (Cambridge, MA: Harvard Crimson, 1941), 22–23, all in box 1, Confy—HUA.

34. C. O. Davis, "Our Test Teachers," *School Review* 34 (December 1926): 757; Christopher P. Loss, *Between Citizens and the State: The Politics of American Higher Education* (Princeton, NJ: Princeton University Press, 2012), 46; *Students Speak Out!*, 85; "Eliminate Detachment," *Pennsylvanian* 49 (9 January 1933): 2; Frederick Rudolph, *The American College and University* (1962; repr., Athens: University of Georgia Press, 1990), 449; "The College Faculty Questionnaire" (MS, 15 January 1940), 59, folder 1, box 11, Dean of the College Records, SCRC—Chicago; John M. Fletcher, "Educational Trobrianders and the Professorial Illusion," *Scientific Monthly* 27, no. 5 (November 1928): 451.

35. *Students Speak Out!*, 110–11; Student Curriculum Committee, "General Report," 6, 10; Earl F. Cox to Athern Park Daggett, "Alumni Letters A–C" folder, box 3, Self-Study Reports, Bowdoin College; Edwards, Artman, and Fisher, *Undergraduates*, 312; *Colby College Bulletin: Reports on Instruction, 1923–24* (Waterville, ME: Colby College, 1924), 14; *Colby College Bulletin: Reports on Instruction, 1927–1928* (Waterville, ME: Colby College, 1928), 8, 15.

36. Richard H. Platt, "Some Practical Aspects of Junior College Work," *Sierra Educational News* 14 (1918): 71–73; Steven Brint and Jerome Karabel, *The Diverted Dream: Community Colleges and the Promise of Educational Opportunity in America, 1900–1985* (New York: Oxford

University Press, 1991), 42; A. Monroe Stowe, "Thesis-Response Teaching in College," *Bulletin of Randolph-Macon Woman's College* 13, no. 4 (September 1927): 14, "Contents Courses of Study Junior College Courses" folder, box 784, American Historical Association Papers, Library of Congress, Washington, DC; Walter Crosby Eells, *Present Status of Junior College Terminal Education* (Washington, DC: American Association of Junior Colleges, 1941), 162–63.

37. Geraldine Joncich Clifford, introduction to *Lone Voyagers: Academic Women in Coeducational Universities, 1870–1937*, ed. Geraldine Joncich Clifford (New York: Feminist Press at CUNY, 1989), 25; Palmieri, *In Adamless Eden*, 162–63; A. Caswell Ellis, "Preliminary Report of Committee W, on Status of Women in College and University Faculties," *Bulletin of the AAUP* 7, no. 6 (October 1921): 21–22; "Second Report of Committee W on the Status of Women in College and University Faculties," *Bulletin of the AAUP* 10, no. 7 (November 1924): 67–69.

38. "Alumnus," "Howard Class 'A' College before Stanley Durkee Became President," *Baltimore Afro-American*, 17 October 1925, 2; "President Durkee Said to Be Seeking $10,000 Pastorate in Brooklyn," *Baltimore Afro-American*, 5 December 1925, 2; David Gold, *Rhetoric at the Margins: Revising the History of Writing Instruction in American Colleges, 1873–1947* (Carbondale: Southern Illinois University Press, 2008), 40, 35; William M. Banks, *Black Intellectuals: Race and Responsibility in American Life* (New York: W. W. Norton, 1996), 95.

39. Guy E. Snavely, "Who Is a Great Teacher?," *Association of American Colleges Bulletin* 15, no. 1 (March 1929): 68–70.

Chapter 4 · "Teaching Made Personal": Reform and Its Limits in Interwar College Teaching

1. Homer L. Dodge, "The Improvement of College Teaching," *Journal of Higher Education* 3, no. 9 (December 1932): 561–62.

2. Max McConn, "When Is a Teacher Not a Teacher?," *North American Review* 228, no. 4 (October 1929): 416; Addison Hibbard, "Our Truant Professors," *Outlook*, 5 December 1928, 1267; Joseph Seidlin, *A Critical Study of the Teaching of Elementary College Mathematics* (New York: Teachers College Press, 1931), 71; John M. Fletcher, "Educational Trobrianders and the Professorial Illusion," *Scientific Monthly* 27, no. 5 (November 1928): 446–47.

3. John Palmer Gavit, *College* (New York: Harcourt Brace, 1925), 86–88; William Bennett Munro, "Quack-Doctoring the College," *Harper's* 157 (September 1928): 481–82.

4. Charles F. Thwing, "College Problems under Wide Attack. Teaching Made Personal," *New York Times*, 8 March 1931, 59.

5. "A Report to the Carnegie Corporation of New York on the Colgate Plan" (MS, 6 June 1933), 2, folder 13, box 107, series IIIA, Carnegie Corporation of New York Papers (hereafter "CCNY Papers"), Rare Book and Manuscript Library, Columbia University (hereafter "RBML—Columbia"); Ralph Barton Perry, "The Preceptorial or Tutorial System: Report by Committee G," *Bulletin of the AAUP* 10, no. 7 (November 1924): 58–60.

6. "Stanford President Doubts Applicability of Tutorial System to Education in the U.S.," *N.S.F.A. News Service* 5, no. 27 (28 April 1934): 3, "News Service 1934" folder, box 1, series II, Archives of the National Student Federation, Special Collections and University Archives, University of Maryland, College Park, MD; *Report of the Harvard Student Council Committee on Education* (Cambridge, MA: Harvard Crimson, 1926), 40; Kenneth B. Murdoch to H. H. Burbank, 1 June 1934, "Committee on Tutorial Instruction" folder, box 11, Harvard Department of Economics General Office Files, Harvard University Archives.

7. Philip C. Beam to Jacques Barzun, 19 October 1945, "The Teacher in America: Correspondence Relating to—Oct. 1945" folder, box 2, series II, Jacques Barzun Papers, RBML—Columbia; Special Committee on Education of the Harvard Student Council, *Harvard Education 1948. The Students' View* (n.p.: Harvard Student Council, 1949), 36; Morton Keller and

Phyllis Keller, *Making Harvard Modern: The Rise of America's University* (New York: Oxford, 2001), 25; John S. P. Tatlock, "The General Final Examination in the Major Study: Report by Committee G," *Bulletin of the AAUP* 10 (December 1924): 613; R. H. Edwards, J. M. Artman, and Galen M. Fisher, *Undergraduates: A Study of Morale in Twenty-Three American Colleges and Universities* (Garden City, NY: Doubleday, 1928), 323; Jacques Barzun, *Teacher in America* (1945; repr., Indianapolis: Liberty, 1981), 57.

8. "Proceedings. Curriculum Conference. Volume I" (MS, 19–24 January 1931), 52, box 2:2, Curriculum Conference 1931 Papers, Archives and Special Collections, Rollins College (hereafter "ASC—Rollins"), Winter Park, FL; Arthur Morgan, "Teaching Methods at Antioch," *Association of American Colleges Bulletin* 14 (November 1928): 401; "A Constructive Rebellion," *New Student* 6, no. 20 (23 February 1927): 1; Burton R. Clark, *The Distinctive College: Antioch, Reed, and Swarthmore* (Chicago: Aldine, 1970), 101, 96; Norman F. Coleman, "How We Teach at Reed College," *Association of American Colleges Bulletin* 14 (November 1928): 408; "A Critique of the Rollins College Conference Plan" (MS, December 1930), 16, "Curriculum Conference 1931. A Critique of the R.C. Conference Plan" folder, box 2:3, Curriculum Conference 1931 Papers.

9. Gayle Prince Rajtar and Steve Rajtar, "The Fierce Competition for Rollins College," http://www.floridahistorynetwork.com/the-fierce-competition-for-rollins-college.html; William H. Honan, "The College Lecture, Long Derided, May Be Fading," *New York Times*, 14 August 2002, "Curriculum Conference 1931—New York Times story 2002" folder, box 2:5; and Frederick Lynch, "The Observer—Revising the College Curriculum," *Presbyterian Advance*, 12 February 1931, "Curriculum Conference 1931. Newsclippings" folder, box 2:3, both in Curriculum Conference 1931 Papers.

10. Unnamed respondents, student survey (MS, [1929?]), folder 10, box 68, Hamilton Holt Papers, ASC—Rollins; Hamilton Holt, "The Rollins Idea," *Nation* 81 (8 October 1930): 373, "Curriculum Conference 1931. Newsclippings" folder, box 2:3; and John Palmer Gavit, "Socrates on the Eight-Hour Shift," *Survey Graphic* 19, no. 3 (June 1931): 249, "Curriculum Conference. Gavit, John Palmer" folder, box 2:5, both in Curriculum Conference 1931 Papers.

11. Unnamed respondents, student survey; Edwin Clarke to Hamilton Holt, 3 November 1941; and U. T. Bradley to Hamilton Holt, 14 October 1941, both in folder 9, box 68, Holt Papers; Gavit, "Socrates on the Eight-Hour Shift," 249; Warren F. Kuehl, *Hamilton Holt: Journalist, Internationalist, Educator* (Gainesville: University of Florida Press, 1960), 192, 202.

12. Kuehl, *Hamilton Holt*, 194; "Wisconsin's Experiment Station," *New Student* 6, no. 1 (29 September 1926): 2; Adam R. Nelson, *Education and Democracy: The Meaning of Alexander Meiklejohn, 1872–1964* (Madison: University of Wisconsin Press, 2011), 140, 168; Jack C. Lane, "The Rollins Conference, 1931, and the Search for a Progressive Liberal Education: Mirror or Prism?" (MS, 1983), "The Rollins Conference 1931—By Jack C. Lane" folder, box 2:5, Curriculum Conference 1931 Papers.

13. *What the Colleges Are Doing* (March 1931), quoted in Kuehl, *Hamilton Holt*, 194; Edward Safford Jones, *Comprehensive Examinations in American Colleges* (New York: Macmillan, 1933), 98–99; University Committee on Educational Research, "College Examinations," *Bulletin of the University of Minnesota* 35, no. 22 (11 April 1932): 20, folder 7, box 60, series IIIA, CCNY Papers; John W. Boyer, *The University of Chicago: A History* (Chicago: University of Chicago Press, 2015), 234.

14. Leon B. Richardson, *A Study of the Liberal College* (Hanover, NH: Dartmouth College, 1924), 224; Wendell W. Cruze, "The Comprehensive Examination," *Peabody Journal of Education* 11, no. 2 (September 1933): 59; "The Opening Wedge," *N.F.S.A. News Service* 6, no. 29 (3 May 1935): 3, "News Service 1935" folder, box 1, series II, Archives of the National Student Federation; John M. Russell, "Report on Colgate University" (MS, 25 May 1933), 6, folder 13, box 107, series IIIA, CCNY Papers.

15. Jones, *Comprehensive Examinations*, 107–8, 149; "Tabulation of the Faculty Question-naire for the Evaluation of Comprehensive Examinations" (MS, [1930?]), 2, folder E9, box 12, Colbiana Collection, Special Collections, Colby College, Waterville, ME; "The College Faculty Questionnaire" (MS, 15 January 1940), 40, 25, 58, folder 1, box 11; and Theodore Weil Shaffner to A. J. Brumbaugh, 21 March 1938, folder 11, box 9, both in Dean of the College Records, Special Collections Research Center, University of Chicago (hereafter "SCRC—Chicago").

16. Frederick J. Kelly, *The American Arts College: A Limited Survey* (New York: Macmillan, 1925), 109; Harry R. Turkel, "The Lecture System, II. Breaking Its Confines at Harvard and Stanford," *New Student* 7, no. 16 (18 January 1928): 4; Clair Wilcox to Frank Aydelotte, [1928?], "Instruction Committee. 1929–1930" folder, box 37, Frank Aydelotte Papers, Swarthmore College Archives, Friends Historical Library, Swarthmore, PA; Jones, *Comprehensive Examinations*, 96–97.

17. Perry, "Preceptorial or Tutorial System," 48; F. J. Kelly, "Educational Principles Stirring the Colleges," *Phi Delta Kappan* 13, no. 6 (April 1931): 163; Student Curriculum Committee, "General Report" (MS, [1930?]), 10, "Com. on Instruction" folder, box 19; Everett Hunt to Professors Dreeden and Spiller, 4 January 1934, "Instruction Committee 1933–1941" folder, box 38; Frederick Manning to Frank Aydelotte, 17 June 1929; and "Proposal for Student Participa-tion in Working Out Matters of Curriculum" (MS, [1929?]), 1, both in "Com. on Instruction" folder, box 19, all in Aydelotte Papers.

18. John Dewey, *School and Society* (Chicago: University of Chicago Press, 1915), 7; AAUP Survey of College and University Teaching, "Report of the Field Director to the Committee," part II, section A (MS, 1 October 1932), 58; and AAUP Survey of College and University Teaching, "Report of the Field Director to the Committee," part II, section B (MS, 2 Octo-ber 1932), 103, both in folder 134, box 12, James Rowland Angell Presidential Papers, Beinecke Rare Book and Manuscript Library, Yale University; "More of This and Less of That" [1940?], folder 4, box 125, Kimon Friar Papers, Rare Books and Special Collections, Firestone Library, Princeton University (hereafter "RBSC—Princeton"); Cruze, "Comprehensive Examination," 60; Jones, *Comprehensive Examinations*, 59–61; "Report of the Committee on College and University Teaching," *Bulletin of the AAUP* 19, no. 5 (May 1933): 99.

19. Kelly, "Educational Principles," 162; Carnegie Corporation press release, "Investigation of College Teaching by the American Association of University Professors" (MS, 20 November 1931); and Homer L. Dodge, "Discussion of the Work of the Committee on College and University Teaching" (MS, 1932), 1, both in folder 3, box 42, series IIIA, CCNY Papers.

20. Paul Klapper, preface to *College Teaching: Studies in Methods of Teaching in the College*, ed. Paul Klapper (Yonkers-on-Hudson, NY: World Book, 1920), iii; "Proceedings. Curriculum Conference. Volume I," 542; Kelly, "Educational Principles," 165; Wilbert J. McKeachie, "Research on College Teaching: The Historical Background," *Journal of Educational Psychology* 82, no. 2 (1990): 190; Melvin Haggerty to Lotus Coffman, 3 October 1927, "Committee on Educational Research, 1924–1926" folder, box 7; and Henry A. Erikson, "Experiments in Class Size in the Department of Physics, University of Minnesota" (MS, [1928?]), 2–4, "Bureau of Institutional Research. Science—Reports" folder, box 23, both in Bureau of Institutional Research Papers, Archives and Special Collections, University of Minnesota, Minneapolis, MN.

21. "Report and Discussion of Committee U" (MS, 28 December 1932), 15, folder 3, box 42, series IIIA, CCNY Papers; "Suggestions, Discussions, and Recommendations" (MS, 7 June 1924), 1–3, "Committee on Educational Research n.d. 1923–24" folder, box 7, Bureau of Institutional Research Papers; H. Gordon Hullfish, "A Problem in College Teaching," *Journal of Higher Education* 1, no. 5 (May 1930): 261; Seidlin, *Critical Study*, 71.

22. "Report of the Committee on College and University Teaching," 59; Allan Burt, "Supervision of Instruction," *Peabody Journal of Education* 25, no. 5 (March 1948): 214, 210; Oberlin College, *The Report of the Committee on Bases of Promotion* (November 1930),

enclosed with Ernest H. Wilkins to William B. Munro, 25 March 1931, folder 3, box 42, series IIIA, CCNY Papers; Harry L. Kriner, "Ways of Improving Instruction in the State Teachers Colleges of the United States," *Peabody Journal of Education* 10, no. 6 (May 1933): 333; Raymond M. Mosher, "The San Jose Plan," *Journal of Higher Education* 4, no. 6 (June 1933): 305; James M. Todd, *The College Conundrum* (New York: Round Table, 1935), 14.

23. James L. McConaughy to Ernest Wilkins, 18 December 1928, "Correspondence with Commission (1928)" folder; and Leon Richardson, "The Inexperienced Teacher" (MS, 1924), "Training of Young Teachers" folder, both in box 92, Ernest Wilkins Presidential Papers, Oberlin College Archives, Oberlin College, Oberlin, OH; "Report of the Field Director to the Committee," part II, section C (MS, 1 October 1932), 102, folder 134, box 12, Angell Papers; Todd, *College Conundrum*, 33; Fernandus Payne and Evelyn Wilkinson Spieth, *An Open Letter to College Teachers* (Bloomington, IN: Principia, 1935), ix.

24. C. B. Boucher, "Honored for Excellence in Teaching" (MS, 1932), 1–3; C. B. Boucher to "Anonymous Donor of the Special College Fund," 30 April 1932; M. C. Coulter to A. J. Brumbaugh, 26 January 1940; F. C. Ward to R. S. Strozier, 3 June 1947, all in folder 8, box 11, Dean of the College Records, SCRC—Chicago.

25. James L. McConaughy to Executive Committee, 3 October 1931; N. Wyman Storer to McConaughy, 30 September 1930; James E. Bryan to McConaughy, 28 September 1931; C. R. Smith to Clinton DeW. Burdick, 23 June 1931; "Report of Committee on Faculty Salaries, Academic Council Minutes, March 1, 1933" (MS, 1933), 1; Burton H. Camp to James L. McConaughy, 28 September 1931, all in folder 11-40, Vertical Subject Files Collection, Special Collections and Archives, Wesleyan University, Middletown, CT.

26. James L. McConaughy to C. R. Smith, 26 March 1935; and William B. Munro to James L. McConaughy, 19 June 1933, both in folder 11-40, Vertical Subject Files Collection; David B. Potts, *Wesleyan University, 1910–1970: Academic Ambition and Middle-Class America* (Middletown, CT: Wesleyan University Press, 2015), 530n17; "Williams Increases Pay," *New York Times*, 6 January 1937, 18; Robert Nisbet, *Teachers and Scholars: A Memoir of Berkeley in Depression and War* (New Brunswick, NJ: Transaction, 1992), 126–27; Victor Butterfield to Albert Johnston, 13 September 1941; "Summary Report on Questionnaires in Regard to Faculty Salaries" (MS, 22 March 1944), 1; Victor Butterfield to Floyd Horowitz, 15 October 1951, all in folder 11-40, Vertical Subject Files Collection.

27. Paul Popenoe to Franz Schneider, 30 March 1941, "Correspondence—January–May 1941" folder, carton 1, Franz Schneider Papers, Bancroft Library, University of California, Berkeley; James McConaughy to Ernest Wilkins, 18 December 1928, "Correspondence with Commission (1928)" folder, box 92, Wilkins Papers; Leon Burr Richardson, "Desirable Types of Graduate Training for Prospective College Teachers," 30; and Leon Burr Richardson, "Deficiencies in College Teaching," 5, both in *The Training of College Teachers*, ed. William S. Gray (Chicago: University of Chicago Press, 1930).

28. Paul C. Packer, "The Selection and Development of College Teachers at the University of Iowa," 179–80; and "Appendix: Reports on Current Methods of Training College Teachers in Various Higher Institutions," 224, both in Gray, *Training of College Teachers*; William H. Allen, *Self-Surveys by Colleges and Universities* (Yonkers-on-Hudson, NY: World Book, 1917), 274; David E. Berg, *Personality Culture by College Faculties* (New York: Institute for Public Service, 1920), 3, 110–18, 81, 6.

29. Hamilton Holt, *The Rollins College Ideal* (1928), 9; David M. Oshinsky, Richard P. McCormick, and Daniel Horn, *The Case of the Nazi Professor* (New Brunswick, NJ: Rutgers University Press, 1989), 11; Christian Gauss, "Student-Faculty Relationships" (MS, 1932), 6, folder 18, box 45, Christian Gauss Papers, RBSC—Princeton; Logan Wilson, *The Academic Man* (New York: Oxford University Press, 1941), 180–82.

30. Sidney E. Mezes, "Professional Training for College Teaching," in Klapper, *College Teaching*, 31; F. J. Kelly, "The Training of College Teachers," *Journal of Educational Research* 16, no. 5 (December 1927): 333; "Report of the Commission on Enlistment and Training of College Teachers," *Association of American Colleges Bulletin* 15, no. 1 (March 1929): 41; Kelly, "Educational Principles," 164; Otis E. Randall, "Enlistment and Training of College Teachers," *Bulletin of the AAUP* 14, no. 4 (April 1928): 277.

31. C. D. Bohannan, "Improvement of College Instruction," *Phi Delta Kappan* 10, no. 6 (April 1928): 161–62; "Report of the Committee on College and University Teaching," 62; R. E. Buchanan to R. M. Hughes, 4 December 1928, enclosed with R. M. Hughes to Ernest Wilkins, 5 December 1928, "Correspondence with Commission (1928)" folder, box 92, Wilkins Papers; Archie M. Palmer, "Educating the Educators," *Journal of Higher Education* 1, no. 6 (January 1931): 335–38; W. W. Charters, "Graduate Schools and College Teaching," *Educational Research Bulletin* 7, no. 16 (14 November 1928): 348–49; Richard Stephen Uhrbrock, "Is College Leadership Bankrupt?," *Journal of Higher Education* 6, no. 1 (January 1935): 8.

32. William S. Gray, "Survey of Current Methods in Training Prospective College Teachers," in Gray, *Training of College Teachers*, 86–87; Harlan H. Barrows to Frederic Woodward, 25 January 1930, folder 2; and "Economics" (MS, 1930), enclosed with Harlan H. Barrows to R. M. Hutchins, folder 1, both in box 96, Office of the President, Hutchins Administration, Records, SCRC—Chicago.

33. "Report of the Field Director to the Committee," part II, section B, 86, 77; Glen Wakeham, "Compulsory Education Courses for College Teachers," *School and Society* 32 (2 August 1930): 157; Todd, *College Conundrum*, 180–81; Homer L. Dodge, "The Place of the Subject-Matter Department in the Preparation of College Teachers" (MS, 13–15 July 1938), 10, folder 1, box 50, Homer Levi Dodge Papers, Neils Bohr Library, American Institute of Physics, College Park, MD.

34. "Report and Discussion of Committee U" (MS, 28 December 1932), 6, 3; "Report of the Field Director to the Committee," part II, Section B, 86.

Chapter 5 · *Expansion and Repression: Cold War Challenges for College Teaching*

1. Theodore C. Blegen, "Education Cannot Stand Still," in *The Preparation of College Teachers*, ed. Theodore C. Blegen and Russell M. Cooper (Washington, DC: American Council on Education, 1950), 7. Blegen's essay reprinted a speech he delivered at a conference in December 1949, sponsored by the American Council on Education and the US Office of Education.

2. "Educators Hear Policies Scored," *New York Times*, 7 March 1956, 33; *Statement by the President Making Public a Report of the Commission on Higher Education* (15 December 1947), https://www.presidency.ucsb.edu/documents/statement-the-president-making-public-report -the-commission-higher-education; *Higher Education for American Democracy* (Washington, DC: General Printing Office, 1947), 4:2.

3. Binder (no title), item 11-b, box 1; and "Reactions of Respondents to Attacks Directed toward Others" (MS, [1955?]), 4, folder 3, box 2, both in series II, Paul Lazarsfeld Papers, Rare Book and Manuscript Library, Columbia University (hereafter "RBML—Columbia"); John T. Wahlquist, "The Improvement of College Teaching" (MS, 1954), 5, folder 33, box 3, Clark Kerr Personal and Professional Papers, Bancroft Library, University of California, Berkeley. The standard history of Cold War repression in American academia remains Ellen Schrecker, *No Ivory Tower: McCarthyism and the Universities* (New York: Oxford University Press, 1986).

4. "Lack of Teachers Hampers Colleges," *New York Times*, 20 February 1947; and Christian Gauss, "Teachers" (MS, [1947?]), 1, both in folder 16, box 38, Christian Gauss Papers, Rare

Books and Special Collections, Firestone Library, Princeton University; George Williams, *Some of My Best Friends Are Professors: A Critical Commentary on Higher Education* (New York: Abelard-Schuman, 1958), 1; Martin A. Trow, "Reflections on the Recruitment to College Teaching," in *Faculty Supply, Demand, and Recruitment. Proceedings of a Regional Conference Sponsored by the New England Board of Higher Education* (Winchester, MA: New England Board of Higher Education, 1959), 51–52, "Com. C—College and University Research and Publications. Jan–April 1960" folder, box 4, Committee C series, American Association of University Professors Papers (hereafter "AAUP Papers"), Special Collections Research Center, George Washington University.

5. Henry A. Perkins, "Paternalism in American Colleges," *Journal of Higher Education* 16 (January 1945): 3; Mark Raeff, "We Do Not Teach Them How to Think," *New York Times*, 26 January 1958, SM7; C. Page Smith to Clark Kerr, 16 December 1958, folder 5, box 75, Dean E. McHenry Papers, Special Collections and Archives, University of California, Santa Cruz (hereafter "SCA—UCSC"); Read Bain, "College Teaching," *Bulletin of the AAUP* 31, no. 1 (Spring 1945): 57–58.

6. "The Conservative Tradition in Education at Bowdoin College. Report of the Committee on Self Study" (MS, 1 September 1955), 77–78, vol. 1, Self-Study Reports Collection, Special Collections and Archives, Bowdoin College, Brunswick, ME; Gilbert Arthur Highet, "Renewal in Teaching," in *Strengthening Education at All Levels: A Report of the 18th Educational Conference, 1953* (Washington, DC: American Council on Education, 1953), 111, "The Immortal Profession—Notes" folder, box 13, Gilbert Highet Papers, RBML—Columbia; *Confidential Guide to Freshman Courses, 1952* (Cambridge, MA: Harvard Crimson, 1952), 3, box 1, Confidential Guide to Courses / Harvard Crimson Collection (hereafter "Confy—HUA"), Harvard University Archives; "Proceedings. Second Work Conference on College Teaching for Purdue Faculty Members, September 16, 1957" (MS, 1957), 22, "Com. C—College and Univ. Teaching Research and Publications 1958" folder, box 4, Committee C series, AAUP Papers; Wilbert McKeachie, "How Do Students Learn?," in *The Two Ends of the Log: Learning and Teaching in Today's College*, ed. Russell M. Cooper (Minneapolis: University of Minnesota Press, 1958), 27; Betty Friedan, *The Feminine Mystique* (New York: Norton, 1963), 145.

7. Christopher Jencks, "The Next 30 Years in the Colleges," *Harper's*, October 1961, 126; David Boroff, "American Fetish—the College Degree," *New York Times*, 14 February 1960, SM11; David Boroff, *Campus U.S.A.: Portraits of American Colleges in Action* (New York: Harper & Brothers, 1960), 36; "Schneider Aims at Better Methods," *Daily Californian*, 27 May 1953, "Franz Schneider" folder, box 60, Kenneth Eugene Eble Papers, University Archives and Record Management, University of Utah, Salt Lake City; Jud Kinberg, "Faults on Both Sides," *American Scholar* 16, no. 3 (Summer 1947): 348; S. M. Vincoor, "The Veteran Flunks the Professor: A GI Indictment of Our Institutes of Higher Education," *School and Society* 66 (18 October 1947): 289; Richard A. Hoge, "Letter to the Editor," *Daily Pennsylvanian* (University of Pennsylvania) 62 (20 April 1949): 2.

8. "The Preparation of College Teachers. Proceedings of the Conference on the Preparation of College Teachers Held at the University of Chicago on May 6, 1948" (MS, 1948), 33, folder 4, box 1, Committee on the Preparation of Teachers Papers, Special Collections Research Center, University of Chicago (hereafter "SCRC—Chicago"); "Lack of Teachers Hampers Colleges"; Frederick J. Kelly, *Toward Better College Teaching* (Washington, DC: General Printing Office, 1950), 45; Earl McGrath, "What's Wrong with College Teaching?," *Boston Globe*, 13 December 1959, B14; "South Faces Teacher Deficit," *Christian Science Monitor*, 12 February 1962, 5; "College Teacher of Electrical Technology Appears on 'Meet the Professor'" (press release, 26 November 1962), folder 2, box 26, Records of the Office of the Chancellor and Executive Vice President, University Archives, New York University.

9. Robert Marsh, "The Road to Major Changes," *American Scholar* 16, no. 4 (Autumn 1947): 486; "Conservative Tradition in Education at Bowdoin College," 97; "Interview with President Thomas Jones of Earlham College, 12 March 1958" (MS, 1958), 3, folder 3, box 1, Bernard R. Berelson Study of Graduate Education Records (hereafter "Berelson Records"), SCRC—Chicago; Stacy Schiff, "The Genius and Mrs. Genius," *New Yorker*, 10 February 1997, https://www.newyorker.com/magazine/1997/02/10/the-genius-and-mrs-genius; Moody E. Prior to F. W. Strothmann, 31 July 1956, folder 1, box 4, Donald Morrison Papers, Rauner Special Collections Library, Dartmouth College, Hanover, NH; "Interview with President Weimer Hicks of Kalamazoo College, March 28, 1958. From H. R. Metcalf" (MS, 1958), 2, folder 3, box 1, Berelson Records.

10. Linda Eisenmann, *Higher Education of Women in Postwar America, 1945–1965* (Baltimore: Johns Hopkins University Press, 2006), 58–59; *Proceedings of an Institute on College Teaching Held at Marquette University, Milwaukee, Wisconsin, 5–7 June 1961* (Racine, WI: Western Printing and Lithographing, 1961), 41; Mrs. Harvey H. Scholl to O. Meredith Wilson [1959?], folder 2, box 470, American Council on Education Papers (hereafter "ACE Papers"), Hoover Institution Library and Archives, Stanford, CA; Patricia Meyer Spacks interview (MS, 30 November 2007), 12–13, Accession 2012-A-054, Oral Histories Documenting Yale University Women, Beinecke Rare Book and Manuscript Library, Yale University.

11. Harry Hoijer to V. O. Knudsen, 23 April 1947, "Teaching Assistants—File #3 (1947–8) folder"; R. B. Allen to Robert Sproul, 20 January 1958, "Teaching Assistants—File #7 (1958–9, n.d.)" folder; V. O. Knudsen to John D. Hicks, 11 November 1946; and Harry Hoijer to V. O. Knudsen, 9 October 1946, both in "Teaching Assistants—File #2 (1940–1946)" folder; J. A. C. Grant to V. O. Knudsen, 31 January 1947, "Teaching Assistants—File #3 (1947–8) folder," all in box 21, Graduate Division Dean Administrative Files, Charles E. Young Research Library, University of California, Los Angeles (hereafter "CYRL—UCLA"); "Kelley" to Clark Kerr, 15 August 1957, folder 34, box 3, Kerr Papers.

12. "Interview with William McElroy, Biochemistry, Johns Hopkins University, April 25, 1958" (MS, 1958), 2, folder 6, box 1, Berelson Records; William G. McMillan to Raymond H. Fisher, 13 January 1961, "Teaching Assistants—File #8 (1960–1961)" folder; K. N. Trueblood, "Some Policies, Problems, and Proposals with Regard to Teaching Assistants" (MS, 11 September 1962), 4, "Teaching Assistants—File #9 (1962–1964)" folder; Vern O. Knudsen to Chairmen of Departments, 7 March 1947, "Teaching Assistants—File #3 (1947–8)" folder, all in box 21, Graduate Division Dean Administrative Files, CYRL—UCLA; Williams, *Some of My Best Friends*, 98.

13. *Confidential Guide to Freshman Courses, 1947* (Cambridge, MA: Harvard Crimson, 1947), 28, box 1, Confy—HUA; Hamilton Brown, "My Son Will Not Go to Harvard," *Harvard Alumni Bulletin* 51, no. 11 (12 March 1949): 470; Mentor L. Williams, "The Place of Teaching in Higher Learning," *Bulletin of the AAUP* 36, no. 4 (Winter 1950): 674; Boroff, *Campus U.S.A.*, 39; Bernard Berelson, *Graduate Education in the United States* (New York: McGraw-Hill, 1960), 67; Gladys Kammerer, "The University's Responsibility for Improvement of College Teaching" (MS, [1959?]), 2, folder 7, box 469, ACE Papers.

14. Sidney Hook, *Education for Modern Man* (New York: Dial, 1946), 175–76; Williams, *Some of My Best Friends*, 239. On overcrowding and poor facilities in Cold War classrooms, see, e.g., "How Can Effectiveness of Instruction Be Improved" (MS, 24 February 1948), 150, "Teaching 1948–1969" folder, box 41, Academic Senate Los Angeles Division, Executive Office Administrative Files, CYRL—UCLA; "Buzzin' Around," *Ithacan* (Ithaca College), 16 May 1947, 2.

15. William P. Godfrey, "The Seven Deadly Sins of Teaching," *Proceedings of the American Society for Engineering Education* 58 (1950–51): 213–15; Williams, *Some of My Best Friends*, 61–67; Lauren D. Reid, "The Improvement of Classroom Morale," in *Toward Better Teaching:*

A Collection of Commentaries on College Instruction, ed. Edward M. Palmquist and Donald F. Drummond (Columbia: Board of Curators, University of Missouri, 1951), 19–21.

16. Elmer Ellis, "The Characteristics of Good Teaching in College," in Palmquist and Drummond, *Toward Better Teaching*, 9; Alvin Kernan, *In Plato's Cave* (New Haven, CT: Yale University Press, 1999), 89; Susan Burton, "English 330" (MS, 16 September 1960), 4, folder 4, box 1, George G. Williams Papers, Rice University Archives, Rice University, Houston, TX; Hook, *Education for Modern Man*, 187; untitled manuscript (1949), 16, folder 4, box E45, Margaret Mead Papers, Library of Congress, Washington, DC.

17. "Intellectual Ennui—III. Insufficient Discussion," *Daily Pennsylvanian* 75 (11 February 1960): 2; Special Committee on Education of the Harvard Student Council, *Harvard Education 1948. The Students' View* (n.p.: Harvard Student Council, 1949), 8; "Kelley" to Clark Kerr, 15 August 1957, folder 34, box 3, Kerr Papers; John Dizikes, "A Life of Learning and Teaching at the University of California, Santa Cruz, 1965–2000" (MS, 1 January 2012), 7, Regional History Project, SCA—UCSC, https://escholarship.org/uc/item/24z7r5bh; E. S. Bogardus, "Behavior Patterns of College Teachers," *Sociology and Social Research* 30 (July–August 1946), 485; Thomas Francis Maher, "Gilt for the Lily," *Bulletin of the AAUP* 34, no. 2 (Summer 1948): 391.

18. Edgar Dale, "New Techniques of Teaching," in Cooper, *Two Ends of the Log*, 194; Robert Berkelman, "Farewell to Passiveness," *Journal of Higher Education* 22, no. 1 (January 1951): 20; J. G. Umstattd, *B. A. U. in Action: Teaching and Learning at Biarritz American University* (Austin: University of Texas Press, 1947), 36, iii; Rexford W. Bolling, "You Bore Me, Prof.!," *Education* 73 (February 1953): 351.

19. James O. Freedman, *The Education of James O. Freedman* (Princeton, NJ: Princeton University Press, 2007), 215–16; Gerald Graff, "Yvor Winters of Stanford," in *Masters: Portraits of Great Teachers*, ed. Joseph Epstein (New York: Basic, 1981), 149; "Dr. Carman Assails College Teaching," *New York Times*, 18 February 1949, 25; Yale Daily News, *Course Critique Pamphlet* (New Haven, CT: Van Dyck, April 1948), 81; Yale Daily News, *Critique of the Humanities* (New Haven, CT: Eastern Press, April 1950), 24; "The Consumers' Report," in Palmquist and Drummond, *Toward Better Teaching*, 72.

20. John Erskine, *My Life as a Teacher* (Philadelphia: J. B. Lippincott, 1948), 204; Dexter Merriam Keezer, *The Light That Flickers* (New York: Harper, 1946), 138; D. Lincoln Harter, "Dr. Lincoln Explains 'ISM' of Teaching How to Make Sense with Three Little Words," *Daily Pennsylvanian* 67 (11 December 1953): 2; "Sympathy," *Yale Daily News*, 19 January 1949, 4.

21. "To Free the Mind," *Yale Daily News*, 14 January 1949, 2; *Confidential Guide to Freshman Courses, 1954* (Cambridge, MA: Harvard Crimson, 1954), 45, box 1, Confy—HUA; William R. Dennes to Frank C. Abbott, 21 November 1955, folder 4, box 397; and "Minutes. Committee on College Teaching" (MS, 7–8 November 1955), 4, folder 10, box 396, both in ACE Papers.

22. "Minutes. Committee on College Teaching," 4; "Wake Up," *Time*, 2 February 1953, folder 18, box 65; and "Earlham Interdepartmental Group Tutorials: A Program for Responsible Discussion of Values" (MS, 25 April 1956), 1, enclosed with Wayne Booth to Robert J. Werth, 27 April 1956, folder 15, box 546, both in series IIIA, Carnegie Corporation of New York Papers (hereafter "CCNY Papers"), RBML—Columbia; "Report of the Special Committee on Improving the Effectiveness of Instruction" (MS, 1 April 1958), 1, "Teaching 1948–1969" folder, Academic Senate Los Angeles Division, Executive Office Administrative Files, CYRL—UCLA; Chancellor's Advisory Administrative Council minutes (MS, 12 May 1954), 1, folder 33, box 3, Kerr Papers.

23. *Harvard Education 1948*, 38; Phillip E. Jacob, *Changing Values in College: An Exploratory Study of the Impact of General Education in Social Sciences on the Values of American Students* (New Haven, CT: Edward W. Hazen Foundation, 1957), 88–89; Aura E. Severinghaus

et al., *Preparation for Medical Education in the Liberal Arts College* (New York: McGraw-Hill, 1953), 199; "College Teachers Talk Too Much," *Argus* (Illinois Wesleyan), 3 May 1950, 1; Nathan Glazer, "The Wasted Classroom," *Harper's*, October 1961, 149; Joseph Axelrod et al., *Teaching by Discussion in the College Program* (Chicago: University of Chicago, 1949), v, 3, folder 6, box 15, Dean of the College Records, SCRC—Chicago.

24. B. S. Bloom, "The Study of Conscious Thought Processes by the Method of Stimulated Recall" (MS, [1950?]), 15, 10, folder 2, box 98, series IIIA, CCNY Papers; John W. Riley Jr., Bryce F. Ryan, and Marcia Lifshitz, *The Student Looks at His Teacher* (New Brunswick, NJ: Rutgers University Press, 1950), 117; Robert A. Brady, "Memorandum on the Teaching of the Social Sciences in the College, University of Chicago" (MS, January 1945), 34, folder 1, box 6, Dean of the College Records, SCRC—Chicago; W. J. McKeachie, "Procedures and Techniques of Teaching: A Survey of Experimental Studies," in *The American College: A Psychological and Social Interpretation of the Higher Learning*, ed. Nevitt Sanford (New York: John Wiley, 1962), 335; Boroff, *Campus U.S.A.*, 68, 170.

25. Severinghaus et al., *Preparation for Medical Education*, 197; Binder (no title), item 11-b, box 1, series II, Lazarsfeld Papers.

26. Paul F. Lazarsfeld and Wagner Thielens Jr., *The Academic Mind: Social Scientists in a Time of Crisis* (1958; repr., New York: Arno, 1977), 192–94; "Reactions of Respondents without a Specific Stimulus" (MS, [1955?]), 2, folder 3, box 2; and Jeannette Green to Staff of Teacher Apprehension Study, 26 November 1956, 7, box 3 (no folder), both in series II, Lazarsfeld Papers.

27. "Reactions of Respondents," 3, 5, 7, 4; Florence Ruderman to Staff of Teachers' Apprehension, 9 December 1955, 30, 40, 46, box 2 (no folder), series II, Lazarsfeld Papers.

28. Ruderman to Staff of Teachers' Apprehension, 9 December 1955, 32; Jeannette Green to Staff of Teacher Apprehension Study, 28 September 1956, 6, box 2 (no folder); and "Reactions of Respondents," 6; Binder (no title), item 11-d, box 1, both in series II, Lazarsfeld Papers.

29. "South Dakota State College of Agricultural and Mechanical Arts" (MS, [1955?]), 4, folder 1, box 3, series II, Lazarsfeld Papers; Ruderman to Staff of Teachers' Apprehension, 9 December 1955, 15, 46; "Tulane University" (MS, [1955?]), 19, folder 1; and "Grinnell College" (MS, [1955?]), 2, folder 2, both in box 3, series II, Lazarsfeld Papers; Lazarsfeld and Thielens, *Academic Mind*, 208.

30. Binder (no title), item 11-d, box 1; and "Williams College" (MS, [1955?]), 17, folder 4, box 3, both in series II, Lazarsfeld Papers.

31. Green to Staff of Teacher Apprehension Study, 26 November 1956, 14; Ruderman to Staff of Teachers' Apprehension, 9 December 1955, 20; Ruderman to Staff of Teacher Apprehension, 24 October 1956, 10, box 3 (no folders), series II, Lazarsfeld Papers.

32. Bogardus, "Behavior Patterns," 489; John B. Judis, *William F. Buckley, Jr.: Patron Saint of the Conservatives* (New York: Simon & Schuster, 1988), 67; William F. Buckley Jr., *God and Man at Yale: The Superstitions of "Academic Freedom"* (Chicago: Regnery, 1951); Yale Daily News, *Course Critique Pamphlet*, 25; Yale Daily News, *Critique of the Humanities*, 17; Howard S. Becker, Blanche Geer, and Everett C. Hughes, *Making the Grade: The Academic Side of College Life* (New York: John Wiley, 1968), 100.

33. John W. Gustad to Nicholas Brown, 26 October 1959, folder 12, box 469, ACE Papers; "How Can Effectiveness of Instruction Be Improved," 151; William D. Patterson, "Urban Work on Teaching Smacks of Ivory Tower," *Times* (Roanoke, Virginia), 16 January 1957, "The Art of Teaching. Reviews (Clippings)" folder, box 7, Highet Papers; Trow, "Reflections on the Recruitment," 62.

34. B. Lamar Johnson to Vern Knudsen, 31 January 1956, "Teaching Assistants—File #6 (1955–1958)" folder, box 21, Graduate Division Dean Administrative Files, CYRL—UCLA;

Carolyn Winchell, "Like Old Times," *Campus News* (East Los Angeles Junior College) 6 (20 April 1951): 2; Alfred H. Fenton to Athern P. Daggett, 4 February 1955, "Alumni Letters D–H" folder, box 3, Self-Study Reports Collection; "Conservative Tradition in Education at Bowdoin College," 88.

35. "Preparation of College Teachers," 28; James Early, "Thoughts on the Current State of the College Teacher," *Educational Horizons* 38, no. 3 (Spring 1960): 180–81; W. H. Cowley, "College and University Teaching, 1858–1958," in Cooper, *Two Ends of the Log*, 117.

36. Bob Abrams and Ed Booker, "Seeing the Scenes," *Lincolnian* (Lincoln University) 8 (November 1947): 4; Joy Ann Williamson-Lott, *Jim Crow Campus: Higher Education and the Struggle for a New Southern Social Order* (New York: Teachers College Press, 2018), 108; Robert Cohen, *Howard Zinn's Southern Diary: Sit-Ins, Civil Rights, and Black Women's Student Activism* (Athens: University of Georgia Press, 2018), 113–15; Dr. Spiro Spero, "Letters to the Editor," *Lincolnian*, 15 January 1962, 2.

Chapter 6 · TV or Not TV? Reforming Cold War College Teaching

1. F. W. Strohmann et al., *The Graduate School Today and Tomorrow* (New York: Fund for the Advancement of Education, 1955), 13; and Sidney J. French to Clarence Faust, 2 February 1955, both in "Fund for the Advancement of Education (Faculty Fellowship Program)" folder, box 27, series II, Dean of the Faculty Papers, Archives and Special Collections, Rollins College, Winter Park, FL. On the origins and activities of the Fund for the Advancement of Education, see Dwight Macdonald, *The Ford Foundation: The Men and the Millions* (New York: Reynal, 1956), 51–56; and Paul Woodring, *Investment in Innovation: An Historical Appraisal of the Fund for the Advancement of Education* (Boston: Little, Brown, 1970).

2. "Educators Hear Policies Scored," *New York Times*, 7 March 1956, 33; B. F. Skinner, "Final Report of a Project at Harvard University Sponsored by the Fund for the Advancement of Education 1956–1957" (MS, 1957), "Correspondence—Teaching Machines [ca. 1953–59]" folder, box 1, Burrhus Frederic Skinner Papers, HUG(FP) 60.25, Harvard University Archives (hereafter "HUA").

3. R. E. de Kieffer to University of Colorado Planning Committee, 26 September 1960, "Committee C—Questionnaire Sent to Institutions, 1961" folder, box 6, Committee C series, American Association of University Professors Papers (hereafter "AAUP Papers"), Special Collections Research Center, George Washington University; "Teacher Put First by Carnegie Fund," *New York Times*, 15 June 1953, 21.

4. C. R. Carpenter and L. P. Greenhill, *An Investigation of Closed-Circuit Television for Teaching University Courses* (University Park: Penn State University, 31 July 1955), 58–61, folder 10, box 1, Warren F. Seibert Papers; and Presley D. Holmes Jr., "A Report on Three Closed-Circuit Television Class Sessions" (MS, January 1958), 6, folder 5, box 1, series 1, Presley D. Holmes Papers, both in Special Collections and University Archives, University of Maryland (hereafter "SCUA—MD"), College Park, MD.

5. "Worse Jam Feared for College Staffs," *New York Times*, 26 January 1948, 14; William R. Dennes to Frank C. Abbott, 21 November 1955, folder 4, box 397; and "Consultation on Preparation of College Teachers," (MS, 1947), 18, folder 2, box 379, both in American Council on Education Papers (hereafter "ACE Papers"), Hoover Institution Library and Archives, Stanford, CA; *Higher Education for American Democracy* (Washington, DC: General Printing Office, 1947), 4:2.

6. The Woodrow Wilson National Fellowships, *Past and Present: A Handbook of Information* (Princeton, NJ: Woodrow Wilson Foundation, 1959), 7–11, no folder; and "Fellowship Program Attracts Recruits for College Faculties," *New York Herald Tribune*, 24 November 1946, "Clippings and Press Releases" folder, both in box 1, Woodrow Wilson National Fellowship Foundation Papers, Seeley G. Mudd Manuscript Library, Princeton University.

7. William C. DeVane to R. B. Patrick, 8 April 1959; R. Smoluchowski to Robert S. Zimmer, 7 April 1965; A. Whitney Griswold, "A Proposal for Teaching Fellowships in Yale College" (MS, 18 November 1957), 2; William C. DeVane, "A Proposal for Teaching Fellows in Yale College" (MS, 20 December 1957), 1, all in folder 131, box 9, Records of the Dean of Yale College, Beinecke Rare Book and Manuscript Library, Yale University.

8. Frederick J. Kelly, *Toward Better College Teaching* (Washington, DC: General Printing Office, 1950), 9; Dexter Perkins, "We Shall Gladly Teach," *American Historical Review* 62 (January 1957): 297; Aura E. Severinghaus et al., *Preparation for Medical Education in the Liberal Arts College* (New York: McGraw-Hill, 1953), 195; "The Preparation of College Teachers. Proceedings of the Conference on the Preparation of College Teachers Held at the University of Chicago on May 6, 1948" (MS, 1948), 7, folder 4, box 1, Committee on the Preparation of Teachers Papers, Special Collections Research Center, University of Chicago (hereafter "SCRC—Chicago"); *Teaching Fellowships in Harvard College* (n.p.: Harvard University, October 1960), 45, box UAIII.10.220.15 (no folder), Committee on College Teaching as a Career Papers, HUA.

9. "The Preparation of College Teachers" (MS, 24 March 1948), 1, folder 4, box 1, Committee on the Preparation of Teachers Papers; *Higher Education for American Democracy,* 16; Michael Chiapetta, "A Recurrent Problem: The Professional Preparation of College Teachers," *History of Education Journal* 4, no. 1 (Autumn 1952): 19; Peter Odegard, "Revolutionary Implications for the Future," *American Scholar* 16, no. 4 (Autumn 1947): 478; Ruth E. Eckert, "A New Design for the Training of College Teachers," *Junior College Journal* 18 (September 1947): 25.

10. Sidney Painter, untitled MS (1958), 34, enclosed with Sidney Painter to Bernard Berelson, 28 March 1958, folder 5, box 1, Bernard R. Berelson Study of Graduate Education Records, SCRC—Chicago; Kelly, *Toward Better College Teaching,* 27; Earl J. McGrath, "The Education of College Teachers: An Editorial," *Journal of General Education* 3, no. 2 (January 1949): 85; Harold A. Anderson and William P. Tolley, "Institutional Programs for the Preparation of College Teachers" (MS, 1950), 6, 11–12, folder 5, box 1, Committee on the Preparation of Teachers Papers; John Robert Greene, *Syracuse University. Volume Four—The Tolley Years, 1942–1969* (Syracuse, NY: Syracuse University Press, 1996), 90–91.

11. "Interview with Kenneth Pitzer, University of California, July 11, 1958" (MS, 1958), folder 6, box 1, Berelson Study of Graduate Education Records; Very Reverend William Troy, "How Should a Good College Teacher Be Trained?," in *Quality of College Teaching and Staff,* ed. Roy J. Deferrari (Washington, DC: Catholic University of America Press, 1961), 115; "Disciplinary Interview with Richard Hofstadter, History, April 1958 (New York)" (MS, 1958), folder 5, box 1, Berelson Study of Graduate Education Records; Bernard Berelson, "Graduate Education and the Preparation of College Teachers," in *Faculty Supply, Demand, and Recruitment. Proceedings of a Regional Conference Sponsored by the New England Board of Higher Education* (Winchester, MA: New England Board of Higher Education, 1959), 92, "Com. C—College and University Research and Publications. Jan–April 1960" folder, box 4, Committee C series, AAUP Papers; Bernard Berelson, *Graduate Education in the United States* (New York: McGraw-Hill, 1960), 89; L. T. Benezet, "Do Changing Conditions Require Any Modification in the Preparation of College Teachers?" (MS, 6 March 1953), 2, enclosed with Frank C. Abbott to Louis T. Benezet, 25 May 1953, folder 17, box 360, ACE Papers.

12. "Special Grant for Teaching Given at U. of C.," *Chicago Tribune,* 10 February 1952; and "University of Chicago. Grant of $100,000 for Preparation of College Teachers" (MS, 1952), 1, both in folder 2, box 98, series IIIA, Carnegie Corporation of New York Papers (hereafter "CCNY Papers"), Rare Book and Manuscript Library, Columbia University (hereafter "RBML—Columbia"); Anderson and Tolley, "Institutional Programs," 10, 7; "The Vanderbilt Program for the Preparation of College Teachers" (MS, [1955?]), 1, folder 8, box 396,

ACE Papers; Joseph Axelrod, ed., *Graduate Study for Future College Teachers* (Washington, DC: American Council on Education, 1959), 14; Kelly, *Toward Better College Teaching*, 32, 40.

13. "Minutes of the Meeting of the University Committee on the Preparation of Teachers" (MS, 15 May 1950), 1, folder 5, box 1, Committee on the Preparation of Teachers Papers; "Notes on Science Panel—Extracurricular Course in College Teaching. Monday, November 13, 1961" (MS, 1961), 2; and Kenneth V. Thimann, "Your Appointment" (MS, 23 October 1961), 4–5, both in "Notes Science Panel Nov. 13, 1961 meeting" folder," box UAIII.10.230.7, Committee on College Teaching as a Career Papers; *Teaching Fellowships in Harvard College*, 49; Everett Case to Carnegie Corporation of New York, 30 December 1947, folder 14, box 107, series IIIA, CCNY Papers.

14. Hoxie Neale Fairchild, "The Scholar-Teacher," *American Scholar* 15, no. 2 (Spring 1946): 207; Edward Fiess, "Antiochians in College Teaching," *Antioch Alumni Bulletin*, November 1955, 6–7, folder 4, box 397, ACE Papers; "Consultation on the Preparation of College Teachers," 20; American Council on Education, "Committee on College Teaching. Minutes. May 2–3, 1952, Chicago, Illinois" (MS, 1952), 3, folder 1, box 347, ACE Papers.

15. "Committee on College Teaching. Minutes. May 2–3, 1952, Chicago, Illinois," 3; Axelrod, *Graduate Study*, 36; "The Preparation of College Teachers. Proceedings of the Conference on the Preparation of College Teachers," 1; Benezet, "Do Changing Conditions," 1.

16. Benezet, "Do Changing Conditions," 3; C. Scott Porter to Richard L. Park, 18 August 1954, folder 33, box 3, Clark Kerr Personal and Professional Papers, Bancroft Library, University of California, Berkeley; "Intercollegiate Program and Graduate Studies. Seven Southern California Colleges" (MS, [1955?]), 1, folder 8, box 396; and Henry C. Herge to Frank C. Abbott, 15 November 1956, folder 8, box 412, both in ACE Papers; "Consultation on the Preparation of College Teachers," 98; Berelson, *Graduate Education in the United States*, 225; "Meeting with Charles Odegaard, Dean of the College of Arts and Sciences, March 4, 1958" (MS, 1958), 1, folder 8, box 1, Berelson Study of Graduate Education Records.

17. Miami University, *Experimental Study in Instructional Procedures* (Oxford, OH: Miami University, 1 October 1956), 47, folder 4, box 1, Seibert Papers; J. L. Meriam, "Comments on the Proposal for the Rating of Teachers" (MS, 23 February 1954), folder 33, box 3, Kerr Papers; Paul L. Dressel, "The Current Status of Research on College and University Teaching," in *The Appraisal of Teaching in Large Universities* (Ann Arbor: University of Michigan, 1959), 11, "Com. C—College and University Teaching Research and Publications. Jan–Sept 1959" folder, box 4, Committee C series, AAUP Papers; Carpenter and Greenhill, *Investigation of Closed-Circuit Television*, 6.

18. Carpenter and Greenhill, *Investigation of Closed-Circuit Television*, 6; Clark Kerr, "Quality of Teaching" (MS, 10 February 1954), folder 33, box 3, Kerr Papers; Meriam, "Comments on the Proposal," 1–2; Ohmer Milton, "College Professors *Can* Learn to Teach" (MS, [1956?]); Hugh Taylor to Frank C. Abbott, 27 February 1957; Ohmer Milton to Frank C. Abbott, 22 April 1957, all in folder 4, box 430, ACE Papers.

19. Frank Finger, "Trumbull, October 1953" (MS, 1953), 1; and Frank Finger, "Improving Undergraduate Teaching" (MS, 24 March 1954), 6, both in "Talks on Teaching: Division 2 Presidential Address" folder, box 41, Frank Whitney Finger Papers, Albert and Shirley Small Special Collections Library, University of Virginia (hereafter "SCL—UVA"), Charlottesville, VA; "Committee on College Teaching. Minutes. May 2–3, 1952, Chicago, Illinois," 3–4; Kelly, *Toward Better College Teaching*, 51; "The Conservative Tradition in Education at Bowdoin College. Report of the Committee on Self Study" (MS, 1 September 1955), 99, vol. 1, Self-Study Reports Collection, Special Collections and Archives, Bowdoin College, Brunswick, ME; H. T. Morse, "Improving Instruction in the College Classroom" (MS, March 1955), 1, folder 14, box 396, ACE Papers.

20. Ralph W. Gerard, "Proposed College Evaluation Study" (MS, [1944?]), 1–3, folder 5, box 7, Ralph W. Tyler Papers, SCRC—Chicago; "Evaluation of the Coll. Outline Plan" (MS, [1944?]), 2, enclosed with Ralph W. Gerard, "Memorandum for Meeting of Subcommittees of the College Evaluation Committee, April 1, 1944" (MS, 1944); "Itinerary" (MS, [1947?]); Ralph W. Gerard to Mary Owens, 27 March 1947; "Colleges Which Have Been Considered for Participation in the Study of Educational Progress during the Period 1944–1947" (MS, [1947?]), all in "College Evaluation Study" folder, box 2, Ralph W. Gerard Papers, Special Collections and Archives, University of California, Irvine; William H. Cowley to Paul R. Hanna, 11 November 1949, folder 49-16, box 21, series 1-B, William H. Cowley Papers, Special Collections and University Archives, Stanford University.

21. Herbert D. Lamson, "Some of Us Teach," *Peabody Journal of Education* 24, no. 5 (March 1947): 261; *Higher Education for American Democracy*, 47; Richard J. Medalie, "The Student Looks at College Teaching," in *The Preparation of College Teachers*, ed. Theodore C. Blegen and Russell M. Cooper (Washington, DC: American Council on Education, 1950), 49–51; Ellsworth Barnard, "More Thoughts on Grading the Professors," *Bulletin of the AAUP* 31, no. 2 (Summer 1945): 269; Kelly, *Toward Better College Teaching*, 65; Al Fuchs, "A Report on the Evaluation of Teaching Effectiveness" (MS, [1972?]), 2, "Faculty Committees: Teaching as a Career, Committee on, 1958–1972" folder, box 1, Roger Howell Administrative Records, Office of the President Records, Special Collections and Archives, Bowdoin College; Fred Helsabeck, *Improving the Quality of Instruction at the College Level* (1951), 9, General Collection, SCL—UVA; "Smitty Haynes' Intercollegiata," *Lincolnian* (Lincoln University), 13 December 1947, 2; Norman A. Reeves, "Student Evaluation," *Lincolnian*, 18 May 1957, 2.

22. "Princeton in Transition," *Nassau Sovereign*, December 1946, folder 16, box 36, Christian Gauss Papers, Rare Books and Special Collections, Firestone Library, Princeton University; LeRoy Hanscum to Clark Kerr, 22 October 1954, folder 33, box 3, Kerr Papers; "Franz Schneider Initiates Plan for Student Appraisal of Instruction," *Daily Californian*, 25 May 1951; and "Help for the Educational Consumer," *Daily Californian*, 29 May 1953, both in "Franz Schneider" folder, box 60, Kenneth Eugene Eble Papers, University Archives and Record Management, University of Utah, Salt Lake City; C. Robert Pace, "The Evaluation of the Teacher," *University of Missouri Bulletin* 53, no. 6 (20 February 1952): 31.

23. John W. Riley Jr., Bryce F. Ryan, and Marcia Lifshitz, *The Student Looks at His Teacher* (New Brunswick, NJ: Rutgers University Press, 1950), 115, 112; Glenn Hughes, "Footnotes to E. R. Guthrie's Report on the Evaluation of Teaching" (MS, [1954?]), 3, folder 4, box 3, Edwin R. Guthrie Papers, Special Collections, University of Washington, Seattle, WA; anonymous survey (MS, [1955?]), question 10c, untitled binder, box 1; and "Reactions of respondents without a specific stimulus" (MS, [1955?]), 70, folder 3, box 2, both in series II, Paul Lazarsfeld Papers, RBML—Columbia.

24. "The CEA Critics," *Critic* (College English Association), September 1953, 2, folder 6; and Glenn Hughes to Edwin R. Guthrie, 14 January 1951, folder 4, both in box 3, Guthrie Papers; Very Reverend Gerald E. Dupont, "The Relation between Teaching and Research," in Deferrari, *Quality of College Teaching and Staff*, 111; Roy G. Francis, "Questions Concerning Closed Circuit Television," *Senate Forum* (University of Minnesota) 2, no. 1 (March 1961): 5, "Committee C—College and University Teaching, Research, and Publication, Jan–May 1961" folder, box 4, Committee C series, AAUP Papers.

25. John D. Millett, "The Use of Visual Aids in Political Science Teaching," *American Political Science Review* 41, no. 3 (June 1947): 518; "War Shows Great Possibilities in Movies," *Washington Post*, 23 September 1945, S6; Malcolm M. Willey to Lt. William Exton Jr., 19 February 1943; and Malcolm M. Willey to W. C. Coffey, 19 February 1943, both in "Visual and Teaching Aids 1942–1945" folder, box 43, President's Office Papers, Archives and Special

Collections, University of Minnesota, Minneapolis, MN. On the education of military servicemen during World War II, the best source is Christopher P. Loss, *Between Citizens and the State: The Politics of American Higher Education in the 20th Century* (Princeton, NJ: Princeton University Press, 2012), 91–120.

26. Charles L. Ponce de Leon, *That's the Way It Is: A History of Television News in America* (Chicago: University of Chicago Press, 2015), 6–7; Jon Herskovitz, "How the JFK Assassination Transformed Media Coverage," *Reuters*, 21 November 2013; Joint Committee on Educational Television, "Talk about Educational Television" (MS, 20 June 1952), 3; "Address by Paul A. Walker, Chairman, Federal Communications Commission" (MS, 19 April 1952), 5; Milton S. Eisenhower, "A Report on Educational Television" (MS, 20 May 1953), 3, enclosed with Ralph Steetle, "Memorandum" (MS, 8 August 1953); "Address of Governor Earl Warren at Conference on Educational Telev. Sacramento, Calif. December 15, 1952" (MS, 1952), 4, all in folder 16, box 2100, Records of the Dartmouth College Treasurer, Rauner Special Collections Library, Dartmouth College (hereafter "RSCL—Dartmouth"), Hanover, NH.

27. R. E. de Kieffer to University of Colorado Planning Committee, 26 September 1960, "Committee C—Questionnaire Sent to Institutions, 1961" folder, box 6, Committee C series, AAUP Papers; *Teaching by Television*, 2nd ed. (New York: Ford Foundation, 1961), 19; "TV Class Opens and a Book Sells," *New York Times*, 24 September 1967; "'Sunrise Semester,' TV's First 'Hit,' Gets 'Renewal,' Unprecedented Space," *Variety*, 9 October 1957; "There's No Question in My Mind" (cartoon), *New Yorker*, 12 October 1957; "N.Y.U. Will Teach Literature on TV," *New York Times*, 18 June 1957, all in folder 10, box 25; Warren A. Kraetzer to John E. Ivey Jr., 11 November 1958, folder 9, box 25, all in Records of the Office of the Chancellor and Executive Vice President, University Archives, New York University (hereafter "UA—NYU"); "Report of the 1964–65 Activities of the Office of Radio-Television" (MS, 1965), 1, folder 7, box 4, Records of the Office of Radio and Television, UA—NYU; Hollis R. Cooley survey, 11 May 1961, "Practices and Attitudes Regarding College TV Courses" folder, box 6, Committee C series, AAUP Papers. On educational television in higher education during these years, see also Loss, *Between Citizens and the State*, 147–56.

28. John K. Weiss, untitled memorandum (MS, 17 September 1957), 2, folder 5, box 25, Records of the Office of the Chancellor and Executive Vice President, UA—NYU; *Inter-Campus Teaching by Television. Report of the Oregon Development of CTV Teaching Experiment* [1958?], enclosed with Glenn Starlin to William P. Fidler, 18 July 1958, "General Educational Television 1965–1968" folder, box 6, Committee C series, AAUP Papers; William K. Cummings, "The 'Teleclass' is Stephens' Contribution," *College and University Business* 20 (April 1956): 29; University of Miami survey (MS, 1 July 1961), "Committee C—Educational TV in Coll. and Universities. 1961" folder; and University of Detroit survey (MS, 18 May 1961), "Practices and Attitudes Regarding College TV Courses" folder, both in box 6, Committee C series, AAUP Papers.

29. "Summary of Report of the Conference on Credit Courses by Television" (MS, 1955), 1, "Television Committee" folder, box 25, Graduate Division Administrative Files, Charles E. Young Research Library, University of California, Los Angeles; R. F. Arragon, "A Report to the Chapters from the Chairman of Committee C on College and University Teaching, Research, and Publication" (MS, 28 April 1960), "Com. C—College and University Teaching Research and Publications. Jan–April 1960" folder, box 4, Committee C series, AAUP Papers; Frederick Mosteller, "Continental Classroom's TV Course in Probability and Statistics," *American Statistician*, December 1962, 1, "Continental Classroom's TV Course in Probability and Statistics" folder, box 17, series III, Frederick Mosteller Papers, American Philosophical Society, Philadelphia, PA; "Summary of Visit of B. Lamar Johnson to Chicago City College" (MS, 19 April 1963), 6; and Chicago Board of Education, *Chicago's TV College: A Report of the Three Year Experiment by the Chicago City Junior College* (Chicago: Chicago Board of

Education, 1960), 5, both in "Chicago: Chicago City Jr. Coll. Dr. Clifford Erickson" folder, box 26, B. Lamar Johnson Papers, Boone Special Collections and Archives, Pepperdine University, Malibu, CA; John W. Taylor, "Television as a Means of Instruction for Credit in Chicago," in Boston University School of Public Relations and Communications, Division of Communication Arts, "International Educational Television Seminar" (MS, 1957), 5, folder 1, box 1, Seibert Papers; Clifford G. Erickson and Hymen M. Chausow, *The Chicago Junior College Experiment in Offering College Courses for Credit via Open Circuit Television. A Report of the First Year of a Three Year Project* (Chicago: Chicago Public Schools, March 1958), 4, folder 19; and *Chicago's TV College: Final Report of a Three Year Experiment* (Chicago: Chicago Public Schools, August 1960), 98, folder 21, both in box 3, series I, Holmes Papers; Flo Brenninger, "The Twenty-One Inch Classroom at Fresno State College" (MS, [1961?]), 9, "Committee C— Questionnaire Sent to Institutions, 1961" folder, box 6, Committee C series, AAUP Papers.

30. "TV Wonders at Westwood," *ULCA Alumni Magazine*, April 1962, folder 7, box 71, Dean E. McHenry Papers, Special Collections and Archives, University of California, Santa Cruz; *Closed-Circuit Television as a Medium of Instruction at New York University, 1956–1957* (New York: Fund for the Advancement of Education, 1958), 41, folder 6, box 1, Seibert Papers; Charles F. Westhoff, "An Evaluation of Sunrise Semester, 1958–59" (MS, 1959), 5, folder 9; Curtis F. Myers to "Gentlemen," 5 October 1957, folder 10, both in box 25, Records of the Office of the Chancellor and Executive Vice President, UA—NYU.

31. "TV Class Opens and Book Sells"; Huston Smith, "Teaching to a Camera," *Educational Record* 37 (January 1956): 49; Hollis Cooley to William Fidler, 21 January 1959, "Gen Educational Television 1965–1968" folder, box 6, Committee C series, AAUP Papers; Mosteller, "Continental Classroom's TV Course," 6.

32. Dressel, "Current Status of Research," 8; Carpenter and Greenhill, *Investigation of Closed-Circuit Television*, 58; University of Missouri Instructional Television, "Guide for Television Teachers" (MS, [1960?]), 6, 8, folder 6, box 3; and Office of Instructional Television (University of Missouri), "'So You Want to Be on Television'" (MS, [1960?]), folder 4, box 4, both in subseries 2, Barton L. Griffith Papers, SCUA—MD.

33. Earnest Earnest, "Must the TV Technicians Take Over the Colleges?," *Bulletin of the AAUP* 44, no. 3 (September 1958): 583–84; Philip G. Davidson, "How Can Available Educational Resources Be Stretched through Better Faculty Utilization?" (MS, 1955), 2, folder 4, box 397, ACE Papers; "LJ Comment on Tentative Draft of Policy Statement on Educational TV, AAUP, Committee C—October 11, 1959" (MS, 1959), 1–2, "Com C.—College and University Teaching Research and Publications. Oct–Dec 1959" folder; Harold B. Dunkel to Bertram H. Davis, n.d. (received 10 April 1959), "Com C.—College and University Teaching Research and Publications. Jan–Sept 1959" folder, both in box 4, Committee C series, AAUP Papers.

34. Francis, "Questions Concerning Closed Circuit Television," 5–7; David Bonnell Green to William P. Fidler, 17 January 1959, "Gen Educational Television 1965–1968" folder; University of Oklahoma survey, 15 May 1961; Michigan State University survey, 15 May 1961; H. C. Childs, "Literature on TV: A Report" (MS, 1960), 4, all in "Practices and Attitudes Regarding College TV Courses" folder, box 6, Committee C series, AAUP Papers.

35. Brenninger, "Twenty-One Inch Classroom," 9; Westhoff, "Evaluation of Sunrise Semester," 5, 6; Holmes, "Report on Three Closed-Circuit Television Class Sessions," 6; Miami University, *Experimental Study in Instructional Procedures*, 2nd report (Oxford: Miami University, 1 October 1957), 46, 55, folder 4, box 1, Seibert Papers; Leonard Kriegel, *Working Through: A Teacher's Journey in the Urban University* (New York: Saturday Review Press, 1972), 72.

36. Alexandra Rutherford, *Beyond the Box: B. F. Skinner's Technology of Behaviour from Laboratory to Life, 1950s–1970s* (Toronto: University of Toronto Press, 2009), 27; E. A. Vargas and Julie S. Vargas, "B. F. Skinner and the Origins of Programmed Instruction," in *B. F.*

Skinner and Behaviorism in American Culture, ed. Laurence D. Smith and William R. Wood-ward (Bethlehem, PA: Lehigh University Press, 1996), 237, 239–41; S. L. Pressey, "A Third and Fourth Contribution toward the Coming 'Industrial Revolution' in Education," *School and Society* 36 (19 November 1932): 672; Sidney Pressey, "Sidney Leavitt Pressey," in *A History of Psychology in Autobiography*, vol. 5, ed. Edwin G. Boring and Gardner Lindzey (New York: Appleton-Century-Crofts, 1967), 323.

37. Urban H. Fleege, "Individualization of Instruction," in Deferrari, *Quality of College Teaching and Staff*, 36; "Part IV. Use of the Machines in Teaching a General Education Course in Human Behavior. Spring Term, 1958" (MS, 1958), 46, 42–43, "Correspondence—Teaching Machines [ca. 1953–59]" folder, box 1, Skinner Papers; *37th Confidential Guide 1962–1963* (Cambridge, MA: Harvard Crimson, 1963), 39; and *36th Confidential Guide 1961–1962* (Cambridge, MA: Harvard Crimson, 1962), 38, both in box 1, Confidential Guide to Courses / Harvard Crimson Collection, HUA.

38. Rutherford, *Beyond the Box*, 28; "Faculty Members to Test New Teaching Machines," *Hamilton Alumni Review* [1958?], "Correspondence—Teaching Machines [ca. 1953–59]" folder; and Isabelle K. Hoose to B. F. Skinner, 24 February 1940, "Correspondence—Teaching Machines 2" folder, both in box 1, Skinner Papers; Donald A. Cook to Fred S. Keller, 19 March 1987, folder 18, box 7, Fred S. Keller Papers, Special Collections, University Archives and Museum, University of New Hampshire, Durham, NH; "Carnegie Grant to Enable Experiments in Teaching," *Covington (VA) Virginian*, 7 January 1960; and "Cross Reference Sheet" (MS, 7 April 1960), both in folder 1, box 612, series IIIA, CCNY Papers; Emily M. F. Cooper to B. F. Skinner, 9 April 1961, "Correspondence—Teaching Machines 3" folder, box 1, Skinner Papers.

39. William A. Hunt and Claude Mathis, "The Use of Programmed Instruction in Introductory Psychology for Teachers" (MS, [1964?]), 1, folder 5, box 14, B. Claude Mathis Papers, University Archives, Northwestern University, Evanston, IL; John D. Kelton et al. to J. Jefferson Bennett, 6 September 1969, folder 5, box 1, series 1, Holmes Papers; "Proceedings. Second Work Conference on College Teaching for Purdue Faculty Members, September 16, 1957" (MS, 1957), 9–10, enclosed with Harold B. Dunkel to William P. Fidler, 26 May 1958, "Com C—College and Univ. Teaching Research and Publications 1958" folder, box 4, Committee C series, AAUP Papers; Arthur I. Gates to B. F. Skinner, 17 April 1962, "Correspondence—Teaching Machines [ca. 1953–59]" folder, box 1, Skinner Papers; Ruther-ford, *Beyond the Box*, 29–30.

40. "Great Teachers. U.S. College Students Select 1950's Outstanding Professors," *Life*, 16 October 1950, "The Art of Teaching. Notes (with Related Printed Materials)" folder, box 7, Gilbert Highet Papers, RBML—Columbia.

41. Moody E. Prior to F. W. Strothmann, 31 July 1956, folder 1, box 4, Donald Morrison Papers, RSCL—Dartmouth; Houston Peterson, "Introductory," in *Great Teachers Portrayed by Those Who Studied under Them*, ed. Houston Peterson (New Brunswick, NJ: Rutgers University Press, 1946), xviii; Claude E. Buxton to B. F. Skinner, 18 November 1954, "Correspondence—Teaching Machines [ca. 1953–59]" folder, box 1, Skinner Papers.

Chapter 7 · The University under Attack: College Teaching in the 1960s and 1970s

1. *Report of the President's Commission on Campus Unrest* (Washington, DC: Government Printing Office, 1970), 13, 78, 200–201; Charles F. Hampton to William Scranton, 16 June 1970, folder 13, box 45, William Warren Scranton Papers, Special Collections Library, Penn State University, State College, PA.

2. Margaret LaPorte to William Scranton, 14 August 1970, folder 9; Edward F. Obert to Scranton, 10 September 1970; and Edward F. Obert to President Richard Nixon, 15 May 1970, both in folder 15, all in box 45, Scranton Papers.

3. Arlen J. Hansen to Kenneth Eble, 20 July 1970, "P–R" folder, box 58, Kenneth Eugene Eble Papers, University Archives and Records Management, University of Utah, Salt Lake City; Anthony Burgess, "My Dear Students," *New York Times*, 19 November 1972, folder 7, box 45, Scranton Papers.

4. Terry H. Anderson, *The Movement and the Sixties* (New York: Oxford University Press, 1995), 95; Brian Haynes, "Black Undergraduates in Higher Education: An Historical Perspective," *Metropolitan Universities* 17, no. 2 (2006): 14; Patricia Gumport et al., "The United States Country Report: Education from Massification to Post-Massification," *National Center for Postsecondary Improvement* (1997), 5, https://web.stanford.edu/group/ncpi/documents/pdfs/1 -04_massification.pdf; Jonathan Zimmerman, "Uncle Sam at the Blackboard: The Federal Government and Education," in *To Promote the General Welfare: The Case for Big Government*, ed. Steven Conn (New York: Oxford University Press, 2012), 53; "'Ancient Curriculum' Hit: Students of Today Won't Be Put On—or Put Off," *Los Angeles Times*, 12 March 1968, 16; Win Kelley and Leslie Wilbur, *Teaching in the Community-Junior College* (New York: Appleton-Century-Crofts, 1970), v. For an overview of college students in the 1960s, see John R. Thelin, *Going to College in the Sixties* (Baltimore: Johns Hopkins University Press, 2018), 85–115.

5. Gene I. Maeroff, "A Kind of Higher Education: This Side of Paradise," *New York Times*, 27 May 1973, 202; Anderson, *Movement and the Sixties*, 95; Martin Trow, "Undergraduate Teaching at Large State Universities," in *Improving College Teaching*, ed. Calvin B. T. Lee (Washington, DC: American Council on Education, 1967), 171; Charlotte Morse interview, 26 May 2008, 184, Accession 2012-A-048, Oral Histories Documenting Yale University Women, Beinecke Rare Book and Manuscript Library, Yale University (hereafter "BRBML—Yale"); J. T. Borhek, "The Sociology of Lousy Teaching and Learning," in Associated Students of the University of Arizona, *ASUA Course Evaluation* (Tucson, AZ: ASUA, 1969), 4:3; E. L. Tennyson to William Scranton, 27 June 1970, folder 13, box 45, Scranton Papers; *Second Conference on Effective Teaching*, ed. Naftaly S. Glasman and Berthold R. Killait (Santa Barbara: University of California, Santa Barbara, June 1974), 54–55, "2nd UCSB Conference on Effective Teaching, May 1974" folder, box 1, Instructional Development Collection, Special Research Collections, University of California, Santa Barbara (hereafter "SRC—UCSB"); Hanno Weber to Marvin Bressler, 7 February 1972, folder 2, box 1, Commission on the Future of the College Papers, Seeley G. Mudd Manuscript Library, Princeton University; Richard Todd, "Voices of Harvard '70," *New York Times*, 7 June 1970, folder 2, box 47, Scranton Papers.

6. "Retiring Professor John Gunning Reflects on Past 38 Years at Ithaca," *Ithacan* (Ithaca College), 12 April 1990, 11; Kenneth E. Eble, "Improving College Teaching," *Phi Delta Kappan*, January 1971, 284, "Project to Improve College Teaching (PICT) 1971–73" folder, box 7, Committee C series, American Association of University Professors Papers (hereafter "AAUP Papers"), Special Collections Research Center, George Washington University; "Pelton Declares War over Shorts," *Daily Iowan* (University of Iowa), 28 June 1967, 1; John Pelton, "Pelton Sees War Ahead," *Daily Iowan*, 28 June 1967, 2; Abraham Maslow, "Humanistic Education versus Professional Education: Further Comments," *New Directions in Teaching* 2, no. 2 ([1970?]): 6.

7. Sidney Simon, "The Frenic [*sic*] Fraud of Finals," *Ithacan*, 15 January 1965, 4; "Student Revolt against Authority Has Long and Productive History," *Los Angeles Times*, 26 April 1965, 1; Alan N. Schoonmaker, *A Students' Survival Manual; or, How to Get an Education, Despite It All* (New York: Harper & Row, 1971), 88; Paul D. Saltman, "How Does It Feel to Be Mediocre?," *Los Angeles Times*, 8 October 1967, folder 51, box 3, Paul D. Saltman Papers, Special Collections and Archives, University of California, San Diego (hereafter "SCA—UCSD").

8. Jonathan Zimmerman, "Tom Hayden's Reforms and Today's Protesters," *Chronicle of Higher Education*, 25 October 2016; Robert Cohen, *Freedom's Orator: Mario Savio and the Radical Legacy of the 1960s* (New York: Oxford University Press, 2009), 190, 202, 206; Mary K.

and Kenneth J. Gergen, "How the War Affects College Campuses," *Change* 3 (January–February 1971), 10; Todd, "Voices of Harvard '70."

9. "Colleges Facing Crisis: A Shortage of Adequate Teachers," *Boston Globe*, 22 September 1963, A71; "News Notes," *New York Times*, 23 June 1963, 151; "Illinois Spawning Junior Colleges," *Chicago Tribune*, 28 May 1967, A1; "Summary of a Conference of B. Lamar Johnson" (MS, 27 June 1963), 3, "Los Angeles Presidents" folder, box 25, B. Lamar Johnson Papers, Boone Special Collections and Archives, Pepperdine University, Malibu, CA.

10. "Make Way for Women Professors," *Boston Globe*, 20 February 1972, F23; Faculty of Arts and Sciences, Harvard University, *Report of the Committee on the Status of Women in the Faculty of Arts and Sciences* (April 1971), 2, folder 6, box 2, Harvard Graduate Students and Teaching Fellows Union Papers, Tamiment Library and Robert F. Wagner Labor Archives, New York University; Jessie Bernard, *Academic Women* (State College: Penn State University Press, 1964), 100, 120; Colette Gaudin, "An Interview Conducted by Jane Carroll" (MS, 19 September 1996), 4–6; and Mary C. Kelley, "An Interview Conducted by Mary S. Donin" (MS, 28 July and 7 August 2008), 8, both in Rauner Special Collections Library, Dartmouth College, Hanover, NH.

11. *Report of the Committee on the Status of Women*, 31–34; Norma Wikler, "The Female Professor: Contradictions in Role Perceptions," *Teacher on the Hill* (University of California, Santa Cruz), no. 10 (February 1979): 10–11; David Riesman to Peter Elbow and Task Force Colleagues, 30 March 1977, "SURC (II) 74–75" folder, box 64, David Riesman Papers, HUG (FF) 99.16, Harvard University Archives; "Make Way for Women Professors."

12. "Ford Foundation to Help Negroes Get Doctorates," *New York Times*, 20 September 1968, 37; "SEP Seeks Recruits for College Teaching," *Baltimore Afro-American*, 30 March 1968, 62; Joy Ann Williamson-Lott, *Jim Crow Campus: Higher Education and the Struggle for a New Southern Social Order* (New York: Teachers College Press, 2018), 104–5, 110; Ann Jones, *Uncle Tom's Campus* (New York: Praeger, 1973), 122.

13. "Teaching Assistants Struggle to Be Heard on U.S. Campuses," *University of Utah Review* 1, no. 6 (March 1968): 1, "Clippings Useful to Project" folder, box 61, Eble Papers; Robert Dubin and Fredric Beisse, "The Assistant: Academic Subaltern," *Administrative Science Quarterly* 11, no. 4 (March 1967): 525, 529, 523; "The Teaching Preparation Program," *UCLA Innovator*, Fall 1972, 1, enclosed with Bob Wilson and Lynn Wood to Members of the Committee on Teaching, 8 March 1972, "Teachers Assistant Training (Past)" folder, box 55, Associated Students Subject Files, SRC—UCSB; "University of Wisconsin (Madison Campus) Faculty Document 183. Report of Committee on Teaching Assistant System" (MS, 5 February 1968), 14, 21, folder 1, box 2, Harvard Graduate Students and Teaching Fellows Union Papers.

14. Yale Daily News, *Course Critique 1963* (New Haven, CT: Yale Daily News, 1963), 73; Yale Daily News, *Yale Course Critique, Fall and Spring Terms* (New Haven, CT: Yale Daily News, 1 April 1965), 52; Yale Daily News, *Yale Course Critique* (New Haven, CT: Yale Daily News, 1 April 1966), 30; *The Seer: An Evaluation of Courses and Professors at the University of Colorado* (Boulder: Associated Students of the University of Colorado, September 1966), 32, folder 1, box 1, Course Evaluations / UCSU Professors Performance Guides Collection (hereafter "Evaluations—Colorado"), Special Collections, Archives, and Preservation, University of Colorado Boulder; Michael W. Ham to James H. Wells, 5 March 1974, "Training Graduate Students to Teach" folder, box 89-7/18, Mathematical Association of America Papers, Briscoe Center for American History, University of Texas at Austin.

15. Paul Monette, *Becoming a Man: Half a Life Story* (New York: Harcourt, 1992), 177; "Summary of Appraisals of the Program by Carnegie Teaching Fellows, 1964–1965" (MS, 15 July 1965), 3, folder 131; and "Summary of Appraisals of the Program by Carnegie Teaching Fellows, 1966–1967" (MS, 5 July 1967), 3, folder 134, both in box 9, Records of the Dean of Yale

College, BRBML—Yale; Franklin W. Knight, "A Caribbean Quest for the Muse of History," in *Becoming Historians*, ed. James M. Banner Jr. and John R. Gillis (Chicago: University of Chicago Press, 2009), 200.

16. Charles H. Monson Jr., "Teaching Assistants: The Forgotten Faculty," *Educational Record* 50, no. 1 (Winter 1969): 60; "University of Wisconsin (Madison Campus) Faculty Document 183," 11–12, 14; Teaching Assistants Association, "Organizing Campus Workers" (MS, [1970?]), 1–2, folder 2; and Teaching Assistants Association, "Is Teaching Assistantship a Scholarship?" (MS, [1971?]), 1, folder 1, both in box 2, Harvard Graduate Students and Teaching Fellows Union Papers.

17. "Professors Teach Less and Less These Days," *Boston Globe*, 1 January 1963, 84; "Preliminary Analysis of Replies to Questionnaire" (MS, [1965?]), 1, enclosed with H. Arthur Steiner to Franklin D. Murphy, 8 December 1965, "Teaching Assistants—File #10 (1965)" folder, box 22, Graduate Division Dean Administrative Files, Charles E. Young Research Library, University of California, Los Angeles (hereafter "CYRL—UCLA"); Wilhelmina Gilbert, "Business Education at Bennett College: A Report on the Departmental Self-Study" (MS, June 1967), 17, Self-Study Collection, Bennett College Archives, Greensboro, North Carolina; "Valley State Seeking 156 to Fill Teaching Vacancies," *Los Angeles Times*, 23 June 1968, SFA1; "Teaching-Job Prospects for Graduates with Doctorates Reported to Be Growing Worse," *New York Times*, 21 January 1976, 30; "Job Crunch in Academia—It's No Time for Tenure," *Boston Globe*, 12 October 1975, A3.

18. Anderson, *Movement and the Sixties*, 97; Jean H. Hagstrum, "The Improvement of Teaching at Northwestern University: The Committee on Curriculum and Teaching of the University Senate," in *Profiles in College Teaching: Models at Northwestern*, ed. B. Claude Mathis and William C. McGaghie (Evanston, IL: Northwestern University Center for the Teaching Professions, 1972), 10–12; "The Kahn-Bowers Report," *Cornell Daily Sun*, 12 November 1965, 1; "Yale Faculty Unit Asks Wide Reforms," *New York Times*, 9 April 1972, folder 92, box 11, Study Group on Yale College Records, BRBML—Yale; Alice Jimenez, "Instructors, Courses Need Updates," *Campus News* (East Los Angeles Junior College) 27 (29 September 1971): 2; "The Quality of Undergraduate Education at Hopkins: A Report by the Education Hearings Committee of the Student Council" (MS, 23 February 1971), 2, folder 2; and Ernst Cloos to Lincoln Gordon, 9 February 1970, folder 1, both in box 65, series 9, Office of the President Papers, Ferdinand Hamburger University Archives, Johns Hopkins University.

19. *UCSC Course Review. Evaluations of 1974–75 Courses* (Santa Cruz, CA: Dharma, 1975), 22, 16; Kenneth E. Eble, *Professors as Teachers* (San Francisco: Jossey-Bass, 1972), 11; *The Seer: An Evaluation of Courses and Professors at the University of Colorado* (Boulder, CO: Associated Students of the University of Colorado, September 1968), 14, folder 3, box 1, Evaluations—Colorado; John J. Monroe evaluation, in *Academic Evaluation in Selected Undergraduate Courses* (MS, April 1968), "Academic Evaluations 1968" folder, box 1, Office of Student Life Records (hereafter "OSLR—GWU"), Special Collections Research Center, George Washington University; *The Guide to Undergraduate Courses* (Princeton, 1966), 7; George A. Dunlap, *Giving It the Good Old College Try* (New York: Carlton, 1970), 72.

20. *Seer* (September 1966), 57, 3, 33, 46; Yale Daily News, *Course Critique 1963*, 10; Emilie L. McGrath, "English 330" (MS, 3 October 1964), 2, 19, folder 5, box 1, George G. Williams Papers, Rice University Archives, Houston, TX; "What College Does to People: A Survey," *Washington Post*, 1 April 1973, G1; *UCSC Course Review*, 65; Borhek, "Sociology of Lousy Teaching," 3.

21. "In Memorium: Vincent Scully, Beloved Teacher 'Helped Shape a Nation,'" *Yale News*, 1 December 2017, https://news.yale.edu/2017/12/01/memoriam-vincent-scully-beloved -teacher-helped-shape-nation; "Remembrances of Vincent Scully," *Yale News*, 2 December 2017, https://news.yale.edu/2017/12/02/remembrances-vincent-scully; *UCSC Course*

Review, 141; Bernard Beck, "Toward a Poor Classroom," in Mathis and McGaghie, *Profiles in College Teaching*, 32, 37; Donald J. Lewis to Wilbert McKeachie, 4 June 1974; and Donald J. Lewis, "Style and Content" (MS, 6 May 1974), 3, both in "McKeachie—Psychology—Correspondence—L" folder, box 1, Wilbert J. McKeachie Papers, Bentley Historical Library, University of Michigan.

22. Anonymous, "September 25," *Teacher on the Hill*, no. 2 (October 1977): 1; W. James Popham, "Higher Education's Commitment to Instructional Development Programs" (MS, 1974), "Higher Education's Commitment to Instructional Development Programs by W. Popham" folder, box 2, Academic Senate, Los Angeles Division, Committee on Teaching Records, CYRL—UCLA; "Committee on Effective Teaching" (MS, 7 March 1975), 4, "Effective Teaching 78–79" folder, box 13, Associated Students Subject Files, SRC—UCSB; Borhek, "Sociology of Lousy Teaching," 3.

23. Schoonmaker, *Students' Survival Manual*, 80, 8; Jerry Farber, "The Student as Nigger," *Ithacan*, 24 October 1969, 2; Donald Strebel to Carl Holstrom, 3 April 1975, folder 1, box 45, Henry C. Booker Papers, SCA—UCSD; *Seer* (September 1968), 35.

24. Yale Daily News, *Yale Course Critique*, 88; *Academic Undergraduate Evaluation* (MS, April 1969), 188, "Academic Evaluations 1969" folder, box 1, OSLR—GWU; Panos D. Baris, "A Lilliputian Dictionary of Campus Unrest in the USA" (MS, [1970?]), 10–11, folder 4, box 46, Scranton Papers; William K. Cahall, "Exchange News," *Lincolnian*, 15 March 1966, 7; "Editorial: Attendance," *ASUA Course Evaluation* (September 1969), 2; "Psychology Department," in *Academic Evaluation in Selected Undergraduate Courses* (April 1968), OSLR—GWU.

25. Yale Daily News, *Yale Course Critique*, 39; Dr. Margaret Sullivan evaluation, in *Academic Evaluation in Selected Undergraduate Courses* (April 1968); Glasman and Killait, *Second Conference on Effective Teaching*, 54–55; William R. Taylor et al., "Seminar to Initiate New Experiments in Undergraduate Instruction. Report of the Working Committee on the Teaching of American History" (MS, 1965), 2–3, "Seminar to Initiate New Experiments in Undergraduate Instruction—Tufts University" folder, box 765, American Historical Association Papers, Library of Congress, Washington, DC.

26. *Education at Berkeley: Report of the Select Committee on Education* (Berkeley: University of California Press, 1968), 96–97; Erwin Mayer to editor, 7 November 1974, in *The Best of FAST: Opinion and Humor at Western, 1963–1991*, ed. Peter Frazier and Robert Keller (Bellingham: Western Washington University, 1991), 80; *Seer* (September 1966), 15; *Guide to Undergraduate Courses*, 10; *The Mirror. Spring 1972* (Carbondale: Mirror Activities Office, Southern Illinois University, 1972), 12, "Committee C. Student Evaluation of Teachers. 1970–73" folder, box 5, Committee C series, AAUP Papers.

27. *Mirror. Spring 1972*, 12; *Seer* (September 1966), 63; *Education at Berkeley*, 97n5; Associated Students of the University of Arizona, *ASUA Course Evaluation 1967* (n.p.: ASUA, 1967), 76; *Bennett College Self-Study: A Summary Report to the Southern Association of Colleges and Schools* (Greensboro, NC: Bennett College, January 1968), 66, box 1 (no folder), Self-Study Collection Bennett College; Sy Schwartz to editor, 8 July 1971, in Frazier and Keller, *Best of FAST*, 63; Ernest A. Strathmann, "Causes of Dissatisfaction with Traditional Letter (or Number) Grading and the GPA" (MS, [1970?]), 3; "Com. C—Grading and Evaluation 1970" folder, box 5, Committee C series, AAUP Papers.

28. James Axtell, *The Making of Princeton University: From Woodrow Wilson to the Present* (Princeton, NJ: Princeton University Press, 2006), 205; Alvin Kernan, *In Plato's Cave* (New Haven, CT: Yale University Press, 1999), 173; Kenneth M. Greene, "Grade Inflation: A Preliminary Report of the Senate of Phi Beta Kappa" (MS, 1976), 3–4, "Eble—Statement on Teaching Evaluation" folder, box 1, Committee C series, AAUP Papers; Thomas B. Bailey, *The American Pageant Revisited: Recollections of a Stanford Historian* (Stanford, CA: Hoover Institute Press, 1982), 37.

29. Lillian S. Calhoun, "Junior Colleges Being Run Like Factories," *Chicago Defender*, 19 October 1964, 4; William Raspberry, "Remedial Education and Academic Standards," *Washington Post*, 1 March 1976, A23; Edward F. Obert to Scranton, 10 September 1970, folder 15, box 45, Scranton Papers; "Committee on Effective Teaching," 7.

30. Edward Wakin, "The Junior College: A Place to Mature," *Sign*, June 1962, "VA. Marymount College" folder, box 25, Johnson Papers; William Raspberry, "Making the Grade in College," *San Diego Tribune*, 30 May 1975, folder 12, box 45, Booker Papers; David Riesman, Joseph Gusfield, and Zelda Gamson, *Academic Values and Mass Education: The Early Years of Oakland and Monteith* (Garden City, NY: Doubleday, 1970), 138–39, 148; David Baldwin, "Commentary: The Student Climate in 1983," *Hilltops* (Hartwick Coll.), 15 September 1983, enclosed with David Baldwin to C. David Gruender, 22 September 1983, "Comm C— Evaluation of Faulty" folder, box 1, Committee C series, AAUP Papers; L. Pearce Williams, "The Decline of Education at Cornell," *Cornell Daily Sun*, 4 March 1974, 7.

31. "Minutes of the Meeting of Predominantly Black Colleges and Universities of North Carolina" (MS, [1971?]), 2, "Atlanta Conference, May 19" folder, box 60, Eble Papers; Brad Humphrey, "Stop Brueckner Prosecution in the Press," *Triton Times* (UC San Diego), 6 June 1975, folder 12, box 45, Booker Papers; William J. Bowers, *Student Dishonesty and Its Control in College* (New York: Bureau of Applied Social Research, Columbia University, December 1964), 32, 36, 193; Bradford Cleaveland, "A Letter to Undergraduates," in *The Berkeley Student Revolt: Facts and Interpretations*, ed. Seymour Martin Lipset and Sheldon S. Wolin (Garden City, NY: Anchor Books, 1965), 68; Simon, "Frenic [*sic*] Fraud of Finals," 4.

32. "Teaching Is Too Important," *Petersburg (VA) Progress-Index*, 5 April 1964, folder 2, box 1, Woodrow Wilson Sayre Papers, Digital Collections and Archives, Tufts University, Medford, MA; E. Alden Dunham, *Colleges of the Forgotten Americans: A Profile of State Colleges and Regional Universities* (New York: McGraw-Hill, 1969), 99; Kenneth Eble to Eugene England, 8 February 1972, "Miscellaneous Letters" folder, box 60, Eble Papers; William Arrowsmith, "The Future of Teaching," in Lee, *Improving College Teaching*, 66, 70.

33. Kelley and Wilbur, *Teaching in the Community-Junior College*, 138, 191; Eugene Garfield, "What Is the Primordial Reference for the Phrase 'Publish or Perish'?," *Scientist* 10, no. 12 (10 June 1996): 11; Emilie Tavel Livezey, "Teach, Publish, or . . . ?," *Christian Science Monitor*, 5 June 1965, 10; "Marcham Assesses 55 Years Here," *Cornell Daily Sun* 95 (26 October 1978): 1; Sheldon S. Wolin and John H. Schaar, "Berkeley and the University Revolution," *New York Review of Books*, 9 February 1967.

34. Robert Nisbet, "Conflicting Academic Loyalties," in Lee, *Improving College Teaching*, 27; "Professors Teach Less and Less These Days," 84; Jacques Barzun, *Teacher in America* (1945; repr., Indianapolis: Liberty, 1981), xii–xiii; Robert A. McCaughey, *Stand, Columbia: A History of Columbia University in the City of New York, 1754–2004* (New York: Columbia University Press, 2003), 295; "New Directions in Faculty Development for Spelman College. A Proposal Submitted to the Bush Foundation" (MS, February 1987), appendix, folder 9, box 10, B. Claude Mathis Papers, University Archives, Northwestern University, Evanston, IL.

35. Robert Cohen, "The New Left's Love-Hate Relationship with the University," in *The Port Huron Statement: Sources and Legacies of the New Left's Founding Manifesto*, ed. Richard Flacks and Nelson Lichtenstein (Philadelphia: University of Pennsylvania Press, 2015), 109; Edward Germain to E. W. Strong, 15 April 1963, "Teaching 1948–1969" folder, box 41, Academic Senate, Los Angeles Division, Administrative Files, CYRL—UCLA; *Report of the President's Commission on Campus Unrest*, 200; "Final Staff Report. State of Michigan Senate Committee to Investigate Campus Disorders and Student Unrest" (MS, 25 February 1970), 110, 114, folder 13, box 47, Scranton Papers; "Quality of Undergraduate Education at Hopkins," 1; *Seer* (September 1968), 17; Judy Yamagata, "Don't Ignore Brueckner Report Lessons," *Triton Times*, 27 October 1975, folder 12, box 45, Booker Papers; *Update 1976. Undergraduate Policies*

Digest and Teacher Evaluations (Los Angeles: Associated Students of the University of California at Los Angeles, 1976), 15, "Undergraduate Policies Digest and Teachers Evaluations 1976" folder, box 60, Associated Students Subject Files, SRC—UCSB.

36. "Sayre Relieved of Tufts Post," *Boston Globe*, 3 April 1964; "Tufts Professor Faces Dismissal," *New York Times*, 3 April 1964; Woodrow Wilson Sayre, "The Case for Not Publishing," *Tufts Weekly*, 17 April 1964, all in folder 2, box 1, Sayre Papers.

37. "Students Picket Ballou, Cohen," *Tufts Weekly*, 15 April 1964, folder 2; "Mountain-Climbing Educator Visits City," *Richmond News-Leader*, 23 February 1965, folder 1; "Snobbery on the Campus," *North Adams (MA) Transcript*, 20 April 1964, folder 3; "A Mere Teacher," *Greensboro (NC) News*, April 1964, folder 3; "The Decline of Teaching," *Wall Street Journal*, 10 April 1964, folder 2, all in box 1, Sayre Papers.

38. "Prof. Sayre Loses New Tufts Round," *Boston Herald*, 29 April 1964, folder 3; John E. Burchard, "Publish or Perish," *Newsweek*, 4 May 1964, folder 4; Richard A. Newhall, "Good Teaching Analyzed," *Berkshire Eagle*, 30 April 1964, folder 2; Bernard R. Carman, "Scholarship Makes Good Teachers," *Berkshire Eagle*, 8 May 1964, folder 4, all in box 1, Sayre Papers.

39. "Let the Teachers Teach," *Berkshire Eagle*, 4 April 1964, folder 2, box 1, Sayre Papers; "Students Begin 3-Day Vigil," *Yale Daily News*, 2 March 1965; and "Faculty Members Enter Yale Protest," *New Haven Register*, 3 March 1965, both in folder 1, box 44; "Publish and Perish," *Pittsburgh Post-Gazette* [1965?], folder 14, box 43, all in series I, Office of the President, Kingman Brewster Jr. Records, BRBML—Yale; Geoffrey Kabaservice, *The Guardians: Kingman Brewster, His Circle, and the Rise of the Liberal Establishment* (New York: Henry Holt, 2004), 225–27.

40. Peter Eisenberg to Kingman Brewster Jr., 4 March 1965, folder 14; Robert T. Connery to Kingman Brewster Jr., 4 March 1965, folder 16; Mrs. James M. Conway to "the President," 5 March 1965, folder 16; Robert L. Clark to "the President," n.d., received 10 March 1965, folder 16, all in box 43; "Something Rotten in Academe," *Wall Street Journal*, 12 March 1965, folder 2, box 44, all in Brewster Records.

41. Clark Kerr, *The Uses of the University* (1963; repr., Cambridge, MA: Harvard University Press, 2001), 49; *Hearings before a Subcommittee of the Committee on Government Operations of the House of Representatives*, 89th Cong., 1st Sess., 14–17 June 1965 (Washington, DC: General Printing Office, 1965), 2, 63; "U.S. Research Criticized," *New York Times*, 31 October 1965, E11; Riesman, Gusfield, and Gamson, *Academic Values and Mass Education*, 6; Seymour Martin Lipset, *Rebellion in the University* (1971; repr., New Brunswick, NJ: Transaction, 1993), 222; Kenneth Keniston, "Remarks Prepared for President's Commission on Campus Unrest, July 24, 1970" (MS, 1970), 4, folder 12, box 45, Scranton Papers.

42. Lipset, *Rebellion in the University*, 221; John W. Boyer, *The University of Chicago: A History* (Chicago: University of Chicago Press, 2015), 374–75; "Students Getting Larger Role in Hiring of Faculty Members," *Los Angeles Times*, 7 June 1970, B1; Fred M. Hechinger, "About Education: Critical View of Universities," *New York Times*, 11 November 1983, C4; Norwood Russell Hanson to Kingman Brewster Jr., 25 March 1965, folder 15, box 43, series I, Brewster Records.

Chapter 8 · *Experimentation and Improvement: Reforming Teaching in the 1960s and 1970s*

1. Wilbert J. McKeachie, "Undergraduate Psychology in the 70s" (MS, 30 April 1971), 3, "McKeachie—Psychology—Speeches—Curriculum—Undergraduate Psychology in the 70s" folder, box 3, Wilbert J. McKeachie Papers, Bentley Historical Library, University of Michigan.

2. McKeachie, "Undergraduate Psychology in the 70s," 5; Billy Rojas, "The Next Target for Student Dissent," *Massachusetts Daily Collegian*, 17 March 1970; and Billy Rojas, "The Future of Education. Suggestions for Individual Projects" (MS, Spring 1970), both enclosed with Billy

Rojas to Kenneth Eble, 23 March 1970, "M" folder, box 58, Kenneth Eugene Eble Papers, University Archives and Records Management, University of Utah, Salt Lake City.

3. Wilbert J. McKeachie, "The State of the Art in Improving Teaching and Learning" (MS, 11 June 1977), 9, "McKeachie—Psychology—Speeches—Faculty Development—The State of the Art in Improving Teaching and Learning" folder, box 3, McKeachie Papers; Stanford C. Ericksen to John Atkinson, 28 March 1972; and Ericksen to Leonard Greenbaum, 10 November 1972, both in "Secretary's Correspondence. 1972" folder, box 1, Center for Research on Learning and Teaching Papers, Bentley Historical Library; Ronald D. Simpson to Wilbert J. McKeachie, 2 September 1986, "McKeachie—Psychology—Correspondence—G" folder, box 1; and Wilbert J. McKeachie, "Learning Teaching and Learning from Teaching" (MS, 18 November 1989), 5, 2, "McKeachie—Psychology—Speeches—Faculty Development—Learning Teaching and Learning from Teaching" folder, box 3, both in McKeachie Papers.

4. Martin Duberman, "An Experiment in Education," *Daedalus* 97, no. 1 (Winter 1968): 318–24.

5. Mildred Magruder, "What Is the Professor's Function?," *Universitas* 1, no. 4 (January 1973): folder 56b, box 9, Six Institutions Consortium Collection, Bennett College Archives, Greensboro, NC; *The Papers of F. G. Marcham*, vol. 1, ed. John Marcham (Ithaca, NY: Internet-First University Press, 2006), 64; "Frederick Marcham, Cornell Professor, 94," *New York Times*, 19 December 1992.

6. H. R. Wolf, "The Classroom as Microcosm," *College English* 33, no. 3 (December 1971): 260–62; Gary Margolis, "Taking It All Off: Teaching in the Therapeutic Classroom," *College English* 33, no. 3 (December 1971): 277–78; George R. Levine to Kenneth Eble, 28 December 1970, "S–U (1)" folder, box 59, Eble Papers; Gerald Grant and David Riesman, *The Perpetual Dream: Reform and Experiment in the American College* (Chicago: University of Chicago Press, 1978), 79–82.

7. Reid Pitney Higginson, "When Experimental Was Mainstream: The Rise and Fall of Experimental Colleges, 1957–1979," *History of Education Quarterly* 69, no. 2 (May 2019): 204–5; "Santa Cruz: Revolt against Assembly-Line Academics," *Chicago Tribune*, 24 July 1966, K20; Jonathan Zimmerman, foreword to *Seeds of Something Different: An Oral History of the University of California, Santa Cruz*, ed. Irene Reti, Cameron Vanderscoff, and Sarah Rabkin (Santa Cruz: Regional History Project, UCSC Library, 2020); Philip Werdell, "Futurism and the Reform of Higher Education," in *Learning for Tomorrow: The Role of the Future in Education*, ed. Alvin Toffler (New York: Vintage, 1974), 287.

8. Dean E. McHenry, untitled ms [1974?], 1, folder 8; and Dean E. McHenry, "The Santa Cruz Campus as a Utopian Venture" (MS, 7 March 1974), 1–2, folder 10, both in box 46, Dean E. McHenry Papers, Special Collections and Archives, University of California, Santa Cruz; Grant and Riesman, *Perpetual Dream*, 108; *UCSC Course Review. Evaluations of 1974–75 Courses* (Santa Cruz, CA: Dharma, 1975), 98, 68, 70, 53.

9. Ralph Keyes, "The New SUNY College at Old Westbury: Can a 'Total Innovation' Be Planned?" (MS, [1969?]), 4, 15, "Student Publications circa 1969" folder, box 7; Harris Wofford, "A Case Study on Planning at Old Westbury" (MS, [1968?]), 2, 4, "Academic Planning and Development 1966–1970" folder, box 4; "The Heckmans Say 'Yes!' to '68 and '69" (MS, 1968), enclosed with Jan Heckman to Harris Wofford, 15 December 1968, "Experimental Colleges. Essay, 1968–1970, Undated" folder; and "Life and Death at a Far-Out College," *New York Times*, 26 April 1971, "Experimental Colleges: Articles, Clippings, Notes" folder, both in box 5, all in Harris Wofford Papers, College Archives, Bryn Mawr College, Bryn Mawr, PA.

10. "UC Santa Cruz Grade System Passes Test," *Los Angeles Times*, 10 June 1974, B1; "Area Colleges Adopt Pass-Fail Grading," *Washington Post*, 16 November 1967, "General Grading" folder, box 5, Committee C series, American Association of University Professors Papers (hereafter "AAUP Papers"), Special Collections Research Center, George Washington

University; Keith E. Justice, untitled memorandum [1969?], 14, enclosed with Keith E. Justice to Curtis Manns, 18 July 1969, folder 47, box 1, Committee on Educational Policy Records, Archives and Special Collections, Williams College, Williamstown, MA; E. David Cronon, *The University of Wisconsin: Renewal to Revolution, 1945–1971* (Madison: University of Wisconsin Press, 1999), 477; "Temple Prof Gives A's to All Students," *Philadelphia Bulletin*, 25 January 1969; and "Temple Denies Punishing Professor," *Philadelphia Bulletin*, 22 March 1968, both in "Temple University, Student Activities, Grading" file, Philadelphia Bulletin Collection, Urban Archives, Temple University, Philadelphia, PA; Paul Lyons, *The People of This Generation: The Rise and Fall of the New Left in Philadelphia* (Philadelphia: University of Pennsylvania Press, 2003), 103.

11. Peter Anton, "Therapy for Credit: The New Higher Education" (MS, 30 October 1972), 8, November 1972 Faculty Forum, Faculty Forum Papers, Oregon State University, https://senate.oregonstate.edu/sites/senate.oregonstate.edu/files/faculty_forum_papers_faculty_senate_oregon_state_university.pdf; R. A. McConnell, "How to Avoid Slovenly Teaching" (MS, 9 April 1970), folder 7, box 47, William Warren Scranton Papers, Special Collections Library, Penn State University, State College, PA; "Teaching: The Uncertain Profession," *Change* 4, no. 3 (April 1972): 57; Grant and Riesman, *Perpetual Dream*, 109.

12. Grant and Riesman, *Perpetual Dream*, 120–21; "Anthropology Department," in *Academic Evaluation in Selected Undergraduate Courses* (April 1968), "Academic Evaluations 1968" folder, box 1, Office of Student Life Records (hereafter "OSLR—GWU"), Special Collections Research Center, George Washington University; "Teaching: The Uncertain Profession," 58; *Academic Evaluation* (1970), 224, 197, "Academic Evaluations 1970" folder, box 1, OSLR—GWU; Charles Frankel, "Professor Finds Old Hopes Endure," *New York Times*, 11 January 1971, 51.

13. William R. Torbert and J. Richard Hackman, "Taking the Fun out of Outfoxing the System," in *The Changing College Classroom*, ed. Philip Runkel, Roger Harrison, and Margaret Runkel (San Francisco: Jossey-Bass, 1969), 176; J. Richard Hackman and William R. Torbert, "Educational Experimentation: A Case History," *Yale Alumni Magazine*, May 1969, "TMC Secondary Materials, 1967–1973" folder, box 2, Teaching Methods Committee Papers, College Archives, Carleton College, Northfield, MN; Henry F. Ottinger, "Lecturer Finds Why Students Can't 'Turn On,'" *Philadelphia Bulletin*, 27 February 1971, "College—Students—1971" file, Philadelphia Bulletin Collection; Duberman, "Experiment in Education," 331.

14. Tom Powers, "Old Westbury Dies Young," *Newsday*, 25 September 1971, 7W, "Experimental Colleges: Articles, Clippings, Notes" folder, box 5, Wofford Papers; Martin Baskin, "Old Westbury's 'Exciting Mess,'" *Newsday*, 16 February 1970; Jay Neugeboren, "Your Suburban Alternative," *Esquire*, September 1970, https://classic.esquire.com/article/1970/9/1/your-suburban-alternative; Lawrence Resnick, "Paper Presented to the Organization of American Historians" (MS, 17 April 1969), 17; and Ralph Keyes, "The College That Students Helped Plan," *Change*, March–April 1969, both in "Critiques" folder, box 4, Wofford Papers.

15. Robert Hampel, "'The Whole Structure Has to Change': Martin Duberman's Experimental Seminar at Princeton University, 1966–1971" (MS, 2019), 10, in author's possession; Douglas T. Hall, "Yale Students and the Classroom," *Yale Daily News*, 11 November 1968, 2; Karin Egan, "Workshop on Innovation and Experimentation in Higher Education Held at the University of California at Santa Cruz, March 23–24, 1970" (MS, 23 June 1970), folder 1, box 458, series IIIA, Carnegie Corporation of New York Papers (hereafter "CCNY Papers"), Rare Book and Manuscripts Library, Columbia University; "Samuel Von Winbush, Interviewed by Carl Quirke at SUNY College at Old Westbury, New York, on October 18, 2012" (MS, 2019), 20, http://www.oldwestburyoralhistory.org/resources/full-transcripts/samuel-von-winbush/#Winbush.

16. Neal W. Anderson to P.S.I. Newsletter, 2 October 1971, folder 11, box 12, Fred S. Keller Papers, Special Collections, University Archives and Museum, University of New Hampshire, Durham, NH; Fred S. Keller, *Pedagogue's Progress* (Lawrence, KS: TRI, 1982), 6–7, 10–14, 29–31.

17. Keller, *Pedagogue's Progress*, 34–35; Manuel Stillerman, "A Demonstration Project in Programmed Instruction," *Transactions of the New York Academy of Sciences* 25, no. 8 (June 1963): 932, "Bronx Community College" folder, box 25; "Report to Dr. Lamar Johnson" (MS, [1963?]), enclosed with J. W. Mears to B. Lamar Johnson, "California Junior Colleges" folder, box 25; "Study Skills at LA Valley," *Inside*, November 1963, 7, "San Bernardino Valley College" folder, box 26; Irving Drooyan and William Wooton, *Programmed Beginning Algebra. United VIII Quadratic Equations* [1963?], vi, "Los Angeles Pierce College" folder, box 25; Carl H. Hendershot, *Programmed Learning: A Bibliography of Programs and Presentation Devices*, 2nd ed. (University Center, MI: Delta College, 1963), 1, "Delta College. University Center, Mich (2)" folder, box 25; Carl H. Hendershot, "Programmed Instruction's Implications and Potential for Michigan," 641; and Carl H. Hendershot, "Save the Day at First Annual Programmed Instruction Conference," 642, both in *Michigan Education Journal*, 1 May 1963, "Delta College. University Center, Mich (2)" folder, box 25, all in B. Lamar Johnson Papers, Boone Special Collections and Archives, Pepperdine University, Malibu, CA.

18. Fred S. Keller, "The History of PSI," in *The PSI Handbook: Essays on Personalized Instruction*, ed. Fred S. Keller and J. Gilmour Sherman (Lawrence, KS: TRI, 1982), 5, 10; Fred S. Keller to William N. Schoenfeld, 18 February 1965; Fred S. Keller to William N. Schoenfeld, 19 March 1965; Fred S. Keller to William N. Schoenfeld, 15 April 1965, all in folder 22, box 3, Keller Papers.

19. Fred S. Keller to William N. Schoenfeld, 19 March 1965, folder 22, box 3, Keller Papers; Keller, *Pedagogue's Progress*, 69; Fred S. Keller, "'Good-Bye, Teacher . . . ,'" *Journal of Applied Behavior Analysis* 1, no. 1 (Spring 1968): 88; Fred S. Keller to J. Gilmour Sherman, 12 June 1972, folder 3, box 4, Keller Papers.

20. J. G. Sherman, preface to *Personalized Instruction in Higher Education*, ed. Robert S. Ruskin and Stephen F. Bono (Washington, DC: Center for Personalized Instruction, 1974), v; Fred S. Keller to Olgierd Celinski, 12 November 1971, folder 2, box 7, Keller Papers; Karin Egan memorandum re "Georgetown University—Center for PSI," 21 March 1973; and J. G. Sherman to Richard Hendrix, 27 October 1976, both in folder 5, box 587, series IIIA, CCNY Papers; Fred S. Keller to Kermit Oberlin, 8 March 1971, folder 12, box 3, Keller Papers; Undergraduate Teaching Committee, "Conference on Innovative Teaching at Rice" (MS, 27 March 1973), 1, 4, folder 4; and H. E. Rorschach to Norman Hackerman, 8 August 1973, folder 5, both in box 1, Committee on Undergraduate Teaching Papers, Rice University Archives, Houston, TX; Drake University press release, 30 August 1972, folder 8, box 8; Edward Cobb to Fred S. Keller, 19 October 1969, folder 8, box 7; Howard Gallup to Fred S. Keller, 14 August 1969, folder 17, box 8, all in Keller Papers.

21. "Colleges: New Pace," *New York Post*, [March?] 1972; and Meredith Plann, "Students Are Teaching Psychology at Hunter. What's It All About?????," *Synapse* (Hunter College Department of Psychology) 2, no. 4 (February 1972): 1, both in folder 18, box 7, Keller Papers; "Modularization: Style for the Future?," *Future Talk: Educating for the '80s* (California State University and Colleges), no. 2 (Winter 1973), "Future Talk" folder, box 84, California State University Reports Collection, Donald R. and Beverly J. Gerth Archives and Special Collections, California State University, Dominguez Hills, Carson, CA (hereafter "CSU—DH"); Stan Nicholson, "P.S.I.—Mastery Learning with the Personal Touch," *Teaching/Learning Newsletter* (University of California Santa Barbara) 1, no. 4 [1974?], "Teaching/Learning Innovations, Teaching/Learning Newsletter, 1974" folder, box 1, Instructional Development Collection, Special Research Collections, University of California, Santa Barbara (hereafter "SRC—UCSB"); "Individualized Instruction Goes to College," *Mosaic* 4 (Winter 1973): 10, 12,

15, "Com. C—ITV 1973" folder, box 6, Committee C series, AAUP Papers; J. Christopher Reid, "Teaching Botany at Purdue University. A Description of the Audio-Tutorial Method of S. N. Postlethwait" (MS, [1970?]), 2, folder 7, box 3, subseries 2, Barton L. Griffith Papers, Special Collections and University Archives, University of Maryland, College Park, MD.

22. *UCSC Course Review*, 29; Arthur L. Robin, "Behavioral Instruction in the College Classroom," *Review of Educational Research* 46, no. 3 (Summer 1976): 322, 315; Billy V. Koen to Fred S. Keller, 11 January 1971, folder 5, box 20; and Edward Cobb to Fred S. Keller, 19 October 1969, folder 8, box 7, both in Keller Papers.

23. *The Challenge of Creative Change: The Program for Innovation and Improvement in the Instructional Process* (n.p.: New Program Development and Evaluation, Office of the Chancellor, California State University and Colleges, March 1975), 12, 11, 39, "The Challenge of Creative Change" folder, box 84, California State University Reports Collection, CSU—DH; Collier Cole et al., "A Comparison of Two Teaching Formats at the College Level," in *Behavior Research and Technology in Higher Education*, ed. James M. Johnston (Springfield, IL: Charles C. Thomas, 1975), 74; W. Scott Wood and Ruth G. Wylie, "Individualized Systems of Instruction Are Better . . . for Whom?," in Johnston, *Behavior Research and Technology*, 382–83.

24. Donald E. Strebel to John H. Goodkind, 15 August 1975, folder 12, box 45, Henry C. Booker Papers, Special Collections, University of California, San Diego; Karin Egan memorandum re "Georgetown University—PSI," 23 April 1973, folder 5, box 587, series IIIA, CCNY Papers; H. H. Rorschach to Undergraduate Teaching Committee, 2 April 1973, folder 4, box 1, Committee on Undergraduate Teaching Papers, Rice University Archives; Fred S. Keller to Ben A. Green, 6 March 1972, folder 16, box 2; and Fred S. Keller to Kermit Oberlin, 29 December 1971, folder 12, box 3, both in Keller Papers.

25. Fred S. Keller to J. Gilmour Sherman, 18 July 1965, folder 2, box 4; and "For Fred S. Keller from Donald A. Cook" (MS, [1971?]), enclosed with Fred S. Keller to Donald A. Cook, 21 September 1971, folder 32, box 1, both in Keller Papers; Susan G. Clark, "An Innovation for Introductory Sociology: Personalized System of Instruction," in Johnston, *Behavior Research and Technology*, 124; D. N. Robinson to Dave Carter, 7 April 1988, folder 6, box 4, Keller Papers.

26. J. Gilmour Sherman to "Dear F and F," 30 November 1988, folder 15, box 12, Keller Papers; J. Gilmour Sherman to Karin Egan, 1 March 1977, folder 5, box 587, series IIIA, CCNY Papers; Fred S. Keller, "Lightning Strikes Twice," *Teaching of Psychology* 12 (1985): 4, 8; Fred S. Keller to J. Gilmour Sherman, 4 February 1983, folder 6, box 4, Keller Papers; Bob Edgar, "Mastery Learning," *Teacher on the Hill* (University of California, Santa Cruz), no. 7 (June 1978): 3; Wilbert J. McKeachie to Fred S. Keller, 14 October 1991, folder 1, box 10, Keller Papers.

27. McKeachie, "State of the Art," 1–2; Egan, "Workshop on Innovation and Experimentation," 1; Wilbert J. McKeachie, "Motivation, Learning, Teaching" (MS, 19 May 1966), 1, "McKeachie—Psychology—Speeches—Research—Motivation, Teaching Methods, and the College Learning" folder, box 3, McKeachie Papers.

28. Kenneth E. Eble and Wilbert J. McKeachie, *Improving Undergraduate Education through Faculty Development* (San Francisco: Jossey-Bass, 1985), 4; Wendell I. Smith, "Faculty Development at Bucknell," *Teaching and Learning* (Bucknell University), no. 3 (October 1976): 2, "Teaching and Learning" folder, box 29, Faculty Records, Special Collections / University Archives, Bucknell University, Lewisburg, PA; Arthur M. Cohen and Florence B. Brawer, *The Two-Year College Instructor Today* (New York: Praeger, 1977), 67; "Teaching Professors to Teach," *New York Times*, 19 August 1985, ES33; Kenneth E. Eble, "Final Report to the Carnegie Corporation of the Project to Improve College Teaching Co-sponsored by the Association of American Colleges and the American Association of University Professors" (MS, 26 October 1971), "PICT II-Com. C" folder; and Kenneth E. Eble, "Improving College Teaching," *Phi*

Delta Kappan, January 1971, 285, "Project to Improve College Teaching (PICT) 1971–73" folder, both in box 7, Committee C series, AAUP Papers.

29. Samuel P. Kelly, "Effective Techniques and Methods of College Teaching" (MS, April 1970), 6, 3, 4, 8, "Atlanta Conference. May 19" folder, box 60, Eble Papers.

30. John Anderson, untitled editorial, *Teaching and Learning*, no. 4 (December 1976): 1, box 29, Bucknell Faculty Records; B. Claude Mathis, "The Lilly Endowment Program at Ball State University. An Evaluation of the Office of Instructional Development" (MS, [1979?]), 14, folder 5, box 13, B. Claude Mathis Papers, University Archives, Northwestern University, Evanston, IL; David Holmes, *Reform from Within: Case Studies of Faculty-Initiated Educational Change at the University of Vermont* (Burlington: University of Vermont Press, 1979), 8; Smith, "Faculty Development at Bucknell," 3; "Abstract" (MS, [1982?]), enclosed with Barbara F. Nodine to Wilbert McKeachie, 21 December 1982, "McKeachie—Psychology—Correspondence—B" folder, box 1, McKeachie Papers; Office of Instructional Development, Ball State University, untitled questionnaires (MS, 1979), folder 8, box 13, Mathis Papers.

31. Office of Instructional Development, Ball State University, untitled questionnaires; Mathis, "Lilly Endowment Program," 11; *Second Conference on Effective Teaching*, ed. Naftaly S. Glasman and Berthold R. Killait (Santa Barbara: University of California, Santa Barbara, June 1974), 56, "2nd UCSB Conference on Effective Teaching, May 1974" folder, box 1, Instructional Development Collection, SRC—UCSB.

32. "Improvement of Undergraduate Teaching: Progress and Problems" (MS, Office of the President memorandum to Regents of the University of California, 16 June 1972), 11, "Evaluation of Teaching [Orbach Facility]" folder, box 2, Academic Senate, Los Angeles Division, Committee on Teaching Records, Charles E. Young Research Library, University of California, Los Angeles (hereafter "CYRL—UCLA"); *The Challenge of Creative Change: The Program for Innovation and Improvement in the Instructional Process*, 2; R. J. Diamond, "Letter to the Editor," *Future Talk: Educating for the '80s*, no. 14 (Spring/Summer 1976): 3, California State University Reports Collection, CSU—DH; David McEntire to Angus E. Taylor, 10 February 1975, "Teaching Undergraduates $1 Million" folder, box 42, Academic Senate, Los Angeles Division, Executive Office, Administrative Files, CYRL—UCLA.

33. *A Report on the Conference on Programs to Assist Predominantly Negro Colleges and Universities Held at the Massachusetts Institute of Technology, April 18 and 19, 1964* (1964), 12; and Allen R. Blackmer, "Summer Institute in History. Carnegie Institute of Technology. June 15 to July 31, 1964" (MS, 1964), 3, both in folder 22; Lewis H. Fenderson, "A Report on the Summer Institute for Teachers of English in Predominantly Negro Colleges" (MS, 1964), 26; and David Riesman to Educational Services, Inc., 13 October 1964, both in folder 21, all in box 36, series IIIA, CCNY Papers.

34. *Project to Improve College Teaching. Special Report #1* [1970?], 1, folder 1, box 420, series IIIA, CCNY Papers; "Nov. 11 ABC Premier of 'Meet the Professor,'" *Atlanta Daily World*, 28 October 1962, 6; David C. Epperson, "The Development-Oriented Scholar: Recruitment, Training, and Renewal" (MS, 8 April 1970), 7–8, 12, "Planning Conference" folder, box 60, Eble Papers.

35. *Danforth Graduate Fellowships for College Teaching Careers, 1965–1966* (St. Louis: Danforth Foundation, 1965); Russell K. Darroch, "Goals and Facts" (MS, 22 October 1965); David Louick, "Statement and Goals in Application for Danforth Fellowship" (MS, [1965?]), all in "Fellowships and Scholarships—Danforth Fellowships, 1963–1972" folder, box 11, Dean of College Office Records, College Archives, Carleton College, Northfield, MN; The Danforth Foundation, "Dorothy Danforth Compton Fellowships for Minority Persons Preparing for College and University Teaching" (MS, 31 October 1979), "Danforth Foundation" folder, box 2.11, series 2, Association of American University Records, Ferdinand Hamburger University Archives, Johns Hopkins University; American Association of Physics Teachers, "Paul W.

Zitzewitz Award for Excellence in K–12 Physics Teaching," https://www.aapt.org/Programs
/awards/Paul-Zitzewitz-Award-for-Excellence-in-K12-Physics-Teaching.cfm; "David Fisher,
RDNA Founder, News Update," http://www.rdna.info/druidinquirer46.pdf.

36. Jane Tompkins, *A Life in School: What the Teacher Learned* (Reading, MA:
Addison-Wesley, 1996), 86, 90; "A Large State University (Berkeley)" (MS, 1974); "A Large
Private University (Stanford)" (MS, 1974); "A Medium-Sized State University (Davis)" (MS,
1974), all enclosed with S. K. Stein to Dear Fellow Members of the MAA-AMS Joint Commit-
tee on the Training of Graduate Students to Teach, 15 May 1974, "Training Graduate
Students to Teach" folder, box 89-7/18, Mathematical Association of America Papers, Briscoe
Center for American History, University of Texas at Austin; "Summary of Recommendations
of Group '2': Pedagogical Development and Evaluation from the Ojai Conference. Chairman: Andrea Rich" (MS, [1976?]), 3, Allegra Fuller Snyder Papers, CYRL—UCLA; Frank W.
Finger, "'Professional Problems': Preparation for a Career in College Teaching," *American
Psychologist*, November 1969, 1048, "Cmte C—Teaching Seminar—Frank W. Finger" folder,
box 1, Committee C series, AAUP Papers.

37. E. Alden Dunham to "LM & AP," 8 November 1968, folder 5, box 542, series IIIA,
CCNY Papers; "Schools Developing a Teaching 'PH.D.,'" *New York Times*, 11 June 1970, 45;
Robert L. Hampel, *Fast and Curious: A History of Shortcuts in American Education* (Lanham,
MD: Rowman & Littlefield, 2017), 93; galleys for "The Doctor of Arts: A High Degree of
Teaching Competence," *Carnegie Quarterly*, Winter–Spring 1970, 2, folder 5, box 542, series
IIIA, CCNY Papers; John Gillis, "The Doctor of Arts Degree: Background Paper for the
Commission on Students and Faculty" (MS, June 1970), 3–4, "Joint Project to Improve
Preparation of College Teachers, 1970–" folder, box 7, Committee C series, AAUP Papers.

38. "The Doctor of Arts Degree Settles into a Small Niche," *Chronicle of Higher Education*,
7 July 1975; and Alvin H. Proctor to Alden Dunham, 15 December 1972, both in folder 2;
Alden Dunham to Paul L. Dressel, 9 November 1972, folder 6, all in box 542, series IIIA, CCNY
Papers; Hampel, *Fast and Curious*, 94; Robert H. Koenker, "Status of the Doctor of Arts
Degree" (MS, 11 November 1974), 8, 9, folder 4; Paul L. Dressel to Joseph Axelrod, 30 October
1974, folder 2; Alden Dunham to Frank Newman, 1 April 1971, folder 3, all in box 542, series
IIIA, CCNY Papers.

39. John Q. Academesis, "Too Many College Teachers Don't Teach," *New York Times*, 21
February 1960, 72, folder 5, box 71, McHenry Papers; Frederick L. Redefer, "To Teach Youth
Better" (MS, [1969?]), 1, enclosed with Frederick L. Redefer to Kenneth Eble, 30 Decem-
ber 1969, "N–O" folder, box 58, Eble Papers; Andrew H. Malcolm, "To Gifted Professor,
Teaching Is an Exchange of Ideas," *New York Times*, 8 December 1969, 29; "Outstanding
Teacher Awards," in *Improving College Teaching*, ed. Calvin B. T. Lee (Washington, DC:
American Council on Education, 1967), 307.

40. "News of Interest to Deans of Arts and Sciences in Ohio's Public Universities," *Stately
Arts and Sciences* 1, no. 2 (April 1972): 2, "Miscellaneous Papers (3)" folder, box 61, Eble
Papers; James E. Finholt to Kenneth E. Eble, 1 September 1970, "Teaching Methods Commit-
tee, 1968–1973" folder, box 18, Dean of College Office Records, College Archives, Carleton
College; Martin Trow, "Undergraduate Teaching at Large State Universities," in Lee, *Improving
College Teaching*, 168; Redefer, "To Teach Youth Better," 5; Emery N. Castle to W. E. Koenker,
12 January 1966; "Recipients of Undergraduate Teaching Awards" (MS, [1966?]); E. K.
Dortmund, "The Mosser Plan at the Oregon College of Education" (MS, [1966?]), 1, 4, all in
Dean of Faculty Records, Microfilm Reel 1, Special Collections and Archives Research Center,
Oregon State University, Corvallis, OR; "The Bookworm Turns: More Collegians Now Grade
Their Teachers," *Wall Street Journal*, 3 January 1966, 1.

41. Bruce A. Kimball, "Historia Calamitatum," in *Teaching Undergraduates: Essays from
the Lilly Endowment Workshop on Liberal Arts*, ed. Bruce A. Kimball (Buffalo, NY:

Prometheus, 1988), 13–14; Glasman and Killait, *Second Conference on Effective Teaching*, 27; *ASSU Course Guide. Winter 1981–82* (ASSU, 1982), 7, folder 17, box 2, series 7, Associated Students of Stanford University Records, Special Collections and University Archives, Stanford University; "Study Claims Lindback Winners Fare Well in Tenure Process," *Daily Pennsylvanian*, 13 October 1987, "Daily Pennsylvanian 1985–89" folder, box 2, Student Committee on Undergraduate Education Records, University Archives and Research Center, University of Pennsylvania; William Arrowsmith, "The Future of Teaching," *Arion: A Journal of Humanities and the Classics* 2, nos. 2/3 (Spring 1992–Fall 1993): 179.

42. Charles J. Hitch to Chancellors, 29 August 1969, in *Report of the Task Force on Teaching Evaluation* (n.p.: University of California, February 1980), 149; "President Hitch's Statement on Improvement of Undergraduate Teaching" (MS, 12 November 1970), in *Report of the Task Force*, 154; "Reforms at UC to Emphasize Teaching Skills," *Los Angeles Times*, 12 November 1970, F1.

43. "Is Old College Try Necessary?," *Philadelphia Bulletin*, 24 January 1971, "College—Students—1971" folder, Philadelphia Bulletin Collection; Jerry G. Gaff and Robert C. Wilson, "The Teaching Environment," *Bulletin of the AAUP* 57, no. 4 (December 1971): 476; Daniel Wilner to School of Public Health Teaching Faculty, 25 November 1970, enclosed with Daniel Wilner to David S. Saxon, 30 November 1970, "Teaching 1970–1972" folder, box 41, Academic Senate, Los Angeles Division, Executive Office, Administrative Files, CYRL—UCLA.

44. Merton J. Peck to Robert L. Herbert, 22 February 1971; and Frederic M. Richards to Herbert, 19 January 1971, both in folder 6, box 9, Records of the Dean of Yale College, Beinecke Rare Book and Manuscript Library, Yale University; W. James Popham, "Higher Education's Commitment to Instructional Development Programs" (MS, 1974), 3, 5, "Higher Education's Commitment to Instructional Development Programs by W. Popham" folder, box 2, Academic Senate, Los Angeles Division, Committee on Teaching Records; and Gabriel Jackson to Angus E. Taylor, 29 October 1970, "Teaching 1970–1972" folder, box 41, Academic Senate, Los Angeles Division, Executive Office, Administrative Files, both in CYRL—UCLA.

45. W. H. Massey to Robert L. Herbert, 22 December 1970; and Frederic M. Richards to Herbert, 19 January 1971, both in folder 6, box 9, Records of the Dean of Yale College; Michael Scriven, "Evaluating Higher Education in California" (MS, 1972), 21, "Excerpts from 'Evaluating Higher Education in California' by Michael Scriven" folder, box 2, Academic Senate, Los Angeles Division, Committee on Teaching Records; "Student Ratings of Professors Held Useful," *New York Times*, 29 March 1978.

46. Charles F. Warnath, "The Uses and Misuses of Student Evaluations" (MS, 26 April 1978), 1, Faculty Forum Papers, May 1978, Oregon State University, https://senate.oregonstate.edu/sites/senate.oregonstate.edu/files/faculty_forum_papers_faculty_senate_oregon_state_university.pdf; David Baldwin, "Commentary: The Student Climate in 1983," *Hilltops* (Hartwick College), 15 September 1983, enclosed with David Baldwin to C. David Gruender, 22 September 1983, "Comm C—Evaluation of Faulty" folder, box 1, Committee C series, AAUP Papers.

Epilogue · The Decade of the Undergraduate? College Teaching in the 1990s and Beyond

1. Randall Bass, "Higher Education's Amateur Hour," *Liberal Education* 79, no. 2 (Spring 1993): 26–31; Ernest L. Boyer, *Scholarship Reconsidered: Priorities of the Professoriate* (Princeton, NJ: Carnegie Foundation for the Advancement of Teaching, 1990), xi. See also David Pace, "The Amateur in the Operating Room: History and the Scholarship of Teaching and Learning," *American Historical Review* 109, no. 4 (October 2004): 1171–92.

2. Steven Brint, "Focus on the Classroom: Movements to Reform College Teaching and Learning, 1980–2008," in *The American Academic Profession: Transformation in Contemporary Higher Education*, ed. Joseph C. Hermanowicz (Baltimore: Johns Hopkins University Press,

2011), 73; James Frank, "Program Teaches Young Professors to Teach," *New York Times*, 14 February 1992, 1; "Opportunities Abound in Teaching Evaluation Revision" (MS, 1992), enclosed with Susan Dorman to Pat Culbertson et al., 16 December 1992, folder 12, box 58, range 63, Office of Academic Affairs Administrative Files, University Archives, Louisiana State University, Baton Rouge, LA (hereafter "UA—LSU"); David L. Kirp, "Balancing Teaching and Research," *Fresno Bee*, 25 April 1990, in California Legislature, Senate Special Committee on University of California Admissions, *Background Material for the Hearing on the Quality of Undergraduate Education at the University of California* (Sacramento, CA: Senate, 1990), app. I. On Donald Kennedy and teaching at Stanford, see also Larry Cuban, *How Scholars Trumped Teachers: Change without Reform in University Teaching and Research, 1890–1990* (New York: Teachers College Press, 1999), 3–4.

3. "In the Battle for Tenure, Research Still Rules," *San Jose Mercury News* [1990?], in *Background Material for the Hearing*, app. I; "Whither College Lectures? Maybe Right out the Door," *New York Times*, 14 August 2002.

4. Steven Brint, *Two Cheers for Higher Education: Why American Universities Are Stronger Than Ever—and How to Meet the Challenges They Face* (Princeton, NJ: Princeton University Press, 2019), 301; "A Dual Teaching Career: An Oral History with UC Santa Cruz Professor Frank Andrews" (MS, 18 December 2014), 119, 30, https://escholarship.org/uc/item/4st5s13x; *T.E.A.C.H.* (Associated Students of University of California Irvine), Spring Quarter 1992–93, inset, Special Collections and Archives, University of California, Irvine.

5. Brint, *Two Cheers*, 317–18, 301–2; Professor X, *In the Basement of the Ivy Tower: Confessions of an Accidental Academic* (New York: Viking/Penguin Group, 2011), 148–49; Diane Bell, ed., *Why Do We Teach What We Teach?* (1990), 60–61, Archives and Special Collections, College of the Holy Cross, Worcester, MA; W. Norton Grubb, *Honored but Invisible: An Inside Look at Teaching in Community Colleges* (New York: Routledge, 1999), 227; Janet Malcolm, "It Happened in Milwaukee," *New York Review of Books*, 23 October 1997.

6. Lewis H. Miller Jr., "Bold, Imaginative Steps Are Needed to Link Teaching with Research," *Chronicle of Higher Education*, 13 September 1989, folder 4, box 570, series I, President's Office Papers, Special Collections, Archives, and Preservation, University of Colorado at Boulder (hereafter "SCA—Colorado"); *Yale College Course Critique* 4, no. 2 (September 1997): 21, 80, 55; *Yale Course Critique* 1, no. 2 (Fall 1994): 91; *Yale Course Critique*, Spring 1996, 48; *Annex* (Pomona College) 11, no. 1 (3 October 1997): 3, folder 20, box 1, Brian A. Stonehill Papers, Special Collections, The Claremont Colleges, Claremont, CA.

7. Thomas Pinney, "Three Moments" (MS, 10 September 1997), 3, folder 20, box 1, Stonehill Papers; Page Smith, *Killing the Spirit: Higher Education in America* (New York: Viking, 1990), 212; Robert Nisbet, *Teachers and Scholars: A Memoir of Berkeley in Depression and War* (New Brunswick, NJ: Transaction, 1992), 112–13.

8. Nisbet, *Teachers and Scholars*, 115; "An Oral History with William (Bil) Banks" (MS, Regional History Office, Bancroft Library, University of California, Berkeley, 2013), 180.

9. Robert Bechtold Heilman, "The Great-Teacher Myth" (1991), in *The Professor and the Profession* (Columbia: University of Missouri Press, 1999), 322, 324, 331; Aaron M. Pallas and Anna Neumann, *Convergent Teaching: Tools to Spark Deeper Learning in College* (Baltimore: Johns Hopkins University Press, 2019), 200–201.

10. D. Kierstead et al., "Report of the Course Evaluation Committee" (MS, 13 May 1985), 1, folder C4, box 7, Colbiana Collection, Special Collections, Colby College, Waterville, ME; Harold Whittington, "The Case for the Abolition of Student Evaluations," *Texas Academe*, Fall 1983, 22–23, "Comm. C—Evaluation of Faculty" folder, box 1, Committee C series, American Association of University Professors Papers, Special Collections Research Center, George Washington University. For recent summaries and critiques of contemporary student evaluations in higher education, see Jason Brennan and Phillip Magness, *Cracks in the Ivory*

Tower: The Moral Mess of Higher Education (New York: Oxford University Press, 2019), 82–108; and Pallas and Neumann, *Convergent Teaching*, 156–65. For a full history, see Scott M. Gelber, *Grading the College: A History of Evaluating Teaching and Learning* (Baltimore: Johns Hopkins University Press, 2020).

11. Cecil Eby to Edie Goldenberg, 25 May 1991, "CLRT. Administration. Faculty. IDQ/ Evaluation and Examinations Office" folder, box 4, Donald R. Brown Papers, Bentley Historical Library, University of Michigan.

12. William F. Waters, "A Response to the Report of the Faculty Senate Ad Hoc Committee on Teaching Evaluation" (MS, 10 November 1993), 2, folder 14, box 58, range 63, Office of Academic Affairs Administrative Files, UA—LSU; Catherine R. Myers, "The Teaching Portfolio: Current Practice" (MS, [1992?]), 4, "Manhattanville College" folder, box 111; and Maynard Mack Jr., "Personal Statement" (MS, [1993?]), 1, "University of Maryland" folder, box 113, both in American Association for Higher Education Papers, Hoover Institution Library and Archives, Stanford, CA; James Wilkinson, "Jim Wilkinson's Report" (MS, [1997?]), enclosed with Pat Hutchings to "Everyone," 29 September 1997, "Fall 1999 Electronic Classroom Syllabi" folder, box 1, Center for the Advancement of Teaching Collection (hereafter "CATC—Xavier"), Archives and Special Collections, Xavier University, New Orleans. For a description and analysis of more recent efforts to promote peer review of college teaching, see Pallas and Neumann, *Convergent Teaching*, 166–72.

13. Brint, *Two Cheers*, 314; Daniel P. Tompkins to Pat Hutchings and Peer Review Participants, 17 June 1997; Daniel P. Tompkins to Peer-ReviewProj@Lists.Stanford.Edu, 30 April 1997; Daniel P. Tompkins to Peer-ReviewProj@Lists.Stanford.Edu, 11 December 1997; Daniel P. Tompkins to Peer-ReviewProj@Lists.Stanford.Edu, 3 October 1997, all in "Fall 1999 Electronic Classroom Syllabi" folder, box 1, CATC—Xavier.

14. Steve Villano to Lisa Luebke, 3 August 1981, "Fac Course Questionnaire Absolute Miscellany" folder, box 70; and Lou McClelland to Alan Ikeya et al., "FCQ" folder, box 8, both in series I, University of Colorado Student Union Papers, SCA—Colorado; "Joe Katz Interview with Blythe McVicker Clinchy" (MS, 27 April 1987), 2, "Ford Fnd. Project Interviews 1987 (1)" folder, box 3, Joseph Katz Papers, Special Collections and University Archives, Stanford University; "U. Classes Examine Issues of Free Expression and Civility," *Daily Pennsylvanian* (University of Pennsylvania) 110 (12 April 1994): 3.

15. "U. Classes Examine Issues," 3; Martha Salas, "P.C. Ends Taping in Class," *Campus News* (East Los Angeles Junior College) 50 (8 February 1995): 2; Bruce L. R. Smith, Jeremy D. Mayer, and A. Lee Fritschler, *Closed Minds: Politics and Ideology in American Universities* (Washington, DC: Brookings Institution, 2008), 152; Jordan J. Titus, "Pedagogy on Trial: When Academic Freedom and Education Consumerism Collide," *Journal of College and University Law* 38 (2011–12): 164. For a brief history and analysis of "political correctness" in higher education, see Jonathan Zimmerman, *Campus Politics: What Everyone Needs to Know* (New York: Oxford University Press, 2016), 23–37.

16. Richard Arum and Josipa Roksa, *Academically Adrift: Limited Learning on College Campuses* (Chicago: University of Chicago Press, 2011), 3, 71; Catherine Rampell, "A History of College Grade Inflation," *New York Times*, 14 July 2011; "New Research Casts Doubt on Value of Student Evaluations of Professors," *Chronicle of Higher Education*, 16 January 1998; "Doonesbury," *San Antonio Express-News*, 27 December 1993, "Teaching vs. Research" folder, box 74, American Association for Higher Education Papers.

17. "Part-Time College Teaching Rises, as Do Worries," *New York Times*, 4 January 1995, A17; Brint, *Two Cheers*, 283; Kirp, "Balancing Teaching and Research"; H. C. Dudley to A. E. Koenig, 24 February 1970, "G–I" folder, box 58, Kenneth Eugene Eble Papers, University Archives and Record Management, University of Utah, Salt Lake City.

18. "'Digital Chalk': A Project to Quickstart the Introduction of Computer Technology as a Teaching Tool in Classes Relying on Manual or Low-Tech Methods of Material Presentation" (MS, 30 May 1994), "MIT2" folder, box 4; and Randall Bass, "What Technology Can Teach Us about Learning," *Faculty Development* 13, no. 3 (Spring 1999): 5, "The Collaboration" folder, box 3, both in CATC—Xavier; "Teacher Evaluations a Welcome Addition," *Daily Reveille* (Louisiana State University), 29 November 1993, folder 14, box 58, range 63, Office of Academic Affairs Administrative Files, UA—LSU; Karen Pasternack, "The Value of Student Feedback," *Daily Pennsylvanian* 114 (12 February 1998): 6.

19. "Summary of Open-Ended Responses to Teach [*sic*] Effectiveness Questionnaire. Spring 1993" (MS, 1993), 5, 2, 1, 4, folder 116, box 58, range 63, Office of Academic Affairs Administrative Files, UA—LSU.

20. Franz Samelson to Wilbert McKeachie, 26 February 1987, "McKeachie—Psychology—Correspondence—S" folder, box 1, Wilbert J. McKeachie Papers, Bentley Historical Library; Richard Bradley, *Harvard Rules: The Struggle for the Soul of the World's Most Powerful University* (New York: HarperCollins, 2005), 274–75; "Who Says?," *Colby Teacher* 1, no. 2 (October 1992): 8.

21. "An Investment Worth Making," *Daily Texan*, 31 January 2012, 4; "New Learning Initiative to Focus on Active Problem Solving," *Daily Pennsylvanian*, 9 February 2014; David Gooblar, *The Missing Course: Everything They Never Taught You about College Teaching* (Cambridge, MA: Harvard University Press, 2019).

22. "Learning to Balance Research and Teaching," *Philadelphia Inquirer*, 15 May 1990, folder 4, box 570, series I, President's Office Papers, SCA—Colorado.

23. On "presence" in the classroom, see James M. Lang, "Waiting for Us to Notice Them," *Chronicle of Higher Education*, 19 January 2015; and Rob Jenkins, "The Four Properties of Powerful Teachers," *Chronicle of Higher Education*, 16 March 2015.